U.S. MARINE CORPS AVIATION

1912 to the Present

3rd Edition

U.S. MARINE

CORPS AVIATION

1912 to the Present

3rd Edition

PETER B. MERSKY

The Nautical & Aviation Publishing Company of America
Baltimore, Maryland

Second printing with revisions, 1987.
Third printing, May 1990.
Fourth printing, April 1991.
Third edition, October 1997

Printed in the United States of America.

Library of Congress Catalog Card Number: 96-28230
ISBN: 1-877853-42-9

Third edition design by James M. Faulkner.

All photos courtesy of the United States Marine Corps, unless otherwise stated. Drawings are by the author.

Library of Congress Cataloging in Publication Data

Mersky, Peter B., 1945-
    U.S. Marine Corps Aviation : 1912 to the Present / Peter B. Mersky. — 3rd ed.

        p.   cm.

    Includes bibliographical references (p. -   ) and index.
    ISBN 1-877853-42-9
1. United States. Marine Corps—Aviation—History.   I. Title.
VG93.M48   1996
359.9'6'0973—dc20   96-28230
CIP

Contents

Photo sections occur on pages 55 to 86, 151 to 182, 247 to 278, and 337 to 368.

Preface to the 3rd Edition

From its first tentative steps in 1912, as part of the Navy's flight training unit, to the tough, experienced, capable and proud entity it is today, Marine aviation has always been unique among the world's flying services. It is the air arm of the United States Marines, an organization of aviators, aircrews and personnel within the larger framework of naval aviation. No other military service or air arm in the world includes such a dedicated group.

My first contact with Marine aviation came not with roaring jet engines and flashing wings, but with the deep, long-cultivated bellow of a Marine Drill Instructor at the Navy's Aviation Officer Candidate School at NAS Pensacola, Florida. On the damp, dark morning of February 8, 1968, this close-shaven, immaculately dressed man thrust my first article of military clothing into my hands, a black plastic raincoat, and yelled at me to "Geddout, geddout, geddout!!" I never thought of it then, but during those strange, hellish weeks, these dedicated people were working hard, preparing me and the others in my class for the road ahead, whatever it might be. They have provided me with a wealth of experience, stories, and pride over the years, and a bonding with others who went through the same educational process. Although the DI was not a pilot, he was as much a part of Marine aviation as the leather-jacketed, gold-winged aviators who followed him in the courses of instruction at Pensacola.

The Marines have had to constantly fight to justify their own air force, and there were times when it seemed that the Corps would lose its planes and pilots. But somehow Marine aviation has lasted.

So much has happened to Marine Corps aviation, indeed all U.S. military aviation, during the decade since the publication of the second and most recent edition of this book, which ended with the raid on Libya in April 1986. Since that event, Marine Corps squadrons have been engaged in actions in the Persian Gulf in 1987, 1988, and 1991, rescued thousands of refugees and other civilians from strife-torn African cities, supported an international relief effort in northern Iraq, and continued their effort to maintain their identity and dedication to the Corps. It has not been easy.

Political events at home and abroad have affected everyone, resulting in downsizing, and in many cases, decommissioning of battle-tested veteran units, some right after the biggest combat action since Vietnam. Old aircraft have been retired along with their squadrons. In other cases, the veteran aircraft have given way to newer types, which have occasionally changed their mission and the unit's home base. Maximum flexibility is the key to survival these days, both in mission readiness, and in personal goals and abilities.

What I wrote in 1983 still holds true, but with a greater degree of guarded optimism. It is still a great time to be a newly designated Marine aviator with a twenty year career ahead, and a strong, vital heritage behind him. Those gold wings still go well with a well-blacked eagle, globe, and anchor. But along with the enthusiasm, changing times and values call for alertness and re-dedication.

Peter Mersky
Norfolk, Virginia, September, 1997

Acknowledgments

I have had help from many people in writing this book. In particular, I would like to thank Mr. Norman Polmar, a highly respected naval and military authority in his own right, and a teacher from whom I have learned much.

Major John M. Elliott, USMCR (Ret) is one of those gems one occasionally discovers during the course of a project. There is probably very little John does not know concerning Marine aviation (indeed, he participated in some of the events presented in this book), and whatever he does not know is most likely stashed away in his prodigious files. He extended every available assistance as well as reading the manuscript.

Lieutenant Colonel H.C. Brown, USMC, whose job today includes running the growing Marine aviation museum at Quantico, regaled me with stories of his pre-Vietnam Shufly days and also provided some of his personal photography taken during his tours in Vietnam. Major Frank Batha, USMC, of the Marine Corps History and Museums Division, has always been a great source of help in projects of mine concerning the Marines.

There is, of course, the small group of people in the Washington Navy Yard forming the staff of the Naval Aviation History Office and *Naval Aviation News,* without whom a great deal of this book would have been impossible. To them goes a special word of appreciation.

Others who have given a lot of assistance are: Captain Charles H. Brown, USN (Ret); Colonel John E. Greenwood, USMC (Ret); Commander Gary W. Riese, USNR; Major Joseph Rice, USMCR; Captain

W.E. Wood, USMC; Major William Curtis, USMCR; Major David Fich-
tner, USMCR; Lieutenant Colonel David Jones, USMC; Lieutenant
Colonel Terry Mattke, USMC; Lieutenant Colonel Dave Seder, USMC;
Major John T. Dyer, Jr., USMC (Ret); Major Fred C. Lash and Captain
Jay Farrar of the Division of Public Affairs, Headquarters, USMC; Lieu-
tenant Colonel Fred McCorkle, USMC; Major Ron Faucher, USMC;
Lieutenant Colonel Earl Bufton, USMC; PHC Fred Gooding, USN; and
IS2 Frank Rucker, USN.

Lieutenant General Thomas H. Miller, USMC (Ret), Major General
John P. Condon, USMC (Ret), and Major General Philip D. Shutler,
USMC (Ret) spent several hours discussing their careers and the policies
which shaped Marine aviation in the post-World-War-II era.

Several representatives of various aircraft companies also came to my
assistance: Harry Gann, McDonnell Douglas; Tommy L. Wilson and
Monte D. Ditmer of Vought; Lois Lovisolo, Grumman Aerospace Corporation; Dick Tipton, Bell Helicopter; and Jeffrey P. Belmont, Sikorsky
Aircraft.

Ann Ferrante and Regina Strother of the Museum Division, Clyde
Gillespie, and Nicholas Williams, who has accumulated much material
on the F4D Skyray, also contributed invaluable aid.

Walt Boyne, Robert Mikesh, and Tim Wooldridge, all of the National
Air and Space Museum, also lent that institution's resources when needed. Robert H. Baker also spent long hours copying many of the personal
photographs lent by various contributors.

In addition to those Marines quoted in the narrative, I would like to
thank the following people who helped gather information, experiences,
and photos for this new edition. Military ranks given are from the time
of their contribution. Mr. Benis Frank, Chief Historian, Marine Corps
Historical Center; Ms. Ann A Ferrante, Marine Corps Historical Center;
Ms. Catherine Kiley and Lieutenant Colonel Henry Dewey of the Office
of Aviation Manpower and Support, HQMC; Mr. W.H. Rever, Jr., Bell
Helicopter Textron; Colonel J.P. Monroe, USMC (Ret), Executive Di-
rector, Marine Corps Aviation Association; Colonel Tim Hill, USMC,
HQMC Safety Division; Major W.G. West, USMC, HQMC Safety Divi-
sion; Major John P. DeHart, USMCR, HMLA-773; Captain Scott S.
Creed, USMC, VMFA(AW)-332; Captain E.A. Sweatt, USMC, Director,
Joint Public Affairs Office, MCAS El Toro; CWO2 N.H. North, USMC
Joint Public Affairs Office, MCAS New River; SSgt. Craig Larson,
HQMC Public Affairs.

I would also like to thank the Marine Corps Historical Foundation for
its support of this updated project.

Lastly, a special note of appreciation to my parents, Leonard and
Muriel.

The Beginning: 1912-1918

 By 1912, when the first U.S. Marine Corps pilots were being trained, naval aviation had been in existence for nearly two years. On November 14, 1910, off Hampton Roads, Virginia, Eugene Ely, a persistent and resourceful test pilot for the Curtiss Airplane and Motor Company, took off from the deck of the *Birmingham* and flew to Willoughby Spit on the opposite shore. The military uses of aircraft, though immediately obvious to some, were somewhat limited by the imagination of the military leaders of the time and the performance of the little contraptions themselves. However, with time the airplane was gaining in reliability and also causing people to think about it more seriously.

Soon after Ely's flight from the *Birmingham*, Glenn Curtiss offered to instruct a naval officer in flying at no charge to the government. The Navy sent Lieutenant T.G. Ellyson to San Diego, California, to take advantage of Curtiss' patriotic offer. Ellyson subsequently became Naval Aviator Number 1. The Navy was sufficiently impressed by the possibilities offered by the airplane to set up a small training camp, funded by a Congressional appropriation of $25,000, at Annapolis, Maryland, across the Severn River from the Naval Academy. The service purchased three aircraft with the money, two Curtiss and one Wright. All three were hydroplanes, for in the early stages of aviation, the hydroplane offered the relative safety of a water landing should the somewhat unreliable engines quit in flight.

The companies trained an officer to pilot each aircraft, as well as an enlisted mechanic to take care of them. Lieutenants John Rodgers and John H. Towers reported to the camp and thus initiated a chain of pilot and mechanic trainees. To keep the operations going year-round, the camp moved to San Diego in December and then returned to Annapolis the following spring.

Something new was added, however, in the spring of 1912: a Marine officer. The Marines had been watching the Navy's progress in aviation with interest. They saw a use for their own aircraft operation as part of their Advance Base Force concept, then emerging after a long gestation period. With the apparent success of the Annapolis training camp, the Marine Corps' Commandant, Major General William P. Biddle, concluded that training Marine Corps aviators might be a "great benefit" to the Marines. Two Marine first lieutenants were ordered to flight training in Annapolis.

The first of these two officers to arrive was Alfred A. Cunningham, born in Atlanta, Georgia, in 1882, and an ardent aviation enthusiast. Assigned to the Marine Barracks in the Philadelphia Navy Yard, he reported on May 22, 1912—which has since become the official birthday of Marine Corps aviation. However, almost as soon as he arrived, he was ordered away for expeditionary duty. When he returned in July, the disappointed Cunningham was told that there was no serviceable aircraft available, and his training would be postponed again. Undaunted, he gained permission to travel to Marblehead, twenty miles north of Boston, where the Burgess Company was building Wright hydroplanes. There were instructors available there and after only two and one-half hours of instruction, Cunningham soloed on August 20, 1912. He cited the reason for the brevity of his instructional period:

There being so few civilian flyers, the factory had to pay them a huge salary to teach us, and they were anxious to make it short and snappy . . . . I had only attempted to make two landings in rough weather, when one calm day they decided to risk the plane rather than continue to pay any instructors large salaries. I was asked if I was willing to try it alone and said I was . . . .[1]

His first solo flight was uneventful, and he returned to the Annapolis camp to train other pilots, including the second Marine to report, First Lieutenant Bernard L. Smith of Richmond, Virginia. By the time Smith reported to the training camp on September 18, 1912, the three Navy aircraft had been repaired and were ready for operations.

At that time, Lieutenant Ellyson, who was designated as officer in charge of the camp, had an additional airplane available, bringing the total to four: two Curtisses—A-1 and A-2—and two Wrights—B-1 and

B-2. (He assigned an individual aircraft to a specific pilot, along with a specific mechanic.) The older Wright B-1 was assigned to Cunningham, while Lieutenant Smith received a Curtiss. In addition, the camp was divided, perhaps unintentionally, into the "Marine Camp"—which included Cunningham and Sergeant James McGuire, the first enlisted man to go through pilot training (although McGuire reportedly did not stay with flying for very long)—and the "Curtiss Camp," with Lieutenant Smith and Navy Lieutenant Towers.

Training was conducted throughout the remainder of the year and most of 1913, the fledgling aviators experimenting with flying and operational techniques. In January 1913, the aviation camp was ordered to join the annual fleet maneuvers off Guantanamo, Cuba. Having already developed some spotting and underwater-detection techniques, the Marine pilots were able to show themselves and their aircraft to the best advantage. During the exercises, the pilots tracked submerged submarines, scouted for enemy surface vessels, took photographs, and dropped aerial "missiles." In addition to their duties of supporting the fleet during the exercises, the Navy and Marine aviators also provided indoctrination rides for over 150 Navy and Marine officers. These included one future Marine Commandant and staunch aviation supporter, then-Lieutenant Colonel John A. Lejeune.

This first operation by the Annapolis contingent was a success and alerted many skeptics that naval aviation was to be taken seriously. But Lieutenant Cunningham was not happy. He chafed at the limitations of his Wright B-1, a plane which had been wrecked and rebuilt more times than he cared to remember, and whose every flight was suspect, even though he had made over 400 flights with it. He pleaded for newer aircraft constantly, citing engine failure and structural problems as the reasons for his dissatisfaction.

By August 1913, Cunningham had one more problem, common among aviators. He asked to be detached from flying duty as a result of his fiancee's fears for his flying safety. "My fiancee will not consent to marry me unless I give up flying," he wrote in requesting a transfer. Accordingly, and perhaps with some personal misgivings, he was assigned to ground duty at the Washington Navy Yard. But his heart and mind were still in the sky, and he remained a vocal and persistent advocate for Marine aviation. (He would eventually return to active flying.)

By the end of 1913, thirteen naval aviators had been trained at Annapolis, providing a cadre of pilots, in addition to the mechanic trainees, to train further personnel. Three of the pilots were Marines: Cunningham, Smith, and Second Lieutenant William M. McIlvain, who soloed in September 1913. The Commandant was sufficiently impressed with his Marines' progress that in October 1913, he recommended the establishment of a Marine flying camp at the Philadelphia Navy Yard to be stationed with the advance base regiment being formed there.

In August 1913, the General Board of the Navy—a senior advisory panel established in 1900, reporting directly to the Secretary of the Navy—called for the formal creation of a naval air service, with appropriate funding in the military budget for 1914. Accordingly, Secretary of the Navy Josephus Daniels created a seven-man board, headed by Navy Captain W.I. Chambers, an early advocate of naval aviation. This panel, called the Chambers Board, which included Lieutenant Alfred Cunningham, Marine Aviator Number 1, advised creation of a section of six aircraft as an advance group, shore-based. The board also recommended that a Marine officer be appointed as a member of the staff of the new Director of Naval Aviation. Navy and Marine aviation were thus getting their share of attention in the military. But implementation of the board's recommendations was slow.

However, several notable events occurred in the next few months. The Annapolis training camp, along with its Marine contingent, was moved to the old Navy Yard at Pensacola, Florida, some fifty miles east of Mobile, Alabama, on the Florida panhandle. Meanwhile, Congress, in its biggest appropriation for military aviation so far, had voted a $1,000,000 budget for naval aviation. The money was to be spent under the eye of the Secretary of the Navy. Soon after, on January 5, 1914, a group of Marine pilots, enlisted mechanics, and equipment, were detached from the main Annapolis group moving to Pensacola. Travelling north to Philadelphia, the group, with Lieutenants Smith and McIlvain among its members, embarked in the Navy transport *Hancock*, and sailed for Puerto Rico to join the Advance Base Brigade in the annual Atlantic Fleet exercises. It was the first time an all-Marine aviation force was to operate as a special part of Marine ground forces.

For the next three weeks, using the Curtiss C-3—an F-model flying boat equipped with a pusher engine and a two-man crew—Smith and McIlvain demonstrated the capabilities of the aircraft in a variety of roles, including scouting and reconnaissance. By the time the exercises ended and the Marines departed for home on February 5, the two pilots had made fifty-two flights and spent nearly twenty hours in the air. The unit was pleased with itself, certain that it had proved the value of Marine aviation. The members even recommended the expansion of the unit to five pilots and twenty mechanics with two aircraft. But it was not to be. Upon their arrival at Pensacola, the Marines found, to their dismay, that they had been disbanded as a separate unit and once more were simply part of the overall larger Navy establishment. There was, evidently, still much highly placed skepticism as to the value of aviation.

In 1914, the United States' long-simmering border dispute with Mexico, which was going through a long period of governmental instability, threatened to erupt into open warfare. Indeed, a small band of Marines was sent to participate in operations against the Mexican cities of Vera Cruz and Tampico in April. Although Lieutenant Smith was stationed with the fleet at Tampico, having been ordered from Pensacola along with several other Marines, he did not fly in support of the Marine brigade's activities. By January 1915, Lieutenant McIlvain was the sole remaining Marine pilot in the Marine Section of the Navy's flying school. (With the outbreak of World War I in August 1914, Lieutenant Smith had gone to France as an observer.) But Cunningham reappeared, reporting in April, evidently having relieved some of his wife's fears of his flying activities. In the summer, a fourth pilot, Lieutenant Francis T. Evans, arrived to begin flight training.

In August, the Marines began training in land planes, through an agreement reached with the Army's Signal Corps, McIlvain being one of the first aviators to receive Army pilot training. There was also more experimentation at Pensacola, particularly with launching aircraft from ships with catapults. Cunningham sustained a serious back injury on November 8, 1916, when, immediately after being shot from a catapult mount on the *North Carolina*, his AB-2 seaplane rolled inverted and crashed into the water.

The news from Europe had not been good during 1916. The war was expanding, and the Germans were on the offensive. Submarine attacks on supposedly neutral American shipping, spy fever in the United States itself, and sympathy for the hardpressed Allies, gave notice that America could not remain neutral for much longer. Things were also becoming increasingly complicated by the possibility of war with Mexico.

With all these combative possibilities, in August 1916 Congress voted $3,500,000 in appropriations for naval aircraft and equipment. A permanent Navy Flying Corps was created, with 150 officers and 350 enlisted men from both the Navy and Marine Corps. By the end of the year, sixty new aircraft, including thirty Curtiss N-9 floatplanes—variants of the famous "Jenny" training biplane—had been ordered, with twenty-five of the tractor-engined planes being at Pensacola by December.

The business of flying aircraft was still new, and there was much to be learned concerning the safe operation of these early aircraft. Several maneuvers which later generations take for granted could be terrifying, even fatal, for a hapless pilot. One of these maneuvers was the loop. A successful loop had been accomplished some years before and, by this time, a loop was a staple of every combat pilot's repertoire in the skies of Europe. However, in the peaceful American skies, no one had successfully looped a tractor-type seaplane. The heavy pontoons, the floats, upon which the aircraft maneuvered on the water, created drag problems, which could prove dangerous, even fatal, if an attempt was made to loop the ponderous craft.

On February 13, 1917, Evans tried to loop his N-9 from an altitude of 3,500 feet. His entry into the maneuver was not smooth, and the airplane went into a stall and then a spin. A spin was another terrifying, little understood, gyration at the time, and it seemed that Lieutenant Evans was going to crash into Pensacola Bay. But, whether by design or instinct—even he was not sure—Evans pushed forward on the plane's control wheel and activated the rudder to slow the rapidly accelerating turn. The spin slowed, then stopped altogether and Evans found himself in control of the airplane again.

Regaining his composure, he again tried to loop the plane and again fell into a spin. But he righted himself as before, and tried another loop. Finally, he managed to complete the maneuver, repeating the entire show over the base to make sure he had witnesses. It was not long before his looping technique and life-saving spin recovery were incorporated into the syllabus at Pensacola, thereby solving a major safety problem and no doubt saving countless young aviators' lives. Evans was awarded the Distinguished Flying Cross nineteen years later, in 1936, for his efforts.

The First Combat Tests

First Lieutenant Cunningham was directed, on February 26, 1917, to organize an Aviation Company at the Philadelphia Navy Yard to be associated with the Advance Base Force. The number of Marine pilots stood at five, with plans to double that number in the near future. With the Army taking most of the tactical side of aviation—bombing, ground attack—for itself, making clear that it did not want the Navy intruding into what it considered to be its territory, the Navy decided that its aviation units could serve best against the German submarine menace. The extraordinarily ambitious program of building 1,700 seaplanes was adopted in October.

The Marines, eager to prove their proud claim of being "first to fight," immediately prepared a brigade to be sent to France. Anxious to take advantage of the rapid wartime expansion affecting all services, Cunningham, newly promoted to captain, strove to obtain more men and equipment, and—most important—to go to France and fight alongside the ground brigade. When the U.S. declared war against the Central Powers in April 1917, he would have that chance.

Renamed the Marine Aeronautic Company, the Philadelphia contingent absorbed men from Pensacola as well as from other Marine units. Its first duty was to fly antisubmarine patrols alongside the Navy. But there was also concern that the Marine aviators fly in support of their fellow Marines on the ground. The Commandant, Major General

George Barnett, therefore, was allowed to authorize formation of a second Marine aviation unit—this one with landplanes—to fly reconnaissance and artillery-spotting missions for the brigade of Marines bound for France.

Cunningham immediately began to fill the slots in the new second unit, personally addressing the incoming classes of officer candidates at Quantico and preaching the gospel of Marine aviation. He was not disappointed; the response was enthusiastic. The young college-age volunteers were naturally taken by the thrill and glamor of flying, and Cunningham was able to have his pick of qualified applicants, eventually choosing eighteen for the two aviation companies. Most of these pilot trainees were, by the nature of the wartime mobilization, civilians rather than career regulars and were commissioned in the Reserves. By October 1917, the First Marine Aeronautic Company had a total of 34 officers and 330 enlisted men with two Curtiss R-6 floatplanes, plus one French-built Farman landplane for flight training.

The First Marine Aeronautic Company, first of the two units ready for service and led by the newly promoted Captain Evans, took its Curtiss R-6s to the Naval Air Station at Cape May, New Jersey, to conduct further training and operational coastal patrols. The unit operated at Cape May from October 1917 to January 1918. On January 9, it left Philadelphia for the Azores, where it was to conduct antisubmarine patrols.

The Company was beefed up with more aircraft, bringing the total to ten R-6s and two N-9s, both derivatives of the JN "Jenny" series of Curtiss biplanes. The N-9 had a second cockpit with a machine gun and a more powerful engine. A further increase brought six Curtiss HS-2L flying boats, which carried a pilot and a crewman at a speed of 90 miles per hour for a range of 400 miles. These single-engine aircraft represented a great improvement over the smaller floatplanes and it was with great anticipation that the Marine aviators set up shop at Punta Delgada on the southwest coast of San Miguel Island. Flying a 70-mile arc from the island, the First Aeronautic Company had an idyllic setting to be at war, although one young pilot was moved to write directly to the Commandant, Major General Barnett, requesting more vigorous duty. The irate general fired back a letter which informed the anxious youth in no uncertain terms that it was his duty to accept his assignment and do his best. Also, the reply continued, although a new assignment had, in fact, been mailed to him, the Commandant was revoking the new orders.

Good weather and friendly inhabitants made the Marines' stay the best it could be. There were some contacts; some submarines were sighted, and even attacked. But no real damage was done and certainly no submarine was sunk.

The second unit of the Marine Aeronautic Company—the landplane section under Captain McIlvain—was to follow a more complicated path to the war. The plan originally called for the unit to receive basic training with Army instructors on Long Island, New York, and then proceed to Texas for futher instruction. After that, the squadron—for it was now the First Aviation Squadron—would go to France.

At first everything went well. In October 1917, the squadron moved from Philadelphia to Mineola on Long Island, and flew JN-4B Jennies with civilian instructors. While the 1st Aviation Squadron was in training, a third Marine aviation unit was formed, under Captain Roy S. Geiger, the fifth Marine aviator, although this unit's mission was, as yet, undecided.

Cunningham was running into a stone wall trying to find a mission for his landplane squadrons. The Army did not want anything to do with the Marine pilots and bluntly told them so. Typically, Cunningham tried to rethink the problem and come up with alternative solutions. Eventually, he decided to concentrate on augmenting the Navy's antisubmarine effort. Apparently, the Navy had thought only in terms of attacking the German submarines while actually at sea. Cunningham came up with a proposal to bomb the sub bases, thereby adding a second form of attack against the U-boat menace. The General Board of the Navy approved the formation of a so-called Northern Bombing Group in February 1918. By March 11, Cunningham had begun to set his plan in motion, combining Geiger's and McIlvain's units in Miami to form the 1st Marine Aviation Force.

The decision to create the Northern Bombing Group was much easier than the actual formation. The unit's mission was changed again and again. If the Group was to be sent against the submarine bases, why couldn't they also fly fighters to escort the bombers? Or perhaps the Marines would be better employed on daylight bombing raids against other targets.

The men and machines still had to get to the war. While the debate evolved concerning the mission of the Northern Bombing Group to which it was assigned, McIlvain's Mineola-based group moved from the deep winter of Long Island—where temperatures had dipped to sixteen degrees below zero, with an accompanying halt in flight operations—to more hospitable southern climes. The Army's Gerstner Field in Louisiana was to host the Marines. There the Marines were also introduced to a new aircraft, the Standard E-1, a small, rotary-engined single-seater.

Captain Geiger's group in Philadelphia also moved to Miami, Florida, in February 1918. To forestall any complication arising from Army interference, Geiger appropriated the entire assets and grounds of the Curtiss Flying School, including the Jenny training planes. He promptly commissioned the civilian instructors as well. (Geiger had help in this unorthodox procedure from Cunningham, who also obtained additional trainers for Geiger.) Finally, McIlvain's squadron flew from Louisiana and joined Geiger's group in Miami, thereby bringing together the two main components of the 1st Marine Aviation Force.

However, Cunningham knew he needed more personnel to complete his grand plan for four squadrons in France, flying and fighting alongside the Navy. Subsequently, the intrepid captain boldly went to the Navy's main training bases at Pensacola and Key West, and recruited eager young pilots, already designated as Naval Aviators, who were anxious to see action in France and did not care whether they saw it wearing a Navy or Marine uniform. Resigning from the Navy to be picked up by the Marines, these men completed Cunningham's requirement for 135 aviators who finally arrived in France. Seventy-eight of the 135 were these transferred pilots, most of them Naval Reserve officers.

As the time for departure for Europe drew near, the pace at the Miami Marine training facility quickened. Everything from seaplane training to aerobatics and gunnery was crammed into a few weeks. By June 16, 1918, Cunningham had reorganized the group into four squadrons, simply designated A, B, C, and D. Geiger, McIlvain, Captain Douglas B. Roben, and First Lieutenant Russell A. Presley were the respective commanding officers. Three of the four skippers left for France to reconnoiter the situation (Presley and his Squadron D remained behind), and on July 10, the 1st Marine Aviation Force received its marching orders, too. They left on the 13th by train for Philadelphia—which gave them a tremendous sendoff—thence to New York and the *De Kalb*, the Navy transport that was to take them to France.

The Marine Flying Field, which was the new name adopted by the Curtiss facility at Miami, was left to carry on continued training as well as complete the formation of Squadron D, which had been left behind to finish its training and then conduct patrols along the Florida coast. The wartime expansion of Marine aviation brought the strength up to 1,500 officers and 6,000 enlisted men. A new program of training enlisted pilots was established to help meet this manning requirement. (European nations, which had been at war for nearly four years, had come to depend on their nucleus of enlisted pilots, and counted several former enlisted men—such as the French ace, Guynemer, who began his flying career as a corporal—among their flying cadre.)

Initial Operations in France

The 1st Marine Aviation Force disembarked at Brest harbor on July 30, 1918. There were problems from the start. Captain Cunningham found himself without means of transporting his men and equipment the

400 miles to the base at Calais. The resourceful Cunningham obtained the use of a train, however, for the two-day trip. After reaching Calais, Cunningham found that now he had no aircraft! After the train trip and sorting out Marine motor-pool assets from a mixup with the Army, this last problem was almost the last straw. Cunningham thought he had arranged the delivery of seventy-two DH-4 bombers, two-place, single-engine craft then being built under license in America. But the planes had arrived unassembled and it would take a great deal of time to put them together, test them, and commence operations. Cunningham discovered that the De Havillands had somehow been shipped to England across the Channel.

Undaunted, he bargained with the British. It was agreed that, owing to the Americans' holding a fair number of Liberty engines—the powerplant used by the DH-4—and the British having an equally large number of engineless DH-9A airframes (the DH-9A was a derivative of the DH-4), the British would deliver one complete DH-9A for every three Liberties supplied by the Americans. With the concurrence of the U.S. Navy, the deal was consummated and, with the eventual delivery of some of the wayward DH-4s in September, the Marines had, by the November 11 armistice, thirty-six aircraft: one-half the planned complement.

But at the initial arrival, when there were no aircraft available for the Marines, how could they begin operations? The Royal Air Force once again supplied the answer. Because of a shortage of pilots, the RAF—which had been formed by combining the original Royal Flying Corps and the Royal Naval Air Service on April 1, 1918—had more aircraft than it could operate. The arrangement was made that each of the newly arrived Marines would fly three bombing missions with their British allies. RAF Squadrons 217 and 218 were only too glad to accommodate the Americans, who were equally pleased to gain experience with these combat-seasoned veterans.

It was not long before the Marines began to see action and some notable milestones were attained. While flying with 218 Squadron, on September 28, First Lieutenant E.S. Brewer and Gunnery Sergeant H.B. Wersheiner scored the first aerial victory for the Marines when they were attacked by German fighters over Belgium, both crewmen sustaining wounds during the dogfight. A week later, on October 2 and 3, again operating with 218 Squadron, Captain R.S. Lytle and Gunnery Sergeant A. Winman, Captain F.P. Mulcahy and Gunnery Sergeant T.L. McCullough, and Lieutenant Frank Nelms and Gunnery Sergeant Archie Paschal conducted the first aerial resupply drop in Marine aviation history. The trio of crews delivered 2,600 pounds of food and supplies to a surrounded French regiment. Lytle, Mulcahy, and Nelms were awarded the Distinguished Service Medal, while their enlisted crewmen received the Navy Cross.

By October, Squadron D, originally left behind, had arrived with additional pilots and men. The 1st Marine Aviation Force's roster now stood at 149 officers and 842 enlisted personnel. The squadrons were renumbered, as 7, 8, 9, and 10. A change in the planned mission also occurred. Because the Germans had evacuated their submarine bases along the Channel coast, due to the pressure of the Allied offensives at the time, the original mission of attacking the German bases was unnecessary. Therefore, the Marine squadrons could operate alongside the RAF in support of the British and Belgian ground forces which were gathering steam for a final assault against the crumbling German army.

By mid-October, the Marines were ready to operate on their own. Having received enough DH-4s and DH-9As, through Cunningham's arrangement with the British, the Marines set out on October 14, 1918, to strike German-held railyards in occupied Belgium. Captain Lytle, now with Squadron 9, led a flight of five DH-4s and three DH-9As. The mission was to have double significance for the Corps, for as well as being the first time the Marines had flown a mission of their own, it was also to yield the first Medals of Honor won by Marines in aerial combat.

The mission against the railyards went without serious confrontation. However, on the return flight, the Marines were attacked by German fighters, a combination of Pfalz D-IIIs—highly maneuverable, though underpowered, fighters belonging to an earlier stage of the war—and Fokker D-VIIs, the top German fighters of the period, possessing speed and maneuverability which made them distinctly dangerous opponents against the slower, less agile Marine bombers. The German fighters all seemed to converge on the machine piloted by Second Lieutenant Ralph Talbot, one of Cunningham's Naval Reserve "thefts" earlier in the year. His gunner, Corporal Robert G. Robinson, shot down one of the Germans, but was severely wounded by another pair of attackers who spattered the struggling DH with bullets.

Although in great pain, Robinson continued to fire his machine guns while Talbot maneuvered the aircraft, trying to throw off the Germans' aim. Hit twice more, in the hip and stomach, Robinson finally collapsed over his weapons, leaving Talbot to face the German onslaught alone. The pilot turned his DH into the German attack and shot down a fighter with his own forward-firing guns (some DHs were equipped with a pair of guns firing forward as well as the normal pair mounted in the rear cockpit.) After this second victory, Talbot put his plane into a steep dive to escape the remainder of the German force, and safely landed at a Belgian airfield close to a hospital, where the wounded Robinson received medical attention. The intrepid pair of flyers were awarded the Medal of Honor for their actions that day.

Captain Lytle had also had a harrowing experience when he tried to go to Talbot's aid. Turning his aircraft around when he saw his squadron-mate under attack, Lytle's engine quit, leaving him to glide towards some Belgian troops he saw on the ground. He made a successful emergency landing. Later, he and Marine ground crews dismantled the aircraft and brought it back to their base.

During the following week, the Marines continued to carry out raids against German positions, usually without benefit and comfort of fighter escort. On October 22, the Corps lost its first aircraft in action against the enemy. A DH-4, flown by Lieutenants H.G. Norman and C.C. Taylor, was shot down by German fighters during a raid.

By the time of the armistice on November 11, 1918, the First Marine Aviation Force had flown forty-three missions with the RAF, besides fourteen of their own, and had accounted for four German fighters, with claims for eight more. Four Marines had been killed in action. It had been a short, but active beginning for Marine aviation; but Cunningham was now concerned with getting his men home before the onset of winter. Prior to the return to America in December 1918, he said: "I think we could accomplish much more at home, getting our Aviation service established under the new conditions of peace."[2] He was going to have his work cut out for him, for hard times lay ahead for Marine aviation.

Between Wars

As in every war, the period immediately following the cessation of hostilities was concerned with dismantling the war machine and bringing the men home. At the end of World War I, the 1st Marine Aviation Force had 282 officers and 2,180 enlisted men distributed among the three groups in the Azores, Marine Flying Field Miami, and Europe. In September 1919, however, the Force disbanded and its remaining assets dispersed from Miami to Parris Island, South Carolina, and Quantico, Virginia.

Cunningham, now a major, began to rebuild his command, forming two squadrons, D and E, even as the Miami operation was shut down. Realizing that the very existence of its aviation section was hanging in the balance, the Marine Corps began lobbying Congress to maintain the force, at least at prewar levels, as well as making Marine aviation a permanent force with its own bases.

Cunningham knew he also faced internal resistance. Many senior Marine officers remained skeptical, if not outright hostile, to Marine aviation. Many were angry that in Europe, the Aviation Force Marines—through no fault of their own—had not supported their brethren on the ground. Cunningham generally sympathized with their frustration, writing: " . . . the only excuse for aviation in any service is its usefulness in assisting the troops on the ground to successfully carry out their operations." [3]

His persuasiveness paid off. After a year and a half of deliberation,

Congress authorized the overall manning level for the entire Marine Corps as 20 percent of the Navy. This came out to 26,380 officers and men. In addition, Congress allowed 1,020 men for Marine aviation, as well as the establishment of permanent air stations at Quantico, San Diego, and Parris Island.

But it was not for Major Cunningham to lead the Marines past 1920. Even though he was the acknowledged spokesman for Marine aviation, a man more senior in rank took over in December. Lieutenant Colonel Thomas C. Turner was, however, well qualified. Having entered the Corps in 1902, Turner, like Cunningham, was an avid aviation enthusiast and learned to fly at San Diego with the Army. During the war, he served at the Army's Ellington Field in Texas, gaining a designation as a naval aviator in March 1918.

Apparently jealous of Turner, Cunningham had sought to bar the senior officer from any participation in aviation matters. But, after a 1919 tour in Haiti where Turner was cited for bravery during a bandit attack, he prevailed on his friend, Major General John A. Lejeune, now the Commandant, to order him to flying duty. Lejeune, who had flown with Lieutenant Evans in 1913, and was an early convert to aviation, recognized Turner's talents and placed him in charge of the Marine aviation department. Cunningham was given command of Marine aviation in the Dominican Republic.

Cunningham remained in Santo Domingo for a year and a half, then returned to ground duty in accordance with existing policy. A five-year tour in a flying status was followed by a non-flying billet. After all his dedication, work, and sacrifice, he would never fly again. In 1928, he asked to be returned to flight status but was turned down. He wrote the Commandant:

I was the first Marine officer to fly and spent the best years of my career working with enthusiasm to advance Marine Corps aviation. I did the unappreciated pioneer work and stuck by it during the time when no one considered it important enough to be desirable duty . . . ." [4]

But it was not enough. He was too old, he was told, to be returned to flight status. Embittered, he continued to serve in the Corps until he retired in 1935. He died four years later, at the age of fifty-seven, of a coronary thrombosis.

Turner became the driving force behind Marine aviation's struggle to remain alive during the 1920s. From 1920 to 1925, and again from 1929 until his death in 1931, Turner served as the chief of Marine aviation. Major E.G. Brainard took over in March 1925, but after four years he resigned to go into private industry. Turner was recalled to his old post. With the sometime-triumverate of Cunningham, Turner, and Brainard lobbying in Washington, the programs began to solidify.

On October 30, 1920, Lejeune had approved a reorganization of the existing group to include groups of two to four squadrons, divided into flights. At the time, four squadrons of two flights were formed: Number 1 was based in the Dominican Republic, Numbers 2 and 3 at Quantico, and Number 4 was stationed at Port-au-Prince, Haiti, to support brigade operations in that Caribbean country. This organization was changed many times, and by 1926 there were also two Aviation Groups, one on either coast, to support respective Expeditionary Forces: the West Coast group based at San Diego, and the East Coast group at Quantico.

The 1920s

With a somewhat more stable organization established, attention could now be given to developing the physical aspect of Marine aviation. It was long overdue. The Marine aviators were still using the war surplus DH-4 for everything from ambulance to bomber to transport. Boeing in Seattle, Washington, one of the major American airplane companies to survive America's transition to peacetime, tried to modernize the DH-4 by rebuilding several with metal-frame fuselages. This model was designated the O2B-1 and was used for observation duties.

The American-designed and -built series of Thomas-Morse MB-3 Scouts were among the first aircraft to be procured especially for the Marines. Basically World War I design, used as trainers in the States, these planes were barely adequate. The MB-3 was a redesign of the war-time S-4C, which used a rotary engine with resulting high torque levels. The MB-3, having used a stationary Hispano-Suiza inline, did not have such torque problems. Actually, only seven of eleven MB-3s were ever assembled, and these only flew four of the twenty-one months they were assigned to Quantico.

With the war's end, the Germans had been required, by direct order in the Treaty of Versailles, to surrender some of their supreme fighters, the Fokker D-VIIs, and the few Marines who flew the handful of D-7s to be assembled were impressed with the German fighter. It was about time, they thought, for some American-designed, American-manufactured equipment.

Trying to answer this need, the fledgling Lewis and Vought Corporation came up with the VE-7 series. These biplanes were successful, due to their reliability and relative agility in the air. They were also tractable, being used in two- and single-seat versions, as well as floatplanes. Vought also produced one of the mainstays of the Navy and Marine air arm during the 1920s and 1930s, the O2U Corsair two-seat dive-bomber.

Not to be outdone, Curtiss initiated its enduring series of Navy "Hawk" fighters with the F6C-1, which was developed from the original Army XPW-8B/P-1 design of 1924. Built as one of the Navy's first carrier-based fighters, the first F6C-1s served only as proficiency trainers until they were transferred to the Marines in 1927. The Marines were never able to get enough of these nimble little biplane fighters, but were enthusiastic about those they were able to obtain. Apparently 1931 was the year when the Corps had the greatest number of F6Cs on board—four of them in the East Coast Expeditionary Force at Quantico, serving with VF-8M and VO-6M (the "M" denoting, naturally, Marine). The other eight were with the West Coast unit at San Diego with VF-10M.

In July 1920, the Secretary of the Navy had established a formal designating system for both Navy aircraft and squadrons; the Marines were included. Aircraft were given three-character basic designators: the first letter indicating the basic mission of the plane, the numeral indicating the number design of the manufacturer, and the third letter signifying the manufacturer itself. Thus, "O2B" denoted the second observation design built by Boeing; "F6C" was the sixth fighter from Curtiss. (It was not until 1941 that the Navy Department also permitted official popular names to be included in an aircraft's designation.)

Navy squadrons were also designated according to their primary mission. The first letter, V, signified a unit using heavier-than-air equipment—as opposed to airship squadrons, signified by a "Z"—and the following letter described the mission, i.e., "F" for fighter or "O" for observation. Marine squadrons were designated by the simple method of adding an "M." Thus, VO-8M was Observation Squadron Eight (Marine). It was not until 1937 that the current method of designation—VMO—was created.

Boeing was also a competitor in fighter design, for both the Army and Navy during this period. The initial design, Model 15, first flew in September 1923 and continued to be developed by the Army as the XPW-9 series. The Navy was also interested in the design, and ordered ten examples for the Marines as the FB. The Marines took these new fighters to China for a while in 1925.

The Boeing design continued to be developed and improved, the F2B and F3B models appearing in 1926 and 1928, respectively. But it was the definitive F4B model which became the symbol of military aviation—Army (as the P-12), Navy, and Marine—in the late 1920s and mid-1930s.

The design refinement which followed the F3B was unusual in that it did not require the installation of a more powerful engine, normally the procedure to increase performance for a newer model of the same design. Enough aerodynamic refinement—such as the addition of an engine cowling (in the case of the -2 model) and different landing gear—gave a 22-mile-per-hour increase in speed over the F3B. The XF4B-1 was also 400 pounds lighter than its predecessor. The F4B-2 was similar to the

Army's P-12C and D fighters, while the final F4B-3 and -4 models followed the P-12E and F, respectively.

One of the prime operators of the little Boeing fighter was VF-9M, stationed at Quantico. Established on September 1, 1925, as VF-2M, with First Lieutenant Lawson H.M. Sanderson as its commanding officer, VF-9M went through a life of ups and downs, feasts and famines, which mirrored the fluctuating status of Marine aviation in general. Along with Sanderson, the unit eventually numbered several future Marine "greats" among its alumni, including First Lieutenant C.F. Schilt who would win the Medal of Honor in Nicaragua, and Aviation Cadet Gregory Boyington who would also win the Medal of Honor, as well as become the Corps' top ace in World War II.

Initially equipped with Vought VE-7s, then-VF-2M obtained Boeing FB-1s in February 1926. It then immediately began to enter service competitions, including the 1926 National Air Races in Philadelphia, where the Boeings were also used in aerial displays. Competition entries were intended to keep Marine aviation before the public eye.

The squadron began to go through a succession of commanders when Sanderson departed in November to attend Company Officers School. He was replaced by First Lieutenant Jay Swartwout, who began training pilots as fast as he could. Several of the new naval aviators were Naval Aviation Pilots (NAPs)—enlisted men who retained their noncommissioned status even after getting their wings.

In December 1926, eight F6C-3s arrived for the rival squadron, VF-1M, and Swartwout wrote Major Brainard, now Officer in Charge of Marine aviation. Brainard promised that the next new batch of fighters would go to VF-2M. Swartwout turned over the squadron to Chief Marine Gunner Elmo Reagan—probably the only time a warrant officer has had command of a U.S. aviation squadron—on January 6, 1927. The "Gunner" was replaced in March, however, by Captain W.T. Evans. One month later, true to his word, Major Brainard sent four new F6C-4s.

By the following June, though, Evans had been relieved by First Lieutenant V.N. Guymon, who had only received his wings six months before! Problems developed with the new Curtiss fighters' landing gear, two aircraft suffering crashes due to structural failure, one aircraft coming to grief twice in one week. Guymon was obviously concerned and hoped that this apparent jinx on his first command would vanish when VF-2M was redesignated VF-9M on July 1, 1927. But the squadron continued to have problems. Aircraft A-7397, having returned from its second stay in the Brown Field repair shop, survived only long enough for First Lieutenant H.C. Busbey to put it into the Potomac River with a throttle stuck in the closed position.

Thankfully, Guymon departed in October for what promised to be less hectic combat duty in Nicaragua. And so it went. VF-9M seemed to be a training squadron for young COs, but on June 15, 1930, First Lieutenant Sanderson returned to Quantico to lead the squadron which had been re-redesignated VF-5M as of July 1, 1928. This change came as a result of a renumbering reorganization. (*This* designation lasted until August 18, 1930, when it reverted to VF-9M.) With the aggressive, professional Sanderson back at the helm again, the squadron seemed to settle down finally into a routine. And Sanderson took his planes and pilots on tour whenever he could. The public had to be kept aware of its Marine aviators.

VF-9M continued to fly Curtiss aircraft, the F6Cs having progressed to F7Cs in 1928. By 1932, the F7Cs were supposed to give way to Boeing F4B-4s, but in August the eight F7Cs still remained. As VF-9M was scheduled to appear at the Canadian Air Races in Montreal within three weeks, new aircraft were needed. The F7Cs had been prohibited from airshow participation due to several crashes involving the type at public displays. The best that could be done was to borrow nine Curtiss O2C-1s from VO-6M. So, VF-9M operated yet another type of aircraft for a short period, painted with a distinctive arrowhead design on the O2Cs' cowlings and rudders.

By mid-September, however, the first three F4B-4s arrived by train, the entire squadron excitedly turning out to assemble the precious cargo. Within a week, on September 23, the engineering officer, Ed Pugh, had taken the first fighter for a test flight and, returning with a huge grin, proclaimed the thrill of flying a really modern aircraft. The end of the month saw VF-9M with six flyable F4Bs in operation.

Even with the influx of new modern equipment, manpower shortages remained a constant thorn in Sanderson's side, as it was for all Marine squadrons at the time. Airshow commitments were always demanding a full complement of airplanes, but without the pilots to fly them it was no matter. Borrowing pilots from other squadrons sometimes provided relief.

In July 1933, VF-9M received an extra batch of F4Bs as VF-10M, a San Diego squadron, was redesignated a light bombing squadron and its twelve Boeings reassigned to a hungry, happy VF-9M. Eighteen aircraft. Nine spares! It was a luxurious feeling, and Sanderson quickly prevailed on the Marines in California to ferry six of the new additions east. It was up to Sanderson to get the remaining six himself, which he did, by ferrying two older multi-place aircraft out to North Island, near San Diego. Actually, by August Sanderson was in charge of a squadron of twenty-eight aircraft. Through an administrative oversight, the Bureau of Aeronautics had alloted six more airplanes in addition to the eighteen already on strength. A further letter authorized an increase in pilots to twenty-two. It was an incredible stroke of good luck and portended good times for the squadron.

Sanderson continued to be the main backer for public display. This, of course, is not to indicate that the Marine squadrons did not keep their primary military skills sharp. In between airshows, maneuvers and practice bombing drills were the order of the day. But these activities gave no chance for the public to watch their Marine aviators in action. Therefore, an active airshow schedule was a must.

The October 1933 National Charity Air Pageant, held in New York, promised to be the biggest airshow yet, and VF-9M and VO-7M, with nineteen Boeings and thirteen Curtiss Helldivers respectively, were to participate. Roosevelt Field on Long Island was to be the host field, and the two Marine squadrons arrived en masse on October 7, after a three and one-half hour flight from Quantico. The huge crowds were thrilled by the noisy, flashy demonstration of Marine airpower, Sanderson having developed special aerobatic maneuvers for the event. The public response was so overwhelming that Rear Admiral Ernest J. King, chief of the Bureau of Aeronautics, quickly revised the budget for Marine aviation.

Sanderson continued to lead VF-9M until July 1934 when he was relieved by Captain Ford O. Rogers, a pilot who had flown in the war under Lieutenant William McIlvain in France. Handling an eighteen-plane squadron, both in the air and on the ground, was no mean trick, but Rogers was equal to the challenge and he quickly won the respect of his squadron. The years to come were typical, more airshows, maneuvers, and developmental exercises. VF-9M had established itself as the premier Marine fighter squadron. To have served in the Quantico unit was a source of great pride for officers and men alike.

VF-9M was even qualified aboard the carrier *Saratoga* (CV-3) in March 1937, off San Diego; the ship's skipper was Captain—later Fleet Admiral—William Halsey. It was the first time most of the pilots had seen a carrier and although difficulties were encountered, the skill and natural ebullience of the Marines saw them through the rough spots.

Time was catching up with VF-9M however. On July 1, 1937, another numbering reorganization redesignated it as VMF-1 (Marine Fighting Squadron 1). Another directive of the same date, ordered 65 percent of VF-9M's personnel to other duties, with replacements coming from newly designated pilots and Aviation Cadets.

The date July 1, 1937, was coming to have considerable significance for VMF-1; Ford Rogers, by now a major, was relieved by Captain W.L. McKittrick. A long-time squadron member who had also commanded Quantico squadrons VO-6M and VO-7M, "Mac" had taken the squadron through the 1930s, and the introduction of the tough new F3F series of fighters, manufactured by Grumman on Long Island, New York. Big, fast, and Grumman-tough, and with two relatively new features, an enclosed cockpit and retractable landing gear, these biplanes were the last such fighters to serve with the U.S. Navy or Marines; but they helped to establish Grumman as the main supplier of Navy aircraft.

McKittrick continued to follow the airshow circuit established by his predecessors, but by July 1941, war seemed very close and a reorganization of Marine aviation was in order, with the establishment of two wings, rather than groups. VMF-1 was now renumbered VMF-111 and continued to serve as one of the leading Marine squadrons.

Combat Operations in the 1920s

The 1920s and 1930s were years of uncertain and erratic growth for Marine aviation. Many times, people involved were left to their own initiative and resources to get things done and also keep the program going. Sometimes, the dedication and enthusiasm of these individuals were all that kept the program alive during the Depression years. These efforts provided America the tight nucleus of trained, experienced personnel which would sustain her through the dark days after Pearl Harbor.

Many of the senior Marine aviators in World War II gained their initial combat experience in action in Central America during the 1920s, especially in Nicaragua, Haiti, and the Dominican Republic. The situation was something like the situation in China at the same time, where a strong, centralized government was a near impossibility and local war lords, complete with their own armies, ruled their own specific areas.

Nicaragua had the traditional economic and political strife, and throughout the late 1800s was an object of hemispheric concern for worried U.S. presidential administrations, the Marines going into the country to protect American interests as early as 1853 at San Juan del Norte on the southeastern border with Costa Rica. Marines continued to go to Nicaragua periodically throughout the early 1900s as well, the political situation becoming more and more intolerable as dictators vied for overall control.

Problems also cropped up in the Dominican Republic and Haiti, the first Marine aircraft arriving in both countries in 1919 to support ground operations which had begun in 1916. Jenny trainers and Curtiss HS-2L flying boats, used for coastal patrols, flew in during February and March. It was during Marine operations in Haiti that development of the dive-bombing technique probably occurred, although it is difficult to pinpoint such an event. Certainly, during World War I pilots of both sides used steep bomb deliveries when the situation warranted. But the need to drop ordnance accurately through the dense jungle cover of the

Caribbean countries gave men such as VO-9M's Lieutenant Sanderson—later of VF-9M and one of the premier Marine aviators of the period—the chance to develop the technique. This was not the steep, screaming, almost 90-degree dive of the German Stukas twenty years later, but rather a more gentle 45-degree dive. Still, for the aircraft of the day, it was a fairly steep angle.

The operations in Haiti and the Dominican Republic were mainly in support of men on the ground—reconnaissance, supply, and medical evacuation, with some primitive close air support. But it was in Nicaragua, eight years later, that Marine aviation had its first real post-World War I test. The political situation in late 1926 erupted into a bloody civil war, and the U.S. sent in the Marines to protect U.S. citizens and property.

In January 1927, additional troops arrived at Bluefields, a town on the southeastern coast, near the Escondido River, and were followed in February by six DH-4s of VO-1M under 42-year-old Major Ross Rowell. The supplies and men poured in, but by late May, a diplomatic arrangement seemed to have been reached through the efforts of Henry L. Stimson, President Calvin Coolidge's personal representative. Bandit raids continued, however, and any hope for a lasting peace was dashed. All of this turmoil only paved the way for the appearance of Augusto C. Sandino who aspired to become the "strong man" of Nicaragua. Afraid of the intervention from America which could prohibit his rise to power, Sandino took his rebel forces into the hills and jungles. It was against the rebels that the Marines had their first taste of combat in Nicaragua; it was strangely suggestive of events half a world away and forty years in the future.

On July 16, 1927, the Sandinistas—the popular name for Sandino's followers—attacked the northwest town of Ocotal, just over the border from neighboring Honduras. The position of the Marine garrison and loyalist defenders was precarious and Marine air units were called in. A 1030 attack by two aircraft kept the rebels' heads down, and by 1435, Major Rowell was leading a group of five DH-4s and Boeing O2Bs in a major bombing mission. Arriving over the besieged town, Rowell immediately struck the enemy positions, dropping bombs while the rear gunners fired curtains of machine-gun bullets. The devastating attack completely disrupted the Sandinistas' operation and they fled into the jungle. It taught Sandino the danger of a massed air strike and he seldom let his forces be caught in such an open position again.

Operations continued on the ground through the summer months, with Marine transports—the De Havillands and five big Fokker TA-1 trimotor transports—dropping onto the rugged landing strips hacked out of the jungle. Skirmishes along Nicaragua's coastal area, however, did not do anything to reduce Sandino's immense popular support in the interior. As in Vietnam, the overwhelming technical and military superiority of U.S. forces meant nothing against an enemy who came and went at will, fading in and out of the jungle aided by the peasant populace.

The decision was made for a major offensive against the Sandinistas in December 1927. Heavy rains and the constant guerrilla action against the Marines and the Nicaraguan National Guard troops made the planned offensive not only more necessary, but more difficult. Action at Quilali, a small village near the Coco River in the northwest border area with Honduras, highlighted both the power of the guerrillas and that of Marine aviation. On December 30, 1927, the Sandinista forces ambushed a Marine ground force near the village, inflicting heavy casualties. Even with Marine air support, the situation became desperate; many men had been wounded and supplies were low. To make matters worse, the relief column, five miles away, was itself under attack. Eighteen Marines at Quilali needed immediate medical attention, and evacuation by air seemed to be their only hope.

The beleaguered troops called for help, and First Lieutenant C.F. Schilt—another stalwart of VF-9M—prepared to go in. After an emergency airstrip had been cleared and his Vought O2U-1 Corsair refitted with oversize wheels from a DH-4, Schilt took off on January 6, 1928, in the first attempt to evacuate the Marines at Quilali. Flying through low clouds and fire from the Sandinistas, Schilt dropped his aircraft onto the short strip, while the troops on the ground ran forward to grab his plane and haul it to a stop, the Corsair not having working brakes. By the time Schilt had completed his tenth flight, on January 8, he had flown in 1,400 pounds of supplies and evacuated all of the eighteen seriously wounded personnel to Ocotal. It was an incredible display of flying skill and Marine courage, for which Schilt received the third Medal of Honor awarded to a Marine aviator.

It was becoming painfully obvious that operations on the ground would have to take a back seat to continued air attacks; the guerrillas were just too powerful and slippery. Major Rowell, leading many air operations, was only too happy to oblige. In fact, he was later to write in a 1929 article in the *Marine Corps Gazette*:

> The primary objective in bush warfare is the enemy personnel. The secondary objectives are his supplies and animal transport. The primary objective is easier to destroy than the secondary ones. [5]

On January 14, 1928, Rowell led a four-plane strike ahead of a major ground attack against San Albino, a rebel stronghold. Splitting his planes into two two-plane elements, Rowell attacked the enemy positions from two different directions. But the Sandinistas were ready. Experience with Marine air power had also taught them the advantages of antiaircraft defenses, however primitive. Flying within range of rifle fire, Rowell's planes ran into heavy attack from the men on the ground. But the Marine flyers still managed to drop their bombs and also to strafe the rebel positions heavily.

The observers behind the pilots were able to drop fragmentation bombs and white phosphorus hand grenades. Writing in the same article, Rowell outlined the use of weapons against jungle-based guerrillas:

The principal weapon used is the fragmentation bomb, which should be about 25 pounds in size. This type of bomb is very satisfactory and can be effectively used in either diving or contour attacks. The fuze has sufficient delay action so that the bomb will penetrate inside buildings before detonating. No troops, guerrilla or otherwise, will stand in the face of a well-directed fragmentation bombing attack. [6]

Throughout the middle of 1928, the Marines pushed and thrust the guerrillas back towards Honduras. The overall plan was to at least take away Sandino's military capabilities and First Lieutenant Merrit A. Edson—who, fifteen years later, would be one of the Marines' most important commanders during the Guadalcanal campaign—led countless patrols and offensives, aided by Rowell's air support. It was an effective, if bloody, combination. Sandino was beginning to feel the pressure by August, having dropped back to the Coco River and the nearby Honduras border.

With Sandino thus occupied, national elections could be held in a fairly open and hopeful atmosphere. However, Sandino's men still continued sporadic harassment of voting registration, and only the presence of protective Marines at each registration place made progress possible. On November 4, 1928, the election was held and José María Moncada achieved a plurality, bringing his Liberal Party into power. But Sandino could not be held off forever, and the Marines' lines were being stretched thin. It was time for military action to resume. For the next two years, Marine aviation continued the supply and air support it had provided during its first years in Nicaragua. On July 23, 1931, enlisted pilot Staff Sergeant Gordon W. Heritage, on a support mission in the interior, was hit by enemy fire and forced to crash-land near rebel strongpoints. He and his observer, Corporal Orville Simmons, managed to set fire to their airplane before beginning a 40-mile trek to relative safety at Puerto Cabezas.

The 1932 national election saw the same protection against the Sandinistas' marauding tactics supplied four years before. The election was held under heavy security due to Sandino's harassment, and a new President was elected. Juan B. Sacasa, an alternative candidate from Moncada for the badly disunited Liberal party, was the victor. Sacasa was inaugurated in 1933, and a new leader of the National Guard, Anastasio

Somoza, was installed. The Somoza family would have a long-lasting, if somewhat questionable, effect on this turbulent little country. But the Marine Corps's involvement had been a success; the Corps learned many valuable lessons during the protracted involvement in Nicaragua, lessons which were to be of inestimable value during the jungle campaigns in World War II.

Prelude to World War II

The decade of the 1930s did not start well for the Marine aviation section. The Depression was a drain on hoped-for programs. And Marine air lost one of its guiding pioneers: Lieutenant Colonel Thomas C. Turner, Marine Aviator 73. Turner was on his second tour as Director of Marine Aviation, having relieved Major Edward Brainard in May 1929. During an inspection trip to Haiti, Turner descended from his Sikorsky RS-1 amphibian. The big twin-engine craft's wheels had mired into the sand and Turner jumped from the plane to see the problem first-hand. However, as he moved to the side of the plane, forgetting to allow for the still-swinging propeller, he was struck by the moving blades and severely injured. He died from his wounds two days later. Forty-nine years old, Turner was the highest ranking Marine aviator and was posthumously promoted to brigadier general.

Turner's place was taken by Major Roy Geiger, Marine Aviator 5, and thus one of the most experienced pilots the Marines had. Geiger would guide the Marine Aviation section through the early 1930s, ever vigilant of cost-cutting measures which affected his office, and he would eventually rise to command the Fleet Marine Force, Pacific, in 1945 as a lieutenant general. Geiger and his successor in 1935, Major Ross Rowell, who had gained much experience in Nicaragua, had their hands full: the Marines, interested in looking after themselves, set about looking for ways to cut costs. Squadrons were either abolished or merged with sister units. Marine assets abroad were relocated back in the States. All the while, the Marines kept a watchful eye on new aircraft available to the Navy, and perhaps the Marines.

The debate over just what the Marines were to be used for was brought to a conclusion in 1933, with the creation of the Fleet Marine Force on December 8. The FMF, which dedicated the Marines to an amphibious-warfare role, in cooperation with the Navy, also abolished the old East and West Coast Expeditionary Forces. Marine air was also incorporated into the FMF; the headquarters units were redesignated Aircraft One based at Quantico, and Aircraft Two at San Diego. The reorganization was another happy circumstance which afforded the Marines an important capability in the great conflict to come.

In 1935, an important treatise, the *Tentative Landing Operations*

Manual, written by Marines, was published by the Navy Department. This manual detailed the necessary steps in conducting an amphibious assault, relationships, roles, and equipment placement and operations. Marine air's roles of reconnaissance, fighter escort, protection of the landing forces, artillery spotting, and close air support were formally established as the aviation units' responsibilities. In the same year, the Aviation Section of the Division of Operations and Training was placed directly under the Commandant, with now-Colonel Rowell as its first Director.

The General Board of the Navy, the senior advisory panel established in 1900, restated Marine air's mission in January 1939: to support the Fleet Marine Force in the amphibious landing operations and support the troops once they had passed the beachhead. Additionally, the Marine aviators were to provide backup squadrons for the Navy's regular carrier squadrons. This secondary carrier mission has always sparked controversy. But most Marine pilots overwhelmingly favor periodic carrier deployment of Marine squadrons, although in recent times, as before World War II, Marine aviators received only sporadic training for the exacting profession of carrier flying. This tended to give some carrier skippers more than the usual number of gray hairs, as they watched the inexperienced Marines' operations—game and enthusiastic but sometimes lacking the necessary finesse.

Aircraft in 1930-1941

Aircraft development in the 1930s was much different from the preceding period, as established designs gave way to experimentation and advancement. World War I had established the formula for most—though not all—successful military aircraft: a one- or two-place biplane with conventional landing gear (two large main wheels and a smaller tail wheel), radial engine, and two rifle-caliber forward-firing machine guns. It was a formula followed throughout the world, with few exceptions, well into the 1930s. However, by 1935, few aircraft designers would deny that the biplane had reached its peak of development and that the monoplane offered greater advantages in speed, design simplicity, and lightness.

In the early 1930s, the Marines flew a wide variety of biplanes. The Curtiss F6C/F7C series was still very much in use, as were the O2C/O3C two-seater dive-bombers from the same manufacturer. Vought was also represented with its hardy O2U/O3U Corsair family of two-seaters, while Boeing F4B fighters and Curtiss R4C transports—military versions of the civilian Condor twin-engine airliner just entering service—continued to serve into the early 1940s.

By 1931, a new name had appeared: Grumman. Working out of Long

Island, New York, this young company was eventually to become the mainstay of naval aircraft development and construction, its aircraft always representing the state of the art and establishing a reputation for tractability, endurance, and extraordinary toughness in combat. Grumman's initial effort was the FF-1, a two-seat biplane fighter with manually retracted landing gear. The "Fifi," as the new plane was inevitably called, served mainly with Navy squadrons aboard the carriers *Lexington* (CV-2), *Saratoga* (CV-3), and *Ranger* (CV-4). The Marines operated a few FF-1s as "hacks" and several SF-1 scout models in their reserve squadrons. (The SF-1 differed from the FF-1 internally, while a later variant, the FF-2, had dual controls.)

A single-seat development of the FF-1 was the F2F, which had the same portly shape as its predecessor, but offered increased performance. The Marines got only a few F2Fs, usually when the Navy was through with them. But it was not until the F3F came along that the Corps got its first real taste of a Grumman product. The last biplane fighter produced for either the Navy or Marines, the F3F served with VMF-1 at Quantico, and VMF-2 at San Diego, from 1937 to 1941.

By September 1937, a hot contest between Grumman and its Long Island rival, Brewster, had developed over new monoplane fighter designs. Responses to a 1935 Navy requirement, the two designs were immediately plunged into a race to see which would fly first. Brewster came up with a tubby, mid-fuselage monoplane with an enormous greenhouse canopy, while Grumman had originally redesigned its successful F3F series into the XF4F-1 biplane. However, Grumman realized that the biplane was on the way out and made the fortuitous decision to change the design to a more advanced monoplane configuration, eventually ending up with the XF4F-2. Even with a late start, the Grumman design flew in September 1937, before the problem-plagued Brewster XF2A-1, as the competitor aircraft had been designated; it did not fly until December.

From the beginning the XF2A-1 displayed a disappointing performance and it was never satisfactorily upgraded. And, although a great deal of effort and publicity were expended, and the plane was actually exported to several European countries, including Belgium, the Netherlands, Britain, and Finland, as well as seeing service with the U.S. Navy and Marines, it was only with the Finns that the fat little Brewster fighter achieved any success. (The Finns loved the Buffalo—as the aircraft was named—as much as the American pilots hated it, shooting down many Soviet aircraft during the 1940 war, and later as reluctant allies of the Germans in 1943.) The Navy's VF-3 took the first delivery of the F2A in January 1939, operating for a time aboard the *Saratoga*. Only the Marines of VMF-221 took on the F2A-2, at their base at Ewa near Pearl Harbor.

The F4F, in contrast, was a success story. Although a contemporary of the unsuccessful F2A, the F4F Wildcat was an important fighter throughout all but the last year of the war, and certainly in the early days—to early 1943—it was the only U.S. fighter plane capable of meeting the Mitsubishi Zero on anything approaching equal terms. The Wildcat did not reach the Marines until May 1941 when VMF-111, VMF-121, and VMF-211 were formed.

Bombing aircraft were also changing in the late 1930s. The ubiquitous Curtiss and Vought biplanes began to give way to monoplane designs, although the Great Lakes Aircraft Corporation secured a production contract for sixty machines with their big BG-1, a two-seater biplane powered by a single 750-horsepower Pratt and Whitney radial. The "Bee-Gee," as the BG-1 was naturally called, remained in service until 1941 when it was replaced by one, then two, very different aircraft, both monoplanes (it served with VB-6M and VB-4M, later VMB-1 and VMB-2). One other biplane scout/bomber put in some minor service with the Marines, the Curtiss SBC series, with the dash-4 version serving with several Marine Reserve squadrons, as well as "hack" aircraft with other units.

Two aircraft of the late 1930s represented the greatest jump in attack capability for the Marines: the Vought SB2U Vindicator and Douglas SBD Dauntless. Both were multi-seat, low-wing monoplanes with retractable gear and a relatively new development in dive-bombing—the bomb "displacing gear." This device, mounted along the centerline of the fuselage below the cockpit, held the large main bomb (lighter bombs could also be carried under the wings) and extended the bomb outside the propeller arc for release. This arrangement permitted a near-vertical, and thus more accurate, dive to be obtained, with the pilot literally aiming his aircraft at his target, on the sea or ground, and releasing the bomb at the opportune moment.

The earlier Vought design resulted from a 1934 Navy Bureau of Aeronautics call for a new scout and dive-bomber, Vought entering the competition along with the Brewster Company. The XSB2U-1 flew in January 1936, and was a low-wing, fabric-covered monoplane, powered by a 700-horsepower Pratt and Whitney radial. Although the prototype eventually crashed, killing its two crewmen, the Navy awarded Vought a production contract for fifty-four machines. The first SB2U-1s entered service with the Navy's VB-3 squadron aboard the *Saratoga* in December 1937. Eventually, it was exported to France where it served for a brief time during the German onslaught in June 1940. However, the Marines did not receive their first Vindicators until March 1941 with the deliveries of the SB2U-3 to VMS-2, a scouting squadron at San Diego. Poorly armed, even for a scout bomber, the Vindicator served without distinction, its only combat action in U.S. service being an abortive attack on Japanese ships during the Battle of Midway.

The 1930s and early 1940s held great promise, and disappointment, for the Marines. New aircraft were not always the best. Even though equipment was supposedly modern and up to world standards, only the F4F Wildcat and one other aircraft gave the Marines anything remotely resembling a modern airplane. Although somewhat forgotten in the initial hectic accounts of the war, that second aircraft, the Douglas SBD Dauntless, was subsequently recognized as one of the simplest, toughest, most capable, and most dependable of all naval aircraft. Designed by the now-legendary Ed Heinemann, and actually the logical outgrowth of several abortive, yet profitable, designs, the Dauntless broke tradition by beginning operations with a Marine squadron rather than the Navy. Marine Air Group 2 at San Diego received its first SBD-1s in June 1940.

The approximately three decades of Marine aviation before December 1941 had seen a fledgling force of a few men and machines grow to two full wings of aircraft and personnel whose skill would be tested to the utmost in the dynamic years of World War II. There had been policy and administrative changes during those thirty years, some not always successful, or popular; but the Marines fortunately found themselves with a nucleus of seasoned, experienced dedicated airmen to fight the conflict suddenly thrust upon them.

World War II:
On the Defensive

The Japanese attack on Pearl Harbor on December 7, 1941, caught most of the Marine Corps aircraft in Hawaii on the ground at Ewa. The only large groups of Marine planes to escape destruction were the F4F-3s of VMF-211, under Major Paul A. Putnam, which had flown aboard the carrier *Enterprise* (CV-6) on November 28 to be transported to the isolated U.S. base at Wake Island, and eighteen Vought SB2Us of VMSB-231 on the *Lexington*, also steaming for Wake. Attention had been drawn to Wake for several weeks among the higher echelons in the U.S. defense establishment, as some sort of Japanese attack, somewhere, seemed probable. It seemed safe to assume that Wake would receive a workover, if not an outright invasion, and its military defenses needed bolstering.

Wake Island, which is really three small islands 2,000 miles southwest of Hawaii, had long been a minor U.S. outpost in the Pacific, serving primarily as a meteorological station and stopping-off point for the pioneering trans-Pacific flights of Pan American Airways. On October 15, 1941, Marine Major James P. Devereux arrived to assume command of the island's Marine garrison, which had only arrived in August to beef up Wake's defenses. Throughout the next two months, Wake was reinforced with men, communications equipment, and aircraft, including the twelve F4F-3s (an early model of the Wildcat without folding wings) of VMF-211, which flew off the *Enterprise* on December 4. The commander of VMF-211, Major Putnam, was also a veteran of combat in Nicaragua, where he had served alongside Major Devereux, although in the later stages. The Michigan native had joined the Marines in 1923 as a private and was eventually to rise to brigadier general.

The pilots of VMF-211 were unfamiliar with their new mounts, having traded in their F3Fs only a few weeks previously. There was also little knowledge or experience amongst the enlisted ground crews, who were primarily ordnancemen drafted from a scout bomber squadron. There were mechanics at Ewa waiting to be flown to Wake, but the deteriorating situation precluded this course. The men on the island had to make do with what they had. The 5,000-foot runway at Wake was barely long enough, but its width of 200 feet permitted only one aircraft at a time to take off. Multi-plane section takeoffs, normal operational practice in military squadrons, were impossible.

The Wildcats had to be fueled by hand—a time-consuming operation—and with no radar available, the Marines were forced to put up continuous patrols of F4Fs to scout for the Japanese fleet they knew was on the move. Action was not long in coming. Captain Henry T. Elrod was leading a four-plane patrol at 12,000 feet over the north side of Wake at noontime on December 8, when he saw the first wave of Japanese bombers approaching from the south. The thirty-six twin-engine bombers had left Kwajalein Atoll, over 600 miles away, and had made their approach undetected through some rain.

The Japanese bombed and strafed the installations at Wake, destroying seven of the Wildcats on the ground, while an eighth was damaged and put out of service while the pilot was taxiing. In the early afternoon, the situation did not look good. VMF-211 had had twenty men killed, including three pilots, with eleven more, among them four pilots, wounded.

On the 9th, the Wildcat patrol, all that was now left of the airborne defense, ran into a second Japanese attack at 1145, and this time, two Marines, Lieutenant David S. Kliewer and Technical Sergeant William Hamilton, each shot down a Japanese bomber, probably the first Marine aerial kills of the war. The ground fire accounted for another bomber, while damaging several more. The next day, December 10, Captain Elrod destroyed two more bombers. But it was rapidly becoming apparent that if reinforcements did not come soon, it was only a matter of time before the Japanese would assault and conquer Wake. There was just too little of everything.

Help seemed on the way. The *Saratoga* was steaming from Pearl with VMF-221, under Major Verne J. McCaul. The eighteen fighters in the squadron were the abhorred, obsolete Brewster Buffalos, good only for training duty in the States. There was also radar equipment, supplies, and ammunition. All of these would be welcomed, even the F2As. The *Lexington* had been tasked with flying patrols searching for the Japanese fleet, and its load of Vindicators would never reach Wake. Due to the horrible state of confusion and indecision in the aftermath of Pearl Harbor, "Sara" was held up from entering Pearl Harbor and did not actually depart until December 15. It was a fatal delay.

Things were rapidly deterioriating at Wake, where it was actually December 16, due to the difference of the International Date Line. The Japanese had, indeed, sent a force of destroyers and cruisers to pound the crumbling defenses on Wake's south coast, while transports prepared to launch their landing craft with invasion troops. As the shore guns were firing at the invaders, Major Putnam and three other pilots, including Captain Elrod, were airborne with small, 100-pound bombs carried on makeshift racks. The Japanese ships had been sufficiently damaged by shore fire that they were retreating from their close-in positions, and the four Marine Wildcats found them. Putnam and his flight immediately began bombing and strafing the enemy ships, eventually hitting most of them.

The destroyer *Kisaragi*, which blew up at 0815, provided one of the continuing legends of the defense of Wake. In one of the first public propaganda releases, it was claimed that the 100-pound bombs and determined attacks of the outnumbered Marine pilots were totally responsible for the sinking of the destroyer. In the light of later examination, it seems more probable that, although severely damaged by the Wildcat attacks, the ship's fate was sealed when one of her own depth charges exploded due to the fires *started* by the aerial attack.

The surviving aircraft of VMF-211 flew ten missions on the 16th, and were involved in the sinking of two destroyers. But two F4Fs, pilots Elrod and Captain Herbert C. Freuler, were put out of commission as a result of Japanese antiaircraft fire. The aerial defense of Wake now rested on only two F4Fs. And the Japanese air raids continued.

The sole contact the beleaguered defenders had with the outside world occurred on December 20, when a Navy PBY Catalina made it through, landing in the lagoon and bringing news of the relief force en route to Wake. But time was running out. The Japanese carriers *Soryu* and *Hiryu*, returning from the Pearl Harbor operation, had joined the fleet offshore and their planes were intended to contribute to the continuing softening-up operation in preparation for the actual invasion.

December 22 saw the last of the Wildcats. Captain Freuler and Lieutenant Carl R. Davidson jumped a force of thirty-three bombers from the enemy carriers and were, themselves, immediately attacked by the Zero escort. Freuler tacked himself onto one of the Japanese fighters and shot it down. But the fragments of the dying Zero damaged his own plane's controls, forcing Freuler to land. Looking around for his wingman, Lieutenant Davidson, he saw him once with another Zero on his tail, and that was all. Davidson was not seen again. Wounded by another Zero, Freuler crash-landed Wake's last Grumman. Now the Marine pilots on Wake became what all Marines are first considered: riflemen.

The situation was now bad enough that the headquarters of Vice Admiral Pye, who was serving as Commander, Pacific Fleet, began to reconsider sending a relief force to Wake. The island's fall was now nearly a certainty. What good would sending more—but not enough—reinforcements do? After initially deciding to continue the rescue operation, even as Wake's aerial defense collapsed, the headquarters at Pearl Harbor changed its mind and recalled Task Force 14, the relief force, at 0811 Hawaiian time.

To the anxious Marine pilots and sailors aboard the *Saratoga*, the decision to leave Wake to its fate was both incomprehensible and shameful. But even as some cried and others railed against the decision-makers, Sara was changing her course away from Wake. There was little the Marines aboard her could do.

The main Japanese attack began in the early hours of December 23, with landing barges disgorging Japanese troops. Bloody combat continued until 0700 when Commander Winfield S. Cunningham, the Navy commander of Wake, and Major Devereux bitterly concluded that further resistance was useless and would only result in needless loss of life. They had not only the lives of their own Marines and sailors to consider, but those of the civilian workers who had joined in the fight alongside the Marines. And so Wake fell.

Among those killed during the Japanese assault was Captain Hank Elrod, who had been involved in some of the siege's worst aerial action. Elrod was shot and killed by a Japanese playing possum. Elrod's performance, only learned after the war, earned him the Medal of Honor. Devereux and Major Putnam, along with the survivors, civilian, sailors and Marines, were herded together by the victorious Japanese. Some would be held as prisoners of war in Japan, while some civilians were held at Wake to work the island's facilities. However, these unlucky personnel, after nearly two years of captivity, were executed in October 1943 by the commander of Wake at the time, in retaliation for American strikes on the Japanese-held base. (Rear Admiral Shigematsu Sakaibara was later tried as a war criminal and executed in 1947.)

The heroic, hopeless defense of Wake Island gave birth to the Marine Corps' modern perception of itself. Although 166 years of Marine Corps history had preceded it, Wake became a symbol to America and the

Marines. A song, composed after Wake's fall, had a chorus which went:

Wake Island, Wake Island.
It's not even marked on the maps.
But who would have thought a few crummy Marines
Could stop the advance of the Japs.

Perhaps Major Putnam put the feeling a little more accurately and objectively when he filed a report which the visiting PBY took out two days before Wake surrendered. He wrote, in part, "All hands have behaved splendidly and held up in a manner of which the Marine Corps may well tell."

Prelude to Midway

The day of the attack on Pearl Harbor, another massive Japanese strike began against the Philippines. (Since the Philippines were over the International Date Line, this attack occurred on December 8.) Carrier-based dive bombers and fighters, as well as aircraft based on the island of Formosa (Taiwan), swept down on the island of Mindanao and U.S. Army and Navy forces in the area, under General Douglas MacArthur, were quickly overwhelmed. The big air base at Clark Field near Manila was particularly hard hit. By Christmas 1941, the Japanese had conquered most of the Philippines, as well as the British colony of Hong Kong on the Asian mainland to the north, and were heading toward the Netherlands East Indies—Java, Borneo, and Sumatra—in the south. The last-ditch stand by U.S. and Filipino forces on the Bataan Peninsula, near the harbor at Manila, made world headlines. But in mid-March 1942, MacArthur was ordered to leave and the Philippines fell. Japan ruled most of the southwestern Pacific.

Smarting from the blow at Pearl Harbor and the unbroken string of Japanese successes, the United States sent a task force into Japanese home waters, in a sneak attack of its own. Conceived by Lieutenant Colonel Jimmy Doolittle, a well-known pre-war race pilot, the plan called for sixteen B-25 Mitchell bombers to take off from the *Hornet* and attack the Japanese capital of Tokyo and several other important cities. Obviously, the value of such an attack would be more spiritual than physical: a strike against the enemy's homeland when he would least expect it.

Thus, on April 18, 1942, the twin-engine B-25s took off from the carrier's pitching deck. (An unfortunate encounter with a Japanese patrol boat had necessitated launching the planes 250 miles from the original launch point.) Doolittle led his men off and the raiders were over Tokyo within four hours. Plans called for the aircraft to fly to China, but the severe weather caused many to stray off course, run out of fuel and crash-land. One came down in Soviet Siberia and the crew was interned. Others had the misfortune to land in Japanese-held territory where their crews were executed. Most, including Doolittle, managed to make the Chinese coast, where their crews survived their landings.

The Japanese were not through, however, and they continued their drive southward, putting pressure on Australia. Early in May 1942, a Japanese task force headed for New Guinea met an American task force, with the *Yorktown* and *Lexington*, in the Coral Sea off Australia's northeast coast. On May 8, in an encounter which was the first naval battle in which the opponents' ships never saw each other, American and Japanese aircraft dive-bombed and torpedoed the other's carriers, the Japanese sinking the *Lexington*—the first U.S. carrier lost in the war—in exchange for the light carrier *Shoho*, and damage to other ships.

Although a tactical defeat for the U.S., in terms of tonnage sunk, the Battle of the Coral Sea was the first strategic defeat of the war for the Japanese, whose steamroller advance had finally been halted. The Japanese realized more than ever that the American carriers must be sunk or disabled, if a Japanese drive was to be sustained. The small mid-Pacific atoll of Midway looked like a good spot for a showdown.

Through mid-1942, the American military forces in the Pacific could be likened to a prize fighter gamely trying to fend off his opponent's blows as he staggers on his feet. He is resolved to remain standing while he looks for an opening, and hopes for the bell which will end the round and give him some breathing space. Until June 1942, there were no campaigns; only specific battles—such as Pearl Harbor, Wake, and Coral Sea—which the Japanese initiated, and with the exception of the Battle of the Coral Sea, easily won. These successes put a tremendous drain on the U.S. forward areas. But these early trials also gave American industry time to gather the steam which Admiral Isoroku Yamamoto, Chief of the Imperial Japanese Navy, feared would be the undoing of Japan's military ambitions, and of the island nation itself, if the war lasted more than six months after Pearl Harbor.

In the early days of 1942, though, the Japanese rolled unchecked across the Pacific. But the original intent of the attack on Pearl Harbor was not only to damage as much of the Navy's Pacific Fleet as possible, but specifically destroy America's carriers. Fortunately for the U.S., the carriers—the *Lexington, Yorktown, Saratoga, Hornet,* and *Enterprise*—were either at sea or serving in the Atlantic, and thus escaped the fury of the Japanese attack.

Japan therefore saw the value of Midway Atoll, halfway between America and Japan, as a way-station for any further thrusts against Pearl and America's west coast. She developed a plan to attack and occupy Midway, thus drawing the U.S. carriers into a battle with a refreshed Japanese battle fleet, which would stage from Midway. With four major carriers and a complete support fleet, the Japanese Navy felt itself invincible as it approached Midway from the northwest on the early morning of June 4, 1942.

Arrayed against the huge Imperial force, besides the carriers *Yorktown, Enterprise,* and *Hornet*—the *Lexington* having been sunk at Coral Sea one month before and the *Saratoga* laid up for repairs stateside—there were the land-based U.S. Army Air Corps assets: four Martin B-26 Marauders and seventeen Boeing B-17 Flying Fortresses. There were also six brand-new Navy Grumman TBF Avenger torpedo bombers of VT-8. (The TBFs were actually on detachment from the main squadron aboard the *Hornet,* which was still flying antiquated Douglas TBD Devastators.)

Marine assets on that morning of June 4 included a total of sixty-four aircraft: nineteen Douglas SBD-2 Dauntlesses, seventeen obsolete Vought SB2U-3 Vindicators; twenty-one nearly useless Brewster F2A-3 Buffalos; and seven Grumman F4F-3 Wildcats. The mixed bag of fighters came from VMF-221, the same squadron which had sailed to relieve Wake on December 15, 1941, only to be turned back when all seemed lost at the isolated outpost. The seven F4Fs represented the only nearly modern fighter equipment available.

Additional manpower and aircraft had been pumped into Midway throughout the first five months of 1942 as Washington became rightly convinced of an impending Japanese attack. One of the more unusual visitors to Midway prior to the battle was an R4D-1 (the Navy version of the C-47 military derivative of the civilian DC-3) of VMJ-252, based at Ewa. The twin-engined aircraft, piloted by Captain Albert S. Munsch, carried much-needed ammunition for the PBY and Buffalo aircraft already on Midway, as well as ten Navy enlisted men to augment the Navy patrol squadrons, VP-23 and VP-44, whose Catalinas flew constant patrols from Midway. By exemplary overwater navigation, the transport reached Midway over eight hours after taking off on June 2. It was a great demonstration of flying skill, but Lieutenant Colonel Ira Kimes, commanding Marine Air Group-22, could not afford to let the R4D crew rest. He greeted them and immediately sent them back to Hawaii with dispatches for Admiral Nimitz.

In early March the Brewsters intercepted some marauding Japanese flying boats, Captain James E. Neefus shooting down one of two Kawanishi Mavis: large, four-engined, parasol-winged boats. These Japanese probes, along with other naval actions—submarines and surface ships shelled Midway sporadically—only reinforced Admiral Nimitz's feeling that a major assault was due. He visited Midway on May 2, and more antiaircraft defenses, gasoline, and communications gear were delivered to the island soon afterwards. By June, Midway had 120 aircraft ready for action against the approaching Japanese. Although the three-day battle which developed on June 4 was primarily a Navy show, the Marines were very much in evidence, especially during the early stages of the action.

The Battle at Midway

As soon as the first PBY reports came in, confirming the approach of the Japanese fleet, the Marines of MAG-22 sent off all available planes, both as a defensive measure, so that they would not be caught and destroyed on the ground, and also to be in a better position to attack when the time came. Circling at 8,500 feet, 20 miles east of Midway, was the combined SBD/SB2U squadron, VMSB-241, under Major Lofton R. Henderson (in an SBD) and his executive officer, Major Ben Norris (flying an SB2U). The fighters of VMF-221, led by their skipper, Major Floyd B. Parks, numbered twenty-five Buffalos and Wildcats. The fighters split into two sections of twelve and thirteen aircraft and orbited, waiting for word of the first attack. Within 15 minutes of getting airborne, the Marines spotted a large force of Japanese bombers from the *Hiryu* and their Zero escorts, all heading for Midway. At 0616 hours, June 4, the section under Major Parks pushed over into screaming dives to meet the enemy 2,000 feet below them. Moments later, the second group, under Captain Kirk Armistead, joined the fight.

It was no contest. The courage of the Marine aviators, the majority of whom were inexperienced, could not offset the inadequacies of their fat old Buffalo fighters against the Zero. And there were just not enough of the newer Wildcats. The faster, far more maneuverable Zeros, flown by seasoned combat veterans of the Japanses Navy—some of whom had seen much combat in China over the last five years—swarmed all over the struggling defending interceptors. There was little anyone could do.

(It might be worth considering, in retrospect, that the Buffalo might not have been totally at fault for its reputation. For after all, consider the Finns' sterling performance with the type. They, however, operated the lighter F2A-1, while the Marines flew the -3, which, while incorporating extra fuel, with its accompanying 900 pounds of extra weight, still retained the -1's powerplant. Added to this additional weight were extra armor protection, increased armament, and self-sealing fuel tanks. Of course, these additions were important and were derived from recent combat experience in Europe. Nearly all Japanese aircraft lost in aerial combat at Midway went down before the guns of the Buffalos and Wildcats. There were only seven of the latter at Midway, flown by Marines, three of which were lost in combat. Those and the remaining four could not have accounted for even a majority of the thirty-four Japanese planes destroyed in dogfights. The little F2As had to have had some hand in the action. Perhaps, the much-maligned Brewster deserves better from historians.)

One young Marine fighter pilot who did survive, and even managed to shoot down two Zeros while flying an F4F, was Captain Marion E. Carl. Having been promoted in May, Captain Carl, who was active throughout the early part of the war, and eventually would rise to major general, found himself the target when two Zeros dove on him. As the Japanese bullets struck his plane, Carl chopped his throttle and skidded the Wildcat around, making the Zeros overshoot. Carl then ducked into a cloud. For his actions that day he was awarded the Navy Cross.

VMF-221 was decimated. Of the twenty-five aircraft which took off at 0600, only thirteen returned, and only two of the returnees were fit to fly again. Major Parks was apparently shot down and did not return.

While the fighters of VMF-221 were doing their best to slow down the Japanese, the Army and Navy air contingents were also running into trouble. Four B-26s were sent out with torpedos to find the Japanese fleet, but although the Army claimed that the hot new bombers had loosed all their torpedos and had scored hits, that was not the case, and indeed, two of the four Marauders were shot down by Zeros or antiaircraft fire.

The Grumman Avengers of the Navy fared little better. In a macabre emulation of their brethren aboard the *Hornet*, the VT-8 detachment lost five of the six new torpedo bombers. (VT-8 sent out fifteen TBDs, all of which were shot down; only one of the thirty crewmen survived.) The Zeros and antiaircraft fire were a veritable wall between the Japanese ships and the U.S. bombers.

Things were not going well for the American defenders in the opening rounds of the battle. The Japanese did seem nearly invincible: too powerful, too experienced. The planes from the carrier *Hiryu*, which had punched through VMF-221's interceptors, although somewhat reduced in numbers, still managed to wreak havoc on Eastern and Sand Islands, the two islands which compose Midway. Besides the human casualties, power facilities, fuel, and aircraft were destroyed in the Japanese bombing and strafing attacks.

Much has been written about the final outcome of the Battle of Midway, forty years ago, concerning the record of the U.S. pilots, and the problems of the Japanese commanders, especially Admiral Chuichi Nagumo, commanding the carrier task force. Basically, the tide of battle turned in favor of the Americans when Nagumo finally chose to rearm and refuel his aircraft for another attack against Midway with bombs, instead of an attack against the U.S. carriers with torpedos. He left his fleet without aerial defense. It was, indeed, a fatal error of judgment. By the time Nagumo received word that there were American carriers in the area and decided to change back to torpedos, it was too late. Dauntlesses from the *Enterprise, Hornet,* and *Yorktown* caught first the *Soryu,* then the *Kaga,* and finally the *Akagi,* and sank them with devastating dive-bombing attacks. Later in the day, the fourth Japanese carrier, the *Hiryu,* was hit after launching an attack on the *Yorktown*; she sank the next day. The Japanese retreated with their first major carrier losses of the Pacific war. The *Yorktown,* though mortally wounded in the Japanese attack, did not sink immediately, and was finally finished off by a prowling Japanese submarine two days later. The losses and subsequent defeat were to have wide-ranging effect on the Japanese, as many of their most experienced personnel, and nearly 400 aircraft, went down with the ships.

However, although the U.S. Navy's dive-bombers won the day—land-based air power really had a negligible effect on the fighting—the Marines could be proud of their own record too. On the early morning of June 4, as Marine fighters tangled with the Japanese raiders, and the Army and Navy torpedo bombers thrust themselves through devastating antiaircraft fire, to no avail, the Dauntlesses and Vindicators of Majors Henderson and Norris were directed against the enemy task force, 150 miles to the northwest. Approaching the Japanese fleet, the bombers immediately were set upon by Zeros. Major Henderson was apparently the first loss, his group of SBDs reaching the target fifteen minutes before Norris' SB2Us. Eight of Henderson's sixteen SBDs were destroyed as they dove towards their targets. One pilot from Henderson's section, First Lieutenant Daniel Iverson, limped back to Midway with 259 holes in his airplane and his throat mike shot away. It is thought that relative inexperience and unfamiliarity with their new planes caused the Marine pilots to go into much shallower dives—almost glide-bombing deliveries—instead of the more direct and faster vertical technique which was the hallmark of the Douglas plane. This failure to use their aircraft correctly left the Marine crews open to deadly antiaircraft fire and interceptors.

The ancient SB2U Vindicators of Major Norris' section were little better off than the SBDs, losing three of the fabric-covered dive-bombers to Zeros and flak. Captain Richard E. Fleming's aircraft sustained 179 holes; Fleming himself was wounded twice.

Regrouping at Midway, the Marines sent out another mission in the early evening. Eleven SBDs and SB2Us, led by Major Norris, who had taken over the squadron after the death of Major Henderson that morning, sought a reported damaged Japanese carrier. Failing to locate the target, the bombers turned back to Midway. However, 40 miles out from Midway, Major Norris was seen to go into a steep descending turn and disappear. Command of VMSB-241 turned over for the second time in 24 hours, this time to Captain Marshall Tyler.

Tyler led his squadron on the first mission of the next day, taking off at 0630 on June 5. The targets were Japanese battleships, 176 miles off to the west. Approaching the enemy ships, some of which had been damaged the day before and were leaking easily-seen trails of oil, the twelve Marine bombers were staggered, with the Dauntlesses at 10,000 feet and the Vindicators at 4,000 feet.

Captain Fleming, who had survived murderous fire the day before, was seen to run into more deadly flak, his SB2U bursting into flames as he dropped his bomb over the heavy cruiser *Mikuma*. Perhaps he was mortally wounded, or perhaps his plane could not climb; whatever the reason, Fleming and his burning aircraft fell onto the rear turret of the damaged Japanese vessel. Whether his destruction was the result of aircraft failure or the last desperate, courageous act of a brave man, will never be known. Captain Fleming was awarded a posthumous Medal of Honor.

The Battle of Midway continued through the 6th, with the Japanese finally retiring for safer waters. The Marines had suffered badly, along with the rest of the American forces. The fighter and bomber squadrons had each lost commanding officers. Enlisted ranks, too, with the loss of rear-seat gunners and ground crewmen—from those Japanese bombers which got through to Midway—were also hard hit. The flight crews of MAG-22 had shot down forty-three enemy planes, twenty-five Val dive-bombers and eighteen Zero fighters; ground fire had accounted for ten more Japanese aircraft.

Cactus in the Pacific: Guadalcanal

 Now that the Japanese advance had been halted at Midway, the "breathing space" which that decisive American victory afforded was put to good use. Plans were made for an American invasion of the Solomon Islands group, 1,300 miles northeast of Australia. The Solomons were chosen for the first Allied offensive in the Pacific because they were within the range capabilities of the limited U.S. carrier forces, and also of the long-range Army and Navy reconnaissance aircraft based at Espiritu Santo. Tulagi Island was originally set to be the sole target, but when word came that the Japanese had begun building an airfield on nearby Guadalcanal, 20 miles across the Sealark Channel, the main target became Guadalcanal. Major General A.A. Vandegrift, commander of the First Marine Division, had five weeks to set up his amphibious force, a monumental task. Operation Watchtower, as the invasion was named, was set for August 1, 1942, then postponed to August 7.

The group of Marine pilots, men, and aircraft picked to provide the Corps' air contribution to the invasion was Marine Aircraft Group 23, composed of VMF-223 and VMF-224, VMSB-231, and VMSB-232, all manned by eager but inexperienced young men. The fighter squadrons had previously operated the hated Brewster Buffalo, and were quickly reequipped with the more modern Grumman Wildcat, the newer F4F-4 model. The scout bombers upgraded their SBD-1 and -2 Dauntlesses for the newer SBD-3.

Captain John L. Smith of VMF-223 and Major Richard Mangrum,

skipper of VMSB-232, were highly experienced aviators and knew that they had only the barest of essentials to take into combat against an experienced and dangerous enemy. (For Mangrum, this was his second tour as commanding officer, for he had led 232, then designated as VF-10M, for the month of September 1930, flying Curtiss F6C-4s.) Captain Smith made the quick decision to exchange twelve of his most junior pilots for a dozen more experienced aviators from VMF-212, based at Efate Island in the New Hebrides, near Espiritu Santo, under Major Harold W. Bauer. Major Mangrum flew the pants off his men, cramming in as much flight time and bombing practice as the month's lead time allowed.

The initial landings of August 7 went fairly well, and five days later, General Vandegrift was able to report that the 2,600-foot airstrip, which had been partially completed by the Japanese, and finished by his Marines, was ready for operations. Named for Major Lofton R. Henderson, killed at Midway leading the Marine dive bombers of VMSB-241, the field received its first aircraft on August 12, when a Navy PBY landed there.

Under constant threat of aerial attacks from the Japanese squadrons based at their huge base at Rabaul, on the northeast tip of New Britain, the Marines on Guadalcanal began calling for their own air support. Transported to the vicinity of Guadalcanal by the escort carrier *Long Island* (CVE-1), VMF-223 and VMSB-232 took their nineteen Wildcats and twelve Dauntlesses down the little carrier's catapults on the morning of August 20 and headed for Henderson Field. (VMF-224 and VMSB-231 remained behind at Espiritu Santo to complete training, and would join their comrades soon.)

It was well that the Marine aircrews arrived on August 20, for early on the 21st, the Japanese attacked less than three miles from the airstrip, and the newly arrived F4Fs and SBDs were quickly in action, bombing and strafing the 900-man enemy ground force. By noontime, the first aerial combat had taken place when Captain Smith led a four-plane section against four Zeros; the result was a trade-off. One Zero and one Wildcat were shot down, although the American pilot was able to make a dead-stick landing back at Henderson.

The next several days were taken up with bringing in supplies and preparing for future battle; American and Japanese forces both used the time to advantage. VMSB-232 was constantly in action, its SBDs harassing the Japanese wherever it found them—on the ground, or at sea on transports preparing to come ashore. Major Mangrum and his crews were getting a great deal of experience.

The Japanese had a variety of aircraft in operation, from the big, twin-engined Mitsubishi land-based bomber—code-named "Betty"—to scouting floatplanes such as the Kawanishi "Alf," a large, single-engine, three-seater. But, of course, above all they had the Zero, ruler of the Pacific skies in the early war.

The Mitsubishi A6M fighter, popularly known as the Zero, resulted from a 1937 specification by the Imperial Japanese Navy for an "escort fighter with dogfight performance superior to that of its opponents . . . . an interceptor capable of destroying enemy attacks . . . ." [7] The new fighter was the creation of Dr. Jiro Horikoshi, a young engineer with the Nagoya aircraft manufacturing plant of Mitsubishi Heavy Industries. The A6M was a trim, light, radial-engined pacesetter with an enclosed cockpit and retractable landing gear. New metal research, attention to weight saving, and other aerodynamic refinements gave the plane breathtaking maneuverability and incredible range. Both would be sorely needed in the vast reaches of the Pacific. Armed with two 20-mm cannon and two 7.7-mm machine guns, the A6M first flew in April 1939 and was operationally evaluated in China in 1940.

Combat results were even beyond the manufacturer's hopes, and incredible to American and British intelligence-gatherers. Although such forward observers as Claire Chennault and his Flying Tigers had much first-hand experience on the Japanese fighter, and tried to alert Allied military leaders to the dangers it posed, they were not believed. The U.S. went into the war firmly believing that the Japanese flew only copies of Western aircraft. (Even today, there are still adherents to the wartime theory that the Zero was "pirated" from such inadequate American designs as the Vultee P-66.)

For three years after its service introduction as the A6M1 in the summer of 1940, the Zero indeed ruled the Asian skies. No Allied fighter could match its quickness of turn and long legs which enabled the Zero to fight far from its base. (The name derived from the official designation of "Type 00" fighter. The "00," in turn, came from the custom of using the current year of the Japanese calendar, 1940 being 2600 by Japanese reckoning, hence, the shortened "0," or Zero, appellation.)

However, the seeds of the Zero's destruction lay in its very design. The fighter's high performance was at the expense of pilot and fuel-tank protection, the type being prone to blowing up in smoke and flames after a short burst of American .50-caliber machine-gun fire. Its dive capabilities were also pretty dismal, and any Allied pilot bounced by Zeros or caught in a turning fight with one, could usually disengage with a quick snap roll and dive. As soon as the U.S. pilots realized the Japanese fighter's weaknesses, and how to exploit them, the Zero—or Zeke as it was code-named—immediately lost its superiority. Although improvements were made to the Zero throughout the war—more powerful engines and armament, increased armorplate and self-sealing fuel tanks—the newer American fighters to come, starting with the F6F

Hellcat and F4U Corsair, were too fast, too powerful and too well supplied. As Allied experience and confidence grew, Japanese capability decreased. Midway had effectively wiped out a good proportion of the Japanese Navy's most experienced flight crews; Guadalcanal took more. By mid-1943, the Japanese were facing the other side of the coin. Although additional aircraft—many of excellent quality and high capability—continued to be produced, there were just not enough experienced pilots and crews to operate them successfully. The Zero was *passé* by 1944. And it all seemed to begin to end at Guadalcanal.

Cactus in the Pacific

"Cactus" was the Allied code name for Guadalcanal, and the Navy, Marine, and Army Air Force squadrons which fought in defense of the Allied invasion through the last months of 1942 were collectively known as the Cactus Air Force. It was a lonely, motley band of brother airmen who formed this group. At the core, however, were the Marines. It was their show. By August 30, the second group of MAG-23—VMF-223 and VMSB-321—had touched down at Henderson, bringing an additional nineteen Wildcats and twelve SBDs, giving the Marines a total of twenty-six F4Fs and thirty Dauntlesses.

One further addition was 57-year-old Brigadier General Roy S. Geiger, Marine Aviator Number 5. Geiger, who had flown in World War I, now found himself in the thick of the most important battle the Marines had ever fought. He was in overall command of the Cactus Air Force. Arriving on September 3, Geiger began consolidating his resources. Action was constant and heavy, the SBDs and F4Fs losing many of their original crews, killed or wounded. The Japanese constantly harassed the troops at night with single-plane intruder flights, and ground bombardment which, if nothing else, prohibited sleep, an effective weapon in its own right. Tropical diseases, supply shortages, and maintenance problems made people grumble; their tempers were on short fuses. Undaunted, General Geiger ordered a Dauntless readied in the afternoon of September 22. With a 1,000-pound bomb mounted on the belly rack, he took off and bombed the Japanese at Cape Esperance, some 40 miles to the west. The General's mission gave a boost to the sagging morale on Guadalcanal.

More squadrons and aircraft began to trickle in: VMSB-141, under Major Gordon Bell, arrived on September 27, as well as flights of Grumman TBF Avengers, the new torpedo planes which had turned in such a poor showing at Midway, but which were to prove to be one of the war's outstanding naval attack aircraft.

Several legends grew out of the constant combat at Guadalcanal, including the competition among the aces. Major Smith and Captain Carl were locked into an unofficial race for top score. Carl, of course, had fought at Midway, claiming two Zeros on June 4. He shot down three more Japanese planes on August 24 over Guadalcanal, with two more on the 26th. Smith had shot down his first Zero on August 21 and had continued a steady scoring rate.

On September 9, with twelve planes to his credit, Carl himself was shot down and listed as missing. However, he had bailed out of his burning Wildcat and landed at sea. Rescued by natives who kept him hidden from patrolling Japanese, he eventually made it back to Henderson. There he found Smith's score now stood at sixteen—four more than his own. For their efforts during the Guadalcanal campaign, the two aces were awarded their country's highest medals: Carl gained his second Navy Cross, and Smith received the Medal of Honor, more for his overall performance than for any one action. As one writer put it years later,

the true measure of John Smith's value . . . is found, not in heroism—of which he had much—but in tactical skill and leadership as a fighter squadron commander . . . . He was a true professional and that was what it took to make fighter pilots out of a dozen boys in fifty days . . . . [8]

By the time VMF-223 and MAG-23 rotated out of Guadalcanal in October, VMF-223 had accounted for eighty-three Japanese planes downed, two-thirds of the total achieved by the entire Cactus Air Force during the period, August to October 1942.

VMF-224, under Major Robert Galer, was not idle during this time. Arriving on August 30, the new pilots accompanied the aviators of VMF-223 for a few missions to gain their combat initiations. On September 2, their first contact with Japanese aircraft saw Major Galer open his squadron's scorecard with two Zeros downed. He would eventually wind up with thirteen kills and the Medal of Honor. (Of the eleven Marine pilots who won the Medal of Honor in World War II, five received the award for action at Guadalcanal during 1942 and 1943.)

VMF-121's advance party arrived in late September, and the entire squadron arrived soon afterwards with combat operations beginning October 11. The skipper of VMF-121 was an Annapolis Marine, Major Leonard Davis; his executive officer was a 27-year-old captain from South Dakota, Joseph J. Foss. Foss would become the Marines' second-ranking ace of the war, with twenty-six victories. Only "Pappy" Boyington, the hard-charging commander of VMF-214, would achieve a greater score of twenty-eight. VMF-121 flew throughout October, with Joe Foss gaining his first kill on the 13th, only to be nearly shot down himself, and making a hot, emergency landing back at Henderson.

The Japanese kept up the day and night bombardment of Guadalcanal; sleep was a luxury seldom enjoyed. On the night of October 13, a particularly devastating shelling from two Japanese battleships had disabled most of the remaining operational SBDs of the

Marines. Only seven Dauntlesses were flyable. Over forty men had been killed, including the commanding officer, executive officer, and three pilots of VMSB-141. The makeshift operations building, nicknamed the Pagoda, was put out of commission and eventually torn down by order of General Geiger, who had long suspected the structure of being used as an aiming point by the offshore enemy.

There were still Navy and Army fighters available, and these would be used to the utmost in the days to come. On October 15, the Japanese began offloading men and supplies only ten miles away from Henderson, in preparation for an offensive to retake the airstrip. Down to their last fuel supplies, the Marines of Cactus mounted what opposition they could against the enemy ships. The nightly bombardment continued and four more SBDs were destroyed. Two of the remaining three were written off in taxiing accidents, and the third, flown by Lieutenant Bob Patterson of VMSB-141, made a desultory solo attack against the transports anchored just offshore.

By this time, like a gift from the gods, a hidden two-day supply of fuel was found—it was probably cached by the Japanese in hopes of a possible return—and at least the Marine fighters were back in business. With no flyable SBDs, the offensive power of the Marine contingent was nil; the enemy transports continued to unload, unhindered, except for sporadic attention by Espiritu Santo-based B-17s and carrier-based Navy dive bombers. Even the fighters of VMF-121, led by Major Davis, made some strafing runs.

But the situation was desperate. The Japanese were coming, and the American resupply efforts that were underway would probably arrive too late to be of much help to the hard-pressed force. Thus, the effort of one Marine major on October 14 was very much appreciated.

Jack R. Cram, aide and pilot to General Geiger, had been using Geiger's personal PBY—the "Blue Goose"—to bring in supplies from Espiritu Santo. On one run to Guadalcanal, he brought two torpedoes, filched from Navy Torpedo Squadron Eight, and he prevailed upon his boss to let him take a crack at the Japanese transports anchored so temptingly nearby. Reluctantly, General Geiger agreed, growling, "Don't get that plane shot up!"

With a jury-rigged bomb-release mechanism, Cram took off in the Catalina and headed for his targets at 6,000 feet, the PBY straining to climb to the altitude. A decoy flight of SBDs—twelve had been patched together by the miracle-workers at Henderson—drew enemy fire away from the lumbering PBY as Cram began his run. Diving to 75 feet above the water, going at what he later said was 240 miles per hour, 90 mph faster than he should have, Cram dropped his two torpedoes while fierce antiaircraft fire and waiting Zeros chased after him. Wringing the straining patrol bomber around, he headed back for Henderson, but not before he had the satisfaction of seeing one of the transports explode in a ball of flame, mortally wounded.

Arriving back over Henderson, Cram saw most of the Zeros depart in the face of concentrated American antiaircraft fire, but one Japanese fighter grimly hung on, determined to scrub the audacious American raider. Then a Wildcat, flown by Second Lieutenant Roger Haberman, entered the landing pattern, its wheels down in preparation for landing, its own engine smoking. Seeing the beleaguered Catalina's dilemma, and with his landing gear still down, Haberman hauled himself around and behind the pursuing Zero and dispatched it with a burst of machine-gun fire.

When he landed the PBY, Cram counted 175 bullet holes in the aircraft; fortunately, none of his crew was hurt. The general was advancing towards Cram, a scowl on his face, as he surveyed his aide and the remains of his personal plane. After reading Cram the riot act, threatening to court-martial him, Geiger could not keep up the charade and broke into a huge grin. He pumped Cram's hand and congratulated his pilot on the success of his courageous mission. On Geiger's recommendation, Cram was awarded the Navy Cross.

The press instantly labeled him "Mad Jack Cram." He later said, "I guess some people thought I *was* mad, or at least unbalanced!" (Cram went on to command VMB-612, a night bombing squadron, and rose to brigadier general before retiring in 1959.) Recalling his mission forty years later, Cram explained his reason for going:

At a time like that you don't think about anything but the situation. You have to remember that at any point there was some question whether we would be able to hold Guadalcanal . . . . It seemed like a reasonable solution to the problem. [9]

Cram's raid gave a much-needed lift to the Cactus Air Force. Although subsequent attacks put a dent in the Japanese supply efforts, the threat of a massive attack continued; indeed, Japanese surface ships cruised along the shore, pumping night-time fire into the lonely base at Henderson. By the morning of October 16, only nine F4Fs remained operational to confront a Japanese attack. Geiger put in a hurried call to Efate for Lieutenant Colonel Harold W. Bauer's VMF-212, which arrived that afternoon with nineteen Wildcats, and even seven fully-crewed SBDs. The only problem was that VMF-212 arrived over Henderson during a Japanese bombing attack. Wasting no time, with his fuel nearly exhausted, Bauer pounced on the Aichi Type 99 "Val" dive-bombers and quickly shot down four of the raiders in rapid succession and within plain view of the grateful witnesses on the field. This auspicious beginning to VMF-212's stay at Guadalcanal earned Bauer the Medal of Honor.

Things were changing in Marine air on Guadalcanal; personnel were rotating home for a much-deserved rest, while others came to take their places. John Smith and Marion Carl, and now-Lieutenant Colonel Richard Mangrum, had left on October 11 and 12. MAG-23 was relieved on October 16 by MAG-14. During its tour on Guadalcanal from August 20 to October 16, the group had claimed 244 Japanese aircraft shot down, while losing twenty-two pilots serving with MAG-23, and another thirty-three who had put in tours of exchange duty with attached Navy and Army units.

The Battle of Santa Cruz

The months of October and November 1942 were to prove crucial in the Battle for Guadalcanal. The Japanese were preparing for a major offensive to throw the Americans off the island. On October 25, the attacks began, with raids on Henderson coming from air, sea, and land. Henderson and its adjacent fighter strip, nicknamed the "cow pasture" because of its propensity for turning into a quagmire during the torrential rains frequently seen in the area, were in for some very hard times.

A carrier battle developed on the 25th, involving two large opposing forces: two American task forces, 16 and 17, with the carriers *Enterprise* and *Hornet* as their respective centerpieces, and a large Japanese fleet with four carriers and major supporting vessels. Operating under its new commander, Admiral W.F. "Bull" Halsey, and after spending most of the previous day searching for the Japanese fleet, the American force drew first blood on the 26th. SBDs from the *Enterprise* found and heavily damaged the carrier *Zuiho*. The SBD Dauntlesses and TBF Avengers of the American task forces pounded the enemy fleet, while screening destroyers attempted to protect the carriers with intensive antiaircraft fire.

The *Hornet*, however, was damaged around 0900 on the 26th by a heavy and determined Japanese air attack which left the carrier gravely wounded and dead in the water. The battle raged back and forth between the carrier fleets, each side trading attack against counterattack, with several ships of all types sunk on both sides. The damaged *Hornet* was struck by a submarine-launched torpedo, and as the *Enterprise* recovered her own aircraft and those of her sister carrier, an afternoon aerial attack by Japanese planes sealed the *Hornet*'s fate. Still floating after attempts to sink her by gunfire had failed, the gallant ship—deliverer of America's first offensive operation, the April 18 Tokyo Raid by Jimmy Doolittle and his B-25s—was abandoned and left to the prowling Japanese who sunk her in the early morning of the 27th.

The Battle of Santa Cruz had cost the Japanese two carriers damaged, numerous support ships, and 100 aircraft; the Americans had lost the *Hornet* and 74 planes, as well as several surface vessels. But for the Americans, the major objective of the confrontation had been achieved: the Japanese had been denied entrance to the Sealark Channel, offshore of Henderson Field, and the Marines still held the "cow pasture."

In the hectic, pressure-filled months of late October and November 1942, there was only one U.S. carrier, the *Enterprise*, in full operation. This situation caused the Navy to fly many of its aircraft to Henderson to operate alongside the Marines, as well as to take advantage of the maintenance facilities, such as they were, on Guadalcanal. This was one of the few times that Navy and Marine pilots flew and fought in the exact same aircraft; the Marines did not have different equipment from that of their Navy counterparts. Their Wildcats and Dauntlesses were the same. Thus, the Navy Department had two "carriers" operating at the "Canal": the mobile *Enterprise*, and the "fixed, zero-speed" carrier at Henderson.

Even though no Japanese victory had been obtained, Admiral Isoroku Yamomoto, Chief of the Imperial Navy, was not through. He had masterminded the Pearl Harbor attack, and now he had supplies and over 14,000 troops in transports headed for Guadalcanal, protected by battleships and cruisers. Target date for a landing was November 13.

The Americans themselves were bringing in new men and aircraft to fortify Cactus Base and Henderson Field. A new air group, MAG-11, arrived on November 1, the SBDs of VMSB-132 arriving first, with VMF-112 landing the next day. Also, a major personnel change occurred on November 7, when Major General Geiger—the quintessential Air Marine—was relieved by newly promoted Brigadier General Lou Woods. Geiger's departure was tinged with bitterness on his part, for he felt he was being unjustly relieved just when the most crucial battles were coming. But the strain on Geiger was there for all to see; he had been there since the beginning, and had no apologies to make for the way he ran things. A younger, fresher man in the slot was perhaps the best thing.

Soon after Geiger's departure, MAG-11 was put to its first combat test when seven SBDs of VMSB-132 were sent out to attack a large destroyer fleet trying to land troops. Covered by twelve P-39s of the veteran 67th Pursuit Squadron—long-time denizens of Henderson—the Dauntlesses pressed their attacks. They were met by ten Rufe fighters, floatplane adaptations of the Zero built by Nakajima. VMF-112, led by Major Paul Fontana, with seven F4Fs, shot down six Rufes, their pilots successfully bailing out. Then, as if by signal, all six Japanese fliers unbuckled their parachute harnesses to drop to their deaths in the water below.

VMF-121 was along, too. Captain Foss shot down a float biplane, probably from one of the destroyers below, and then turned to meet another Japanese aircraft. The crew of the second floatplane was more cunning and the pilot cut power to make Foss overshoot and give the rear gunner a good target. Hit in the cowling and cockpit canopy, Foss swung his Wildcat around and finally dispatched the enemy aircraft with a burst. Foss shot down another two-seat scout, for a total of three kills that afternoon, and suddenly found himself very much alone in the sky. Disoriented, his fuel low and his aircraft's engine running rough, he was forced to ditch offshore of little Malaita Island, where some natives sheltered him for the night. The next day, Jack Cram flew up to transport Foss home to Henderson. Foss was also to receive the Medal of Honor for his overall contribution during his time at Guadalcanal, rather than for a specific action, similar to John Smith's award.

The Battle for Guadalcanal

On the night of November 12-13, American ships fought a classic naval battle against a larger Japanese force, in what has been called the First Battle of Guadalcanal. Steaming south towards Florida Island, the Japanese delivered a tactical defeat to the American fleet, sinking a cruiser and four destroyers, and damaging several other ships. During the battle, two American rear admirals were killed, Daniel Callaghan on the bridge of his flagship *San Francisco,* and Norman Scott, on the bridge of the cruiser *Atlanta*. These men, their commands, and the sacrifice, albeit unintentional, of their ships, kept the attention of the Japanese away from their objective, Henderson.

On November 14-15, the Second Battle of Guadalcanal was fought, some of it in daylight. The Japanese were sending a huge reinforcement group down The Slot, the channel between the northern shores of New Georgia and Guadalcanal, and the southern coasts of the islands of Choiseul and Santa Isabel. This looked like it could be *the* battle. Planes from the *Enterprise* made continuous attacks, along with land-based raiders from Cactus, starting at 0830, right until sunset. Even B-17s from Espiritu Santo flew some missions. Six transports—one-half the transport fleet—were sunk. However, by midnight, another night engagement had developed as a second Japanese force, coming from the north, had been discovered by a small American fleet of two battleships and four destroyers. When it was over, the Japanese had lost two battleships, a cruiser, three destroyers, and ten transports, as well as 4,000 troops and their equipment.

Henderson continued to suffer nightly bombardment. The Army Air Force's resources had been augmented by the arrival of eight Lockheed P-38s on November 12, and the big, twin-engined, twin-tailed fighters were welcome additions to the always hard-pressed P-39 squadron, the 67th.

SBDs from VMSB-142 attacked the old battleship *Hiei*, one Marine Dauntless planting a 1,000-pound bomb squarely amidships. Joe Foss led six Wildcats as escorts for a second attack by VMSB-131, and also to try their luck at strafing the struggling *Hiei*, which had suffered over 85 hits and had lost steering control. TBF torpedo planes bracketed the *Hiei* for good measure. The Japanese ended up scuttling the ship.

Strikes on the 14th were on a shuttle schedule, with Marine and Navy dive and torpedo bombers taking off for runs on the advancing Japanese, meeting with varying degrees of success and opposition. However, a major loss was that of Lieutenant Colonel "Indian Joe" Bauer—who was part Indian, hence the nickname—commanding officer of VMF-212, who had put in such a spectacular opening performance upon his arrival. Flying escort for the last attacks on November 14, Bauer and his F4Fs were jumped by Zeros, one of which Bauer shot down. He was then apparently hit by antiaircraft fire from the ships below and had to ditch his fighter. The last Joe Foss and another pilot saw of Bauer, he was swimming away from his sinking airplane, seemingly okay. Although search missions were launched, no trace of Bauer was found. In a few brief weeks, he had shot down eleven Japanese aircraft, and gained the respect and admiration of all who flew and fought with him.

The Second Battle of Guadalcanal permanently denied the Japanese any major landing on the island and a chance to retake their airfield. Admiral Halsey wrote later:

Now, nearly five years later, I can face the alternative frankly. If our ships and planes had been routed in this battle, if we had lost it, our troops on Guadalcanal would have been trapped as were our troops on Bataan . . . the enemy would have driven south. . . . [10]

This is in the clear light of historical perspective. At the time, however, the Japanese had a few thoughts yet on Guadalcanal; but their supplies had now to be *floated* in on the tide.

New blood was being supplied to the Marines, too. For the combat-weary wonders of the First Marine Division—the mud Marines—the Army sent in its 25th Infantry Division. Brigadier General Woods was relieved as COMAIRCACTUS, a somewaht unofficial title, by Brigadier General Francis P. Mulcahy, Marine Aviator Number 64, another old hand. The first units of the Allies' air resources made their appearance on November 26 when a Royal New Zealand Air Force squadron of Lockheed Hudsons—twin-engine, land-based patrol bombers—landed at Henderson.

December saw aerial action continue, though at a somewhat reduced pace from the earlier hectic months. On December 1, Major Joe Sailer, tireless commander of VMSB-132 was shot down by a Zero after making an attack on some Japanese destroyers. Sailer had flown twenty-five mis-

Menu

Appetizer

Juice   ~~Soup~~
Tossed Salad   Dressing

Hot Entrée
Or
~~Cold Turkey
Sandwich/Lettuce/Tomato~~

Potato   Vegetable
White Bread   Saltines

Gelatin   ~~Dessert of Day~~

Beverages

Coffee   4 oz Skim
~~Tea~~   4 oz Low Fat
Decafe Coffee   ~~4 oz Whole~~
Decafe Tea   ~~Creamer~~
Non-Dairy Creamer

Condiments

~~Salt~~   Margarine
~~Pepper~~   Butter
~~Sugar~~   Lemon
~~Sugar Substitute~~   Catsup
Herb Seasoning   Mustard
      ~~Mayonnaise~~
      Parm Cheese

Name: _Jordan_ Room: _One_
Diet Order:_____

sions in five weeks and had scored six hits on enemy ships. His loss was that of a future leader and highly skilled dive-bomber pilot.

By Christmas 1942, the Japanese position was really untenable. Their troops remaining on Guadalcanal were sick and short of food, medicine, and ammunition, and the American base at Henderson was searching out and destroying the enemy everywhere. January brought some increase in Japanese strength and activity, but it was not the same as the early summer and fall days of the past year.

The Marine units, VMF-112, VMF-121, VMSB-144, and VMSB-234, were active. And on January 31, 1943, Lieutenant Jeff DeBlanc flew a mission which gained him the Medal of Honor when he escorted a strike over Vella Lavella, near Bougainville, a main Japanese staging area. Leading six Wildcats, DeBlanc, flying at 14,000 feet, sighted a number of Zeros and Rufe floatplanes heading for his charges. The Louisiana native immediately dove to break off the Japanese attack, shooting down three Rufes and two Zeros which had joined the fight. His skill and bravery enabled the bombers to complete their mission, although DeBlanc and another pilot, Staff Sergeant James A. Feliton, had to abandon their Wildcats over Kolombangara Island to the west. They were cared for by a coast-watcher on Kolombangara until a plane could be sent up from Guadalcanal to get them.

By early February 1943 it was all but over. Japanese ships began evacuation on the 7th, continuing until the next day. Japan had been handed its first major land defeat after six months of the bloodiest fighting in the history of warfare. Because of the intensity of the fighting, as well as lack of record-keeping during and immediately after the battle, the cost for both sides is open to conjecture. Estimates of Japanese aircraft lost during the campaign range from 36 fighters and bombers to 263, including 75 various types, such as floatplanes and transports. The American estimates of the Cactus Air Force's losses are put at 101 aircraft, a ratio of 1.3:1 or 2.6:1. Ninety-four American pilots were killed at Guadalcanal. However, as Brigadier General Samuel B. Griffith II, who, as a lieutenant colonel, commanded the much-feared and -admired Marine Raiders on Guadalcanal during some of the fiercest fighting on the island, later wrote:

In the cold perspective of history, the relative importance of a military campaign is not judged by statistics. . . . it is the ultimate effect which the battle . . . exerts on the conduct and result of the war that should be considered. [11]

As satisfying and deserving a victory as Guadalcanal was for the Americans, it is also important to note that the Japanese seemed to have the momentum knocked out of them. The vital force which had carried the island nation from China to Pearl Harbor and the Philippines was lost, along with Guadalcanal. As the search for reasons began in Tokyo, many accusing fingers were pointed. But, one who would not be there—and who would have certainly come in for his share of criticism—was Admiral Isoroku Yamamoto.

This brilliant tactician was shot down and killed in his transport on April 18, 1943, while on an inspection trip in the Solomons area. In a beautifully executed mission, Army Air Force P-38s caught the two Betty transports and their Zero escorts in a surprise strike, and shot down the two bombers, killing Yamamoto. (The wreck of his plane still survives in the jungle.) The Japanese were denied the mind and leadership of this professional soldier, at a time when they could not afford such a loss.

An interesting sidelight to the Yamamoto mission was the fact that it was a Marine who actually plotted the intercept course for the Army fighters. Major John P. Condon was the Fighter Command Operations officer for ComAirSols and he duly laid out a route which would take the eighteen P-38s in through the back door at Kahili, 50 feet above the water, to avoid Japanese radar detection. Because the Japanese code had been broken, Yamamoto's itinerary was known, down to the last detail—takeoff times, route, and number of escorting Zeros.

The P-38s were divided into two sections, escorts and "shooters"—those Lightnings which would actually go after the admiral's transport. As they drifted out of communications range on the morning of the 18th, there was little anyone on the ground could do but wait. Finally, the excited voices of the Army pilots began to come in, telling of their success. As the fighters approached their home field, Captain Thomas G. Lanphier and his wingman, Lieutenant Rex T. Barber, swung into victory rolls. Lanphier radioed Major Condon that "that S.O.B. would never dictate anything in the White House—or anywhere!" It was a proud moment for everyone concerned. The Japanese were understandably furious, for that night they pounded the Americans from sunset to sunrise. It was a sure thing, as far as U.S. servicemen were concerned, that Yamamoto was indeed dead.

5

Island-Hopping

The campaign for Guadalcanal gave proponents of Marine aviation ammunition in making their case for a beefed-up air arm. Outgoing Marine Corps Commandant, General Thomas Holcomb, had named General Vandegrift as his successor, but Vandegrift had to take temporary command of I Marine Amphibious Corps (I MAC). He later turned over this important job to Major General Geiger.

After Guadalcanal, the drive through the Solomons to gain the bases needed to support a strategic bombing campaign against the Japanese home islands—hopefully with the powerful new B-29 Superfortresses that were beginning to roll off various Boeing assembly lines—began to take shape. New aircraft had also begun to arrive in Marine fighter squadrons to replace the dependable, but obsolescent, F4F Wildcat. The first of these new fighters was the big Chance Vought F4U Corsair. Known variously as "Hose Nose," "Hog," "Bent-wing Bird," or just plain "U," the Corsair was one of the greatest naval aircraft of the war.

The prototype XF4U-1 first flew in May 1940, with an inverted gull wing enabling the 2,000-horsepower Pratt and Whitney radial to swing a 13-foot-diameter propeller without correspondingly long landing gear. The huge fighter was an obvious world beater, but the massive nose and resulting limited visibility gave rise to fears that carrier landings could present dangerous problems. Reluctant to accept the new fighter for carrier operations, the Navy handed it over to the Marines. By June 1942, Corsair production was in full swing and September brought the first carrier qualification tests. Fears about the plane's handling around the ship were borne out, the F4U developing a stall and resulting loss of control during the close-in, slower-speed phase of the landing approach. Modifications were instituted, but in the meantime, the plane was desperately needed in the Pacific, and it was determined that it would operate from land bases, with both Navy and Marine units.

Accordingly, VMF-124, under Major William E. Gise, flew their new F4U-1s to Guadalcanal in February 1943, and began combat operations in company with Army P-38s and P-40s, acting as escorts for an attack by Navy PB4Y-1s, the Navy models of the B-24 Liberator four-engined bomber, against Kahili, a big Japanese airfield on Bougainville. The combat debut of the Corsair was hardly auspicious. Over fifty defending Zeros met the attack head-on, shooting down ten American aircraft, including two of the new F4Us, for the loss of only four of their own.

Shaken, the Marines of VMF-124 determined to utilize their new mount's superior speed and firepower to combat the lighter, more maneuverable Zero. By September 1943, all eight Marine fighter squadrons in the Pacific were transitioned to the Corsair. Indeed, as far as the public at home was concerned, the F4U was the only aircraft flown by the Marines. The average American could hardly be blamed for thinking so, with names like Walsh, Hanson, and Boyington—all winners of the Medal of Honor for action in the Corsairs—constantly in the headlines and movie newsreels. Once its pilots learned its idiosyncrasies, and adjusted for the lack of view forwards, the F4U did everything: bombing, strafing, rocket delivery, photo reconnaissance, and of course aerial combat. The Corsair accounted for 2,140 enemy aircraft in the Pacific, with a loss of 189 F4Us (this total includes both Navy and Marine victories), second only to the Grumman Hellcat in total kills for a single type. The Corsair was to continue in production until January 1953, when the last of 12,571 "Us" rolled off the line.

Bougainville and the Solomons

After Guadalcanal, Navy carrier resources in the Pacific were at an all-time low. Only the *Enterprise* and *Saratoga* were operational, and it would be mid-summer before any newer flattops would join the fleet; the Marines would have to shoulder much of the burden for the Navy's air contribution to the war effort. In February 1943, Rear Admiral Charles P. Mason was chosen to head the newly established post of Commander, Aircraft, Solomons (ComAirSols). This new organization had control of all land-based naval air assets—excluding search and rescue—which accounted for thirty-two fighter and bomber squadrons, including six

(Text continues on page 87.)

First Lieutenant Alfred A. Cunningham, the first Marine officer to be designated a Naval Aviator, stands in front of a Curtiss "Jenny" trainer at NAS Pensacola in March 1914.

First Lieutenant Bernard L. Smith, Marine Aviator Number 2, stands near the tail of the Curtiss C-3.

The Curtiss C-3 on the catapult of the *North Carolina* in July 1916. The aircraft was assigned to the Marines for maneuvers off Puerto Rico. (U.S. Navy)

A Curtiss N-9 floatplane shown at Pensacola in 1918. This type was the first seaplane ever looped. First Lieutenant Francis T. Evans accomplished the feat on February 13, 1917.

DH-4Bs of the Northern Bombing Group, during the winter of 1918. Note the early attempts at identifying these planes as Marine aircraft. The second DH from the left, 012, carries the eagle, globe, and anchor symbol on the rear fuselage.

A DH-9A of Squadron "A," First Marine Aviation Force, France, 1918.

A view of the Lewis gun on a Scarff ring mount in the rear cockpit of a DH-4 in France. Some aircraft carried two machine guns, as well as a forward-firing gun. Note the wind vane front sight, designed to lead a moving target.

A Standard E-1 assigned to the Marines for training during 1918. These rotary-engined single-seaters were also flown by Marines training at the Army field at Gerstner, Louisiana.

A Boeing-manufactured O2B-1, an improved version of the DH-4, with a metal fuselage. Photograph was taken at Quantico in 1926. Note globe-and-anchor insignia below rear cockpit.

Master Sergeant B.T. Belcher, first enlisted pilot in the Marines, sits in the cockpit of his VO-1M DH-4B at Santo Domingo City, Dominican Republic, 1922. Note that the front cockpit has been covered, perhaps as a baggage compartment.

A Thomas-Morse MB-3 of Flight "F" warming up at Quantico in 1921. Only eleven of these small fighters were assembled and flew for a very short time. They were, however, the first aircraft procured especially for the Marines.

Photographed at Quantico in October 1922, this Fokker D-7 was the best German fighter to be operated in large numbers during World War I. The Marines obtained six for postwar training and evaluation.

A Curtiss HS-2L over the harbor in Guam, 1922. These flying boats were used for long-range patrols by the Fourth Air Squadron.

Lieutenant Colonel Thomas Turner, director of Marine Corps Aviation, dismounts from his DH-4 while on a visit to Camp Meade, Maryland, in August 1925.

The Martin MBT was used for training parachute jumpers, probably because of its stability in the air. These two views of parachutists in 1927 give a good idea of the size of the MBT and the maze of struts and wires characteristic of most aircraft of the period.

Personnel of Quantico-based VF-2M in 1926 standing beside a squadron FB-1. Lieutenant W.L. McKittrick, second from left, eventually commanded the squadron, as VMF-1; Sergeant R.E. Fry, fourth from left, left the service to fly for the airlines, and was the pilot of a Fokker airliner which crashed in 1931, killing all on board, including football great Knute Rockne. "Sandy" Sanderson, twice commander of the squadron, is second from right, talking with another member of the squadron in front of the FB-1.

A Boeing FB-1 of VF-1M in 1925. The circled "F" denoted a Marine fighter squadron instead of a Navy unit. The FB-1 was powered by a Curtiss D-12 engine and was developed from the Army's XPW-9.

VF-10M FB-1 at the Tientsin Landing Field in China, 1927. Note the "Winged Devil" diamond insignia of VF-3M which had been redesignated VF-10M in June 1927, shortly after arriving in China. It was renumbered once more to VF-6M one year later.

An F4B-4 of VF-10M with two bombs mounted under the lower wing. The F4B series, the most successful of biplane fighters, served with Navy and Marine squadrons, as well as Army Air Corps units as the P-12. Many of the senior military fighter pilots of World War II cut their teeth on these nimble little aircraft.

The follow-on to the F6C was, naturally, the F7C of 1928. This example is operated by VF-5M which was renumbered VF-9M and based at Quantico in 1930.

One of the most sought-after aircraft during the late 1920s was the Curtiss F6C-4. This example served with VF-10M, based at San Diego in the early 1930s.

A 1931 view of Brown Field, Quantico, showing the VF-9M flight line. The aircraft are Curtiss F7Cs.

Aircraft and crews of VF-9M in formation in August 1932. VF-9M had to borrow the aircraft from VO-6M to meet its airshow schedule. The squadron's own F7Cs were barred from participation because several of them had crashed.

A Vought VE-7F of VO-1M shown at Santo Domingo, Dominican Republic, 1922. The VE-7 series was another long-lived design which served in both single- and two-seat versions.

68

Shown as a major general during World War II, Ross Rowell participated in combat in Nicaragua in the 1920s and was a member of the small group of Marine aviation pioneers.

Shown on the day he was awarded the Medal of Honor, First Lieutenant C.F. Schilt flew his Vought O2U into a small jungle landing strip in Nicaragua to transport wounded Marines to safety in January 1928. The mission called for the utmost in bravery and skill.

An O2U of the type piloted by Lieutenant Schilt takes off from a field at Managua, Nicaragua, in 1928. Two-seat Corsairs were active during the 1920s and 1930s.

Colonel Thomas C. Turner, Marine Aviator Number 73, and second director of Marine aviation. A dedicated and capable administrator, Turner was viewed as a competitor by Cunningham and only by intervention of the Commandant, a personal friend of Turner's, did Turner assume overall authority for Marine aviation. He was killed in October 1931 while on an inspection of Marine squadrons in Haiti.

70

Annual inspection in May 1932 shows squadrons at San Diego. Curtiss F6C-4s and OC-2s await the inspecting party in the far right.

The Sikorsky RS-1 Amphibian of Colonel Thomas C. Turner. Jumping out of this plane, which had become mired in mud, Turner was struck on the head by the still-turning propeller, and eventually died from his injuries. The RS-1 carried a two-man crew and seven passengers.

A Boeing F4B-4 and Ford JR-3, two important aircraft of Marine aviation in the 1930s. The big tri-motor transports did valuable work out of the primitive landing strips in Central America.

View of an R4C-1 in California. Note the two nose-mounted landing lights. Between-the-wars aircraft were immaculately maintained, as can be seen by the gleaming silver finish on this Condor.

A Curtiss F8C-5. After serving with the regulars in the late 1920s and early 1930s, the remaining F8Cs went to the Reserves in mid-1931.

One of the classic fighters of all time, this F4B-3 of VB-4M is shown in October 1933. Note the telescopic gunsight protruding through the windscreen, and the curious bomb rack between the main landing-gear struts. This arrangement was deleted on the later F4B-4, which used underwing bomb racks.

VMF-2 operated the F3F-2. The F3F used the Wright Cyclone, which developed 200 more horsepower than the Wasp of the earlier F2F.

Vought SU-2s of VO-8M, 1933. The San Diego-based squadron had just taken delivery of these new aircraft. SU-2 scouts served through the remainder of the decade. (William T. Larkins)

The Grumman F4F-4 Wildcat, in competition with the Brewster Buffalo, proved to be the only American fighter, Army or Navy, capable of fighting the Japanese Zero during the opening stages of the Pacific war.

Curtiss SOC-3s of VMS-2 at San Diego, 1939. Although operated mainly by Navy squadrons, the SOC did serve with a few Marine units. The type could operate either as a land plane or, with some changes, as a catapult floatplane. It served on several capital ships from 1938 to 1944. (William L. Swisher)

The big, tough Great Lakes BG-1 were used as dive bombers during the mid-1930s. This "Bee Gee" of VMB-2 carries the "Winged Devil" insignia of VB-4M, the squadron's designation until July 1937. (William T. Larkins)

The last biplane bomber by Curtiss, the SBC-3 served with only a few Marine units, mainly with Reserve squadrons. This well-proportioned dive bomber never saw combat, although the French were in the process of obtaining the type when they surrendered to the Germans in 1940. (Rudy Arnold Photo Collection of the Smithsonian Institution)

Vought SB2U-3s of VMSB-131 based at Quantico in July 1941. This fabric-covered monoplane was to prove a great disappointment to both the Navy and Marines during its very few combat actions, notably at Midway in 1942. (Rudy Arnold Photo Collection of the Smithsonian Institution)

A Douglas R2D-1, military version of the civilian DC-2 airliner, in VMJ-1, photographed at Boston in August 1939. The R2D was assigned to the Marines in 1935 as a paratroop trainer and as a general transport.

A Grumman J2F-5, better known simply as a "Duck," shown in February 1942, still carrying the "neutrality" star markings, pre-war rudder striping, and dark gray paint. This particular aircraft is serving with the American Aviation Mission to Central and South America. Colonel V.E. Megee, left, served throughout the Pacific war, eventually taking charge of all Marine close air support in the Okinawa campaign. The J2F also served through the war, in several versions, mainly as a rescue aircraft.

A North American SNJ-2 trainer of Base Air Detachment (BAD), Quantico, immediately before U.S. entry into World War II. The SNJ, the Navy version of the T-6 Texan, trained thousands of naval aviators, and several actually found their way to the war zones for use as proficiency trainers and "hacks." (Rowland P. Gill)

One of America's first air heroes of the war was Captain Henry T. Elrod, who fought in the skies above Wake Island, and then on the ground where he was killed by a Japanese Marine. Elrod was awarded the Medal of Honor.

Grumman F4F Wildcats of VMF-211 immediately after the surrender of Wake to the Japanese. The all-gray fighters served the Marine aviators well during the hectic, hopeless battle.

One of the few photographs showing the SB2U in action. Two Vindicators of VMSB-241 take off on the morning of June 4, 1942, to attack the Japanese fleet. Note the unusual placement of the fuselage star.

A Brewster F2A-3 Buffalo is directed out of its ramp position prior to takeoff at the Marine base at Ewa in early 1942. Oversize fuselage star and rudder striping are characteristic of the non-standard markings applied to Navy and Marine aircraft during the opening stages of the Pacific war.

Three important personalities of the Guadalcanal campaign are shown together in early 1943. From left to right, Major John L. Smith, Lieutenant Colonel Richard C. Mangrum, and Captain Marion E. Carl.

Two important figures in the fighting on Guadalcanal. On the left, Major General Roy S. Geiger, commanding the Cactus Air Force, and Captain Joe Foss of VMF-121, who gained most of his twenty-six kills during the Guadalcanal campaign.

Marine Wildcats on Henderson Field, Guadalcanal, 1942. This open-air "garage" was the maintenance area of the field. Note the tents in the background which served as a living area.

The Mitsubishi Zero, main opponent of Marine fighters over Guadalcanal. This is an A6M2 model, the first true production variant, and the one which flew through the early stages of the war until mid-1943. With a single belly tank, the Zero possessed incredible range and frequently flew missions of over 1,000 miles round trip. (Robert Mikesh)

A Wildcat positions itself for takeoff from Guadalcanal in February 1943. The dust and low-hanging clouds are characteristic of the weather and operating conditions.

Marine SBDs fly to their target from Henderson Field in 1943. Aircraft carry a single 500-pound bomb on the main belly rack.

Grumman TBF Avenger torpedo bombers taxi on Henderson Field and take off for a mission in 1943. The big TBF, nicknamed "Turkey" by its crews, served in several Marine squadrons as a torpedo bomber and, later at Okinawa, as a close air support aircraft.

Marine units. AirSols was composed of Army, Navy, Marine, and New Zealand officers, and the post of commander rotated among them with fair regularity.

The Japanese, after their humiliating defeat at Guadalcanal, organized a massive punitive sweep against Guadalcanal and New Guinea, called the "I Operation." To begin the offensive, fifty-eight Zeros attempted to raid Guadalcanal on April 1, 1943. They met a force of American fighter pilots, including the eager young Marines of VMF-124, anxious to rack up some kills with their new Corsairs. Among the Marines of VMF-124 was First Lieutenant Ken Walsh, a former enlisted Naval Air Pilot (NAP), who had been commissioned after Pearl Harbor and posted to the squadron. Walsh had nearly been killed a few months before when he had to ditch his F4U after the engine quit. The heavy aircraft sank like a stone, taking its pilot down with it; but keeping his cool, Walsh quickly unstrapped underwater and bobbed to the surface.

On April 1, Walsh had ample opportunity to test the Corsair's reliability and combat prowess, shooting down two Zeros. A second ditching, however, followed a few days later, but did not lessen his enthusiasm. On May 13, he became the first Corsair ace when he destroyed three more Zeros. By mid-August, he had doubled his score to ten. On August 30, Walsh fought an incredible battle against fifty Japanese aircraft, which he originally mistook for the bombers he was tasked with escorting.

He shot down four enemy fighters in the melee before another Zero tacked itself onto his tail and proceeded to shoot holes in his airplane, mortally wounding the struggling Corsair. With his engine crippled, Walsh prepared for his third water landing in six months! But the Zero kept hammering him from behind until another Corsair and an Army P-40 arrived to scare off the Japanese pilot, leaving Walsh to ditch in peace. Rescued, Walsh was returned to the U.S., where President Franklin D. Roosevelt awarded him the Medal of Honor for his exploits. He finished the war with twenty-one kills to his credit, most of which were obtained during the intense period of combat in mid-1943.

On April 7, another massed Japanese attack found seventy-six Army, Navy, and Marine defenders waiting. The American pilots piled into the Japanese formations, First Lieutenant James E. Swett, flying an F4F, shooting down seven Val dive bombers, the greatest number of kills on a single mission scored to that time. Swett too was forced to ditch his battered fighter and await rescue. He was also awarded the Medal of Honor.

The I Operation was not a very successful venture for the Japanese, and after two large attacks on New Guinea, the operation was recalled by Admiral Yamamoto. This was his last official act as commander of the Japanese fleet resources.

Marine fighter squadrons, with an increasing number of Corsairs, were in action continually. VMF-213 was especially active. Its pilots had some incredible experiences, including Lieutenant Gil Percy's 2,000-foot fall with a streaming parachute on June 7 (he lived to talk about it) and Staff Sergeant William Coffeen's odyssey by raft after being shot down on April 13 near Munda. With his survival equipment lost when his raft capsized, Coffeen paddled to a deserted island, rested for two days, and then struck out for another island. Existing on whatever food he found, he was rescued in a state of delirium, by a native who looked after him until a PBY came for him. Coffeen had been missing for seventy-three days!

Lieutenant Sheldon Hall, also of VMF-213, was shot down on July 18. After the enemy pilot strafed him in his raft, Hall paddled to an island which turned out to be held by the Japanese. He spent the next four days hiding out, eventually finding a native village whose inhabitants proved helpful—it was not always that way—and fed him. They finally took him to a coastwatcher, who called a PBY to rescue Hall and a TBF crew the coastwatcher had been guarding. The Pacific theater was full of escape, evasion, and rescue stories like these.

"Pappy" Boyington

The assault on Bougainville, largest of the Solomon Islands, began on November 1, 1943, catching the Japanese off guard, but they counterattacked on the 7th. The battle continued through the interminable rain, mud, and jungle heat which taxed attacker and defender alike. The storming of Bougainville received generous air support. ComAirSols was now Major General Ralph J. Mitchell, who had been Director of Marine Corps Aviation from 1939 to 1943. He had fifty-two squadrons at his command, including fourteen Marine units, and 728 aircraft. Army fighters and bombers—B-24s, B-25s, and P-40s—pounded the Japanese daily, while Marine squadrons, all now converted to the Corsair, participated in fighter sweeps, the main practitioner of which was a 29-year-old major named Gregory R. Boyington from Idaho. His squadron, VMF-214, called him "Grandpappy," or "Gramps," due to his "advanced" age for a fighter pilot; the newspapers shortened it to "Pappy." His older associates referred to him by his pre-war monicker of "Rats," while what some of his superiors may have called him is best left unsaid.

Boyington was one of a kind, the archetypical fighter pilot: cool, self-confident almost to abrasiveness, sure of eye, and always ready for a fight, in the air or on the ground; the opponent made no difference. He had been an aviation cadet with VF-9M, flying Boeing F4Bs, and was usually in some sort of light-hearted trouble. As a first lieutenant, he resigned his commission in 1941 to join the Flying Tigers, or American

Volunteer Group (AVG) as Chennault's band was actually known. (The Flying Tiger sobriquet was attributed to the highly spirited remarks of Chiang Kai-shek's wife, a patron of the AVG.) Boyington claimed six kills in China, making him one of the first American aces, albeit not under American colors, before the U.S. entry into World War II.

Ultimately returning to the States after Pearl Harbor, Boyington was shocked and angered to find that he was labeled a traitor and malcontent who had left his country in time of crisis. Even though he was an experienced fighter pilot, with six kills, he was told that his services were not needed. While he parked cars, Boyington fumed, sent off a letter to the Assistant Secretary of the Navy, and he found himself with orders to active duty and a commission as a major.

Shipping overseas to Guadalcanal in May 1943, Boyington found himself a squadron. He later wrote:

I finally thought my break had arrived . . . for Elmer Brackett was able to get me into his squadron as an executive officer . . . . We had no more than arrived when Elmer was promoted out of the squadron and I was assigned as commanding (officer). . . . [12]

He was with VMF-122 flying intensive patrols in the Solomons but he had no combat kills to show for it. After several weeks alternating between different squadrons, Boyington prevailed on an old acquaintance, now-Colonel "Sandy" Sanderson, a friend from Boyington's VF-9M days, to get him into a real combat squadron. Boyington was given command of VMF-214, which was, at that, even a loaner, the original VMF-214 having just completed a cruise. VMF-214's crew has been described as an outfit of misfits, brawlers, and washouts nobody else wanted. It certainly seemed that way, as Boyington tried to form them into a cohesive unit with himself, an aging fighter pilot, as the skipper.

They needed a nickname. Boyington's Bastards sounded alliterative but the newspapers would never have printed it, and so the name they settled on was the "Black Sheep," with an appropriate insignia. The squadron was equipped with the F4U which Boyington called "a sweet flying baby if ever I flew one," and went into action in the Solomons late in 1943.

On December 17, 1943, he led the first fighter sweep over Rabaul, hurling goading challenges over the radio to the Japanese below to come up and fight. By the end of the year, he had tied the existing score of Foss' twenty-six kills and found himself the object of much publicity. Some of the attention was a little too much for his pugnacious nature, and Boyington did not take his new-found fame too easily. But time was running out for Pappy.

He led a Black Sheep flight over Rabaul on January 3, 1944, from their strip at Vella Lavella. Japanese fighters were waiting and though he brought down two more Zeros to bring his score to twenty-eight, his wingman was shot down, and Boyington himself finally had to jump from his burning Corsair. Wounded, he floated in the water until he was taken prisoner by the crew of a Japanese submarine. Sent to a prison camp in Japan, Boyington waited out the last 20 months of the war. Listed as missing in action, the fact that he was alive was learned only when his name was painted in huge letters on the roof of one of the camp huts for pilots of American aircraft to see when they dropped supplies to the prisoners of war, after the Japanese surrender in August 1945.

Returning home, Boyington found he had been awarded the Medal of Honor. Somewhat belatedly, the Marines gave him the Navy Cross and sent him on a Victory Bond tour. As tough and realistic a man as he was, Boyington took the awards with a touch of cynicism and anger, but his war record remains one of the most colorful of all American combat pilots. The top Marine ace, he later wrote a book, which has become a minor classic of wartime autobiography, *Baa Baa Black Sheep*, published in 1958.

Captain John M. Foster, a Corsair pilot with VMF-222, a neighbor fighter squadron to Boyington's VMF-214, was one of the "other" aviators who flew, although sporadically, with Boyington. He knew the Marine ace from a distance, and his own book *Hell in the Heavens*, published in 1961, throws some interesting light on how the other pilots viewed Boyington, his reputation, and his flying skill. Foster first saw Boyington as the VMF-214 commander was reporting a score of four kills to intelligence officers, and later recounts one of the various stories which involved Boyington. The tale concerns a hectic combat during which his squadron mates inquired over the radio as to the ace's whereabouts. He replied that he was occupied.

> "I've got five Zeros surrounded."
> "Where are they?"
> "Outside this cloud they've got me in!" [13]

Foster denied being struck by any hero worship or awe.

I was only interested in Boyington for what information I could learn from him about fighting . . . .
When you're actually associating with such men . . . you do not look upon them with awe. They are just other pilots who sit across the table and eat with you, whom you shower with, get bombed with, and sometimes fight with. [14]

When Boyington was reported missing, Foster admits, the loss was taken pretty hard by everyone, but especially, quite naturally, by the men of VMF-214.

That evening, his heartsick friends went out in the face of a storm to search for Boyington, but they found nothing, not even a trace of wreckage . . . .
Every time I saw Boyington I always seemed to think of a bulldog. Perhaps it was the set of his jaw. Perhaps it was the legend he had built around himself. [15]

Several veteran Marine fighter squadrons returned to their old Pacific haunts during this time, among them VMF-223, now led by the redoubtable Major Marion Carl, veteran of Midway and Guadalcanal. VMF-223 left its base at El Toro, south of Los Angeles, in July and slowly made its way west, through Alameda, Ewa, and Midway. While working-up at Midway, the squadron lost four Corsairs and one pilot, largely to engine malfunctions, and was airlifted back to Hawaii to reequip, subsequently being reassigned to MAG-23.

After getting new aircraft, VMF-223 sailed for Espiritu Santo, arriving on November 11, and by the end of the month it was firmly ensconced at Vella Lavella, alongside other F4U squadrons, including 214 and 222. VMF-223's first combat action of the new tour occurred on December 23, four kills being registered by Bulldog pilots. But the pickings were slim. Early February saw Carl reassigned to a staff job in MAG-12.

While the aircrews were fighting their way up from Guadalcanal, the Japanese abandoned Bougainville by early 1944 and attention could now be directed towards Rabaul. The decision was made to land an amphibious force at Cape Gloucester on the west end of New Britain; Rabaul was on the northeast tip, directly across the island. Guarded by a natural barrier of five volcanoes, Rabaul Harbor had been a natural place for the Japanese to set up their huge staging base in January 1942, after taking it from a small Australian garrison. It had been a thorn in Admiral Halsey's side, and he was determined to remove it.

It was during this campaign—"Ring Around Rabaul" it was quickly dubbed—that pilots like Boyington and First Lieutenant Robert Hanson were especially active. Hanson probably was one of Boyington's closest competitors. The son of missionaries, Hanson called the small town of Newtonville, Massachusetts, 10 miles west of Boston, his home, although he spent most of his early life following his parents from India to Vienna. Enlisting in the Marines in May 1942, he was designated a naval aviator in early 1943 and joined VMF-215 at Vella Lavella, flying the Corsair. Although a friendly, outgoing sort on the ground, the burly Hanson disdained in-flight discipline, so necessary in combat involving large groups of aircraft. He preferred to lead rather than follow as a wingman and would frequently find excuses to break formation and go after a kill on his own, although he was not a glory-seeker in any sense.

Hanson's first kills came while he and his squadron were covering the landings at Bougainville on November 1, 1943, the 23-year-old pilot shooting down a Val dive bomber that was attempting to bomb the Navy ships during the landing. The next several days saw Hanson bringing down Japanese planes at an almost unbelievable rate—three, four, and five at a time. The newspapers picked up his story and labeled him "The One-Man Air Force," and "Butcher Bob." His squadron mates took it in stride, but as his score approached the magic twenty-six, Hanson became all-too-aware of the constant publicity. (The American World War I ace, Captain Eddie Rickenbacker, obtained twenty-six kills in 1918 and the number had become the goal of all U.S. fighter pilots.)

On January 30, 1944, Hanson shot down four Zeros, part of the intercepting fighter force against a large raid. His score now stood at twenty-five; he had been in continuous combat for nearly three months. One day before his 24th birthday, on February 3, Hanson participated in a sweep over Rabaul, but the Marines found the target obscured by clouds and returned to their base. On the return flight, Hanson asked permission to strafe a lighthouse which had proved troublesome as a Japanese flak tower and observation post. Captain Harold Spears, the flight leader, consented and Hanson broke away to begin his run. The next thing his horrified friends saw was Hanson's aircraft shudder from flak hits, its wing disintegrating. Hanson apparently tried to ditch, but lost control of the cartwheeling Corsair and crashed into the ocean, leaving only scattered debris.

Captain Foster knew Hanson, and wrote in his book:

He had flirted with death so often he could laugh at her, but this, the third day of February 1944, she decided to embrace him, and nothing remained behind, only some debris and an oil slick and a record. [16]

Robert Hanson was awarded a posthumous Medal of Honor on August 1, 1944, for his performance during his three months of intensive combat in the Solomons: twenty-five kills during that period, twenty in only seventeen days. He became the third-ranking Marine fighter ace of World War II.

The landing at Cape Gloucester took place on December 26, 1943, the veteran First Marine Division storming ashore and meeting very little initial resistance. But by afternoon, the Japanese launched a large air raid, much of which was dispersed by Army P-38s. One little-known Marine operation, which took place for the first time, was the use of small Piper Cubs designated for artillery-spotting. Flown by officers and enlisted men, the ten little single-engine craft did valuable work during the later stages of the landings.

The Japanese were pounded by Army, Navy, and Marine air power continuously. VMTB-232, newly redesignated and reequipped VMSB-232 of Guadalcanal fame, flew its TBFs on daily raids against enemy shipping in Simpson Harbor. The squadron had arrived in New Caledonia in August and then went to Espiritu Santo in September, operating in the vicinity of Bougainville, assigned to MAG-24.

By mid-February, under constant attack, the Japanese had had enough and began pulling out, even as American Navy and Marine squadrons took over recently captured airstrips. The Japanese had, by some estimates, lost 400-700 aircraft during the Bougainville/Rabaul operation, 393 of which were claimed by Marine aircrews. The real numbers, due to the huge free-for-all aerial battles of December 1943 and January 1944, will never be known.

Charles A. Lindbergh's Combat Tour

A world-famous personality appeared in the Pacific in the spring of 1944. At forty-one, he might have been considered pretty old to be flying combat missions in a Corsair; what made the situation even more unusual was the pilot's civilian status. But Charles A. Lindbergh was no stranger to unusual situations. And as far as his "advanced" age is concerned, he was flying before many of his future wingmen had even been born. His 1927 New York-to-Paris flight had established his life and fortune. As highly acclaimed as he was in the 1930s, the pendulum swung in the opposite direction later in the decade as Lindbergh was reviled for his stand in favor of American isolationism and his professed admiration for Nazi Germany. (Some speculated that he was really involved in spying for American interests during his contacts with the Germans.) But when war came in 1941, he immediately offered his services to the military.

Not knowing exactly what to do with so famous a personage, the War Department made Lindbergh a consultant with United Aircraft, of which Chance Vought was a part. By January 1944, he was heavily involved with Corsair development and had checked out in the F4U. He flew to various stateside Marine installations to discuss his theories with senior Marine aviators. After going through several weeks of combat training with the Corsair, Lindbergh flew out to the Pacific in April 1944 and spent several days with Marine units working-up with his aircraft in Hawaii and Midway.

May found him at Espiritu Santo, and on May 22, he flew his first combat mission—still in a civilian status—with VMF-222. It was a strafing run over islands near Rabaul. He eventually flew with most of the active Corsair units, VMF-218, VMF-223, and VMF-212 of MAG-24, VMF-224 and VMF-311 of MAG-31. In all, it is estimated that Lindbergh flew over fifty missions with the Marines, and later with the Army Air Force's P-38-equipped 475th Fighter Group. (With the latter organization, the trans-Atlantic pioneer shot down a Sonia observation plane.)

Lindbergh was convinced that the powerful Corsair could carry much more ordnance than it was normally fitted with. On September 8, he flew an aircraft with a specially modified belly rack, carrying a 2,000-pound bomb. Taking off from Roi Island, he flew out to Wotje Island, which had been the recipient of recent Marine attention, and dropped the weapon on a Japanese installation. Subsequent missions with increased payload proved Lindbergh's contention, although some difficulties were experienced in releasing the big bombs in dives. He was still not satisfied that the Corsair had reached its limit.

Accordingly, on September 13, 1944, Lindbergh had his plane, an F4U-1D, loaded with one 2,000-pound bomb and two 1,000-pounders. Using up almost every foot of runway, he managed to pull the shuddering plane into the air and proceed to Wotje where he dropped the heaviest load carried by a single fighter up to that time. Lindbergh described his dive in his wartime diary.

I flew upwind over my target . . . at 8,000 feet, rolled over and started my dive. I was pointed downward at an angle of about 65 degrees, the steepest I have used with a heavy bombload . . . . There was just time. I tripped the bomb releases and pulled up steeply.

When the period of grayout was over, I looked back to see the black column of debris rising above the main naval-gun installation in that area of the island . . . . I could not have selected a better target area even if it had been intentional, with plenty of time to consider. My bombs had completely wiped out the southern portion of the gun position and probably dislocated the gun itself. [17]

The Night Fighters

During this intense year of action, the Marines were in the forefront of a new theater of combat for Americans, night fighting. Aerial combat at night was not new, of course. World War I had seen night bombing attacks by both British and German squadrons, which drew the appropriate development from the opposing sides: the night fighter. At that time, this defensive aircraft was usually a single-seater such as the Sopwith Camel, modified to fly and fight in the dark. Normally, these modifications were limited to cockpit lighting and flame-dampeners for engine exhausts or machine-gun muzzles; a good pair of eyes also helped.

However, the German aerial blitz on London in 1941 encouraged the British to develop their new weapon of radar, to be carried by the larger, twin-engined aircraft in service, such as Bristol's Blenheim bomber and Beaufighter multi-seated fighter. An unsuccessful single-engine day fighter, the Boulton-Paul Defiant, armed solely with a four-gun turret behind the pilot, was also utilized with radar. The British also had taken to bombing at night, and naturally the Germans countered with their own stable of night fighters, usually Bf-110s and Ju. 88s, twin-engined products of the Messerschmitt and Junkers concerns, respectively. But single-engine fighters such as the Bf-109 and Focke-Wulf 190, and lesser aircraft like the Dornier-217, and a later night fighter, the Heinkel 219, were also used and were, unfortunately for the British, very successful.

While the development of aerial combat at night was proceeding in the European theater, the Pacific saw little of it, until the introduction of Marine squadron VMF(N)-531 on January 1, 1943. Nighttime intruder raids at Guadalcanal, by one or two Japanese planes, were accomplishing their objectives: harassment of American troops, loss of sleep, resulting in reduced combat effectiveness and morale. A way of dealing with these marauders had to be found. But it was not until March that the initial contingent of VMF(N)-531 arrived in the Pacific. On April 1, Marine Night Fighting Group 53, MAG(N)-53, was formed, splitting VMF(N)-531 into two squadrons, VMF(N)-531 and VMF(N)-532. VMF(N)-531 had been operating the Lockheed Vega PV-1 Ventura, a twin-engined development of the prewar Lodestar transport. The Marines were not happy with their mount's capabilities, especially its low operating ceiling of 15,000 feet. However, the PV-1s went into service and on December 6, 1943, the executive officer of VMF(N)-531, Major John D. Harshberger, scored the first kill, destroying a Japanese floatplane near Bougainville. In close radio contact with the GCI (Ground Control Intercept) site on Vella Lavella, the night-fighter crews were vectored towards their quarry with directional-bearing information until visual contact could be made.

On February 9, 1944, Major Harshberger was up over Rabaul and was quickly vectored towards two Japanese bombers. The enemy crews were alert, however, and raked the Ventura with 20-mm cannon fire, one shell entering the cockpit just behind Harshberger's head. With most of his forward-firing guns knocked out, Harshberger closed in on the Bettys, allowing his turret gunner, Staff Sergeant Walter Tiedman, a good shot. One Mitsubishi eventually burst into flames and went down; the other escaped in the night. Coming back to Bougainville, jittery "friendly" antiaircraft gun crews almost finished the job the Japanese bombers started.

The other night-fighter squadron of MAG(N)-53, VMF(N)-532, was much better equipped than its sister unit, and was one of only three squadrons to use the F4U-2 model of the Corsair, the other two squadrons being the Navy's VF(N)-75 and VF(N)-10. The F4U-2 was a dedicated night fighter, incorporating wing-mounted scanner radar enclosed in a nacelle on the right-wing tip. The radar was manufactured by Sperry and operated in the X-band range, 5.2 to 10.9 megacycles. After much testing and development, the first F4U-2, converted from an existing dash 1 with the familiar "birdcage" canopy, flew in January 1943 at the Naval Air Station, Quonset Point, Rhode Island, across from Newport. Exhaust-flame dampeners, IFF/transponder beacon, VHF radio, and a radar altimeter were installed in the night fighter. An oddity was the deletion of one .50-caliber machine gun in the right wing, presumably to accommodate the radar unit, leaving the aircraft armed with five guns instead of the normal six, still lethal enough. The aircraft was also left in the normal day-fighter scheme of three-tone blue, there being no provision for a regular night-fighter paint scheme. Thirty-two

F4U-1s were converted to dash 2s. Twelve of them went to VMF(N)-532, commanded by Major Everette H. Vaughn, once an airline pilot for TWA.

By December 1943, the twenty-one pilots of VMF(N)-532 had completed training and had shipped out to the Pacific, arriving in Hawaii on Christmas Day aboard a transport ship. Another ship carried them to the Gilbert Islands, arriving there on January 14, 1944, at Tarawa Atoll. Tarawa welcomed the newcomers, having been the recent subject of attentions from Japanese intruders.

The Navy's ground radar was in desperate need of repair, but was finally fixed to some extent, and functioned sporadically for the next several nights, the pilots of VMF(N)-532 trying their best to make do with the situation. Finally, a detachment of eight aircraft was sent down to Kwajalein in the Marshall Islands. Major Vaughn led the Corsairs to Roi, where they stayed for the next three months, having little initial success until the night of April 13-14, 1944. In their first successful interception, VMF(N)-532 pilots shot down two Bettys and scared off the remaining ten. One pilot apparently got lost in the dark and was listed as missing in action.

Two definite kills and one probable were gained that night, although Lieutenant Joel Bonner was forced to parachute from his plane after taking hits from a Betty. Bonner spent the night in his raft and was rescued by a destroyer escort the next afternoon.

In May, Vice Admiral Marc Mitscher paid a visit to the Marine night-fighter detachment and was so impressed with them that he later took two of the Corsairs, having them flown out to his task force for inspection, promising to deliver two brand-new replacements. He was as good as his word; however, the new F4Us were day fighters and had to be modified for night operations.

July saw the entire squadron loaded aboard the *Windham Bay* (CVE-92) and landed on Saipan where they were tasked with conducting night-time patrols as well as pre-dawn bombing raids on Japanese positions. This last type of operation did not sit too well with Major Vaughn, who knew how much training was involved in making a good night-fighter pilot, only to have that hard work thrown away simply to deliver bombs. Eventually, VMF(N)-532 was returned to the States to work-up on Grumman F7Fs. The squadron record was not impressive at first sight, however, because they had accomplished their objective of denying the nighttime skies to the enemy during important operations, the pilots and crews of VMF(N)-532 had accomplished their task.

The War Continues

The relentless march northward towards Japan began to gather steam with invasions of the Gilbert Islands, the Marshalls, and the Marianas.

Names like Tarawa, Kwajalein, and Peleliu were etched into the public consciousness by the blood used to buy each of these island groups. For the Marines who were in the van of almost every invasion, it was the ultimate test of combat for the 160-year-old Corps. At Tarawa, the tough and bloody battle for the airfield runways on Betio Island from 20-24 November 1943 cost 3,318 American casualties with 1,085 deaths, of which 984 were Marines. The battle for Kwajalein began on January 31, 1944, and by February 5, the island group was declared secure. 8,400 Japanese died; 500 American GIs, Army and Marine, were killed. Marine aviation had taken a back seat to these frantic amphibious operations. The "mud-Marines" had to take these islands themselves.

Something interesting, and perhaps unfortunate for the Marines on the ground, had transpired during the island invasions. Marine aviation resources—aircraft, crews, pilots, and support—had become so tied to the more traditional roles of land-based air power that the purpose for which Marine aviation had been developed had been subordinated, if not completely forgotten: providing close air support for the men on the ground.

The Marines, perhaps, were partly to blame for this turn of events. The gusto with which their fighter pilots and bomber crews went after the Zeros or bombed Japanese shipping served to push close-air-support functions into the background. The Navy, always the watchful and jealous big brother, was only too glad to let the Marines take care of things from land bases, leaving Navy air to its rightful dominion: carrier-based operations. Of course, the Marines could also operate from carriers. Adding fuel to the controversy was the Army's jealousy of a Marine air arm and the Corps' expansion into what the Army viewed as its own territory: land warfare. Lieutenant General Holland Smith, ever the vocal advocate for the Marines, proposed a combined Army-Marine amphibious organization under *his* command with Major General Roy Geiger's III Amphibious Corps as its nucleus.

Not surprisingly, Admiral Nimitz, with Commandant Vandegrift's approval, rejected Smith's proposal, but did authorize creation of a consolidated logistical and administrative group under Smith, known as Fleet Marine Force, Pacific. Included in FMFPac was Aircraft, Fleet Marine Force, Pacific, which covered the supply and administrative aspects of Marine aviation in the area. Nimitz wanted the operational control of Marine air to remain with the Navy, under Commander, Air Force, Pacific Fleet.

But the vast distances involved in some Pacific island operations, especially those in the Gilberts and Marianas, forced the Navy's hand. The Marines were brought aboard some of the escort carriers now beginning to populate the various task forces. With fifty-four flattops, the Navy seemed to have enough ships, and with 10,000 pilots and 126 squadrons, the Marines certainly had enough manpower and resources to fly from them. Their new job was not welcomed by Major General Ross Rowell, the senior Marine air commander in the Pacific. Rowell became so negative that he was relieved by Vandegrift on September 16, 1944, and sent to Lima, Peru, as the chief of the Naval Air Mission there, certainly a sorry end to a dedicated man's career. Major General Mulcahy took Rowell's place in the Pacific.

Marine Carrier Groups, Aircraft, Fleet Marine Force, Pacific, was born on October 21, 1944, and had its headquarters at MCAS Santa Barbara, California, Colonel Albert D. Cooley commanding. This organization was composed of two air groups, each group containing a complete set of two squadrons for each of four carriers: an eighteen-plane fighter squadron and a twelve-plane torpedo squadron. By summer, the order to carrier-train Marine pilots had been given and the Marines finally brought the battle-tested F4U home. With several improvements added since its initial carrier approach in September 1942, the Corsair had become more docile around the ship, but still retained its reputation as fairly unforgiving of lackadaisical treatment. Although most of the pilots were thrilled about carrier flying, the impression their little escort carriers—CVEs—gave was less enthusiastic. A song probably composed during Korea went:

> The *Midway* has 1,000-foot runways.
> The *Leyte* 810.
> But we still wouldn't have much of a carrier
> If we laid two of ours end to end.

In actuality, the Marine carrier program did not really get going until January 1945, but by the middle of the month the carrier Marines were in the thick of Pacific combat. On January 12, Marine fighter pilots aboard the *Essex* (CV-9) claimed their first kills off Okinawa. There were other areas of combat with names which would become all-too-familiar to another generation of Marine aviators twenty years later. Names like Saigon, Bien Hoa, Than Son Nhut, the South China Sea, and Hanoi, all in what was then French Indochina.

Aircraft and Missions

As the hierarchy wrestled with the weighty problems of organization and deployment, the war went on. By mid-1943, the Marine Corps had been the beneficiary of American over-production. Too many North American B-25 Mitchells had been turned out, and the Army could not find enough work for the twin-engined, twin-tailed bombers. Ever anxious for more planes, the Marines grabbed the first B-25s, which were designated PBJs, and quickly established eight squadrons by mid-October to operate them. VMB-413, under Lieutenant Colonel Andrew

B. Galatian, Jr., arrived at Espiritu Santo in January 1944 with their PBJ-1Ds, and by March, the Flying Nightmares were bombing Japanese installations at Rabaul, Kavieng, and on Bougainville, losing five aircraft and thirty-two crewmen by May in combat action. Five PBJ squadrons deployed overseas.

One of the more unusual PBJ outfits was VMB-612, in the central Pacific, skippered by Jack Cram, now a lieutenant colonel. The PBJ-1Hs (B-25Hs) and PBJ-1Js (B-25Js) of Cram's squadron were specially fitted with zero-length rocket launchers under the wings, radar bomb sights, and other electronics gear; the mission of VMB-612 was to harass Japanese shipping at night. The squadron arrived at Saipan in November 1944, and prior to beginning operations, the Mitchells were again modified by having the dorsal turret removed, as well as other components which were not essential to flying or navigation. Range and endurance were all-important; the night missions promised to be long. It took a lot of patient training to get the green crews combat-ready, but by April, with Iwo Jima secured and ready for American flight operations, VMB-612 began flying against Japanese harbors. Between April 10 and July 28, 251 sorties were flown, with claims for 53 ships damaged and five sunk.

Two aircraft which began to appear in Marine squadrons, although in limited numbers and roles, were the Grumman Hellcat and Curtiss Helldiver. Of the two, the former was much more successful. Derived from operational experience gained from the F4F Wildcat, the Hellcat was a big flying barrel of a fighter, supported by huge broadchord wings which carried the heavy single-seater without correspondingly high wing-loading factors; the wings and the relatively low wing loading gave the big Grumman the agility to meet the still-dangerous Zero on near equal terms, although the Mitsubishi still held the edge in maneuverability. (The Zero's combat superiority had begun to wane by early 1943, with the introduction of the Corsair, and disappeared with the advent of the Hellcat. However, in the hands of the few experienced Japanese aces still alive in 1944, the Zero could still be a formidable opponent and was to be treated with respect by Allied fighter pilots.)

Powered by the big 2,000-horsepower Pratt and Whitney radial engine, the F6F-3 went to the Navy's VF-9 aboard the *Essex*, and VF-5 in the new *Yorktown* (CV-10). The two squadrons took the Hellcat into action on August 31, 1943, and the aircraft immediately established itself as the Zero's nemesis. The Marines operated three versions of the Hellcat: the basic F6F-3/5 fighter, which flew from land bases and sporadically from carriers; the F6F-5P, photo reconnaissance; and the F6F-3/5(N) for night-fighting.

Interest in night-fighting techniques was still high in mid-1944, and

VMF(N)-541 was detailed to the Philippines to combat the Japanese Hayabusa (code-named Oscar), a fighter many mistook for the Zero because of its great maneuverability and light construction. The Nakajima-built Army fighter (the Zero flew only with Imperial Navy units) had been used as a nuisance raider, proving too fast for the U.S. Army Air Force P-61 Black Widow night fighters. VMF(N)-541 arrived at Tacloban on San Pedro Bay on the northeastern coast of Leyte Island in December, led by Colonel Peter Lambrecht. After some initial problems stemming from the inexperienced Army radar operators, Lieutenant Rodney E. Montgomery scored the first kill on December 5, shooting down an Oscar while he was covering a four-ship convoy. (One of VMF(N)-541's collateral duties was providing night-time combat air patrols (CAPs), something which did not sit well with the pilots.) Two more Oscars were downed on the 6th, but these were the squadron's last night kills since it was put on regularly scheduled daytime patrols and convoy protection. However, seventeen more kills were scored through the remainder of December, the early-morning mission of the 12th resulting in eleven Japanese planes downed in a single mission. Seven Bateye Hellcats were airborne at 0650 and covering a convoy when the ground radar detected a large enemy force approaching. Arranged in three- and four-plane divisions, the Marine fighters pounced on the Japanese bombers, numbering thirty-three aircraft, and during three passes, destroyed one-third of the attacking planes, with no losses themselves.

Other night-fighter units, VMF(N)-533, 542, and 543, flew during operations in the Philippines, and during the operations around Okinawa beginning in April 1945; these squadrons were flying the new F6F-5N Hellcat. VMF(N)-533 ended up with the high score among Marine night-fighter squadrons with thirty-five confirmed kills, achieved during the Okinawa campaign. Captain Robert Baird became the only Marine night-fighter ace with six kills, the last of which was obtained using the new mixed armament of 20-mm cannon and four .50-caliber machine guns.

Marine Hellcats also flew from the *Block Island* (CVE-106), VMF-511 operating a mixed bag of Corsairs and Hellcat reconnaissance and fighter aircraft. Operating in conjunction with a British task force, the *Block Island* was supporting operations off Okinawa using its planes against small water craft. VMF-511 lost its skipper, Major Robert Maze, when his Corsair was hit by flak and crashed into the sea.

The Curtiss SB2C Helldiver was this company's last operational design; there were other products but the Curtiss company finally closed its doors in 1947 after a 40-year period of supplying military and civilian aircraft to the world. The SB2C was a problem right from the beginning, for both the Navy and Curtiss. Loaded down with constraints and requirements, Curtiss had trouble meeting the Navy's demands. Derived from a 1938 design requirement, the XSB2C-1 did not fly until December 18, 1940. Its development and contractual problems plagued the Helldiver, to the extent that the first production aircraft did not reach VB-17 aboard the *Yorktown* until late 1942. The Navy squadron did not take their new dive bombers aboard the carrier until July 1943 and into combat until that November. Intended to replace the obsolescent SBD Dauntless, the SB2C never lived up to expectations, being difficult and unforgiving to fly and vastly underpowered in view of its burgeoning operational weight and ordnance loads. Development proceeded with the -2 and -3 models.

The Marines first made the acquaintance of the SB2C in a typically off-handed manner. The Army gained several hundred aircraft, designating them A-25As (the SBD had been used in New Guinea in 1942 as the A-24.), deleting the Navy's wing-folding mechanism; but the Army quickly became unhappy with their new dive bombers and hurriedly gave them to the Marines as SB2C-1As. The Marines took the almost 400 new aircraft and used them in the States as trainers in several VMSB squadrons; the -1 never flew in combat with the Corps. Like their Navy counterparts, the Marines never developed the respect and affection for the big-tailed Curtiss, which many pilots called derisively "the Beast," that they had for the SBD. By May 1945, however, many VMSBs had traded their trusty Dauntlesses for the Helldiver. VMSB-244 and VMSB-245 were probably typical of the 1945 version of the Marine Scout/Bombing unit, and were active during the invasion of the Philippines. May 19, 1945, saw VMSB-244 trade its SBDs for SB2C-4s and use them in support of ground units, toting bombs and 5-inch rockets.

Carrying the War to Japan

By mid-1944, having secured the Gilberts, Marshalls, and Marianas, Allied commanders could now see that ultimate victory in the Pacific was in sight. The battles on Saipan and Guam, especially Saipan, presented some of the bloodiest fighting yet encountered, as Japanese troops entrenched themselves in caves, waiting to rain mortars and machine-gun fire on the advancing Marine landing parties which stormed ashore in June and July 1944. In time, the new island bases for the oncoming B-29 offensive were secured, however, and it was time to allow General MacArthur to make good on his promise to "return" to the Philippines.

Intelligence reports told of weak Japanese air power in the Philippines area. According to Far East Air Force (FEAF) intelligence, there were sixty-five known operational Japanese airstrips throughout the islands with 692 aircraft, 340 of which could be expected to be operational. But considering the low experience level and manning shortages of the Japanese units, it was estimated that only 130 of these planes could be fielded at any one time; hence, the threat to a U.S. invasion was minimal. MacArthur was given the green light. October was the target month and the initial invasion would be on Leyte Island in the central Philippines. After securing Leyte, the Allies would head north towards Luzon and the capital city of Manila.

Lieutenant General George C. Kenney, in charge of MacArthur's air operations, told Marine Major General Ralph J. Mitchell, ComAirNor-Sols (Commander, Air, Northern Solomons) to get his 1st Marine Aircraft Wing (MAW) ready to support the Leyte operation which would be spearheaded by Army troops. Kenney had seen Marine dive bombers at work in the Solomons and greatly admired their skills; he wanted them for his operation. Mitchell ordered MAGs 24 and 32 to stand by.

Although the invasion on October 20, 1944, went off well, the Japanese response was to send its Combined Fleet into action. This turned out to be the last time this once-invincible armada would come out in force, and its sortie resulted in the climactic battle for Leyte Gulf, October 23-26, which would include the first planned use of *kamikaze* suicide aircraft by the desperate Japanese.

The first air strip opened for U.S. operations was at Tacloban, taken from the Japanese during the initial landings on October 20. Three major typhoons in late October and early November, however, brought operations down to a minimum as the strips turned into oceans of mud. It was not until late November that the first Marine air elements arrived to begin working up to operational strength and capability. In addition to the previously mentioned Hellcats of VMF(N)-541, Corsairs of MAG-12—VMFs 115, 211, 218, and 313—were in action by December 7, 1944, flying against Japanese shipping and providing CAP for U.S. convoys. (These units were actually operating FG-1s, Corsairs built by Goodyear which deleted the wing-folding mechanism.)

On December 7, twenty-one FG-1s of the four fighter squadrons struck a seven-ship convoy, sinking four freighters and one troop transport in a deluge of 1,000-pound bombs. Two Corsairs made mast-level attacks on the accompanying destroyers, seriously damaging two. It was a hectic battle for the Japanese, accomplished without a single American loss.

All of the Corsair squadrons were kept busy covering the U.S. convoys or attacking the enemy. The orders were to get past the protecting Japanese air cover, and concentrate on the ships below. Naturally, however, there were times when the Zeros could not be safely ignored. Aerial combat took place particularly during Japanese attacks on Allied convoys, the covering FGs usually having their hands full. On December 11, four VMF-313 aircraft engaged sixteen bomb-laden Zeros headed for ships at only 2,500-foot altitude under the cover of a rain squall.

Radar had not detected the approaching enemy formation hidden behind the highly reflective water-laden clouds. It was not until the Japanese were little more than a mile from their targets that they were spotted by a screening destroyer which gave a frantic call for the CAP aircraft. The four Corsairs plunged into the Zeros, flaming five on the first pass; the survivors dropped their bombs and fled. Every Marine pilot shot down at least one Zero, while Second Lieutenant Clyde R. Jarrett scored twice.

With all the aerial action evidently occurring over water instead of land, there was very little close support for the ground troops, one of the main reasons for bringing Marine air power to the Philippines in support of what was largely an Army show. Marine Corsairs, when they were involved in action against ground targets during the early stages of the action, seemed to be used against selected targets, as opposed to ground liaison-directed attacks against Japanese troops or fortifications immediately impeding an advance. In other words, the Marines were given their targets before leaving the ground, never receiving any instructions which would characterize a direct close air support mission. On December 17, thirty-two "Corsairmen," as one Marine writer called them, carried 1,000-pound bombs with instantaneous fuzes to a road intersection, causing a lot of smoke, but little ascertainable damage to enemy installations. VMF-211 aircraft did apparently hit a local warehouse, and VMF-115 planes demolished a building, but the actual benefits of such a massive strike were negligible.

However, the Marines were learning their trade for the invasion of Luzon. The "training" had not been without cost, for while MAG-12 fighters had flown 264 missions of all types—CAP, strikes, and ground support—nine pilots and thirty-four aircraft had been lost; on the other side of the ledger, over forty Japanese planes had been destroyed in the air and on the ground, and twenty-two ships, from destroyers to transports, had been sunk, with eleven others damaged. December 25, 1944, with the capture of Palompon on Leyte's west coast, saw the remaining Japanese sealed off, with no hope of rescue or reinforcement, and the island was effectively secured the next day. There were, of course, many mopping-up operations, lasting well into 1945, but attention could now be directed northward for the January invasion of Luzon.

Even as the Hellcats of VMF(N)-541 continued to deal with the Japanese at night through the first weeks of the new year, destroying twenty-two enemy aircraft in the air, preparations had begun for the invasion of Luzon, the next step in the liberation of the Philippines. The Sixth Army landed at Lingayen on January 9, 1945, under the sheltering support of MAG-12 and MAG-14, while the trusty SBDs of MAG-24 and MAG-32 flew into an airstrip hacked out of the rice paddies by the ground crews of the 1st MAW. By the end of the month, seven Dauntless squadrons were in the country flying support for the Army.

The men and pilots of the Marine squadrons did not mind flying support for the Army, instead of their own Marines. Here, at last, was an opportunity to prove their theories on close air support. With visionaries like Lieutenant Colonel Keith B. McCutcheon—one of the driving forces of future marine aviation developments, right through the Vietnam War—the Marines were anxious for any chance to prove themselves. McCutcheon was the operations officer for MAG-24, which included VMSBs-133, -236, -241, and 341; MAG-32 was newly formed from MAG-12's VMSB-142 and VMSB-243, and MAG-14's VMSB-244. McCutcheon saw close air support as a "tool," an "additional weapon" which was only effective if it were used by the ground commander on the scene, or close to it, to be tasked, directed, and coordinated as he saw fit. There was no need for inflexible pre-flight briefings which left no room for the inevitable changes of a major battle, and therefore rendered ineffective those missions which had been called close air support.

The Marines in the cockpits were in total sympathy with the concept as put forth by McCutcheon; before he is a pilot, a Marine aviator is, of course, a Marine, a rifleman, a "grunt." Whether from actual combat or at least from rigorous training prior to his ever seeing an airplane, a Marine pilot has gone through ground soldier training, and he knows what it means to advance on an enemy machine-gun nest or other fortification, or engage in hand-to-hand combat. Therefore most Marine aviators felt that if there was any way they could better serve their compatriots on the ground, so much the better. With men like Lieutenant Colonel McCutcheon, the way seemed clear.

The first missions were flown on January 27 with a 0900 strike against San Fernando, which served as a fuel dump and bivouac area for the Japanese. Eighteen SBDs of VMSB-241, under escort of four Army P-47s, obliterated the target area. In the afternoon, VMSB-133 sent eighteen aircraft against targets north of Manila. The other squadrons got into action in the following days, dive-bombing enemy airfields and positions. In one week, five squadrons flew seventeen missions and dropped 207,800 pounds of ordnance, ranging up to 150 miles from the airstrip at Mangaldan.

The Marines were still not involved in true close air support; the communications facilities, supposedly provided by the Army, were not in place in mobile jeeps. The Army was perhaps still afraid to allow Marine crews to go in so close to its troops. Thus, the initial missions had to come down from Sixth Army Headquarters itself, rather than from the field commands. But proof of the Marines' expertise was soon to come. In the meantime, the Dauntlesses bombed and strafed far ahead of the Army squads on the ground.

Veteran VMF-223 was also in action in the Philippines, having arrived on January 12. The Bulldog Corsairs ranged throughout the region on combat sweeps. During one of these missions, on January 23, Second Lieutenant Kenneth G. Pomasl became lost and, running low on fuel, he made a controlled ditching off Cebu. Hustling over the side of the cockpit, he saw a trio of native canoes coming towards him. The natives were friendly and pulled the Marine pilot into one of their canoes, just as fire from Japanese watching from shore began. Startled, everyone dove back into the water. Suddenly, Pomasl found himself very much alone and under fire. However, he paddled to shore and hid from the Japanese for almost two days. He was found by more natives on the 25th, and cared for until they sailed him to a contact point to be finally rescued by Americans.

True Marine close air support finally arrived during the February drive to the Philippine capital, Manila, on the central west coast of Luzon. Preliminary meetings between Sixth Army commanders and their Marine counterparts provided for equipping jeeps with radios and operator/drivers. Together with a group of support personnel, these jeeps would accompany the 1st Cavalry Division as it moved through the field, relaying messages and requirements back to MAG headquarters where Lieutenant Colonel McCutcheon was running operations.

On February 1, 1945, at 0001 hours, the Army units moved out along with the Marine radio jeeps from MAG-24 and MAG-32. These Marines rode with the 1st CavDiv as it thrust towards Manila and beyond. During the initial drive, February 1-3, the Dauntlesses were directed twenty to thirty miles ahead of or behind the Army columns, looking for enemy troops and reporting instantaneously to the radio jeeps. These aerial scouting missions also enabled the Army to know the best ways to proceed towards any given objective, allowing for natural obstacles such as rivers, bridges, and blocked trails.

February 2 saw forty-five aircraft of VMSBs-133, -142, and -241 diverted from a pre-arranged strike. The aircraft were already airborne when they got the call to change their target to the town of San Isidro which lay directly ahead of the advancing Army troops. The SBDs achieved great accuracy and left the town in smoking ruins, clearing the way for the men on the ground and proving the effectiveness of radio-jeep/airborne liaison. The same day, Army units ran up against a well-entrenched Japanese battalion. The patrolling SBDs were called down by the company commander. Because of the proximity of American forces, the Dauntless crews made several runs on the enemy positions without firing. This so unnerved and distracted the Japanese that the U.S. soldiers were able to overcome the enemy with very little resistance.

By the time the 1st CavDiv entered Manila on February 4, the Army was sold on Marine close air support. The division commander, Major General Verne D. Mudge, said:

The Marine dive-bomber pilots on Luzon are well-qualified for the job they are doing, and I have the greatest confidence in their ability. On our drive to Manila, I depended solely on the Marines to protect my left flank from the air against possible Japanese counterattack. The job they turned in speaks for itself. We are here. . . . I cannot say enough in praise of these dive bomber pilots and their gunners and I am commending them through proper channels for the job they have done . . . .[18]

Throughout the following week, the Army consolidated its position in Manila, the Marine SBD squadrons supporting the progress with pinpoint bomb deliveries directly ahead of the American troops.

While Manila was being secured, operations in the southern Philippines began to heat up. MAG-32 was ordered to pack and head south to support the Eighth Army at Mindanao and Zamboanga; MAG-24 would remain on Luzon to continue supporting the Sixth Army, at least for a time. VMB-611 was also ordered to bring its PBJs from the Solomons; MAG-12 would bring its Corsairs as well. Meanwhile, operations around Manila continued through early February, MAGSDAGUPAN (Marine Aircraft Groups, Dagupan) crews launching a forty-eight-plane strike against enemy ships still in Manila harbor on February 19.

Naturally there were developments in the way the close air support missions were flown. Radio-jeep communications had developed to the point where the single VHF channel could not carry all the traffic and the Marines switched to medium-frequency channels. Napalm was one of the most successful weapons in the Philippines, causing the Japanese the greatest discomfort, as can well be imagined. The jellied gasoline mixture stuck to anything it touched and spilled and flowed into even the safest of entrenchments, bursting into almost unquenchable flame.

Although landings were accomplished on March 10 at Zamboanga, MAG-32 with its four SBD squadrons (VMSB-224 had been transferred from MAG-24) remained on Luzon until an airstrip was ready at their new base. This suited the Sixth Army just fine, as it gave the Army troops more use of the Marine dive bombers. Finally, however, on March 23 word came for the first echelons of MAG-32 to depart for the south. By March 26, the group was in place after a 56-day campaign on Luzon. MAG-24 continued to fly in the north until late April, when it completed the move behind MAG-32.

During the Luzon operation, the Marines of both MAGs flew 8,556 individual sorties. An indicator of how active the SBDs were is the fact that, although the Dauntlesses comprised only 13 percent of Luzon-based U.S. aircraft—a total of 1,294 aircraft, including much of the Fifth Army Air Force—they flew nearly 50 percent of the total individual sorties during the campaign.

The Southern Philippines

Colonel Clayton C. Jerome, commanding MAG-32, was put in overall charge of the four MAGs in the southern Philippines by General Mitchell. It was a good choice, for the seasoned Jerome was "a man full of ideas," as one fellow officer called him later. MAG-14—VMFs -115, -222, -223, and -251—was to provide close air support from its base on Samar, northeast of Leyte, as it was known that the group was going to Okinawa only a few months later. Aircraft of MAG-12, in company with 13th Army Air Force bombers, strafed the beaches on Zamboanga on March 10, but the 41st Infantry Division encountered little opposition even as it moved inland. The only notice the Japanese appeared to take was to drop mortar fire sporadically on the invasion force.

As the Army troops kept moving, it would have been good to move the MAG to a bigger, finished airstrip like the nearby airfield at San Rogue, but Colonel Jerome kept the fighters at the temporary airstrip at Dipalog until the larger field could be secured. Finally, VMF-115 brought its planes into San Rogue, closely followed by the other squadrons. By March 15, the first missions had been flown from the new strip, renamed Moret Field in honor of Lieutenant Colonel Paul Moret who died in a crash at New Caledonia in 1943. The Marine groups under Colonel Jerome were also lumped together under the improbable title MAGSZAM (Marine Aircraft Groups, Zamboanga). The number of planes eventually totalled 293, including F4Us, PBJs, SB2Cs, various single types and, of course, the trusty SBDs.

The collective name for the Southern Philippines operations was Victor. Throughout the Victor invasions, Corsairs of MAG-12 and MAG-14 were active in every type of mission, from convoy CAP to strafing and close air support for the Filipino guerrillas, which greatly enhanced the U.S. Army's capabilities on the ground. The Corsairs had the ability to carry bombs and rockets as well as their normal fixed armament of six .50-caliber machine guns. They were naturally much faster than the SBDs, and also had the luxury of both VHF and MHF radios which enabled them to be quickly integrated into the air/ground liaison teams. The Corsairs could also take care of themselves after delivering their ordnance, and thus could also escort the less agile Dauntlesses.

By this time, there was no need to sell the Army on the value of close air support, and links between the various field commands and the Marine squadrons were close. Frequently, Marine pilots would travel up to the front to observe the situation first-hand and discuss points of interest with their Army counterparts. There were also the rare situations when the Army returned the visits, such as on March 27. Guerrillas had run up against a Japanese troop concentration near Dipalog and word was received by VMF-115 that an air strike might dislodge the enemy. However, without photos, maps, or proper communications gear, it was going to be nearly impossible to point out the target to the Marine pilots. Undaunted, Army Major Donald Wills climbed into a VMF-115 aircraft! First Lieutenant Winfield Sharpe followed and, sitting on Wills' lap,

Sharpe took off, leading three other squadron planes. With the Army officer providing *direct* liaison, the four-plane division strafed the Japanese positions, dispersing the threat.

Late March and early April saw MAG-24 participating in a growing number of close air support missions, working closely with coordinators in 13th Air Force B-24s. The big bombers would lead the fighters towards the target and point out special objectives. Even bad weather in April failed to put a dent in operations: each group aircraft put in the unusually high average of nine hours in the air every day, for a monthly total of 5,800 hours. Replacement aircraft were doled out sparingly; when a squadron was short an airplane—though not a pilot—it was not uncommon for a neighboring commanding officer to lend an aircraft, but only if one of his pilots flew it. MAG-14 continued to fly until mid-May when orders were received to begin packing for Okinawa. On June 1, 1945, VMF-251 was disestablished and its pilots were absorbed by the remaining squadrons of the group. On June 7, MAG-14 said goodby to the Philippines and headed for Japan. The operational record for the group for its four-month tour on Samar included 7,396 individual sorties, totalling 22,671 combat hours.

Victors I and II—operations against the islands of Panay and Cebu—had been successfully concluded; Victor III, against the island of Palawan, westernmost of the Philippine archipelago, had been conducted on February 28, while Victor IV against Zamboanga, had been a big success. Victor IV continued through most of April with additional action on Jolo and Sanga Sanga islands—the Sulu Archipelago. MAG-32 SBDs and MAG-12 Corsairs flew close air support for the men of the 41st Infantry Division once again. Only Victor V, the invasion of Mindanao, remained.

Landings on Mindanao were scheduled for April 17, and for two weeks prior to the date, MAGSZAM crews went over the area with Filipino guerrillas until the Marines were thoroughly briefed on the region. The invasion went off as scheduled, SBDs and PBJs dropping 500-pound bombs on the Japanese while Corsairs flew CAP over the beaches. MAG-24 had finally arrived from Luzon on April 20, and had set up shop at Malabang, 150 miles across the Moro Gulf, east of Zamboanga.

The operation on Mindanao saw the use of airborne coordinators increase as the last remnants of Japanese resistance were dive-bombed. Whole wooded areas were literally blown away, as SBDs and SB2Cs blasted them with bombs and napalm. By June 30, operations on Mindanao had ended and the Philippines were almost entirely secure. July 16 was an important day for the men of MAG-24; it was the day when their beloved SBDs were finally retired in favor of what many felt was a much less capable successor, the SB2C Helldiver. This left the four squadrons of MAG-32 to continue flying the Dauntless until the end of the war itself. On August 1, MAG-32 stood down.

The Philippines had been liberated, due in no small part to the efforts of the Marines. The main beneficiaries of the Marines' work, the men of the 41st Infantry Division, gave MAGSZAM a six-by-four-foot plaque, decorated with a Japanese machine gun and various captured Japanese flags. On the huge trophy, the simple words "In Appreciation— 41st Infantry Division" were inscribed. Major General Jens A. Doe, commanding the 41st, gave an address during the presentation ceremonies. He expressed the entire division's gratitude to the assembled Marines:

The readiness of the Marine Air Groups to engage in any mission requested of them, their skill and courage as airmen, and their splendid spirit of cooperation in aiding ground troops has given the division the most effective air support yet received in any of its operations.[19]

Years later, the commanding general of the Eighth Army, General Robert L. Eichelberger, wrote:

Nothing comforts a soldier, ankle-deep in mud, faced by a roadblock or fortified strong-holds, as much as the sight of bombs wreaking havoc on stubborn enemy positions. It puts heart into him.[20]

General Eichelberger was writing in praise of the MAGSZAM Marines.

Return to Carriers

The last six months of the Pacific War, February to August 1945, were like a final examination for Marine aviation; all the skills learned in the preceding three years of tough combat were to be tested in two major confrontations: Iwo Jima and Okinawa. In between these two important battles, carrier-based Marine air was further refined.

Marine airplanes aboard carriers had always been an option the Navy was reluctant to consider. However, by 1943, the march across the Pacific towards Japan showed the need for more carrier support. The ships were there, but there were not enough squadrons to adequately man them. This situation proved especially true during the late fall of 1944 when the Japanese unleashed their terrifying new weapon, the kamikaze. The call for more fighters aboard the carriers to protect the fleet against this effective new threat was answered by placing two Marine fighter squadrons aboard the *Essex*; VMF-124 and VMF-213 joined the men and ships of Task Force 38 as it made its way through the South China Sea. These Marine squadrons were in the midst of carrier strikes against Indochina in mid-January 1945. Weather played a major role in the loss of thirteen aircraft and seven pilots in navigational and deck-landing accidents. The Marines said that overwater navigation and carrier approaches could not be learned in a week or two, which was certainly an accurate statement, but they pressed on with the fast carriers.

VMF-124 and VMF-213 claimed ten to twelve Japanese planes destroyed on the ground during the January 12 raid on Saigon. In an unusual circumstance, the *Essex* air wing was skippered by a Marine officer after Navy Commander Otto Klinsman was shot down by flak, Lieutenant Colonel William A. Millington, commanding VMF-124, taking over command of the wing.

As the task force ran northward along the China coast and then turned east towards the Philippines, the Marines proved particularly adept at shooting down snooper aircraft—mostly Japanese multi-engine bombers—which were tasked with suicide missions against the fleet. On January 20, the Marine CAP destroyed eight out of fifteen aircraft shot down, Lieutenant William McGill accounting for three in as many minutes.

By early February, three other carriers—the *Bennington* (CV-20), *Wasp* (CV-18), and *Bunker Hill* (CV-17)—had joined the *Essex* as part of Task Force 58. The *Bennington* had VMF-112 and VMF-123 on board; the *Wasp* had VMF-216 and VMF-217; the *Bunker Hill* carried VMF-221 and VMF-451. There were now eight Marine Corsair squadrons aboard four carriers. The task force left the big staging area at Ulithi Atoll on February 10, bound for Tokyo, with a later stop at Iwo Jima to support the big invasion there on the 19th. On February 16, the carriers all launched a massive strike against Tokyo and Yokosuka, aimed at several airfields which could be used as staging areas for Japanese aircraft defending Iwo Jima against the American invasion. The strike in the early hours of the 16th was moderately effective; Tokyo was covered by weather. But enough damage was done on the ground and in the air to make the effort worthwhile. The next day the weather worsened, and only a few missions were flown, VMF-112 sending eight F4Us over Tokyo, followed by other squadrons. All types of enemy aircraft were encountered, from Bettys to Zeros. For the two-day offensive, the carrier Marines claimed twenty-one aerial kills, and sixty planes destroyed on the ground before the operation was cancelled and the task force turned towards Iwo Jima, 800 miles to the south.

Iwo Jima

The Battle for Iwo Jima needs little introduction. Most people have heard of this bloody, hand-to-hand struggle between the Marines and Japanese defenders which lasted thirty-six days. One of the war's most famous photographs—that of the raising of the American flag on Mount Suribachi—has come to symbolize the very essence of the Marine Corps, to the outside world and to the Marines themselves. Although Iwo Jima was largely a Marine operation, the aerial support delivered before and during the battle came, for the most part, from Army and Navy air power. Marine aviation was only available through the eight squadrons aboard the carriers of Task Force 58, and an unusual but abortive experiment with LST-borne Consolidated OY liaison/spotter planes. The latter consisted of aircraft from VMO-4 and VMO-5 which sailed with the LSTs. The little planes were launched from the LSTs by a contraption named after its inventor, Army First Lieutenant James H. Brodie. This so-called Brodie Gear consisted of upright beams and cables from which the planes hung, slid along, and launched themselves into the air. It took great skill and courage to go through a takeoff and the OYs, although they gave great service during the invasion, usually ended up as the targets for mortars as they landed on makeshift landing strips on Iwo. These little Grasshoppers, as they were called by the troops, conducted nearly 600 spotter missions in nineteen days.

On the early morning of D-Day, February 19, Colonel Millington led forty-eight Navy and Marine fighters on a strike at the beach areas, just prior to the actual invasion. This softening-up had been going on for three days and the Marines who actually stormed ashore did so with very little opposition. By 1000 all seven battalions were on the beach and moving inland.

That afternoon *Bunker Hill* aircraft made more strikes, and the *Bennington* sent her air group in on the 20th, along with Marine Corsairs from the *Wasp*. February 22 saw other missions but by noontime, the weather had closed down operations and effectively ended Marine air's contribution to the three-week battle on Iwo Jima. But the task force was not through. Turning back towards Japan on February 25, the carriers launched a big strike in concert with a B-29 raid against Tokyo which was still protected by weather. The Marines scored aerial victories; Colonel Millington shot down a George, one of the newest of the Imperial Navy's fighters, and a very dangerous opponent, even for the maneuverable Hellcat and powerful Corsair. Turning back to Ulithi, the task force made a pass at Okinawa, obtaining photographic coverage of the island in anticipation of the invasion to come.

When TF 58 returned to Ulithi on March 10, the *Wasp* gave up its Air Group 81, including VMF-216 and VMF-217. Many of the non-pilot maintenance personnel of the Marine squadrons elected to remain on board the carriers to assist the Navy Corsair squadrons now beginning to make their appearance. Four days later, the task force departed again for the war zone, with the new carrier, the *Franklin* (CV-13) carrying VMF-214 and VMF-452. (VMF-214, of course, was the famous "Black Sheep" squadron of Pappy Boyington's Bougainville crowd. The Marine ace was cooling his heels in a Japanese prison camp, and was no doubt witness to many of the raids over the Japanese homeland at this time.)

The task force made hit-and-run raids against the island of Kyushu, many of the 102 kills claimed by the flight crews going to Marine aviators. There was a reason for these quick thrusts against the airfields on the island: it was reckoned that these fields would be the staging areas for many suicide missions during the upcoming Okinawa operation. Perhaps, when the big battle did open, the kamikazes were delayed because of these preemptive strikes.

However, luck was not with CV-13. Shortly after 0700 on March 19, a single Japanese plane snuck up on the carrier and dropped two bombs, which burst among aircraft on the flight deck preparing for a mission. The inferno which resulted created a living hell for all aboard the *Franklin.* For four hours the big carrier lay dead in the water, only fifty-five miles off the coast, while her men fought the flames. The cruiser *Pittsburgh* was finally able to take the carrier in tow back to Ulithi. The casualty figures were high. Of the 772 dead, 65 Marines died in the blaze, all from the two fighter squadrons. VMF-214 and VMF-452 were out of the war with only two days of combat operations to show for their troubles.

Only four Marine squadrons were left on two carriers. Both the *Bennington* and *Bunker Hill* launched strikes even as their sister carrier fought for her life. Corsairs from VMF-451 in the *Bunker Hill* escorted Avengers and Helldivers against the remnants of the Imperial fleet, hitting three carriers as they sat at the piers. In a prelude to the Okinawa landings, the *Bennington*'s VMF-112 and VMF-123 contributed to a strike against the island on March 23 and again on the 29th.

The Battle of Okinawa

The Battle of Okinawa drew upon every facet of Marine aviation, from fighter escort and CAP to torpedo- and dive-bombing, as well as defense against the hordes of kamikaze aircraft, and even ground suicide squads. It was the finale for Japan and she grimly cast everything she had left into the combat arena. Okinawa was the most horrible battle, lasting two and a half months; it drained invader and defender alike.

Admiral Raymond A. Spruance, who had led the American carriers at Midway, had charge of the fast carriers offshore, while Lieutenant General Simon Bolivar Buckner, Jr., commanded the 10th Army and related Expeditionary Forces, including Major General Geiger's III Amphibious Corps. (General Buckner was well qualified to lead this momentous invasion. He had been in command of American ground and air forces during the year-long battle in the Alaskan Aleutians. This drawn-out battle—the only fighting on anything which could be called United States soil—saw the Americans and Japanese trading punches in some of the most inhospitable weather, and ended in a Japanese withdrawal in mid-1943.) Over 182,000 troops were under Buckner, of which 81,000 were Marines. The initial landings hit the beaches at 0830, April 1, 1945, Easter Sunday. To their surprise—and relief—the beaches were undefended and nothing of consequence was heard from the Japanese until April 4 when the enemy counterattacked.

During the initial phases of the Okinawa landings, the carrier Marines flew several support missions along the beaches, as well as meeting Japanese aircraft in the sky. But April 6 and 7 brought over 300 kamikaze attacks against the task force offshore. TF 58 aircraft and ship air defenses claimed 300 Japanese aircraft shot down. It was April 6 when the giant battleship *Yamato* made her long-awaited sortie from Tokuyama to attack the American fleet. Her crew considered themselves already dead men and therefore this was another suicide mission; they were right.

As she cleared the southernmost point of Kyushu after noontime, the world's biggest battleship was set upon like a bear by a swarm of bees. Navy and Marine fighters and torpedo bombers made run after run on the *Yamato* until she blew up and sank at 1423 under the weight of ten torpedos—nine on the port side—and six direct bomb hits; 3,063 of her crew died with her, including the captain. This action was probably more of a psychological victory for the U.S. aviators, since the huge battleship could have done little to disrupt the Okinawa operation, either at sea or by bombarding the beaches.

The kamikazes kept coming in droves, hurling themselves through the flak and CAP fighters. It was one of the oldest Japanese ploys: strength through numbers. For every ten aircraft shot down, perhaps one would break through to its target. The desperation of the Japanese at this time can be seen in the battle slogan of the 32nd Army on Okinawa: "One plane for one warship. One boat for one ship. One man for ten enemy. One man for one tank."[21] It was a brutally honest approach to war, and one which bore terrible fruit. The slaughter at Okinawa was all the more terrible because of these unrelenting suicide attacks. The carriers *Enterprise* and *Intrepid* (CV-11), with several exchange Marine pilots serving with Corsair squadrons, as well as other ships, were damaged by kamikazes. The *Bennington* and *Bunker Hill,* however, plowed right through these harrowing experiences without a scratch.

On May 11, the *Bunker Hill's* luck ran out. A lone Zero, followed by a Judy dive bomber, crashed themselves on the carrier's flight deck. Through the late afternoon, the crew fought to save their ship. The fires were brought under control, but the *Bunker Hill* was out of action—as was her air group, including VMF-221 and VMF-451. Only the *Bennington's* Marines remained. But help was coming.

Besides additional land-based squadrons, two escort carriers—the

Block Island (CVE-106) and *Gilbert Islands* (CVE-107)—were on the way, the former arriving in the war zone on May 10, with an all-Marine air group. On board was a mixed squadron, VMF-511, of Corsairs and night-fighter Hellcats, and a twelve-plane torpedo squadron, VMTB-233, equipped with Avengers. The *Gilbert Islands* arrived a week later with VMF-512 and VMTB-143. Other squadrons flying towards Okinawa included Jack Cram's VMB-612, with their specially modified PBJ Mitchells, and VMOs -2, -3, -6 and -7 with Consolidated OYs for spotter duties and general hack work. VMTB-232 and VMTB-231 also arrived with their Avengers, originally for antisubmarine duties, but these found themselves employed against land-based targets in the thick of the fighting.

All of these units and more, including four MAGs, were under the command of Major General Francis P. Mulcahy, as commanding officer of the 10th Army's Tactical Air Force (TAF), which was directly subordinate to General Buckner. TAF included fifteen day and night fighter squadrons, operating 700 aircraft, 450 of which were to be used in actual combat.

The first TAF aircraft, OYs of VMO-2, landed on April 2, flying from the carriers offshore. The other spotter squadrons followed later. Marine aircraft flew from other carriers which had transported them to their objectives. MAG-31 (VMFs -224, -311, -441, and VMF(N)-542) launched from the *Sitkoh Bay* (CVE-86) and *Breton* (CVE-23), and landed on Yontan, one of the first operational fields on Okinawa. The Corsairs of VMF-311—new cannon-armed F4U-1Cs—had had to contend with a single bomber's kamikaze attack on their carrier, but the bomber was dispatched fifty yards from the little *Sitkoh Bay*. VMF-311, which had spent most of the war attached to MAG-31 in Samoa, far behind the front lines, had seen only sporadic combat, flying strike and escort missions in the Marshalls. In March the word came to bring their new cannon Corsairs aboard the CVE which would transport them to Okinawa. The first aerial engagement for the squadron resulted in the destruction of the kamikaze, credit going to Captain Ralph G. McCormick and First Lieutenant John J. Doherty. Landing at Yontan, VMF-311 operated as part of TAF through April and May, scoring 71 aerial kills by the end of the war, second only to VMF-323 which tallied 124 victories.

Another squadron which was new to combat was VMF-312, operating Goodyear-built FG-1s, as part of MAG-33, 2nd MAW. On their first mission, VMF-312 aviators accounted for eight Zeros with only four Corsairs, the rudders of which were painted with a distinctive checkerboard pattern which became the squadron motif.

VMF-312's First Lieutenant Robert R. Klingman figured in one of the more bizarre combat victories of the late Pacific war. Together with Captain Ken Reussen, Klingman spotted a high-flying Japanese reconnaissance plane somewhere around 38,000 feet, 13,000 feet above the American patrol. After laboriously climbing to get above the enemy plane, Klingman and Reusser attacked, firing off most of their ammunition, obtaining some hits. In frustration, Klingman pursued the fleeing Japanese and proceeded to saw off the tail of the enemy plane with his own plane's propeller. The Japanese aircraft went down after Klingman's third pass. The two Marines turned quickly for the safety of Kadena airfield where Klingman made an emergency landing. Kadena and Yontan had been the primary objectives of the April 1 landings, and the two airfields were finally, though tentatively, declared secure on April 7. MAG-33 began operating from Kadena with VMFs -312, -322, -323 and VMF(N)-543. All squadrons were kept very busy intercepting the constant kamikaze raids which had sunk fourteen American ships by April 16. May 11 brought another big suicide attack as Buckner's 10th Army seemed to slow down, and the ships standing offshore to support the ground action became tempting targets for the kamikazes. Night fighter Marines shot down nineteen Japanese, but two other enemy planes plowed through towards the lonely little picket destroyers. Two Kadena Corsairs, probably of VMF-323, closed on a large enemy formation around 0830 on the 11th. The two Marines shot down four Japanese planes apiece in the midst of heavy fire from the ships which were the intended targets. The fighter-director on board the *Hadley* said, in reporting this particular action:

The highest award for flying skill and courage is not too much for this pilot. His wingman stayed at masthead height in the flak and assisted in driving the planes away from the ship.[22]

May 11 was a costly day for American ground forces. General Buckner's offensive against a Japanese line—the so-called Shuri line, extending across the width of Okinawa's southern tip—failed. The fiercely defended line was not overcome until May 28. By this time, 20,000 Americans had been killed or wounded, and 63,000 Japanese had died, most at the Shuri line action. Unfortunately, one of the later American casualties was General Buckner himself. Buckner went up to observe front-line action on June 18 and while at a forward observation post, he was struck by shell fragments and killed. His death was, naturally, a heavy blow for the U.S. forces fighting desperately but successfully on the island.

Close air support during the Okinawa campaign, although far from minimal, was not all it could have been, or was originally intended, because of the preoccupation with the kamikaze threat. On April 13, TAF aircraft flew the first regular close air support missions against Japanese artillery, but for the next three weeks only 20 percent of the total sorties flown by Marines were in the close air support role. The terrain was partly to blame for the lack of support missions: the close proximity of the opposing sides on the tiny island, the great amount of artillery fire which made controlling operations dangerous and sometimes impossible, and the very nature of the Japanese defense, again the network of caves and warrens which required methodical and extremely dangerous hand-to-hand treatment, precluded the freewheeling type of close air support actively used in the Philippines. Nonetheless, TAF provided as much support as it could under the circumstances.

As previously related, two CVEs had arrived by mid-May with all-Marine air groups. The *Block Island* with MCVG-1 (VMTB-233 and VMF-511) began operations on May 10 with a small close air support mission by four TBMs (General Motors-manufactured TBFs). The *Gilbert Islands* arrived on May 17 with MCVG-2 (VMTB-143 and VMF-512), and four days later began operations in company with the *Block Island.* Two other CVEs with all-Marine air groups barely made the war zone before the war ended. The *Cape Gloucester* (CVE-109) with MCVG-4 left Okinawan waters for a protracted sortie along the China coast, while the *Vella Gulf* (CVE-111), MCVG-3, arrived off Okinawa on August 9. (The CVEs were going to play big support roles in Operation Olympic, the planned invasion of Kyushu, but the atomic bombs on Hiroshima and Nagasaki made their use in such a role unnecessary.)

As the fighting on Okinawa progressed through May, developing into a war of attrition for the hard-pressed Japanese defenders, more airfields were taken and reopened by U.S. forces. More fields meant more airplanes; the flood was overwhelming. MAG-22 arrived at Ie Shima on May 6, with VMFs-113, -314, and -422, while VMF(N)-533 and VMTB-131 arrived sometime later. Together with aircraft from the Army Air Force, these Marines brought the total number on Ie Shima to over 200. VMF(B)-533's arrival was especially welcome because of the large number of night-time nuisance flights by the Japanese. With a ring of radar sites set up on the little islands around Okinawa, Ground Control Interception (GCI) facilities were perhaps the best in the war. VMF(N)-533 was in the process of converting to the brand-new Grumman F7F-3N Tigercat, the Navy's first specially designed night fighter, but only a handful of the twin-engined aircraft arrived before the cessation of hostilities.

A large kamikaze attack of 165 planes occurred on May 25. U.S. interceptors shot down 75 of the raiders, Marines scoring 39 kills. VMFs-312, -422, -322, and -323 all shared in the action. Two days later, another big raid of 150 aircraft struck U.S. ships in a day-long procession. Bad weather, however, hampered the performance of Marine air's primary mission on Okinawa. Carrier and land-based aircraft flew over

14,200 specific sorties in support of the ground forces from April 1 to June 21, when Okinawa was officially declared secure. Landing Force Air Support Control Units (LFASCUs) were shipboard controlling authorities under Colonel Vernon E. Megee; some ground units, however, which knew of the great coordination possibilities chafed at having to go through a larger, more distant authority instead of having aircraft in direct communication with the field commands.

In fairness to those on the ships, there were times when several air strikes were going on together, and to have had each strike individually controlled by different commands would have probably resulted in tremendous confusion and very little positive gain. As it was, the proximity of the opposing forces led to several instances where U.S. troops were in the line of fire, with resulting casualties. There were shining examples however. On May 20, four TBMs of VMTB-232, along with Navy Avengers, flew runs in support of Army infantry. The big Grummans flew over American troops at only 15 feet altitude, seemingly diving below the crests of hills hiding Japanese. Corsairs joined in the strike with strafing runs. In a fantastic display of flying skill and coordination, all the bombs and bullets fell in the target area, and all the planes returned safely.

General Mulcahy was relieved as head of TAF on June 11 by Major General Louis E. Woods. On the 18th, General Geiger was named as interim commander of the 10th Army when General Buckner was killed. This was probably the only time a Marine was in command of a U.S. Army unit. On June 23, Geiger was, in turn, relieved by General Joseph "Vinegar Joe" Stilwell—the old "China hand"—when Okinawa was declared secure on June 21. It was a fitting finale for the Pacific war, the largest amphibious operation in history. At a terrible cost in men and material, the last link in the island chain of the Pacific had been won and Japan lay naked across the East China Sea.

Victory

With Okinawa firmly in Amercian hands, plans were solidified for the final massive invasion of the home islands; victory in Europe in May had released armies and resources which would crush the Japanese. The outcome, however bloody it might be, was not in doubt. Japan was doomed. With their work basically done, the Marines of TAF stood by waiting and watching as Army bombers—B-25s, A-26s, and B-24s—descended on Okinawa. B-29s were also to operate from the captured island as part of the rejuvenated Eighth Air Force, fabled victor in the daylight bombing campaigns against Germany.

Japan itself was gathering its remaining resources for a last-ditch defense, spearheaded by thousands of kamikazes. There were estimated to be 11,000 aircraft of all types remaining in Japan, with more than enough pilots to man them. But by the time the last Marine aerial kill was scored early on the morning of August 8, by Lieutenant William E. Jennings in a Hellcat, all but the most fanatical diehards in the islands realized the war was over. The overwhelming strength and technology of the U.S.—as witnessed by the August 6 and 9 atomic bombings—were undeniable. The last Marine air combat missions were probably flown by VMB-612, Jack Cram's PBJs only recently arrived from Iwo Jima. From August 1 to August 15, the squadron flew thirty-one sorties around the Sea of Japan. With the formal surrender aboard the *Missouri* on September 2, 1945, World War II was, indeed, officially over. And, as Brigadier General E.H. Simmons wrote:

Standing little-noticed on a deck filled with U.S. and foreign dignitaries was one solitary senior Marine, Lieutenant General Roy Geiger, who had succeeded Holland Smith as commanding general, Fleet Marine Force, Pacific . . . .[23]

In 1939 there were but two aircraft groups, with a total of nine squadrons, representing the whole of Marine aviation. By September 1944, there were five wings, including thirty-one Marine Aircraft Groups and 145 squadrons. Even at war's end, the five wings included twenty-nine MAGs and 132 squadrons. From a 1939 total of 232 designated pilots—officer and enlisted—the number had grown by January 1945 to 10,412. There had been eleven Medals of Honor won by Marine pilots. Marine crews had shot down 2,355 enemy aircraft while 367 Marine aviators had died in combat; 198 were listed as missing in action.

The ground Marines had developed into the world's foremost amphibious force, and Marine air had closely allied itself as the most experienced practitioner of close air support. However, the sobering fact was, as Allan R. Millett writes, the Marines flew

in support of the general naval campaign rather than in support of amphibious operations. Even when Marine squadrons went to sea aboard carriers in the war's closing stages, they flew proportionately few close support sorties. After the Philippines experience, there was no question that Marine pilots could deliver close air support with unmatched effectiveness . . . .[24]

Postwar Activities

 With the Army taking direct charge, both administratively and physically, of the occupation of Japan, the Marines self-deflated. There were many retirees in the senior ranks; others chose to revert to a lower rank to remain on active duty. Pilots were ordered to serve tours of duty with ground units, unless they wanted to resign. The occupation of Japan, approached with apprehensive caution by all the services, turned out to be a smooth-running, dignified operation because the Japanese kept their own national dignity and grace even in defeat. While the Marine air squadrons still on active alert contributed low-keyed security patrols, their brethren on the ground tended to rather mundane activities, gathering war material and releasing Allied prisoners of war.

However, things were not going all that smoothly or peacefully across the water in China. Although the troops loyal to Chiang Kai-shek and those under Mao Tse-tung had fought together against the Japanese, the civil conflict flared anew once the Japanese had surrendered and withdrawn from China. Attempts by the U.S. to arrange a lasting truce were to no avail, and the Marines were sent in to the troubled areas in September 1945, arriving at Tientsin, 50 miles southeast of Peking on October 1. The First Marine Aircraft Wing, under Major General Claude E. Larkins, arrived on the 6th, with components of MAGs-12, -24, -25, -31, and -32. The planes were largely for security patrols to let the U.S.

presence be seen by both sides. F7Fs and OYs flew over the rocky terrain, keeping watch on the situation, but rarely did anything else. Attempts were made to get the Communists and Nationalists to the conference table, but there was really very little movement towards a peaceful solution.

In February 1946, it was decided to return most Marine ground and air units to the United States. By March VMF(N)-541, VMTB-134, and part of MAG-12 had left. VMF(N)-533 and VMF-115, as well as VMO-6, left for Hawaii later in the year. VMO-6 had reached Tsingtao on the coast, 300 miles southeast of Peking, by October 1945. The squadron was reassigned to AMG-32, 1st MAW, and began flying reconnaissance and rescue missions with its OYs. By mid-1946, VMO-6 was preparing to return to the U.S., but was ordered to remain in China due to increased Communist activities. It was reassigned to MAG-25, under the operational control of the 3rd Marine Brigade. VMO-6 stayed in China throughout 1946, serving in various liaison roles with distinction. The missions were hazardous because of the intense Communist ground fire periodically experienced. But on January 3, 1947, VMO-6 finally left the embattled Chinese to return home. The Communists, watchful and resentful of U.S. aid to the Nationalists, bided their time. By December 1948, the fall of Chiang's government was all but assured, and evacuation of U.S. personnel became essential. VMF-211's Corsairs were to cover the evacuation. In April, the Communist drive to Nanking, the Nationalists' capital, was accomplished and the Communists were in control of China; there was not much a few thousand Marines could do about it, except provide for the security of U.S. citizens and interests. There would be plenty of time and opportunity for the Chinese and Marines to fight in Korea, in little more than a year's time.

New Developments

Meanwhile, Marine aviation was experiencing two major developments which would shape its course for the foreseeable future: the advent of the jet aircraft and the helicopter. Of course, the jet-propelled aircraft had seen combat in the closing stages of World War II in Europe. Germany had the greatest success, while England used its few operational jets to combat the V-1 buzz bomb menace. Even the Japanese had been experimenting with a jet fighter of their own, and a rocket-propelled interceptor, virtually a copy of the frightening German Komet. The U.S. had built its first jet aircraft, the Bell YP-59A Airacomet in 1943, and by war's end had several worthy designs on the boards as well as under construction. The most notable of these early jets was the Army's Lockheed P-80. However, the Navy had a jet design of its own, the McDonnell XFD-1 Phantom, later redesignated the FH-1.

Powered by two small Westinghouse turbojets, the aircraft flew in early 1945, with initial carrier-qualification testing being conducted in July 1946. Major Marion Carl, one of the top aces to remain on active duty after the war, first flew the FH-1 in March 1947. Carl was not new to jets, though. He had been responsible for testing the new P-80 to determine its suitability for carrier operations in November 1946, and was probably the first Marine to make an arrested landing in a jet aboard a carrier. He was promoted to lieutenant colonel and given command of VMF-122, the first Marine jet squadron. In August 1947, Carl set a world's speed record of 650.6 miles per hour in the scarlet-painted Douglas D-558-1 Skystreak, for which he was awarded his fourth DFC. While with VMF-122, Carl even formed the world's first jet aerobatic team from members of his squadron; its name was, inevitably, The Marine Phantoms.

The second Marine jet squadron, and the first on the west coast (VMF-122 was stationed at MCAS Cherry Point, North Carolina), was to be VMF-311 at MCAS El Toro, California, recently returned from duty as part of the occupation forces in Japan. However, it was not until mid-June 1948, after nearly a year's training and preparation, that VMF-311, under Lieutenant Colonel John P. Condon, received two Lockheed TO-1s, similar to Air Force F-80Cs. By August, a full complement of twelve of the single-seat Shooting Stars had arrived and initiation flights and training began in earnest, several enlisted Marine pilots receiving their initial TO-1 indoctrination at MCAS El Toro in the fall of 1948.

There had been a growing problem in retaining young, eager Marine pilots who saw their fortunate Air Force counterparts getting racy new jet aircraft, while the Marines were forced to make do with outdated Corsairs. Colonel Condon finally prevailed upon the Marines to obtain fifty of the Air Force's F-80C Shooting Star fighters for a cost of $13.5 million. Although his plan ran up against initial opposition from the Bureau of Aeronautics, when Admiral J.D. Price took over as Deputy CNO(Air) the plan was immediately put forth and acted upon. Price directed the stubborn BuAer to stop dragging its feet and obtain the jets. Fifteen of the TO-1s actually went to the Marines; twenty-five went to the Navy at North Island, and the remaining ten were scattered around the country at various development centers.

These first jets gave valuable service as training tools. During a recent interview, General Condon referred to these first days of Marine jet aviation as a "turning of the corner," indoctrinating Marine pilots, ground crews, and record-keepers into the new world. There were different maintenance considerations. For instance, an engine change or periodic inspection normally took the airplane out of service for several days.

However, while he was C.O. of VMF-311, Colonel Condon instituted the procedure of always having a spare engine ready to go, and when an aircraft's engine came up for a change, the standby was merely inserted in the airframe in a matter of hours, and the plane remained in service. VMF-311 gave many ground crewmen their first jet instruction, and thereby laid the groundwork for generations to come.

Colonel Condon and Colonel Paul J. Fontana, a Guadalcanal veteran and ace, had been in friendly competition for command of a jet squadron. The two men being equal, it was decided to flip a coin. Colonel Condon won and assumed command in April 1948. Colonel Fontana relieved him in July 1949. Up to this time VMF-311 had independent status as a training squadron, apart from any group association. But on October 1, 1949, the squadron was reassigned to MAG-12 and soon afterwards, in February 1950, was given its first real Navy jet fighter, the F9F-2 Panther.

The F9F series was Grumman's first jet venture, the XF9F-1 being an abortive twin-engined, two-seat night fighter which was never built. The XF9F-2 was a complete redesign, a single-engine, single-seat day fighter, characteristically Grumman—tubby and strong. The -2 flew for the first time in November 1947, and was first issued to Navy fighter squadron VF-41, and then to the Marines' VMFs -311, -115, and -451. The type was to be major workhorse during the next several years, especially in Korea.

Two lesser designs, although their association with the Marines was to prove surprisingly long-lived, were the McDonnell F2H Banshee and Douglas F3D Skyknight. Originally the XF2D-1, the Banshee, was an obvious development of the early Phantom and first flew in January 1947. It was to fly primarily from Navy carriers (providing the basis for James Michener's realistic novella *The Bridges at Toko-ri*), but it also found employment with the Marines as a reconnaissance aircraft in the F2H-2P version. The Douglas Skyknight was a big, twin-engined, multiseat fighter, which flew in March 1948, but was found to be vastly underpowered. The F3D-2 incorporated larger engines and weight-saving measures. The -2 was issued to the Marines in 1950, although they had been using the -1 as a trainer. The F3D-2 was to be used as a night fighter, and as such was to score the first successful night-fighter kill by a U.S. jet.

The Helicopter Arrives

Postwar developments arose concerning the role of Marine troops, especially their traditional role in amphibious operations with air support. Nuclear warfare presented a clear and present danger to the long, involved amphibious invasion where incoming troops were exposed for long dangerous periods to enemy defense fire. The Communists, both the Chinese and their Soviet patrons, posed a large and distinct threat, and traditional service rivalries made the Fleet Marine Force's development, indeed existence, tenuous at best. To make matters worse and more involved, the Army was lobbying for control of all land-based air assets, leaving the Navy to pursue its traditional role of protection of the sea lanes.

The development of the helicopter by the Marines as an expansion of their amphibious-invasion role had the greatest overall impact on them. They had experimented with rotary-winged aircraft as far back as 1932, under actual combat conditions in Nicaragua. The aircraft involved was the Pitcairn Autogyro, which used a normally mounted radial engine to pull the craft to operating speeds at which it could drive the vertically mounted rotor blades to pull it up more or less vertically after a short takeoff run. The Autogyro worked, but could carry virtually no useful payload, and then-Lieutenant Colonel Roy Geiger recommended that its development by the Marines be curtailed.

It was only when Igor I. Sikorsky, who had made a name for himself in his native Russia for building large conventional aircraft, flew his VS-300 in 1939 that a practical helicopter appeared. Under an Army contract, Sikorsky developed several refinements of his basic design, and the Army actually used these aircraft for rescue and observation in the Pacific during late 1944 and 1945. Other developers of helicopters soon appeared, Bell and Piasecki being the most noteworthy. It was Frank Piasecki who designed the first experimental helicopter for the Navy, the XHRP, a tandem-rotored (a Piasecki hallmark), banana-shaped airplane which could carry 900 pounds of useful payload, although it would not be delivered to the Navy for two years. Sikorsky had in the meantime designed an aircraft which would serve well into the 1950s, the HO3S-1, the shape of which would come to mean "helicopter" for the public.

With the infant helicopter industry growing by leaps and bounds, the Marines under General A.A. Vandegrift, the 18th Commandant, were quick to profess interest in the new form of aerial transportation. Lieutenant General Geiger, who had seen early A-bomb tests, was very concerned that one of these horrible weapons could quickly obliterate a Marine invasion force. He urged Vandegrift to seek alternatives to the traditional amphibious landing. (This was probably one of the last of Geiger's major official inputs to Marine policy, as he died in January 1947, one week short of his retirement, at age 61. A Congressional bill elevated him to four-star rank, the only Marine aviator to attain such a position, albeit posthumously, up to that time.) The helicopter seemed to hold great promise, and the seeds of modern vertical assault were sown at this time.

A special board under Major General R.C. Shepherd, later the Corps'
20th Commandant, drew up the Marines' specifications for a practical
helicopter—sort of a "wish list." Basically, the board envisioned a craft
which could carry 5,000 pounds of payload for 200-300 miles at 100
knots, at altitudes from 4,000-15,000 feet. It was a very optimistic set of
demands, but Sikorsky and Piasecki said they could build such an aircraft.

The Shepherd board issued its report in early December 1946, recommending two paths of research: the helicopter, and a large transport
seaplane, which could also act in concert with any envisioned helicopter
invasion operation. The paper also called for the establishment of a
Marine helicopter squadron for training and indoctrination. The Commandant quickly endorsed the report and forwarded it up to the Chief of
Naval Operations. After a lengthy period of correspondence and refinement of the original proposals, the CNO finally decided that, because of
postwar budgetary constraints, a separate Marine helicopter program
was impractical; however, a section of the overall 1949 Navy budget
could be set aside with approval for the Piasecki-designed HRP.
Development of a separate Marine heavy transport helicopter was thus
restricted to some desultory research efforts.

However, approval was given to create HMX-1, the Marine helicopter
development squadron, with Colonel Edward C. Dyer as the commanding officer. Dyer chose Quantico as the site for his squadron because of
its relative proximity to the Sikorsky and Piasecki plants in Connecticut,
and to the Marine Corps' Schools from which he planned to draw most
of his unit. HMX-1 was established in January 1948, with HO3Ss and
HRPs, with a first test of its capabilities coming in May. Five aircraft
transported sixty-six troops from the carrier *Palau* (CVE-122) to Camp
Lejeune, North Carolina, during a school exercise. The five HO3Ss
could only carry three troops apiece, so it was necessary to make thirty-
five flights to carry all the Marines to the landing zone. But the operation, which was called Packard II, clearly indicated the possibilities of
the helicopter. Packard II was the first chance the Marines had to try out
the new doctrine of vertical assault which was being assembled in a
publication titled *Amphibious Operations—Employment of the
Helicopter (Tentative)*, but known colloquially as *Phib-31*. The
helicopter, stated the report,

possesses certain distinctive characteristics which, if exploited, can enhance greatly the speed and flexibility of the amphibious assault, while at the same time per-
mitting a desirable increase in the dispersion of the attacking Naval
forces . . . . its ability to circumvent powerful beach defenses, and to land
assault forces accurately . . . endow helicopter operations with many of the
desirable characteristics of the conventional airborne attack while avoiding

undesirable dispersal of forces which accompany such operations . . . . the evolution of a set of principles governing the helicopter employment cannot await the perfection of the craft itself . . . .[25]

By 1949, HMX-1 was heavily involved in spreading the helicopter gospel, participating in additional demonstrations of rapid troop insertion and deployment, including Packard III in May 1949. Overflying the choppy seas which swamped several landing craft, the HRPs quickly deposited their troops—230 in all, as well as 14,000 pounds of cargo. It was a tremendous success for HMX-1, the Marines, and the helicopter itself.

Colonel Dyer turned over command to Lieutenant Colonel John Carey in June, but by the end of the year, the HRPs had to be grounded due to mechanical problems, leaving the HO3Ss to carry the load until the following April. In June 1950, all the aircraft were back in operation and they provided a flyby for ceremonies accompanying the change of command of the Marine Corps Schools. The ceremonies were attended by many senior military and civilian dignitaries, including President Harry S Truman. As outgoing Lieutenant General Shepherd relinquished command, thirteen helicopters of HMX-1 chopped their way across the field, in front of the reviewing stand.

The relative success of the helicopter, at least in basic terms, and seen with the help of some imagination for the future of the machine, had been the bright spot in an otherwise dim postwar economic picture for the Marines. It would seem that during the immediate pre-Korean years, the fixed-wing community was suffering, to some extent, at the expense of the new helicopter visionaries. With zealous government-sponsored budget cuts affecting everything from manpower to equipment supply—even, at times, the very existence of the Marine Corps itself—Marine aviation in general had very few things to cheer about. Contained within two MAWs, the Marines flew outdated, though not totally obsolescent, Corsairs, whose usefulness and modernity had been rendered questionable almost overnight by the jet airplane. The Marines were, of course, having some opportunity to try the new jets, but the aircraft and support were slow to come into squadron usage.

The Marines had decided to make as strong a case for the development of the helicopter as possible, as a new and necessary tool for the FMF itself, and as the wave of the future. Successes like Packard II and III helped the cause, but there were a few basic problems which still had to be addressed. The big problem was, of course, the budget, followed by the lack of a satisfactory aircraft—one which could carry a meaningful payload—and then the provision for required helicopter squadrons and training facilities had to be considered.

Colonel Dyer, the commanding officer of HMX-1, suggested that the joint Navy/Air Force program responsible for the Piasecki XH-16 be considered for the Marines as well. Until the XH-16 was ready, Dyer further advised, an additional program aimed at a smaller aircraft capable of carrying 3,000-pound payload, or fifteen troops for 100 miles, should also be considered. A negative reply to Dyer's detailed letter was almost a certainty, given the economic conditions for the Marines in 1949, but when the reply came, although it did refute Dyer's suggestions, it did suggest a conference to determine the Marines' position and requirements for a future helicopter program.

A study group had been formed to consider various points of contention and formulate a list of requirements for a helicopter to be procured in 1952-53. The final list included: a 3,000- to 3,500-pound payload carried for 250 nautical miles, or a 13-15 combat-troop capability, in addition to a two-man crew. The aircraft was also to be carried and stowed aboard the CVEs. The last point was important, as the board also stated that the big Piasecki XH-16 would not fit aboard a little escort carrier. Additional requirements included provision in the 1953-54 budget for two Marine assault transport helicopter squadrons, and that HMX-1 would develop an organizational structure for such squadrons.

The joint conference—called the Marine Corps Board—recommended by Colonel Dyer and Lieutenant Colonel Carey, convened in March 1950, with fourteen members from CNO and Marine agencies. The board members basically desired further development of a specific Marine aircraft with an uprated capacity of twenty troops. The helicopter was also to be multi-engined and still operated from CVEs. (This new helicopter proposal would result in the Sikorsky XHR2S-1 of 1956.)

Attempts by the Marines to upgrade the priority of the proposals met with some success, with a two-section program being developed. This program gave attention to cancelling participation in the faltering XH-16 program, marshalling support for the XHR2S, and finding an interim helicopter.

Thus, as Korea erupted in June 1950, and the Marines and the United States found themselves once again involved in a major war on the Asian mainland, the Corps had also come to several developmental forks in the road. Immediately after World War II the Marines had been in distinct danger of being disbanded, lost in the tidal wave of postwar budgetary cuts. But war in Korea provided them with more than enough ammunition for their case, and Marine aviation, both fixed-wing and rotary wing, was to play a big part in the operation.

8

Another War in Asia: Korea

 The Communist takeover in China in 1949 made it clear that civil strife on the Asian mainland was far from over; Korea promised to be next— and soon. The Korean peninsula had been invaded by Russian troops on August 12, 1945. The Soviets had declared war on the already prostrate Japanese corpse on the 8th to make sure of getting a share of the postwar spoils in Asia. As the Japanese were surrendering, Russian troops swept into Korea, bolstered by Korean and Chinese Communist sympathizers, and installed a puppet government at Pyongyang, above the 38th parallel. The American forces arrived in the south on September 8, only to find the situation fairly well set regarding Russian position and influence; Korea was thus permanently divided at the 38th parallel, creating North Korea and South Korea.

Kim Il-sung, the North Korean prime minister and dictator, immediately focused his country's attention on the perceived struggle with the South, which was bound to come soon. Border raids by Northern troops made matters worse and it was only a matter of time before hostilities began.

On Sunday afternoon, June 25, 1950, North Korean troops and armored units poured across the dividing line into South Korea, spearheaded by sporadic strafing attacks by Russian-built Yakovlov prop fighters, seconded to the North. The objective of the drive was Seoul, capital of South Korea. Like a replay of a tired old movie, the

U.S. and its Republic of Korea allies were ill-prepared to meet the onslaught. The task of repelling, or at least stalling, the invasion fell to the U.S. Army. The veteran 24th Infantry Division provided the only reasonably effective ground opposition, holding as best it could until reinforcements were sent.

The U.S. forces were far-flung throughout the Far East. Air Force fighter units in Japan and the Philippines totalled over 550 aircraft, 365 of which were F-80C jet fighter-bombers. Navy forces included units of TF 77 in Japan and at sea, with the carrier *Valley Forge* (CV-45) being the only flattop available when the North Koreans invaded. With Carrier Air Group 5 aboard, the carrier had eighty-six aircraft embarked, including F9F Panthers, F4U-4B Corsairs, and AD-4 Skyraiders. The *Valley Forge* replenished in the Philippines and by June 27 was headed north into combat, joined by a British carrier, HMS *Triumph*, on July 1.

On July 3, the two carriers arrived seventy-five miles off the Korean coast and launched the first carrier strikes of the war, at 0545 and 0600. The *Valley Forge* aircraft rocketed Pyongyang, while the *Triumph*'s planes—Fairey Fireflies (two-seat, single-engined prop fighters) and Supermarine Seafires (shipboard versions of the famous Spitfire)—went after airfield and rail targets at Haeju, just above the 38th parallel, to the south. The enemy was completely surprised by the devastating attack. More strikes were launched in the afternoon, and for the next two days the North Koreans were given a convincing demonstration of carrier airpower.

As the small carrier task force pounded the North Koreans, the decision was being made in the U.S. to send the Marines. The First Provisional Marine Brigade, consisting of the Fifth Marines and MAG-33 (VMF-214, VMF-323, VMF(N)-513, and VMO-6) left San Diego on July 12. MAG-33 rode on two transports and the escort carrier *Badoeng Strait* (CVE-116). In total the brigade had 6,534 officers and men, pilots, and ground-support personnel. (VMO-6 would have the honor of being the first U.S. helicopter squadron in the fighting with their four HO3S-1s.) The 1st Provisional Marine Brigade's formation and departure had been a marvel of logistical coordination, involving activation of Reserve components and creation of new ground units almost overnight.

The brigade landed at Pusan on Korea's extreme southeast coast on August 2, 1950. The F4U-4Bs of VMF-214 aboard the *Badoeng Strait* and another group of the gull-wing World War II fighters from the carrier *Sicily* (CVE-118) which had arrived from Guam, began flight operations immediately upon arrival, flying close air support missions for U.S. and Republic of Korea (ROK) soldiers near Pusan. With the arrival of the *Valley Forge, Philippine Sea* (CV-47), and *Triumph*, the number of carriers off Korea was five, with 250 aircraft.

Fighting along Korea's southern coast from Pusan westward to Masan and Chinju intensified, and the 1st Provisional Marine Brigade was thrown right into battle on August 7, with VMF-323 and VMF-214 Corsairs flying constant close air support strikes ahead of the Marines and Army troops on the ground. During one mission, four VMF-214 aircraft delivered their bombs at the end of a canyon, climbing up over the cliff above. The target was a concentration of enemy troops, and the Corsairs made repeated rocket and strafing runs only to have the North Koreans dart into half-concealed caves at the end of the canyon. The strike leader, Major Ken Reusser, received permission to fly right into the canyon and drop his napalm tank, where another airplane could set the weapon afire with machine gun fire. The routine worked and the enemy troops were wiped out.

Corsairs, rockets, and napalm, were an effective combination during these early operations. In fact, the prop-driven Us were probably the most valuable aircraft in the Marine inventory at the time. The short-legged jets could not loiter above the battlefield, and airfields in-country were not yet available; the carriers from which the fighters operated allowed more fuel and more on-station time, as well. So, it fell to the veteran Corsairs—both Navy and Marine—to carry the war at this time.

VMO-6's helicopters were very active, too. Brigadier General Edward A. Craig, commanding general of the 1st Provisional Marine Brigade, said "Marine helicopters have proven invaluable . . . . They have been used for every conceivable type of mission." One of the first helicopter rescues by Marine crews occurred on August 10, 1950, when an HO3S-1 flown by Lieutenant Gustave F. Lueddeke picked up Captain Vivian M. Moses of VMF-323. Moses' Corsair had been hit by enemy ground fire, lost oil pressure, and he had to ditch. (In a sad twist, Captain Moses volunteered for another mission the following day, only to be shot down again. After being thrown from his aircraft on crashing in a rice paddy, he drowned: the MAG's first combat death.)

Lieutenant Leuddeke continued rescuing downed pilots, sometimes behind enemy lines. On one mission, he carried General Craig along. Craig had wanted to see the helicopter operation for himself. The pilot hovered over Second Lieutenant Doyle H. Cole also of VMF-323 and pulled the young pilot to safety. As Cole entered the cabin, he slapped what he thought was an enlisted man on the back and said, "Thanks, Mac." He was somewhat chagrined to find he was addressing the brigade commander.

VMO-6 also operated several OYs, artillery-spotting aircraft-grasshoppers, as they had been called in World War II. Although these little planes were usually unarmed, their line of work was highly dangerous, and after taking ground fire, several spotter pilots retaliated.

Captain Francis A. McCaleb took to carrying hand grenades, tossing them out over any small group of enemy troops which fired on him.

But VMO-6's immediate claim to fame were the helos. The success of the "pinwheels," as the aircraft were called at the time, led General Craig to recommend the formation and deployment of a new transport helicopter squadron with Sikorsky S-55s, HRS-1s as they were designated in Navy service. The Marines had become quickly interested in the larger HRS, with its unique front-mounted Pratt and Whitney engine, which made maintenance much easier. Official support gathered momentum, taking in along the way provision for observation helicopters like the Sikorsky HO5S-1, and the little bug-like Bell HTL-4, which was to go to VMO-6 until the larger HO5S arrived.

As the action pushed the Communists back, the two squadrons of MAG-33 aboard the carriers (VMF-214 and VMF-323) and the shore-based night fighters of VMF(N)-513, flying Grumman F7F Tigercats (about which more later) contributed morale-building and strategically important close air support missions. From August 3 to September 14, 1950, the three squadrons flew a total of 1,511 support missions, of which 995 were of the close air support variety. VMO-6, of course, was in a class by itself, pioneering new tactics and procedures on a daily basis. For its continued record during the opening conflict, the 1st Provisional Marine Brigade was awarded the first Presidential Unit Citation for action in Korea.

The action at Pusan pushed the North Koreans back from their lightning gains of the summer. The Marines, however, were suddenly ordered to disengage and hurry to another battle shaping up, where they met Communist T-34 tanks for the first time. On August 17, MAG-33 Corsairs, in conjunction with the Marines' M-26 tanks, helped destroy five of the World War II tanks.

The Inchon Operation

Plans were being rapidly developed for a Marine landing at Inchon, on the west Korean coast, which served as the port facility for Seoul, now under Communist domination. A joint task force of U.S., British, and ROK assets began assembling for the invasion, while the 1st Marine Aircraft Wing, under Major General Field Harris, left MCAS El Toro by September 1, with MAG-12 (VMFs -212 and -312, and VMF(N)-542).

There was a great deal of planning for Inchon. The great tides moving on the harbor, with differences of as much as thirty-five feet, were of prime consideration; in fact, the tides actually set the invastion date of September 15, when the flood tide would be highest. There were differences between Army and Navy and Marine planners as well. But General Douglas MacArthur, overall commander of forces in the

Pacific, wanted the invasion, which had been dubbed Operation Chromite; and so planning went ahead on schedule.

Marine aviation support initially came from carrier-based squadrons aboard the *Badoeng Strait* and *Sicily*. In company with regular Navy carrier planes, elements of MAG-33 would be under Tactical Air Control (TAC), with VMF-212 and VMF-312, and VMF(N)-542 waiting to come ashore to the airfield at Kimpo, which would be the main target objective of the initial landing. So, as the invasion date approached, 230 ships assembled off the coast, including six carriers. There were five U.S. flat-tops: the *Philippine Sea, Valley Forge, Boxer,* (which had just arrived from the West Coast with sixty-four Corsairs, sixteen ADs, and fourteen other aircraft), and the two workhorse CVEs *Badoeng Strait* and *Sicily*. The sixth carrier was the veteran British *Triumph*. This mighty armada of ships, aircraft, and men from America, England, New Zealand, Korea, Japan, and France, was designated Joint Task Force 7, with Task Force 77 actually numbering the U.S. carriers within its complement.

Carrier strikes softened up the Inchon-Seoul area prior to the actual landings. The initial target was the little island of Wolmi-do, connected to Inchon by a causeway. VMF-323 and VMF-214 Corsairs made early-morning strikes on September 10 with napalm to clear away trees which were shielding North Korean artillery. Attacks kept coming throughout the morning as the CVEs concentrated on Wolmi-do. The Corsairs also served as naval gunfire spotters for the Navy ships' offshore bombardment. This softening-up continued through the evening of September 14, as the invasion force prepared for action the following morning.

Finally at 0633, September 15, 1950, the Marines hit Green Beach on the northwestern tip of Wolmi-do under a covering umbrella of close air support, the Corsairs hosing enemy positions not fifty yards ahead of the assault columns with machine-gun fire. Men and tanks poured ashore, but resistance was surprisingly light or poorly coordinated. The North Koreans had badly underestimated the U.S. capability to mount such a massive invasion so soon after World War II. They had also guessed wrong concerning the American commanders' resolve to gamble with the dangerous tides and currents of the Inchon shore.

The action shifted to the mainland area and met with stiffer, though not insurmountable, resistance. At 0700, on September 16, North Korean tanks were moving through a village on the outskirts of the city. Eight Corsairs of VMF-214 swept in and inundated the T-34s in napalm, in full view of cheering Marines on the ground. The enthusiasm was somewhat dampened when one of the F4Us crashed, the pilot apparently failing to pull out of his dive soon enough. Additional anti-tank strikes effectively neutralized enemy armored threats with rockets and bombs.

The invasion force fought northeastward, battling towards the major objective of Kimpo Airfield. In the meantime, a second front had been opened in the South at Pusan by American and South Korean units. The North Koreans were caught in a vise and their resolve and resources were rapidly dissolving. Action on September 17 and 18 secured the airfield, and at 1000, September 18, a VMO-6 HO3S-1 with Lieutenant General L.C. Shepherd, Jr., Commanding General FMFPAC, touched down to find several North Korean aircraft scattered about, mainly Russian-built Yak fighters and Ilyushin IL-10 ground attack aircraft. That evening MAG-33 was ordered to occupy Kimpo. There was some initial confusion, as MAG-33 and MAG-12 apparently switched squadrons. Major General Harris, perhaps, wanted veterans VMF-214 and VMF-323 to remain on the carriers doing the job they were doing so well, and thus allow relative newcomers VMF-212, VMF-312, and VMF(N)-542 to come to Kimpo and start operations almost immediately. Close air support was becoming more and more important as North Korean units began to dig in and hit back. On the 18th and 19th alone, nearly fifty CAS missions were flown even before the fighter squadrons had arrived at Kimpo.

The first squadron to arrive at Kimpo was VMF(N)-542, led by Lieutenant Colonel Max J. Volcansek, Jr. Six twin-engined F7F-3Ns landed in the early evening, coming from their base at Itami, Japan. At 0735, the next morning, VMF(N)-542 flew the first combat missions from Kimpo, as four Tigercats shot up enemy railroad traffic. Some time later, Colonel Volcansek had a harrowing experience. Just prior to beginning an attack, he attempted to blow away his underwing fuel tank, only to have the tank jam between the fuselage and right engine nacelle. The airplane became uncontrollable, and at only 1,000 feet Volcansek tried to leave the airplane, but was forced back by the slipstream. In desperation, he kicked the control stick with his foot, sending the F7F into a steep dive, and forcing himself free. His chute opened at only 500 feet, but he landed safely and was picked up by the intrepid Lieutenant Leuddeke in a helicopter.

VMF-212 and VMF-312 also landed at Kimpo on the 19th, and went into action on the 20th, right behind VMF(N)-542. The commanding officer of VMF-212, Lieutenant Colonel Richard W. Wyczawski, also had a narrow escape when his Corsair developed an oil leak on takeoff, and as Wyczawski turned back to the field, the plane burst into flame. The pilot crash-landed and jumped out of the burning plane, but collapsed only a few feet away. With the flames coming closer to the napalm and rockets, there did not seem to be much time for a rescue, but Navy Hospital Corpsman 3rd Class Charles B. Stalcup, rushed into the inferno and pulled the unconscious pilot out of danger, seconds before the napalm exploded.

With Kimpo secured and operations begun, the liberation of Seoul was a matter of time, although the 1st Marine Division was finding the going rough, encountering the stiffest resistance of the operation in house-to-house fighting in the capital city itself. But, backed up by solid close air support, both from shore and carrier-based aircraft, the 1st and 5th Marine Regiments marched into Seoul on September 24th, and by the 27th the city was declared secure.

Thus the Inchon Operation was a complete success; it proved that the Marine amphibious operation was alive and well, and most importantly it routed the Communists from the South Korean capital. Operation Chromite also upheld the hard-won doctrine of Marine close air support, the Marine Corsair squadrons especially coming in for high praise from Army and Marine commanders. The action figures speak for themselves. In a 33-day period, September 7 to October 9, the four F4U squadrons—VMF-214 and VMF-323 (aboard the carriers) and VMF-212 and VMF-313 (at Kimpo)—flew 2,163 individual sorties, while VMF(N)-542, basically a night-fighter squadron, flew 573, for a grand total of 2,736 missions. Eleven aircraft had been lost to enemy ground fire, with six pilots killed in action. VMO-6 came in for its own special commendation, for many of the 139 seriously wounded men were evacuated to hospitals by helicopters of this pioneer unit. The operation had been a success, but difficult times were coming in subsequent action at Wonsan and Chosin.

Wonsan and the Chosin Reservoir Breakout

After succeeding at Inchon, General MacArthur's attention turned northeastward to the harbor at Wonsan, on the east coast of the Korean peninsula, some eighty miles above the 38th parallel. It was all part of the drive to regain lost territory; indeed, MacArthur had strong thoughts of crossing the Yalu River and attacking Red China. By September plans were laid for the Wonsan operation. The harbor had been heavily mined by the Communists, and while Navy PBM Mariner flying boats and surface mine sweepers conducted neutralizing operations, MAG-12 moved from Kimpo (which was later designated K-14) to the airfield at Wonsan, VMF-312 and VMF(N)-513 arriving on October 14, 1950.

The invasion took place on October 26, with VMF-312 providing close air support. The action worked its way north towards the crucial Chosin Reservoir. Unexpectedly stiff resistance from fresh troops of the Red Chinese Army, who fought with guerrilla tactics, had slowed the Marine advance. But the 1st, 5th, and 7th Marine Regiments finally defeated the Chinese and North Korean forces after five days of heavy combat.

By mid-November the Korean winter, with its horrible cold, had begun to descend, creating a new danger for friend and foe alike. The Marines faced a huge enemy force of ten Chinese divisions, totaling 100,000 men. Names such as Hagaru-ri and Koto-ri have been etched into Marine Corps history, for it was in these little villages and towns that Marine fortitude, dedication, and skill, were tested to the utmost in the bitter cold. Outnumbered, fighting against the unexpected Chinese offensive, the Marines began to withdraw against heavy Chinese attack from Chosin—"frozen Chosin," as it was called. It was an epic story of survival and courage.

The main force fell back to Hagaru-ri to regroup and be resupplied, then go south to Koto-ri. This withdrawal was accomplished under heavy enemy attack, as well as the immobilizing cold. The MAG-33 squadrons did their best to hamper the enemy, VMF-312 accumulating nearly 2,000 flight hours, while losing four aircraft and one pilot, even while moving to Yonpo airfield near Hamhung on December 1. By November 28, the situation was becoming quite desperate as Chinese troops harassed positions at Hagaru-ri, where a 2,900-foot airstrip had become crucial to the resupply effort. On December 6, the 7th Marines led the so-called Chosin Breakout, making for Koto-ri in the south.

Essential to the final outcome of the breakout was the air supply operation mounted by Marine transports. Twin-boomed Marine R4Q-1s— designation for the Air Force's Fairchild C-119 Flying Boxcar twin-engined transport—of the First Air Delivery Platoon made the majority of supply drops to Marines at Hagaru-ri and Koto-ri, some 800,000 pounds being dropped at Hagaru-ri and 1,000,000 pounds at Koto-ri, including a 19-ton bridge in eight sections. During the breakout, Corsairs from all the Marine squadrons participated in day-long strikes; VMF-212 and VMF-312, VMF(N)-513, and VMF(N)-542 from Wonsan and Yonpo, and the carrier-based VMF-214 and VMF-323 lifted off even with the sky still completely black, to be over the battlefields at daybreak, helping Marine and Army troops battle their way south. VMO-6 OYs flew artillery-spotting missions, while squadron helicopters performed their usual, but no less valuable, medevac and rescue duties, sometimes behind enemy lines. VMF-212 was very active on November 28, when ten FAC-controlled strikes were made in the morning and afternoon around the Reservoir area against Chinese positions, the Corsairs running in with rockets and napalm, as well as making strafing runs with machine guns perilously close to the overhanging ridges which ringed the area. The next day, the 29th, after a six-inch snowfall had covered the airfields at Wonsan and hindered early-morning operations at sea, the Corsairs struck Chinese troops again, on sixty-one separate occasions, VMF-212 and VMF-312 moving up and down the line between Hagaru-ri and Koto-ri in search of targets. The crowded air above the Allied lines was filled both with cargo planes, dropping much-needed supplies, and the Corsairs diving and wheeling over enemy positions; the FACs were obviously very busy.

As has been previously stated, the value of the Chance Vought F4U Corsair cannot be overestimated. Rugged and powerful, the dependable Corsair was in constant action, from sea and land bases. It was viewed with real affection by the men on the ground. One of the innumerable songs of the period paid tribute to the Corsair and its role in the Chosin campaign.

> Up in Korea midst rocks, ice, and snow,
> The poor Chinese Commie is feeling so low,
> As our Corsairs roar by overhead,
> He knows that his buddies will all soon be dead.

> Lin Pao went way up to cold Koto-ri,
> His prize Chinese Army in action to see,
> He said that his soldiers no battle could lose,
> But all that he found was their hats and their shoes.

Of course, the chauvinism might be understood and forgiven by less interested parties, but the verses do convey the feeling.

It was a tired lot of Marines that left Hungnam in December 1950, aboard Navy transport ships; others had gone by airlift. The Chosin campaign had been one of the bloodiest, yet proudest stories in the Corps' history. There were 4,400 casualties—730 killed—in exchange for estimated Chinese losses of 25,000 dead. But the initial steam of the surprise Chinese offensive had been destroyed. Of course, a large part of the story was the contribution of Marine aviation. Close air support—Marine style—under Forward Air Control had become an accepted tool during the campaign. Both Army and Marine commanders praised the skill of the Corsair pilots, who operated in much less than ideal conditions, where a shootdown, even though the pilot was not initially wounded, could eventually prove fatal. The bitter cold of either the inhospitable land or the icy China Sea made survival as much a skill as flying. Two VMF-212 pilots almost took a dip in the water after making an attack against Chinese positions. Captain Irving Barney and Technical Sergeant Charles Radford encountered icing conditions off the coast. With their gyros inoperative, their pitot tubes frozen—which made flying on instruments difficult—and their fuel down to nothing, the pair found the carrier *Badoeng Strait*, and landed, Radford actually running out of gas just before he touched down.

The weather hampered flight operations at sea, as well as on land; 68-knot winds, ice, and snow periodically blew across the carrier decks, closing down all flight operations. The land bases at Kimpo and Wonsan were also subject to the effects of weather, and Marines and their Air Force neighbors (the Air Force conducted its own effective operation, usually from the same airfields as the Marines, though with its own distinctive rules) would combine to clear the snow from the runways and aircraft.

Airlift missions were generally considered greatly responsible for the successful withdrawal down to the coast, naturally under the protection of Marine Corsairs, and again VMO-6 rung up an impressive tally, making reconnaissance and rescue missions under the most trying of conditions. There were times when the tireless pilots of the little OYs and helos were the only link between units which had become separated under fire.

As 1950 drew to a close, and no matter how great the success and relief at the conclusion of the Chosin operation, it was obvious that the "home for Christmas" hopes of the men of the task forces and ground divisions would not become fact. There was still a lot of fighting left to do.

The Marines at this time were flying some fifteen different types of aircraft in Korea, including Bell and Sikorsky helicopters, Douglas and Fairchild transports, the workhorse F4U Corsair, the unsung OY grasshopper, and even the occasional Grumman TBM (used for liaison and hack work), and the Douglas AD Skyraider. The new Grumman F9F Panthers of VMF-311 had appeared during the closing days of the Chosin campaign as well. But there was also a plane whose record has been largely overlooked, perhaps because it was active for only a relatively short period of time and was eclipsed by its better-known contemporary, the Corsair, and the newer, more glamorous jets. This lonely performer was the Grumman F7F Tigercat.

The Grumman Tigercat descended from the company's XF5F-1/XP-50 designs of early 1940. The Navy issued further authorization for the progressive development of the XF7F-1 in 1941, with the prototype's first flight occurring on December 2, 1943. A graceful, well-proportioned two-seater, the twin-engined Tigercat boasted a top speed in excess of 400 miles per hour, but was considered too hot a plane to operate from aircraft carriers. The Navy therefore decided to give the entire production run to the Marines, to fly from land bases. Twelve squadrons were planned and some of the aircraft were actually en route to the Pacific when the war ended in August 1945, a few F7Fs getting to Okinawa with VMF(N)-533, a mere day before the August 15 ceasefire.

The F7F found a place in postwar Marine squadrons, especially as a night-fighter in the -3N model which incorporated nose-mounted radar and a taller vertical tail. (The F7F-3 was a single-seat model used primarily as a fast ground-attack aircraft.) When the Korean War broke out VMF(N)-542 brought its Tigercats to Japan, and then to Korea itself to be used as night-fighters, although the pace of action dictated their use during the day as well.

Starting usually around sunset and continuing well into the night and pre-dawn hours, the two-man crews took off in search of Communist truck traffic wandering down from Manchuria and China, delivering supplies under the cover of darkness, much like the infamous Ho Chi Minh Trail of Laos and Vietnam two decades later. (Sometimes the parallels between Asian wars are so striking that one wonders if the people involved have not discovered the secret of immortality.) The F7Fs were usually under Forward Air Control—usually FACs of the Air Force as in Vietnam—and would be called down on targets from rail traffic to troop concentrations. It was dangerous work. Sometimes the Communists would string cables across known flight paths to entangle unwary fighters. Captain Don Derryberry of VMF(N)-513 was out one night making strafing runs when he hit a cable, 200 feet of which wrapped itself around both engines, necessitating one powerplant being shut down. Derryberry struggled with the staggering plane, fighting to maintain control with his windshield shattered, and eventually brought the Tigercat back to an emergency field.

The F7F scored two air-to-air kills at night, although against somewhat unworthy game. On July 1, 1951, VMF(N)-513's Captain Edwin B. Long and his radar operator, Warrant Officer Robert C. Buckingham, spotted an ancient North Korean PO-2 biplane engaged on an intruder mission. The F7F pilot made three passes before downing the slow old craft, north of Kimpo. VMF(N)-542's Major E.A. Van Grumby shot down another PO-2 on September 23. These were the only aerial kills scored by the Tigercat, but the type was a valuable member of the Marine close air support team during the Wonsan/Chosin operation, bombing and strafing Communist positions around the clock, if needed. During March 1951, VMF(N)-513 set a record of 2,010 night-combat flight hours, during which time its F7Fs and F4Us destroyed nearly 400 Communist trucks, and damaged 193 more. (When VMF(N)-542 was rotated back to the States, its Tigercats were given to VMF(N)-513, which accounts for the two types in one squadron.) The Tigercat was also used as a photo reconnaissance aircraft in its -3P model.

However, by the time Major General Christian Schilt—one-time Medal of Honor winner from the Nicaraguan campaign, and now commanding general of the First Marine Air Wing—flew his F7F-3 Tigercat over the combat lines on November 10, 1951 (the 176th birthday of the Marine Corps), the F7F was well on its way to retirement, having been finally overtaken by jet aircraft now operating from land bases. (As commanding general of the 1st MAW, Schilt had exclusive use of an AirPac day-fighter which was maintained in spit-and-polish condition by the troops at K-3. The general would often climb into the Tigercat in the early evening and put on a show for the men on the ground, zoom-climbing to 3,000 feet before rolling over in a split S. The troops loved it.) The twin-engined Grumman had fared somewhat better than its company stablemate, the lithe little F8F Bearcat, which saw little U.S. Navy service, and then not during combat operations. The Tigercat was available when it was needed during the hectic first eighteen months of combat in Korea, and it did its demanding, somewhat tedious, job well.

The Jet Squadron: VMF-311

By early 1951, the two CVEs *Badoeng Strait* and *Sicily* (whose skipper was Captain John S. Thach, famous Navy World War II fighter ace and tactician) had returned to the States, having been in action almost from the beginning. The *Sicily* had sometimes been known as the "Black Sheep Jeep," because it was the home of the Corsairs of VMF-214, Pappy Boyington's old outfit. F4Us from the carrier had flown over 8,100 combat hours between July 4, 1950, and January 4, 1951, against every type of target the North Koreans and Communist Chinese had, including locomotives and camel-drawn convoys.

The new year of 1951 saw the intensified use of jets from land bases. VMF-311 had arrived at Yonpo near Chosin by December 10, 1950, and that afternoon two F9F-2 Panthers flew the first Marine jet combat missions. With the successful withdrawal from Chosin, VMF-311 was ordered south to Pusan East (Airfield K-9), where it flew missions all over Korea, usually under Forward Air Control, or even airborne air controllers in T-6 "Mosquito" aircraft. Although the squadron accumulated over 400 hours of combat flying in December alone, by January 16 all of its aircraft were grounded due to difficulties with the Pratt and Whitney engines, the unit being ordered back to Japan to take care of the problems.

In February, VMF-311 was reassigned to MAG-33, from MAG-12, and relocated to Pohang's Yongil-man Airfield (K-3), fifty miles north of Pusan, originally built by the Japanese as a Zero fighter base. By February 19, the "Panther Pack," as the squadron called itself, was back in combat, flying close air support and armed reconnaissance. In March 1951, MAG-33 consisted of VMF-212 and VMF-311, while MAG-12, which had moved to Bradshaw airfield, Pusan West (K-1), had VMFs -214, -312, -323, and VMF(N)-513. Only VMF-311 had jets, however. During March and April, the F9Fs evolved the practice of maintaining 10-minute standby alerts with four ready aircraft, the pilots in the cockpits. This arrangement allowed the unit to respond to unforeseen scrambles and calls for close air support from the Tactical Air Control Center (TACC). However, a better system allowed four aircraft to be already airborne where they could be briefed and arrive over the target ready to go.

On May 9, 1951, VMF-311 put up twenty Panthers as part of the largest U.S. raid on North Korea to that time. Three hundred aircraft, including seventy-five Corsairs and Panthers from the 1st MAW, attacked airfields at Sinuiju, on the southern Yalu shore. There were some MiG sightings but the Russian-built—and perhaps Russian-flown—fighters kept their distance. (The Marine pilots were hungry for air-to-air combat, and were anxious to chalk up a score next to the Navy's first MiG kill—and the second U.S. jet kill, one day behind an Air Force score—by VF-111's skipper, Lieutenant Commander W.T. Amen, on November 9, 1950.) But aerial encounters by Marine-piloted planes were somewhat rare, and MiG kills by Marines were, for the most part, registered while flying exchange duty with the Air Force.

Until February 1952, VMF-311 was the sole Marine jet squadron in Korea, and the Panthers did yeoman service up and down the length of Korea, wherever close air support was needed. VMF-115 arrived that month with F9Fs, and in March VMJ-1—Marine Photographic Squadron 1—brought its McDonnell F2H-2P Banshees for reconnaissance work. By the time Korean action ceased on July 27, 1953, VMF-311 pilots had racked up 18,851 combat sorties in two and one-half years, and even after the ceasefire, the squadron remained on station, overseeing the repatriation of prisoners.

VMO-6 and HMR-161

VMO-6 continued its unique record of rescues during this period. On Friday, April 13, 1951, a VMO-6 HO3S-1 crew, Captain Valdemar Schmidt, Jr. and Corporal Robert Sarvia, was called in to rescue a downed Air Force F-51 pilot north of Kwachon Reservoir. With a combined group of Air Force Mustangs and Marine Corsairs flying escort, the Sikorsky flew out to the downed pilot. But enemy groundfire struck the helicopter and it crashed near the waiting pilot. The Air Force pilot and the two Marine crewmen huddled in some nearby bushes as the Chinese combed the area.

Captain Frank E. Wilson flew another chopper out at dusk with four VMF-214 Corsairs, which attacked the Chinese positions, thereby allowing the helicopter to hover over the Americans. In a slow, arduous process, the first helo's enlisted crewman pulled himself into the trembling chopper. Wilson found a clearing where he was able to land, allowing the remaining two pilots to scramble inside. All was not over yet. With five men the HO3S became nose-heavy, and without hesitating, Captain Schmidt, pilot of the first helicopter, leaped out so that Captain Wilson could regain control and shift sandbags around to retrim the aircraft. With everything set, Schmidt got back into the helicopter. All of this action took place at night under heavy enemy fire.

First Lieutenant Robert E. Mathewson was flying a Bell HTL-4 when he was shot down, crash-landing among a group of mud-Marines. Without a helicopter, Mathewson quickly became an infantryman when his brethren handed him an M-1 rifle. For most of the day, he fought alongside the others, fighting his way out of a Communist Chinese trap.

VMO-6 helicopters set a record of seventy-seven casualties evacuated in one day in April 1951. Flying their bubble-topped Bells, squadron pilots shuttled in and out of the rugged mountains of the Kwachon Reservoir which had become the scene of the Chinese spring counteroffensive. The area, which included a big valley ringed with ridgelines, was nicknamed the "Punchbowl." First Lieutenant Joseph C. Gardiner, Jr. brought seventeen wounded Marines out during this period.

VMO-6 logged a record 2,626 combat hours in May 1952, which saw the second phase of the Chinese offensive, the squadron operating three types of helicopters—Sikorsky HO3S-1s and larger HO5S observation aircraft, and Bell HTLs—as well as Cessna OE-1s, the high-wing tail-draggers later known as Birddogs which the squadron had begun to receive in May. The normal amount of time was between 1,500 and 1,750 hours a month. This action usually included artillery-spotting missions by the OEs, equipped with wing-mounted flares to mark targets, as well as the rescue missions usually flown by the helicopters whenever required. The OEs were engaged in highly dangerous work. Master Sergeant John R. Stone's aircraft was hit by 85-mm-shell fragments which blew out one of his main tires.

All of these actions and more were accomplished under primitive living conditions in what amounted to a tent city, 100 yards from the flight line. The runway was only 1,100 feet of hard-pressed gravel. Rescue operations were accomplished day and night.

The HRS-1 Arrives With HMR-161

Although the gallant Bell and Sikorsky aircraft of VMO-6 were doing a tremendous job in Korea, a larger, more capable aircraft was needed. By September 1951, HMR-161, equipped with the larger HRS-1, had arrived in Korea. The time had come to combat-test fully the developing doctrine of vertical envelopment: the moving of Marine combat troops and their equipment to the battlefield, and the continuing supply of these men for as long as necessary, all by helicopter.

Established on January 15, 1951, Marine Helicopter Transport Squadron 161, equipped with the latest helicopter the Navy could offer, was the result of the Marine Corps' stated requirement for an offshoot of HMX-1. The HRS-1, Sikorsky's model S-55, was a revolutionary aircraft with its engine mounted in the nose, below and in front of the cockpit, behind two clamshell doors. With a top speed of 90 knots, it could carry 1,500 pounds of cargo with a crew of two. Still a long way from the dream of a 3,000-pound payload, but the best available.

Working up, the squadron got its first HRS in April 1951 and was alerted for overseas duty in July. Travelling to Korea on board the carrier *Sitkoh Bay*, which was also ferrying Air Force F-86s across, the fifteen Sikorskys and 270 squadron personnel left the U.S. on August 16, arriving at Pusan on September 2. HMR-161 was quickly attached to the First MAW and stationed first at K-18, near Kang Nung, and then relocated to auxiliary field X-83, where VMO-6 operated. Within two weeks, the unit flew its first resupply mission, the first such helicopter mission of the war, on September 13. September 19 saw another successful resupply mission, and it was decided to use the HRS-1s on a tactical airlift on September 21. In Operation Summit, an effort to relieve an embattled Republic of Korea unit, HMR-161 helos carried 224 troops and 17,772 pounds of cargo to a hill overlooking the action. In addition to inserting troops, the HRSs also carried telephone wire to connect reconnaissance teams with the command post. The operation was a total success. The Marine Corps Commandant, General Lemuel C. Shepherd, Jr., was lavish in his praise of the highly publicized event.

From these early efforts, including airlifts at night on September 28, HMR-161, under Lieutenant Colonel George W. Herring, and then Colonel Keith B. McCutcheon, helped establish the helicopter as a major tactical weapon. October 11, 1951, saw Operation Bumblebee, wherein reinforcements were helicoptered in, with only one pilot per aircraft. Twelve HRS-1s made 156 round trips with 958 troops. Squadron aircraft also took care of the men in the field by airlifting such niceties as Marine Corps birthday cakes (on November 10th) and Thanksgiving turkey dinners to the front lines.

The HRSs also took up the challenge of combat rescue. A May 1952 rescue involved HMR-161 aircraft in trying to reach a stranded navy pilot who had bailed out of his Corsair after it was hit by antiaircraft fire. Initial rescue attempts by Navy helos were unsuccessful and the larger aircraft of HMR-161 were called out to the carrier *Valley Forge* for briefings and another assault. Escorted by Corsairs, two HRS-1s made their way on May 28 to the plateau where the Navy pilot was supposedly waiting. Communist troops were around, and high winds made flying very treacherous. Approaching the rescue site, the first helo was stopped cold by a downdraft and dashed to the ground, fortunately without injuries among the crew. Rain then moved in and the rescue mission was halted for two days.

With the clouds still obscuring much of the area, a second Marine helicopter took off for the windy plateau. Rather than attempt a landing, the helo crew dropped a 40-foot rope ladder. One Marine on the ground grabbed the ladder and climbed into the HRS. The second had trouble, being weakened by his ordeal of the last few days, and had to be assisted into the aircraft by the third man, the helicopter pilot. The tragic part of the story was that the Navy pilot was nowhere to be seen, and under enemy fire, the helicopter had to turn for home or risk being shot down itself.

A similar mission occurred in February 1952, when a Navy pilot and crew of a Marine helicopter were down 40 miles behind Communist lines. A second chopper had been driven away by intense ground fire. A third HRS-1 and eight escort aircraft flew out and found the ridges overlooking the rescue site jammed with enemy troops. The fighters were called in to strafe the Chinese positions, while the rescue helo snuck in from another direction. However, the rescue crew could not see any signs of life from the Americans on the ground and reluctantly flew back to base.

In February 1952, the squadron aircraft were grounded after a series of accidents involving tail-rotor drive shafts. A design modification in March returned the helicopters to service status. In April HMR-161 moved to Army field A-17 on the western front and began to supply Marines of the 1st Division. The next several months involved a series of operations to move various Marine groups in and out of the battle areas.

The Skyraiders and MAG-12

It was used by only three Marine squadrons in Korea—VMA-121, VMA-251, and VMC-1—but the extent of its use, its great success in other military services, and its incredible longevity, made the Douglas AD (later A-1) Skyraider unique among the world's combat aircraft. Created by Douglas' master designer Ed Heinnemann during the closing days of World War II, and originally designated XBT2D-1, the AD flew some of the first attack missions of the Korean War from the deck of the carrier *Valley Forge*, with VA-55, on July 3, 1950. The type continued serving throughout the Korean conflict as a vital part of the Navy's carrier wings and right through the early part of the Vietnam War in the mid-60s. And even when the Navy finally retired its A-1s in 1968 for the new A-7 Corsair II, the Air Force continued using the type as rescue coordinators through the early 1970s. It was an impressive record of service for any military combat aircraft. The Marines' only combat use of the type, however, came in Korea.

The squadron was originally a reserve VMF squadron based at Naval Air Station, Glenview, Illinois, flying Corsairs and F8F Bearcats. In mid-1951, the unit received mobilization orders and moved west to El Toro where it transitioned to AD-2s and was redesignated VMA-121. After arriving in Japan, -121 travelled to Korea, arriving on October 19, 1951. K-3 airfield at Pohang was the only strip which had cement runways with the strength necessary to support the heavily loaded ADs, which could carry over 5,000 pounds of ordnance in addition to the airplane's two wing-mounted 20-mm cannon.

Assigned to MAG-33, the squadron's first mission came on October 27, 1951, and before the Wolfraiders left Korea, they had flown thousands of sorties against airfields, supply dumps, railyards, and bridges. In June 1953, sixteen aircraft of VMA-121 set a record for a single day's ordnance delivery: 156 tons. (It should be noted that several squadrons had been redesignated by June 1952, from fighter to attack. Thus VMF-323 became VMA-323 and VMF-311 became VMA-311.)

VMA-121 pilot Second Lieutenant Ted Uhlemeyer, Jr. had a narrow escape in the summer of 1952 when his Skyraider was hit by flak, which tore a tremendous hole in his wing, flipping the plane upside down. With his controls severely damaged and his landing gear jammed in the up position, Uhlemeyer wrapped both arms and a leg around the control stick, and after dropping his two 1,000-pound bombs on the enemy positions, he flew his battered AD home to K-6, Pyongtaek, which had become the home of MAG-12 on April 20, 1952.

As mentioned, there were two other Marine Skyraider units in Korea. VMC-1, Composite Squadron One, utilized AD-2Qs which carried two-man crews for radar countermeasures duties. VMA-251, which relieved VMA-323, arrived at the very end of the war, in July 1953.

These squadrons were part of MAG-12. VMA-121 was reassigned by the time the group moved to K-6, which was commanded by World War II ace, Guadalcanal veteran, and Medal of Honor holder, Colonel Robert F. Galer. MAG-12 actually came under the control of the Fifth Air Force, which determined when and where the VMAs would go, except for the sorties of VMA-312, which was stationed offshore aboard the Navy ship *Bataan*. VMA-323 had brought a new, and as it turned out, the final, variant of the veteran Corsair to Korea, the AU-1, a model made especially for ground attack, with more armor and a more powerful engine. Only 110 AU-1s were produced, although several comparable F4U-7s were produced for the French through January 1953, bringing the total production of the fabulous U-bird to 12,571.

Colonel Galer, who shot down thirteen Japanese airplanes, went on missions several times a week, and was shot down for the fifth time in his career in August 1952. As Galer pulled out from his bomb run, his Corsair was hit by Communist flak in its wings and engine. The powerplant quit soon afterwards, and Galer bailed out. However, his foot caught in a strap in the cockpit and the Corsair went into a steep dive, dragging the struggling pilot with it. Galer finally managed to free himself, but as he fell from the plane, he struck its tail. Opening his chute only 150 feet above the ground, he landed by the wreck of his plane, and under fire from nearby Communist troops. Galer was rescued but required hospitalization and rotation back to the States. He was awarded the Legion of Merit for his performance in leading MAG-12; Colonel John P. Condon, another experienced Pacific veteran, succeeded Galer as MAG-12 commander. (Galer retired in July 1957 as a brigadier general.)

Colonel Condon had had MAG-33 for several months, and when Galer was wounded, there was a dilemma as to who would replace him as leader of MAG-12; there were not enough experienced aviators to go around. Fortunately, Condon had been sufficiently impressed with his new executive officer, Colonel Herbert Williamson, to recommend to Major General Jerome, commanding the 1st MAW, that Williamson take over MAG-33 and that he, Condon, replace Galer at MAG-12. Jerome was initially skeptical, but eventually agreed to the suggestion. Colonel Condon became one of perhaps only two Marines to command both MAGs.

VMA-312 pilot Major David Cleeland figured in an unusual rescue on February 23, 1953. On a strike against some bridges, Cleeland's F4U-4B was shot up by ground fire, and he made a successful crash landing on frozen Annyong Reservoir. As he climbed out of his plane, his three squadron mates circled overhead for protection. Suddenly a unit of Mongolian cavalry appeared and plunged towards the surprised pilot, who started to run. The Marine pilots overhead immediately dove to the rescue and bombed and strafed the Communists, dumping the horsemen in the icy water of the reservoir as the ice broke under the barrage of bombs and bullets. This gave time for a helicopter to move in, rescue Cleeland, and return him to the *Bataan*.

9

Korean Stalemate

 Air-to-air combat for the Marines in Korea was not the free-wheeling affair it had been in World War II. As previously mentioned, the high degree of usage of Marine fighters for combat in the Pacific actually worked against the Corps, since the aircraft were not involved in close air support, their *raison d'etre*. In the last year of the war and afterwards, there were many senior officers who questioned the need for a Marine air arm. Therefore, in Korea great pains were taken to keep aerial combat to a minimum, although certainly if the opportunity arose it was proper for a Marine aviator to engage the enemy. For the most part, however, aerial combat was left to the Air Force, and, to a lesser extent, the carrier Navy, while the Marine planes supported the men on the ground. Very few chances arose for Marines to fight in the air and those who did score against Russian-built Yaks or MiGs were usually, though not always, on exchange duty with the Air Force.

The first aerial victory for the naval service involving an enemy jet aircraft in Korea came on November 9, 1950, when Lieutenant Commander W.T. Amen, commanding officer of VF-111 aboard the *Philippine Sea*, shot down a MiG-15 with his F9F Panther. The kill came one day after the Air Force had the honor of scoring the first U.S. kill over a jet with another jet; Lieutenant Russell Brown shot down a MiG-15 in a Lockheed F-80. Aerial combat was sporadic at least from the Navy's

147

standpoint, most of the action in Korea occurring with the Air Force's F-86 squadrons operating from Kimpo and Suwon. In the early months of the war, the enemy was reluctant to commit its modern MiG-15 fighters to combat, preferring instead to use up its old World War II-vintage Yakolev prop fighters, usually Yak-9s, in hit-and-run raids against U.S. positions. (Actually, the Yak-9 was one of the best, if not *the* best, Russian fighter of the last war, but of course it had been rendered obsolete nearly overnight by the advent of the jet.) It was almost inevitable that the Yaks should tangle with Marine fighters.

On April 21, 1951, VMF-312 pilots Captain Phillip C. DeLong and First Lieutenant Harold Daigh were jumped by four North Korean Yaks. Daigh quickly shot down one of the enemy planes, and DeLong, a World War II ace with eleven kills, shot down two more in rapid succession. Daigh damaged the fourth plane which fled. VMF-312 was flying from the *Bataan* at this time.

VMF-312 scored again on September 10, 1952, when Captain Jesse G. Folmar shot down a MiG-15, quite an achievement since Folmar was flying a prop-driven F4U. Flying from the *Sicily*, Folmar and his wingman, Lieutenant W.L. Daniels, were jumped by four MiGs who probably considered the Marine aircraft easy prey. Folmar later described the action for the magazine *Naval Aviation News*:

They attacked in pairs. The second section had just passed and was in a climbing left turn. I turned inside them and gave the nearest one a five-second burst of 20-mm. The MiG belched black smoke and the pilot flew into the air from his ejection seat. His chute opened but it was already on fire.[26]

(VMF-312 had exchanged its F4U-4s with machine guns for VMF-323's cannon-armed F4U-4Bs in March because of logistics problems with maintaining adequate ammunition supplies aboard ship.) Folmar did not have much time to feel elated about his kill, as the MiG's wingman came around and poured cannon fire into the Corsair, forcing Folmar to bail out. He was rescued shortly afterwards by an Air Force Albatross amphibian. (There were other instances of prop aircraft destroying MiGs; the Air Force's F-51 Mustangs claimed several, and even the Royal Navy scored a kill with a powerful Hawker Sea Fury.)

The Corsair was not the only Marine prop fighter to score aerial kills in Korea. As previously mentioned, Grumman F7F Tigercats of VMF(N)-513 shot down two PO-2 biplanes at night. Another VMF(N)-513 pilot, First Lieutenant John Andre, a naval aviator in World War II, shot down a Yak-9 on June 7, 1952, flying an F4U-5N. This kill was Andre's fifth, as he had shot down four Japanese aircraft in the Philippines, making him an ace. Spotting the North Korean aircraft while he was on an interdiction mission, Andre swung his Corsair onto the Yak's tail and shot it down. Even an AD Skyraider, flown by Major

Robert H. Mitchell, shot down a PO-2 on June 15, 1953, six weeks before the war ended.

The Marines were anxious to score against the MiG-15, hottest operational fighter in the world at that time. To some extent, the high-tailed MiG-15 had established a mystique comparable to the Japanese Zero of the last war. It was an unknown quantity and its introduction and tremendous performance capabilities came from an unexpected source, the Soviet Union. Russian aircraft designers were thought to be stodgy old bureaucrats incapable of creating anything which could compete with Western designs; they had even had to borrow a British Rolls-Royce Nene jet engine to get started. But the MiG-15 (the term "MiG" is an acronym derived from the last names of the two men—Mikoyan and Gurevich—who founded the design bureau) which flew in July 1947 was a world-beater, fast and heavily armed. The only western aircraft capable of meeting it with a good chance of winning was the U.S. Air Force's North American F-86 Sabre. Even then, many thought that the Sabre's edge was not the plane itself, but the level of experience and training of its pilots, many of whom had flown during World War II.

It was the F-86 which provided the Marines with most of their MiG-15 kills, for, of the twenty-seven Russian jets shot down by Marine crews (twenty-six MiGs and one Yak-15), all except six were downed by Sabres. (The Corsair, of course, and the Douglas F3D Skyknight also shot down MiGs.) Captain William F. Guss was the first Marine to get a MiG, on November 4, 1951, followed by Captain V.J. Marzelo on March 5, 1952; both pilots were on Air Force exchange duty. During a three-month tour, Major Alexander J. Gillis scored three times, with one probable and three others damaged. On October 6, 1952, the last day of his tour, Gillis got a MiG on two separate missions, although the second hop ended with his being shot down himself, just as he finished off the second MiG-15. He ejected over the Yellow Sea and floated for four hours in his raft before being rescued. At that time Gillis was the leading MiG-killer for the Marines.

A new phase of the air war in Korea opened on the night of November 3, 1952, when a crew from VMF(N)-513 shot down the first enemy jet at night with a Douglas F3D-2 Skyknight. Major William T. Stratton, Jr. and his radar operator Master Sergeant Han C. Hoglind shot down a Yak-15, an early-model Russian jet with a single engine buried in the fuselage below the cockpit. The squadron had given up its mixed bag of Tigercats and Corsairs in June 1952 for the big twin-jet Skyknight, obtained from VMF(N)-542. The aircraft were painted flat black with red tail code letters and numbers. The F3Ds could have been in immediate operation after their June arrival at K-6 airfield at Pyongtaek, south of Seoul, but a shortage of parts and faulty vacuum tubes for the radar sets delayed their introduction until November 1. The big jets, with their state-of-the-art avionics, were soon tasked with escorting Air Force B-29s which had been decimated by MiGs. From the first mission, the F3Ds proved their worth and never lost a B-29 to enemy aircraft. The MiGs would try to lure a Skyknight away from its charges to where two other fighters lay in ambush. But the additional MiGs would show up on the F3D's tail warning radar and the Marine plane could escape before the enemy got within firing range.

On the night of November 3, Major Stratton and Master Sergeant Hoglind were directed to a contact flying at their altitude of 12,000 feet at 320 knots. Stratton opened fire with his 20-mm cannon, scoring direct hits on the Yak-15 which exploded and went down. On November 9, Captain O.R. Davis and Warrant Officer B.F. Fessler downed a MiG-15 with cannon fire. Major E.P. Dunn and Master Sergeant L.J. Forten got a second MiG on January 15, 1953; Captain J.R. Weaver and Master Sergeant R.P. Becker got another on the 18th. The third MiG night kill in January was scored by Lieutenant Colonel R.F. Conley and Master Sergeant J.N. Scott on January 31. Conley, the commanding officer of VMF(N)-513, also claimed a "probable" in March, though that claim was never confirmed. All in all, VMF(N)-513 shot down eleven Communist aircraft, the squadron's F3Ds accounting for seven, including six MiGs, more enemy aircraft than any single Navy or Marine Corps type.

It might seem as though the Marines had their fill of aerial combat in Korea, but such was not the case. In fact, the Corps gained only one ace during the three years. Major John F. Bolt, another Marine pilot on exchange duty with the Air Force, was the only Marine to gain five or more kills in Korea alone; in fact, he is credited with six MiG-15s. A Florida native, Bolt had flown eighty-nine missions in Panthers when the Fifth Air Force invited him for a 90-day tour with one of its squadrons of the F-86-equipped 51st Fighter Interceptor Wing.

Bolt chalked up his first MiG kill on May 16, 1953, when his squadron tackled twelve enemy planes south of the Yalu. (It should be pointed out that the Americans were forbidden to cross the river to pursue the MiGs, which took sanctuary in neighboring Manchuria and China, a situation very much like the stiff engagement rules laid down by an ignorant government during the Vietnam War fifteen years later.) On his eleventh mission with the Air Force, Bolt swung onto the tail of a MiG and quickly shot it down. June 22 brought another score, as well as an additional MiG damaged. June 24 and 30 each saw him add to his tally. With four MiGs and 800 hours of jet time, Bolt had considerable experience. His chances of making ace looked good. But bad weather and unaggressive enemy pilots kept him from gaining that important fifth kill until July 11, 1953.

(Text continues on page 183.)

A squadron of Nakajima A6M2-N Rufe floatplanes at their base somewhere in the Solomons, circa 1943. Rufe was floatplane version of famous Mitsubishi Zero, which was produced by rival Nakajima firm. Despite the heavy, drag-producing floats, the Rufe retained much of the legendary maneuverability of the land-plane Zero. (Courtesy Robert Mikesh)

A Corsair production line in 1942. The massive 2,000-horsepower Pratt and Whitney engine and various ''plumbing'' behind the engine are shown. (Vought Photograph)

First Lieutenant Ken Walsh of VMF-124, who won the Medal of Honor in a Corsair in August 1943 when he tangled with fifty Japanese airplanes. Walsh, a former enlisted pilot, ended the war with twenty-one kills.

153

A Consolidated PB4Y-1, a Navy version of the B-24 Liberator, at Henderson Field in late 1942. Marine squadrons VMD-154 and VMD-254 used the big four-engine bomber as a photo-reconnaissance aircraft in the Solomons. VMD-154 was originally VMD-254. However, when the time came to deploy, 254 did not have a full roster, while the original 154 did not have enough planes. Thus, VMD-254, under Major Elliot E. Bard, took some of 154's people, exchanged numbers and went to war. The new VMD-254, led by Major Edwin P. Pennebaker, relieved the new VMD-154 at Espiritu Santo in January 1944. Both squadrons flew several hundred missions over Japanese bases in the area, especially over the big enemy base at Truk. This aircraft also carries a 37-mm cannon "borrowed" from an Army P-39, and mounted in the bomber's nose.

Marine fighter pilots scramble. The squadron, possibly VMF-214, flies early "bird-cage" F4U-1As. National insignia on fuselage consists of "star and bar" with red outline. Note the huge parachute packs carried by the pilots.

"Pappy" Boyington, flamboyant commander of VMF-214, poses in the cockpit of his Corsair with a member of his squadron. A tough, capable leader, Boyington became the Marines' top ace of the war with twenty-eight kills, the last two of which he obtained during the same mission in which he was shot down and imprisoned by the Japanese.

First Lieutenant Robert Hanson, left, stands with two other aces of VMF-215: Captain Donald N. Aldrich, twenty kills (center) and Captain Harold L. Spears, fifteen kills (right). In three months, Hanson scored twenty-five victories and was awarded a posthumous Medal of Honor. Spears was his flight leader on the day Hanson was shot down by flak while on a strafing run.

An F4U-1A—note early "bird-cage" canopy—on a takeoff roll at the Marine base at Munda in the Solomons, August 1943. The aircraft possibly belongs to Boyington's VMF-214. Humidity accounts for the visible vapor describing the propeller arc.

Charles A. Lindbergh walks with two of the Marines' leading aces, Joe Foss, with mustache, and Marion Carl, center. Lindbergh made a whirlwind tour of the various fighter units in the Pacific, Marine and Army, and brought new operating techniques for the Corsair and P-38 Lightning. He also shot down a Japanese Sonia scout plane, but was never officially credited, as he was serving in a civilian capacity.

156

An F4U-2 pilot prepares for a catapult launch from the *Long Island* (CVE-1) in May 1944. Aircraft may be from a Navy unit. Note the taped-over wing gun ports and the large radar fairing on the starboard wing. The long nose of the Corsair is shown to advantage in this view.

Two future leaders sit with squadronmates at El Centro, California, prior to leaving for the war zone in 1943. Tom Miller, second from left in the front row, ultimately rose to lieutenant general and was a record-setting aviator in the early 1960s. He also became Deputy Chief of Staff (Air). On his left is future astronaut and U.S. senator, John Glenn. The two became fast friends and served together during their careers in war and peace.

An F4U-1 taxis on an island airfield in April 1944.

An F6F-5N of VMF(N)-533 from the *Block Island* on patrol in 1945. The war was very close to Japan by this time and the Marine fighters aboard the CVEs were called upon to fly missions during the day, as well as at night. VMF(N)-533 was the top-scoring Marine night-fighter squadron with thirty-five confirmed kills.

F4U-2s of VMF(N)-532 aboard the *Windham Bay* (CVE-92) in July 1944 on their way to Saipan. One of the few photographs of this squadron's night-fighter Corsairs, it gives a good view of the radar fairing on the starboard wing, the early cockpit canopy, and the difficult view over the long nose which made approaches in the Corsair very demanding.

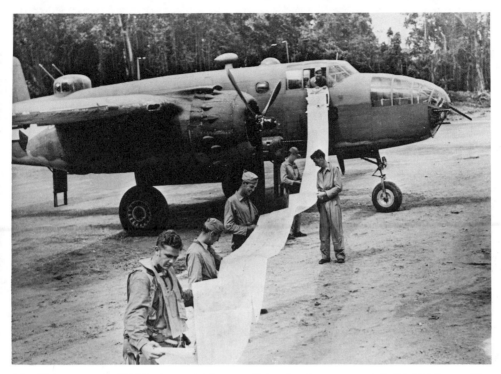

The flight crew of a PBJ look at a 65-foot scroll bearing the names of 35,000 Oklahoma City school children who contributed to the purchase of the bomber. The scroll was dropped over Japanese positions, as requested by the young contributors. PBJ was the Marine version of the Army's B-25 Mitchell, a highly successful, heavily armed light bomber which served in every theater of the war.

A VMF-124 Corsair comes aboard the *Essex* in January 1945. Note second carrier in the background and the *Essex*'s landing signal officer (LSO) in the right foreground.

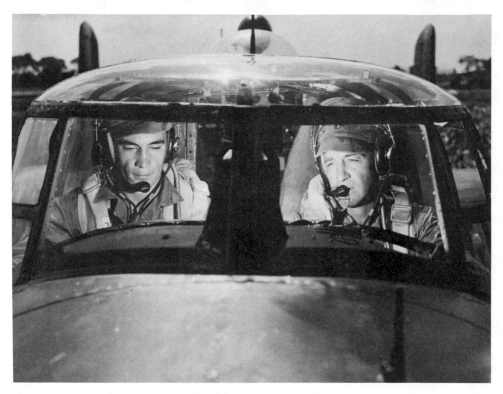

Lieutenant Colonel Jack Cram, right, skipper of VMB-612, gets ready to take off on a mission. Cram flew a heroic raid against Japanese shipping at Guadalcanal and was awarded the Navy Cross for his efforts. He later led this squadron of specially modified PBJs.

An excellent view of a VMB-612 PBJ, painted dull black. Note the bomber's painted-over nose windows and the huge radar blister immediately in front of the cockpit. VMB-612's PBJs probably flew the last Marine mission of the war.

"The Beast." A view of a Marine SB2C-4 Helldiver in April 1945. The Curtiss dive bomber was a big, underpowered brute and never satisfactorily replaced the SBD Dauntless, at least as far as the Marines were concerned. Note the rear gunner's deployed weapons and the huge vertical tail, hallmark of the type.

Marine crewmen load napalm containers on a VMF-114 F4U-1D on Peleliu in September 1944. Corsairs flew the majority of close air support missions during this bloody campaign.

A Corsair drops napalm on Japanese positions. Note that the pilot has not retracted his landing gear because of the proximity of enemy to the landing field.

This little Consolidated OY-1 was the first aircraft to land on captured Iwo Jima. Tiny "Grasshoppers" did valuable work in the later part of the war, flying artillery-spotting and ambulance/rescue missions, right under the guns of the enemy. Here a Marine rifleman sits on the wing strut to guide the aircraft pilot to a protected area.

The Kawasaki Ki. 100, code-named Tony, was a radial, air-cooled derivative of the earlier Ki. 61, the only major Japanese aircraft powered by a liquid-cooled engine (which was more vulnerable to ground fire). The Ki. 100 served in limited numbers near the end of the fighting. Both variants were formidable adversaries. (Courtesy Robert Mikesh)

The Kawanishi N1K1-J Shiden, codenamed George, was one of the Imperial Navy's late war hopes to combat the superlative Mustang and Corsair. The hope was well-placed, but there were never enough of the new fighters available. Those that did enter combat with Allied aircraft gave more than a reasonable account of themselves. (Robert Mikesh)

An F7F-3N two-seat night fighter with nose-mounted radar, part of VMF(N)-531 in 1950. The Tigercat was too late to see action in the Pacific, although a few examples did arrive only a few days before the cessation of hostilities in August 1945. VMF(N)-531 was assigned to the 2nd MAW at MCAS Cherry Point, NC.

A Grumman F9F-2 Panther of VMF-311 photographed on May 19, 1950, Armed Forces Day. In less than six months, VMF-311 would be the first Marine jet squadron to go into combat in Korea.

A Lockheed TO-1, Navy version of the Air Force F-80C Shooting Star, belonging to VMF-311, the second Marine jet squadron. Note the small Marine Corps insignia just forward of the canopy.

A 1932 photograph of a Pitcairn Autogyro of the type tested by the Marines in Nicaragua. Although the aircraft functioned well, it did not carry a useful payload, and development was halted.

McDonnell FH-1 Phantoms of VMF-122, the first Marine jet squadron, commanded by World War II ace Lieutenant Colonel Marion Carl. The FH-1 was a small, twin-engined jet which served for a few years, giving the Marines their first experience with the new type of plane.

Marine troops rush from Piasecki HRP-1s of HMX-1 during maneuvers at Quantico in the late 1940s.

A tandem-rotored Piasecki HUP-1 demonstrates a rescue lift. Little HUPs were fairly common aboard Navy aircraft carriers of the period as well as at Marine air stations.

Night action aboard the *Sicily* in September 1950, as ordnance crewmen check this Corsair's armament prior to launch. In addition to the four 20-mm cannon in its wings, the aircraft carries eight air-to-ground rockets.

An F4U-4B of VMF-214 prior to launching from the *Sicily* during the Inchon invasion, September 1950. Carrier-based air power pounded the Communist positions before the landings. Note that the pilot has his canopy slid back, to facilitate an exit from the aircraft if needed.

A Fairchild R4Q-1 transport of VMR-252. Along with other aircraft, these twin-boomed cargo planes performed valiantly during the Chosin breakout in December 1950.

A VMO-6 HO3S-1 takes off with a wounded passenger (note the litter projecting from the cabin window). The HO3S's payload was limited. This aircraft is equipped with a headlight for night operations and a rescue winch, mounted immediately above the cabin in the stowed position.

A Bell HTL-4 of VMO-6 waits as a wounded Marine is strapped to one of its two outrigger stations for transportation to a hospital ship. (Thanks to the success of the television show "M*A*S*H," these little bubble-topped helicopters are among the best-known aircraft of the Korean War.)

On the field at Seoul in 1951, Grumman TBMs sit in front of a crashed B-29. Once used as torpedo bombers, the Avengers served as personnel transports and general "hack" aircraft during Korea.

Major General C.F. Schilt, winner of the Medal of Honor in Nicaragua in 1928, commanded the 1st MAW in Korea during the early stages of Marine involvement. On the 176th birthday of the Marine Corps, he flew his personal Tigercat over the front lines, much to the chagrin of his staff. This 1955 photograph shows him at his final rank of lieutenant general.

A black Grumman F7F Tigercat on a forward strip in Korea. Too late to see action in World War II, the F7F scored two aerial kills during the war in Korea, at night against Communist harassment aircraft.

A rocket launcher is transported by an HMR-161 helicopter during operations in Korea. HRSs brought equipment, food, and medical supplies to units at the front.

Marines help load litter patients aboard an HTL-4. This scene was repeated countless times during the war. Note fairing for the litters on the ground.

An HRS-1 of HMR-161 lands the first wave of assault Marines on a Korean hilltop. Introduction of helicopters gave new capabilities to the Marines.

A Sikorsky HRS-2 of HMR-161 flies over the *Sicily* on its way to an assault landing in Korea in 1952.

A Douglas AD-2 Skyraider of VMA-121 heads for home after a mission in Korea. Although Skyraiders flew with many Navy squadrons, only a few Marine units operated the type in Korea. Nevertheless, the Skyraider compiled an enviable record, hauling incredible ordnance loads for the Marines.

A black-painted F3D-2 Skyknight of VMF(N)-513, the first squadron to shoot down an enemy jet at night. These big twin-engined aircraft carried a two-man crew and four 20-mm cannon. Tail code letters and numbers were in red.

Corsairs of VMF-312 are prepared for a mission by crewmen on the *Bataan* in 1952. Squadron marking of checkerboards is still carried by present-day F-4s.

Colonel John P. Condon, in cockpit, is congratulated by his executive officer, Lieutenant Colonel Darrel D. Irwin, after leading the largest Marine jet strike of the war. Condon, commander of MAG-33, went on to lead MAG-12 a short time later.

Major John H. Glenn of VMF-311 had a reputation for attracting flak. On March 25, 1953, his Panther was hit by ground fire which covered his plane with 375 holes. Glenn was uninjured and returned to base. He has good reason to be smiling in this photograph. Note the early jet flight helmet and oxygen mask. An ambitious MiG hunter, he eventually shot down three MiG-15s, and received his fourth DFC in the process.

An OY-1 of VMO-6 flies over the rugged Korean terrain during a spotting mission. OYs flew dangerous low-level missions throughout the war; their pilots, several of whom were enlisted NAPs, were exposed to some of the most intense concentrations of flak and small-arms fire.

A McDonnell F2H-2P Banshee of VMJ-1 in 1952. This photo-reconnaissance squadron's outstanding record is reflected by the numerous mission symbols—small cameras—on this one plane's fuselage, 122 in all. The squadron flew over 5,000 such missions.

Boston Red Sox outfielder Ted Williams was one of several personalities recalled to active duty in Korea. Here, Williams receives the Air Medal for bringing his flak-damaged Panther back to VMF-311's base on February 16, 1953. Williams flew thirty-eight missions in Korea and returned to major-league baseball in 1954.

The end of the Korean War is symbolized by this F9F Panther of VMF-311. With a total of 445 mission markings, this aircraft was credited with dropping over 400,000 pounds of ordnance during its combat career, which began in November 1950 with the arrival of the squadron in Korea. VMF-311 flew nearly 19,000 combat missions.

A Sikorsky HR2S—later CH-37—approaches a landing site somewhere in the U.S. Southwest. At one time, this was the largest helicopter in the U.S. inventory. Note the national insignia on the underside of its rear fuselage. (Sikorsky Photo)

A CH-37 of HMH-462 is inspected by a Havasupai Indian while five of the squadron's helicopters were flying 50,000 pounds of school-building supplies to the Arizona tribe's reservation. (Sikorsky Photo)

A UH-34 from the *Randolph* (CVS-15) hovers over the space capsule of astronaut Virgil I. Grissom on July 7, 1961, after Grissom made the second American sub-orbital flight. (U.S. Navy)

A Grumman F9F-8P Cougar of VMCJ-3. The elongated nose contained reconnaissance cameras. The Cougar was a development of the F9F-2/5 Panther of Korea, but had 35-degree swept wings.

The Douglas F3D Skyknight continued to serve with Marine squadrons. This version is the F3D-2M, indicating a missile-armed aircraft. This particular plane belongs to VMF(AW)-542 and carries four Sparrow air-to-air missiles, which were entering service at the time, 1956.

Major Ed Lefaivre stands by his F4D-1 Skyray in which he set five world climb records in 1958. Lefaivre went on to command a MAG in Vietnam. (Nick Williams)

A Skyray of VMF(AW)-115 taxis along the deck after landing aboard the *Independence* (CVA-62). F4Ds of Marine squadrons deployed several times with Navy carriers during the early 1960s. (Nick Williams)

The long-lived Gooney Bird—this is an R4D-8, later C-117—photographed at Quantico in 1957. Note squared tail of the C-117.

Two Douglas A-4Bs of VMA-533 practice air-to-air refueling in October 1962. Aircraft were based at Cherry Point, North Carolina, as part of the 2nd MAW. This "buddy pack" type of refueling was to prove invaluable in Vietnam.

A VMF-232 FJ-4 photographed in 1958. The FJ-4 had several refinements and was capable of carrying an increased payload.

Then-Lieutenant Colonel Thomas H. Miller in the cockpit of his record-setting F4H Phantom-II. (Lieutenant General Thomas H. Miller, USMC, Ret.)

Brand-new F-4Bs of VMFA-513 flying off the California coast in 1962. The F-4B was the first true production version and served throughout the war in Vietnam, with the Navy and Marines. (Lieutenant General Thomas H. Miller, USMC, Ret.)

An HR2S lifts a rocket launcher to demonstrate the big helicopter's load-carrying capability in 1960.

UH-34s load Marine troops during an exercise. Vertical assault from LPH/LPDs was a relatively new doctrine, but has been steadily refined to the present day.

The *Princeton* (LPH-5) maneuvering in 1959, with a deckload of UH-34s neatly arranged on her deck. Note that the ship still carries gun mounts, immediately fore and aft of the island.

Leading a flight of F-86s up the Yalu— that area had become known as "MiG Alley"—he spotted four MiGs taking off across the river and heading south. Diving to the attack, he pulled behind an enemy fighter, a favorite tactic of his by now, and his machine guns slammed the MiG into the ground from only 1,500 feet. He had five, and went after number six. Bolt later described his second kill of the day:

I made the second kill of the day when this other dude drifted over my way. I pulled up my nose and started firing into his tailpipe, getting within 500 feet of him. He started burning immediately. I was so close I was nearly blinded by the dense smoke so I pulled out and just made it in time. I watched the pilot eject himself and float to the ground.[27]

In only a few minutes, Bolt had scored his fifth and sixth jet kills—he had six Zeros to his credit when he flew with Pappy Boyington and VMF-214 during World War II—to become the Corps' only jet ace, to the present day. He was also the first, and one of only two naval aviators, to become a jet ace.

Perhaps the most famous Marine MiG-killer to come out of Korea was then-Major John H. Glenn. Of course, Glenn's activities as one of America's first astronauts and as a U.S. Senator from Ohio are well known. But prior to these experiences, John Glenn was a combat pilot, first in World War II and then in Korea. It is not generally known that he is credited with three MiG-15s while on an exchange tour with the Air Force's 25th Fighter Squadron.

Prior to his tour with the Air Force, Glenn had flown several ground attack missions with VMF-311. A fairly senior pilot, in view of his experience in World War II, Glenn was still given to periods of recklessness which sometimes put his life in grave danger and earned him the early sobriquet "Magnet Ass," because of his seeming ability to attract flak. On two occasions, he brought his Panther back, riddled with over 250 holes. Once, a 75-mm Communist shell punched its way through his tail section and exited, leaving a gaping hole and shreds of twisted metal which greatly inhibited the movement of the aircraft's elevators. It was only with brute strength that Glenn was able to regain his field.

The second time, Glenn screamed back up to what he thought was a safe altitude after dropping his ordnance, out of the range of most small-caliber weapons. He also quit jinking to throw off potential gunners' aim. Leveling off at 7,000 feet, he flew right into a 90-mm antiaircraft barrage, again limping back to his base.

John Glenn could be determined and loyal, as well as aggressive. During his tour with the 25th Fighter Squadron, he flew a MiG-hunting mission with his CO, Major John Giraudo. Finding no MiGs, the flight began looking for targets of opportunity on the ground, as per standing orders. Glenn spotted three Communist trucks situated near a knoll and called them to his leader's attention. Giraudo responded and dove on the trucks only to be bracketed by flak from the knoll. The F-86s had flown into a "flak trap." Giraudo's aircraft was hit and he bailed out, circled all the way down by an anxious John Glenn. There was little the Marine pilot could do for his skipper, except make sure Giraudo made a safe landing. Giraudo was almost immediately surrounded by North Koreans who had a well-earned reputation for taking very few prisoners and violently mistreating the ones they did capture. Giraudo was beaten and even shot in the shoulder not once but three times, before a Chinese group appeared and took the American pilot themselves. (Giraudo was eventually repatriated in 1953 and rose to the rank of brigadier general.) John Glenn circled above his downed leader as long as he could, but his plane was low on fuel and he barely made K-13; in fact, he flamed out on final approach and glided to the runway. As his F-86 rolled out to a stop, Glenn leaped from the cockpit to another fighter and took off back to the scene of Giraudo's parachute descent. It was too late.

Glenn flew Corsairs in the Marshalls campaign in 1944 and then Panthers with VMF-311, accumulating sixty-three missions in Korea in early 1953 before joining the Air Force for an exchange tour. Up to that time, Glenn had gained four Distinguished Flying Crosses for his activities in the Pacific and Korea, as well as several Air Medals. Quietly aggressive, he was anxious to go after MiGs. It was a different batch of MiG pilots he was to face than had been the case previously.

As in any "small" war, the opposing sides used Korea as a testing ground for new weapons and tactics to gain experience. The Communists were no exception, and after the free-wheeling dogfights of 1952, the MiGs to some extent withdrew, as their leaders assessed the situation and ordered more training for their pilots and uprating for their aircraft. The Chinese also discovered that the American Sabres were limited in fuel capacity and range. Having to fly up to the Yalu in search of MiGs or as escort for other aircraft didn't leave the F-86s much time to loiter around for MiGs or engage in heated combat when the enemy was sighted. The MiG tacticians therefore decided to catch the F-86s when they turned for home, cutting the U.S. jets off with MiG patrols in front and behind the Air Force formations. The tactic worked to some degree for a while.

One afternoon, Glenn led three Sabres up to MiG Alley, just as sixteen MiGs had taken off from their Manchurian base at Antung. Under Ground Controlled Intercept (GCI), the Communist fighters swung in towards the F-86s; a fight was a certainty. Without hesitation, Glenn led his flight to the attack. (His ground crew had his F-86's fuselage emblazoned with the name "MiG-Mad Marine" in bright red letters, so well known was his desire to get MiGs and surpass his fellow Marine, John Bolt.)

He lined up on one MiG, but the enemy pilot was good and eventually got on Glenn's tail, pumping 37-mm cannon shells into the Marine's Sabre. Fortunately, one of the other F-86 pilots picked the MiG off and riddled it with machine-gun bullets, forcing the Communist fighter into a fatal spin. However, the rescuer apparently picked up some of the MiG's disintegrating fuselage, as the Air Force pilot began to experience problems with his aircraft. Glenn shepherded the Sabre back to their base.

As the pair flew back, they were attacked by six MiGs which had been waiting as part of the new "box-in" tactics. Glenn succeeded in downing a MiG, but then found he was out of ammunition. The Marine pilot flung his plane all over the sky, trying to bluff the MiG pilots away from the other F-86. His efforts succeeded long enough for a fresh group of Sabres to come to the rescue, the MiGs fleeing before the new formation. Low on fuel, and with both F-86s suffering from battle damage, the two pilots made emergency landings at K-13. Glenn received his fifth DFC for the action that day.

The last Marine aerial kill in Korea had a tragic ending, as Major Thomas M. Sellers, flying with the USAF's Fighter Interceptor Wing (FIW) on July 20, 1953, scored two MiG kills, but disappeared and was declared missing in action.

In general, air-to-air combat was not really the main activity for the air arm of the Corps. Even though Marine aviators are among the most zealous practitioners of aerial combat training, especially today, they rarely get a chance to use their training for real; even in Vietnam, as will be seen, those Marines who scored kills were again on exchange duty with the Air Force. Only one Marine crew scored a kill against North Vietnamese aircraft while flying a Marine aircraft on a Marine mission, and that event did not occur until the war was nearly over.

The Flying Sergeants: Enlisted Aviators in the Marines

One area where the Corps was probably alone among the aviation services was the degree of use it made of its enlisted pilots, especially in combat. Enlisted pilots, of course, were not new. Indeed, France in World War I and the Axis powers—Germany, Japan, and Italy—in World War II had made considerable use of their enlisted aviators. The Royal Air Force would have been in even worse condition during the Battle of Britain in 1940 had it not been for its sergeant-pilots. For the most part, however, the U.S. required its pilots to be commissioned officers and, with few exceptions, that is the way it continues to be. (The Navy had instituted its NAP designation in 1919 due to a pilot shortage. The Marines, too, authorized selection of enlisted members to become pilots, First Sergeant Benjamin Belcher becoming the first Marine NAP in 1923.)

However, with the country's hurried and somewhat unexpected entry into World War II, the need for pilots transcended the niceties of rank and tradition. Therefore all the services, at one time or another during the war, made use of enlisted pilots, sometimes elevating them to commissioned rank later. (Marine ace Ken Walsh, who scored twenty-one kills and earned the Medal of Honor during World War II, was an enlisted pilot until he was commissioned in 1942.)

The Marines probably had the greatest number of non-commissioned aviators (131 in 1942), and not in second-line transport squadrons; many of these NAPs (naval aviation pilots) flew helicopters and jets in very heavy action in Korea. Flying sergeants flew Corsairs and Tigercats at Pusan and Chosin, Panthers in close air support against the Chinese, and OYs in dangerous artillery-spotting missions. Technical Sergeant Robert A. Hill accumulated seventy-six combat missions as an OY pilot, earning the moniker "Bulletproof" after coming home in planes that were more holes than aircraft. He won a Distinguished Flying Cross for evacuating wounded Marines near Chosin under extremely heavy enemy fire. Several of the R4D(C-47) transports which also evacuated wounded from Hagaru-ri and Koto-ri during the epic Chosin Breakout were piloted by Marine NAPs.

But, of course, the jet pilots were the glamor boys. NAPs were among the first Marine jet pilots, taking their training in Lockheed TO-1s along with their commissioned squadron mates in the late 1940s, providing a cadre of experienced and motivated personnel to draw upon during the action in Korea. When VMF-311 first brought its F9F Panthers to Chosin and Pusan, several of its pilots were enlisted aviators. Master Sergeant Avery C. Snow was the first NAP to complete 100 combat missions in a jet. (Snow had been a captain with VMTB-232 during World War II.)

One specialized squadron which made heavy use of its NAPs was VMJ-1, Marine Photographic Squadron One, established on February 25, 1952, flying McDonnell F2H-2P Banshees especially modified with a long nose to accommodate several reconnaissance cameras. VMJ-1 established an enviable record in Korea. Several of its pilots—who were specially trained volunteers—were enlisted men who could double as lab technicians if the situation warranted. An unusual setup. Aerial photo reconnaissance is one of the most exacting and dangerous jobs in all of military aviation. The recon pilot must be more than just a good pilot; that's just a base from which to start. He must be a crackerjack navigator, and know his camera systems inside and out, their capabilities and their limitations. And he must be resourceful, as well as having an inexhaustible supply of courage. Sometimes these last qualities are all that enable him to bring the film home and successfully complete his mission.

Most jet reconnaissance aircraft are unarmed, relying upon their speed to get them home before being intercepted. (During World War II, there were no specifically dedicated reconnaissance aircraft, merely modified fighters which had cameras stuck in the most convenient space, sometimes behind the pilot in the cockpit, or below him in the belly. The F6F Hellcat and P-51 Mustang are examples of such modification. Usually, these aircraft retained most, if not all, their machine-gun armament and could therefore fight their way to and from the target if need be.) During Korea, however, the dedicated photo-Banshees of VMJ-1 were toothless and needed escorts. Sometimes another Banshee would go along, both as an escort and sometimes to ensure the coverage of the target with another camera. Air Force F-86s were sometimes called upon to shepherd the recce pilot. And sometimes the photo pilot found himself alone.

Master Sergeant Lowell T. Truex had made his photo runs against installations near the Yalu River in 1952, thinking that his F-86 escort would look out for any Communist fighters which might try to come after him. However, as he looked around he found that the Sabres were nowhere to be seen, and he also spotted a gaggle of MiG-15s taking off across the river. Hurriedly, he finished his photo runs and ran for home. (He found later, that the F-86s had been watching from above, had the MiGs in sight and were, in fact, ready to jump the Chinese fighters had they come after Truex.)

Master Sergeant James R. Todd was the squadron's high-mission man, completing 101 photo missions before rotation home. A squadron mate, Master Sergeant Calvin R. Duke, who laid claim to being the oldest Marine NAP in Korea, was set upon by two MiGs near Chosin. In a dogfight which went from 10,000 to 30,000 feet, Duke outmaneuvered the Communist fighters, and ran for home at 600 miles per hour.

As can be seen, Marine enlisted aviators formed an integral part of their service's capability. However, by the time Vietnam came along, there were only a few NAPs on active duty, and fewer still actually involved in flying duties. Some of these pioneers served with distinction throughout Vietnam. But by 1973, only four NAPs were still on active service with the Marines, and all four were simultaneously retired on February 1, 1973, bringing to a close a colorful era in naval aviation and Marine Corps history.

The first few months of 1951 saw a buildup by the Communists in anticipation of a spring offensive. Estimates of 750 aircraft were made for the boosted North Korean and Chinese strength. (The Air Force's B-29 crews would certainly have agreed that there were more enemy planes in the air.) On the night of April 22, 1951, the Chinese 20th Army plunged through the U.N. lines and by the 26th had launched their main drive towards Seoul. All of American air power was called into action, trying to hold the onrushing Chinese. Navy carriers' Corsairs and ADs struck railway lines and bridges, while Air Force F-86s battled the MiGs and mounted their own bombing effort with F-80 Shooting Stars and F-84 Thunderjets.

The Marines found themselves in action along the line of the Hwachon Reservoir north of the 38th parallel. By June, the Chinese offensive drive had slowed and as the two sides faced each other at Kwachon, word came that after lengthy and secretive negotiations between Washington and Moscow, truce talks were set to begin at the old city of Kaesong, 35 miles northwest of Seoul. However, the truce talks made very little progress, and with the U.N. and Chinese forces in a stalemate, the war ground to a virtual halt. Action took place, but by mid-1952, very little real estate changed hands. As Brigadier General E.H. Simmons wrote:

. . . The line had solidified and it was trench warfare now, very much like World War I. There were no general offensives or big attacks, just nasty localize' actions growing out of patrols or raids, or the loss or capture of aı. outpost . . . .[28]

The air war settled down to various uses of close air support tactics, as dictated by the individual service—Marine, Navy, or Air Force. (The Marines came up with the idea of using searchlights to pinpoint targets at night. By July 1953, a small unit was experimenting with 3,000,000-candlepower lights aimed at offshore islands. The teams were working up with Air Force F-86s, Marine Corsairs, and British Meteors, when the ceasefire brought a halt to the experiment.) The Air Force tried interdiction, in an effort to cut off the North Koreans' supply routes. First MAW aircraft flew close air support for the U.S. Eighth Army. However, by this time the Air Force had control of Marine missions. First MAW commanding generals, Major General Clayton C. Jerome and then Major General Vernon E. Megee, quickly made sure that the Marines would receive top priority on arranging air strikes.

In October 1951, the truce talks were moved to Panmunjom and the laborious process began anew. The Chinese continued to throw night artillery barrages at the Marines and Army troops, who suffered hundreds of casualties in the dark, huddled in their damp, stinking trenches and dugouts.

The End of the War in Korea

During this time, several veteran Marine squadrons started to be rotated home. VMA-312, now on board the *Bairoko* (CVE-115), left Korea in June 1953; their place, and their aircraft, were taken by VMA-332, made up of 80 percent reserve personnel. VMA-332's nickname was the "Polkadots," while VMA-312's was the "Checkerboards." The newer squadron lost no time in repainting their veteran Corsairs' checkered cowlings.

VMF-311's Panthers, now in company with VMF-115, continued to pound enemy positions. VMF-311 had taken delivery of six new F9F-5s and flown them to Korea in January 1953. (The -5 featured a more powerful engine.) Flying on one of these ground-attack missions one day was a recalled Marine reservist, Captain T.S. Williams, better known as Ted Williams to millions of baseball fans. Prior to becoming a famous major-league player, Williams had joined the Navy in 1942 as an aviation cadet, and was commissioned a second lieutenant in the Marines when he got his wings on May 2, 1944. After a period of instructing at Pensacola, he finished the war in Hawaii, and was released from active duty in January 1946. He subsequently joined the Marine reserves.

At 34, Williams was not a young man when he was recalled to active duty in Korea in 1952. Of course, he was not alone in being recalled, but his visibility as a public figure made his case special. The baseball player himself took the event stoically. In a later magazine article, he said: "The recall wasn't exactly joyous news, but I tried to be philosophical about it. It was happening to a lot of fellows, I thought. I was no better than the rest . . . ."[29] The press was not so understanding. Many could not understand the need to recall "second hand warriors," as one reporter wrote somewhat unkindly. Most sports writers bemoaned the fact that Williams was really kind of old for a ball player as well as for a combat jet pilot.

However, the Boston outfielder reported for duty on May 2, 1952, was given a checkout in Panthers with VMF-223 at MCAS Cherry Point, North Carolina, and assigned to VMF-311, MAG-33, 1st MAW, Korea. His squadronmates got used to having a celebrity in their midst, and tagged Williams with the sobriquet "Bush," or "Bush leaguer," teasing him about his baseball activities and reputation.

On February 16, Williams was part of a thirty-five plane strike against Highway 1, south of Pyongyang, North Korea; it was his third combat mission. As the aircraft from VMF-115 and VMF-311 dove down on the target, Williams felt his plane shudder as he reached 5,000 feet.

Until that day I had never put a scratch on a plane in almost four years of military flying. But I really did it up good. I got hit just as I dropped my bombs on the target—a big Communist tank and infantry training school near Pyongyang. The hit knocked out my hydraulic and electrical systems and started a slow burn . . . .[30]

Unable to locate his flight leader for instruction and help, Williams was relieved to see another pilot, Lieutenant Larry Hawkins, slide into view. Hawkins gave his plane a once-over and told Williams that the F9F was leaking some sort of liquid (it turned out later to be hydraulic fluid). Joining up on the damaged Panther, Hawkins led Williams back to K-13, calling on the radio for a clear runway and crash crews. The baseball player was going to try to bring his plane back, instead of bailing out. With most of his flight instruments gone, Williams was flying on instinct and the feel of the plane as he circled wide of the field, setting himself up for the approach.

It took a long few minutes for the battered Panther to come down the final approach, but perhaps his athlete's instincts and control enabled Williams to do the job. At any rate, the F9F finally crossed over the end of the runway, and slid along its belly, as Williams' hand flicked switches to prevent a fire. As the plane swerved to a stop, the shaken pilot blew off the canopy and jumped from his aircraft, a little worse for wear, but alive.

Williams was awarded the Air Medal for bringing the plane back, and flew a total of thirty-eight missions during his time in Korea. But an old ear infection acted up and he was eventually brought back to the States in June. After convalescence, Williams returned to the Boston Red Sox for the 1954 season, eventually retiring in 1960.

Another famous baseball player, New York Yankee Jerry Coleman, was also recalled in Korea. An SBD pilot in World War II, Coleman flew Corsairs in Korea, totalling sixty-three missions, as Captain Coleman. Younger than Williams, whom he never encountered overseas, the 29-year-old second baseman had one or two close calls while in Korea. He narrowly averted a collision with an Air Force F-86 which had been cleared from the opposite end of the same runway for a landing; later, he experienced an engine failure while carrying a full bomb load. With no place to go, he continued his forward direction to a crash landing. The bombs miraculously failed to detonate but the Corsair flipped over, and the force jerked the straps of Coleman's flight helmet so tight that he nearly choked to death. Fortunately, a quick-thinking Navy corpsman reached him in time.

As the summer months of 1953 proceeded, the Marine squadrons of MAG-33 and MAG-12 kept up the pressure, flying countless sorties against Communist lines and pressure points, sometimes making the difference between a Communist victory and a Marine outpost remaining in Marine hands. April, May, and June were particularly active months for

VMF-311. Communist antiaircraft fire took its toll on squadron aircraft, as did the heavy monsoon weather. In July, flying was completely cancelled for a total of twelve days due to rain and heavy cloud cover. But there were signs of a coming ceasefire.

Even so, Chinese troops made one or two last-ditch efforts against Marine positions. On July 25, VMF-115 and VMF-311 flew strikes against enemy concentrations. Finally, word came that July 27 was to be the final day of the war. Even as the 7,000 men of the First MAW prepared to stand down, wing aircraft flew 222 sorties on the 27th. Captain William I. Armagost of VMF-311 flew the last jet mission of the war against Chinese supply areas in the late afternoon, thirty-five minutes before the ceasefire was to take effect at 1910 hours.

VMF-311 had contributed 18,851 combat sorties to First MAW's grand total of 127,496. Over 39,000 of these sorties were combat air support; the wing's helicopters had evacuated more than 9,800 personnel. There were 436 Marine aircraft of various types lost. HMR-161 had flown over 30,000 hours in combat and had pioneered helicopter tactics and operations which were to be the basis for Marine operations for years to come. The HRS-1s and newer, more powerful -3s were used after the ceasefire to shuttle repatriated prisoners of war back to their home bases.

The war in Korea had given the Marines in general, and Marine aviation in particular, a much-needed shot in the arm. Although the record of World War II spoke for itself, the air arm of the Corps had been very close to disbanding. But when the first shots were fired in June 1950, the Marines were the first to be sent. They were also among the last to leave.

10

Post-Korean Developments

The ceasefire in Korea brought the inevitable post-war soul-searching peculiar to American society and also the just-as-predictable round of cost-cutting measures. The Marines, while maintaining several air squadrons in Korea as peacekeepers, were somewhat protected. In 1952, a third wing based at El Toro, had been established to support Pacific operations, with the 1st MAW in Japan, and the 2nd MAW dedicated to Atlantic responsibilities, based out of Cherry Point and Miami, Florida. The helicopter remained at the heart of Marine aviation programs, having proved its worth in Korea, and several more squadrons were created by mid-1952. By June 1952, each of the three MAWs was composed of three MAGs and a helicopter group—MAG (HR)—containing three helicopter squadrons. Each MAW also included a two-squadron transport group (fixed-wing), a photo-reconnaissance squadron, a composite unit, and an observation squadron; quite an impressive force, obviously meant to be self-sufficient, self-contained, and self-reliant in combat.

New helicopters being considered or added to the Corps' capability included the little Kaman HOK, a twin-engined, twin-rotor design; up-rated versions of the Sikorsky HRS, as well as the HUS, a progressive development of the earlier HRS with more than twice the horsepower and capability of the HRS; and the huge HR2S, a Sikorsky aircraft which was the largest helicopter ordered for the Marines to date.

However, post-war cost-cutting finally reached the Corps, and by late

1956, the Marines' total manpower strength had dropped to 200,000. Rank restructuring, particularly among the enlisted personnel, helped a bit, but the Marines found themselves in budgetary trouble once again. The Air Force was being given the role of strategic-weapons delivery, while the Army and Navy carried on their traditional roles of land warfare and sea-lane protection respectively. Even the Navy lost a round to the younger, politically powerful Air Force when its own strategic-delivery squadrons were deprived of their stated *raison d'etre*—specifically the early North American AJ Savage turboprops, the Douglas A-3 Skywarrior and the unique North American A3J Vigilante carrier-based heavy attack aircraft. The Navy, however, still kept a place in the triad of strategic weapons by maintaining a very potent force of the new underwater-launched Polaris ICBMs carried by nuclear submarines. Where, then, were the Marines?

The future lay in helicopters. In the fall of 1953, at the direction of Commandant General Shepherd, a special team met to consider specific Marine Corps problems and requirements in the amphibious-warfare area. This Advanced Research Group (ARG) also decided to consider the future role of the helicopter as part of the Fleet Marine Force. The upcoming HR2S was the focal point, the ARG recommending that no less than 180 of these big aircraft would meet the board's requirements for a transport helicopter capability in the late 1950's. The aircraft would equip nine squadrons. Admittedly, this figure was somewhat inflated, and the Marines had to expect considerable whittling.

Another board, chaired by Lieutenant General Oliver P. Smith, convened in January 1955 to consider a definitive medium helicopter. This group of senior Marine officers decided that the HR2S was overly large and required much more area to operate in a battlefield than was desirable; however, 180 of these "heavy" transport helos was still the agreed number. When the Smith Board ended in May, its recommendations included a medium helicopter to complement the HR2S, with two medium-helicopter squadrons per wing. The HUS was the prime contender for standard medium helicopter and was to equip several units.

All these meetings, boards, and recommendations, of course, really constituted a Marine "dream list," and when the cold, hard decisions had to be made, the number of HR2Ss was substantially reduced to about 46, but the total number of HUSs was pegged at 140 by FY 1959.

Fixed-Wing Developments in the 1950s

While the Marine Corps created a place for the helicopter, several fixed-wing aircraft were finding their way into the inventory; most of them would be considered classics in the years to come, and indeed, one, the Douglas A-4 Skyhawk, still serves the Corps today.

The battle-tested Grumman F9F series continued to serve after Korea, having established a reputation for toughness in combat with VMF-115 and VMF-311, as well as several Navy carrier squadrons. As the war drew to a close, the more powerful F9F-5 was entering combat overseas. The next variant, the F9F-6, was radical enough to warrant a new name—the Cougar. (Many U.S. companies by this time had tried to establish an image for their aircraft by using a common series of names. Therefore, Grumman used "cat" names—Wildcat, Hellcat, Panther, and Cougar; Douglas used a "Sky" prefix—Skyknight, Skyray [the F4D], and the Skyhawk; and McDonnell entered the spirit world with names like Phantom, Demon [the Navy's F3H fighters], and Voodoo [the Air Force's heavy fighter, the F-101]. The routine was quite effective as a public-relations tool.) The XF9F-6 utilized swept wings, at an angle of 35 degrees, and first flew on September 20, 1951. By December 1952, the straight-wing Panther had been supplemented on the production lines by the -6 Cougar, and ultimately the -7 and -8 models. There were several modifications of these aircraft, including a two-seat trainer and long-nosed photo-reconnaissance variants. (The two-seater served in combat—the only model of the Cougar to do so—and only in Vietnam as a two-seat recon/Forward Air Control platform.) Although used mainly by Navy carrier squadrons, the Cougar did fly with a number of Marine units, especially in the attack role and the photo-reconnaissance role, as the F9F-8P.

VMA-312 had returned from Korea in June 1953 and had been reassigned to the newly created 3rd MAW, as part of MAG-32. On February 15, 1954, the squadron was redesignated as a VMF. During this period it had traded in its veteran F4U Corsairs for the more modern F9F-4 Panther. However, by November, VMA-312 had a new aircraft, the North American FJ-2 Fury, basically a navalized F-86. The original straight-winged FJ-1 served with only a few Navy squadrons, for only a few years, with limited success. Its main purpose, along with its contemporary the FH-1 Phantom, was to indoctrinate the Navy in jet carrier operations. The FJ-2 was a completely different aircraft, being basically an F-86E with an arrestor hook and strengthened landing gear. Armament had also been changed from the standard Air Force battery of six .50-calibre machine guns to four 20-mm cannon. The new Fury first flew in December 1951, and the aircraft entered service with VMF-122 in January of 1954. Intended as a carrier aircraft, the FJ-2 was considered a little too hot to operate from carriers, and was mainly relegated to Marine units to fly from land bases, although many of these Marine squadrons periodically deployed to carriers for landing-qualification periods.

The Checkerboards of VMF-312 also received later variants of the

Fury, the -3, and -3M, which was the first Navy fighter to include Sidewinder air-to-air missiles as standard armament. The Fury served with a number of squadrons. VMF-235 and VMF-323 were prime operators, along with VMF-312. VMA-223 which had remained stateside during Korea, serving as a training squadron for combat-bound Panther pilots, had also begun operating the Fury in its definitive FJ-4B model by August 1957. With increased avionics, the -4B could deliver an atomic bomb and also carried a sizeable bombload on six wing stations, which made it an obvious candidate for close air support. VMA-212 and VMA-214 also flew the -4B, as did VMF-232, a descendant of the Red Devil Dauntless drivers of VMSB-232. VMA-334, VMF-235, and VMF-451 also flew the Fury. VMA-333 had been flying AD-6 Skyraiders, but exchanged its prop-driven aircraft, along with its "attack" designation, for FJ-3s in January 1957, becoming VMF-333. The Fury also had a fairly active career in the Marine Reserves after its retirement from fleet service.

  Another aircraft which played a major role in Marine aviation during the late 1950s was the radical delta-winged Douglas F4D Skyray, a 1947 design which set a world speed record on October 3, 1953, of 753.4 miles per hour. Marine Major Ed Lefaivre also flew an F4D-1 to five world climb records in 1958. The bat-winged fighter entered Navy service with VC-3 in April 1956, but despite its spectacular performance, the short-ranged aircraft never really developed into a satisfactory carrier fighter. The only viable alternative, as it always seemed to be, was to give the Marines some of the new planes. So, VMF-115 received its first "Fords" also in April 1956. VMF-115 unfortunately experienced an early series of accidents which resulted in all aircraft being grounded until the problems could be solved. The faults were eventually traced to the fuel-transfer system and structural weaknesses. By the end of the year, the planes were flying again, and the squadron was redesignated VMF(AW)-115, to indicate its all-weather capability with the new radar-equipped Skyray.

  The next two years saw the Marines of VMF(AW)-115 operate their planes during several exercises and also in the Far East as part of MAG-11, 1st MAW, based at Atsugi, Japan. In September 1958, the unit was put on an alert status, as the Chinese Communists caused considerable turmoil on the island fortress of Taiwan by shelling offshore islands and threatening the Nationalist Chinese with invasion. Skyrays flew from Taiwan on 24-hour combat air patrols (CAPs), guarding vital air-transport traffic from MiG interference. Chinese MiG-17s did tentatively challenge the Americans from time to time, running for home at the last minute. VMF(AW)-115 aircraft achieved several radar lock-ons, and hungrily closed to intercept the threat, only to have the bogeys turn tail and flee.

Two F4Ds were airborne over Taiwan at dawn on one occasion, having scrambled to a threat call of thirty-two MiGs orbiting Quemoy Island. Reaching their "perch" altitude of 50,000 feet, the Skyray pilots knew it would certainly be a one-sided fight, but their mixed bag of four 20-mm cannon and two Sidewinder missiles apiece gave them some measure of confidence. Flying to within twenty-five miles of Quemoy, the Marine aviators spotted the MiGs' contrails but, to their consternation and disappointment, the quarry turned back towards the mainland, the chance of a kill immediately gone. The squadron returned to Atsugi in March 1959, and to the U.S. in May, after a 14-month deployment. VMF(AW)-531 arrived to take their place, as well as their aircraft.

Arriving back in the States, VMF(AW)-115 was reassigned to MAG-24, 2nd MAW. It was further reassigned to MAG-11, 1st MAW, in Japan during June 1960. The squadron returned to MAG-24 at Cherry Point in July 1961, having completed another overseas tour. However, the spring of 1962 saw the unit take the place of a Navy carrier fighter squadron and sail with CAG-7 aboard the *Independence* (CVA-62) for a Mediterranean deployment. The colorfully marked F4Ds formed an integral part of the Navy carrier air group until August. Hardly had the men and aircraft of VMF(AW)-115 returned home, than they were redeployed to the Naval Air Station at Guantanamo Bay, Cuba, the American bastion surrounded by Communist Cuba. The reason for the turnaround was the October Cuban missile crisis, when the world stood perilously close to nuclear war. VMF(AW)-115 remained in Cuba until January 1963. By that time, however, many Marine units were re-equipping with more modern aircraft, namely the McDonnell F-4 Phantom II or the Chance Vought F-8 Crusader. VMF(AW)-115 was somewhat behind schedule, but finally traded its Skyrays for Phantoms in early 1962, also being redesignated VMFA-115 to denote its ground-attack capability with the powerful Phantom.

VMF(AW)-115 was, of course, not the sole Marine operator of the delta-winged Skyray. VMF(AW)-114, -314, -513, and -542 all flew the aircraft, although VMF(AW)-115 flew it longer than any other Marine squadron. The Skyray had been an advanced concept from its inception, but had never found widespread acceptance during its career, either in the Navy or the Marine Corps. (The plane also saw a few years' time with reserve components.) One veteran Navy pilot wrote that the Skyray was "one of the worst Dutchrollers ever to fly (at carrier approach speeds) . . . . The vertical tail was too small, and tended to get blanked out by the wings at the high angles of attack required for slow speed flight . . . ."[31]

However, as the same aviator pointed out, the Skyray gave a lot of pilots their first taste of truly high-performance jet time:

The big manta-ray wing was great in a high-altitude dogfight, when it could be horsed around and stall provide lift at almost any altitude . . . . the tremendous power available could be used to climb like a rocket . . . . The APQ-50 radar was one of the first really good modern airborne sets—Its very descendants were used in almost all the F-4 Phantom models . . . .[32]

The Skyray was also accorded the honor of serving with the North American Air Defense Command, with San Diego-based VF(AW)-3, a Navy squadron.

There was another aircraft, developed during the mid-1950s, which set a rugged, simple standard for any type of ground-attack aircraft to come after it. This small jet, the Douglas A4D series, first flew in 1954 and quickly joined U.S. Navy and Marine squadrons, forming the basis for a strong attack capability. The Marines made the Skyhawk's acquaintance in January 1957, when the first aircraft reached VMA-224 at El Toro. Improved A-4Bs, A4D-2s in the pre-1962 system, joined VMA-211, the Wake Island Avengers, in September. Each new variant of the ubiquitous little Skyhawk brought new Marine squadrons into contact with the bantam bomber. Indeed on the eve of Vietnam in 1964, twelve front-line Marine attack squadrons were flying the A-4, in addition to various H&MS (Headquarters and Maintenance Squadron) and training organizations, as well as reserve units. Marine Skyhawks replaced Navy aircraft on various cruises, either to give the Navy squadrons a break or to save the regular squadrons transitioning to other aircraft, as in the case of the A-6. During the early 1960s, prior to Vietnam, several Navy squadrons were switching over the ultra-sophisticated Grumman A-6A Intruder, leaving their carrier air wings with reduced attack representation. The Marines were happy to oblige, and sent a number of VMAs to fill in for their Navy brethren.

The F-8 and the F-4

The late 1950s was a time of transition for many Marine squadrons. By the end of the decade, plans for reequipping with the next generation of aircraft had been fairly well completed and by the early 1960s most of the three major new types—A-4, F-8, and F-4—were in place, their predecessors relegated to reserve units. In 1959 several fighter squadrons gave up their FJ Furies for F8U Crusaders—VMF-312 in June and VMF-333 in November, to name a couple. VMF-232 did not receive F-8s until early 1962.

The Chance Vought F8U Crusader was quite a success story for this pioneering company. Vought had had troubles connecting with a solid design after its F4U series. The company was in the forefront of jet design with some radical innovations such as the F6U Pirate—the first production Navy aircraft with an afterburner—and the big F7U Cutlass, a twin-tailed bat of an airplane which, although certainly an original design, never even came close to its intended role as a missile-armed fleet defense fighter. The F7U was underpowered and dangerous, even for the Marines, who only got a chance to evaluate a single example.

So, it was with understandable enthusiasm and relief that Chance Vought greeted the first flight of its XF8U-1 in March 1955. It was an impressive aircraft and won several aviation development awards, kudos, and best of all, pilot acclaim; the Navy and Marines lined up to place orders. Of course, the Crusader did have some initial problems, especially around a carrier. It took a fairly fine hand to fly the skittish thoroughbred down the pipe to the flight deck, and several fatal accidents occurred during beginning stages of the type's career. However, adjustments were forthcoming and by the time VMF(AW)-122 took the first Marine delivery of Crusaders in December 1957, the F-8 was well on its way to creating an enviable reputation.

Project Bullet

On July 16, 1957, a young Marine major set a speed record, flying west to east across the U.S. in an F8U-1P, the photo-reconnaissance version of the Crusader. (The basic airframe had been modified to accommodate four aerial cameras in the armament bay forward of the wing. The resulting F8U-1P variant was one of the most successful and long-lived tactical military aircraft in aviation history.) During the mid-summer of 1957, Major John H. Glenn took off with another Crusader—a straight fighter F8U-1, piloted by Navy Lieutenant Commander Charles Demmler—as part of Project Bullet. The idea was to set a record for a cross-country flight, gaining photographic coverage of the entire country along the way. The end point of the flight was Floyd Bennett Field in New York, 2,446 miles to the east. Glenn and Demmler took off and rendez-voused with a waiting Navy tanker to refuel. However, Demmler damaged his refueling probe and had to abort the mission, leaving Glenn to continue alone. Glenn refueled three times in the air, and three hours and 23 minutes after takeoff, touched down in New York, setting a new record, with an average speed of 726 miles per hour; this speed was little better than Mach 1, the speed of sound, at cruising altitude. It was a record which went largely unnoticed, except for some immediate press coverage.

Marine Crusaders were active during the July-August 1958 Lebanon crisis, when President Dwight D. Eisenhower sent elements of the U.S. Sixth Fleet to the Mediterranean. VMF-333 was aboard the *Forrestal* (CVA-59), which had arrived to relieve its sister carrier *Saratoga* (CVA-60). However, the Crusader's finest hour in Marine colors was probably four years later during the 1962 Cuban missile crisis. Twenty years later, it is perhaps a little difficult for those too young to have lived through those agonizing two weeks beginning October 14 to realize how very close the world was to nuclear war. But the Russians had gambled that the U.S., under a fairly untried President, would not respond strongly to a move to insert medium-range ballistic missiles on Cuba, 90 miles from Florida. President John F. Kennedy had not done well in foreign policy. Although he had put on a strong show of words during August 1961, when the Soviets and their East German allies threw up the Berlin Wall, precipitating a worldwide alert, his personal credibility had suffered during the abortive Bay of Pigs invasion of Cuba earlier during the same year. To the Russians, under the colorful, mercurial Nikita Khrushchev, it seemed a calculated risk. They were not, however, prepared for total war, nor for Kennedy's rock-hard ultimatum to remove the offending missiles at once, or face a showdown.

Evidence of missile-site construction had been brought back first by high-flying Lockheed U-2 reconnaissance aircraft, and the President huddled with his cabinet to devise a course of action. Several military aerial reconnaissance squadrons, from all services, descended on the southeastern U.S. to fly continuous missions over Cuba. VFP-62, the east-coast Navy photo squadron, and VMCJ-2, Marine Composite Photo Squadron Two, were the senior service's contribution to the effort. The Marines were actually substitutes, called in to help VFP-62, which did not have enough aircraft and personnel to support the massive effort, due to having several detachments on cruise.

The Navy/Marine operation was code-named "Blue Moon," and began October 23, as RF-8As dashed over Cuba at low level, to avoid radar and surface-to-air missiles (SAMs) which had already claimed at least one U-2 at higher altitude. The Crusaders landed at the Naval Air Station at Key West, Florida, where their film was quickly developed. The prints were then rushed to Washington. The combined Navy/Marine unit flew eighty individual missions during a six-week period; the last missions were on November 26, as the aircraft made surveillance runs to make sure the Russians were, in fact, dismantling the sites as they had finally promised. All the Marine and Navy pilots received Distinguished Flying Crosses for their contributions during this most difficult period.

The Mighty Phantom

One more aircraft remains to be mentioned in the pre-Vietnam era. Like its frequent stablemate, the A-4, the McDonnell Phantom earned a special place in Marine aviation, and, like its little brother, still serves the Corps today, twenty years after its introduction with VMF(AW)-314.

The F-4 started life in 1953 as a single-seat, missile-armed fighter, designated the AH-1, but eventually evolved into a twin-engined, two-seat, radar-equipped monster redesignated the F4H-1. Chance Vought fielded a major redesign of its F8U, the XF8U-3 Crusader III, which was a very advanced speedster with many technological innovations. However, the Phantom appeared at a time when the single-seat, gun-armed fighter was going into partial eclipse, and the McDonnell aircraft's layout was more promising for future development than the Crusader III. As a result, the Phantom won the 1958 decision, and eventually became something of a legend in military aircraft design. Over 5,000 F-4s had been produced by the time the line shut down in 1978, and even the Navy's arch-rival, the Air Force, was, at first, forced into buying quantities of the new airplane. (Of course, the junior service quickly realized what a fabulous plane the F-4 was, and gladly ordered squadrons-full of the wonder fighter.) The F-4 garnered many performance records during its initial stages of service introduction. Marine Lieutenant Colonel (later Lieutenant General) T.H. Miller set a world speed record on September 5, 1960, in an F4H-1, flying a 500-kilometer course at 1,216.78 miles per hour, 400 miles per hour faster than the previous record set in 1959 by an Air Force plane. Vice Admiral Robert B. Pirie, DCNO(Air), had become concerned that the Soviet Union seemed to be garnering a great many aeronautical performance records; others were concerned as well. Pirie, therefore, decided that the U.S. should attempt to regain several speed and altitude marks, and what better way to do it than with the world-beater McDonnell F4H Phantom about to enter U.S. Navy and Marine service? And who better to set the records than the actual project officer/pilots in Washington, rather than some civilian test pilot?

Accordingly, Tom Miller, the F4H desk officer in the Bureau of Aeronautics, soon found himself headed towards the west coast along with other Navy pilots to make several record attempts. Miller was to try for the 500-kilometer speed record, and a triangular course was meticulously laid out which would enable him to get to the optimum altitude of 50,000 feet, punch off his underwing tanks, then finally his centerline tank, make his record dash, and regain March Air Force Base before he ran out of fuel. For above all, the speed record was actually a fuel-management exercise. A tremendous amount of gas was needed to climb to 50,000 feet, to say nothing of the amount gulped by the J-79 engines during the actual run. Miller made a number of practice runs, with Air Force pilot Jim McDivitt, later an astronaut, flying an F-104 as a chase plan.

The day of the actual attempt, Miller zoomed up to altitude and made his run, anxiously watching the rapidly decreasing fuel indicated on his gauge. The carefully calculated lines on his chart indicated that he would have less than 1,000 pounds of fuel left as he went "through the gate," and ended his run. But he would still be at 50,000 feet. As his controllers on the ground told him he was at the end of his run, the Marine aviator immediately pulled back the throttles and split-essed, rolling on his back directly over the desert town of Mojave, and pointed the nose of the Phantom straight down. The resulting sonic boom broke several whiskey bottles in the local bar, he was told later by the barkeeper. As he approached the runway, he gave a little more throttle to bring the aircraft down safely, and as he finally touched down and began his roll-out, the engines quit; he had finally flamed out through lack of fuel. It had been close. Colonel Miller was awarded the Distinguished Flying Cross for his record flight.

During a recent interview, Miller told the author that the Phantom was probably never flown at its top airspeed because of the fear that its directional stability would be lost to such an extent that both the plane and its crew would have been in grave danger. In the early stages of the aircraft's career, test pilots had flown the F4H up to Mach 2.5, but had been recalled by their controllers upon reaching that speed because static tests had shown Mach 2.7 would have posed a major hazard. There was no doubt, however, that the plane could have reached that higher speed and beyond. "The F-4 was an airplane which never quit accelerating," Miller said.

VMF(AW)-314 received its first Phantoms in 1963, and the number of squadrons reequipping with the new plane multiplied rapidly. Two variants served the Marines—the F-4B fighter and the RF-4B tactical reconnaissance version, bigger and faster than the RF-8, but initially engendering some fear of flying aboard carriers due to its elongated nose which prohibited forward vision. Thus the F-4 provided, along with the A-4 and F-8, the triangular backbone for Marine tactical aviation on the eve of Vietnam.

Marine transport aviation was due for a big boost in the early 1960s with the advent of the Lockheed Hercules. Until the first deliveries in 1960 of GV-1s (KC-130Fs), the Marines had depended on a mixture of piston-engined transports, ranging from the ubiquitous R4D(C-47) and Super-Gooney, the R4D-8(C-117), to the four-engine Douglas R5D-Navy version of the C-54-R6D(C-118) and Fairchild R4Q(C-119) Packets of Korean War vintage. With the arrival of the turboprop C-130, the Corps not only had a highly capable heavy hauler, but a viable air-to-air refueling platform. The last capability allowed Marine squadrons to fly long distances with the help of their own aerial gas stations. It was a big help close to a battlefield because jets could now take the maximum bombload, with reduced fuel, and once in the air could top off their tanks for maximum range and effectiveness.

The C-130 had first flown in August 1954 and had quickly interested customers from all the U.S. military services, as well as several foreign countries. In fact, in the opinion of many, if ever there was a replacement for the C-47, it was the Herk. Its exploits in Vietnam, whether in Air Force or Marine colors, were legion, and it continues to serve today.

Thus, as the specter of greater American involvement in Southeast Asia began to take shape, the Corps was in the process of modernizing its air arm in every aspect—from rotary wing to fixed wing, tactical to logistical. The most important event for the Marine helicopter community was a 1956 board presided over by Major General Robert E. Hogaboom. Like preceding gatherings, the Hogaboom Board was tasked with determining the requirements for the Fleet Marine Force, this time from FY 1958. The board homed in on the status and future of the helicopter, and decided that although helicopters were certainly a vital part of amphibious operations, they were by no means the only recommended means for dispersing assault troops on a beach; there was still room for the traditional seaborne invasion, especially after the initial insertion by vertical assault. The board's findings also affected Marine organizational structure as well as other hardware areas, and were in keeping with the new mood of austerity pervading the Corps in the late 1950s.

One aspect of Marine helicopter theory during this time period was the helicopter-carrier concept, the LPH. Anxious to have its own Navy ships, the Marine Corps eagerly accepted an offer to convert several *Essex*-class World War II carriers to meet the immediate requirement for a helicopter carrier. New, built-for-the-purpose ships were several years away. The *Thetis Bay* (CVE-90) had been the experimental vessel in 1956, accommodating twenty HRS helicopters. Three other veteran carriers—the *Boxer, Princeton,* and *Valley Forge*—were eventually converted by 1961, while the Marines waited anxiously for the *Iwo Jima* class of LPH to be built.

With the implementation of the Hogaboom Board's recommendations and the accompanying measures of austerity, Marine aviation was lean and trim immediately prior to Vietnam. Its leaders, crews, and equipment were in the best shape, many observers believed, since World War II, even better than Korea. There were even newer aircraft—fixed-wing and helicopter—in the near future. The highly capable Grumman A-6A Intruder was being touted as a sophisticated bombing and electronic intelligence (ELINT) platform, while the little Bell UH-1E "Huey," the Vertol CH-46 Seaknight medium, turbine-powered transport helicopter, and the big Sikorsky CH-53A Sea Stallion heavy transport helicopter were in various stages of pre-service development. They would join operations very soon. As what has been called "The Longest War" began to rumble more and more loudly in Vietnam, these new machines would be needed desperately.

Prelude to Vietnam

Before entering the Vietnam War, which is generally dated from 1964-73, it is necessary to step back to the eventful year of 1962 for some perspective. From the standpoint of Marine aviation, 1962 was somewhat of a watershed. There were 341 helicopters in service in several MAGs, including MAGs -13, -16, -26, and -36, although the size of the helicopter population varied considerably from group to group. There were also several other units, including the "granddaddy" HMX-1, which had been tasked, since September 1957, with providing VIP flight service with its Presidential flight. (Eisenhower was the first President to use helicopter service for short-range trips.)

Although there were six types of helicopters in service at this time, only three—the HUS, HOK, and HR2S—were operating with any significant numbers. Indeed, by 1962, the HUS—soon to be redesignated UH-34—was the most numerous helicopter, some 225 aircraft being in service. Originally intended as a Navy antisubmarine platform, the HUS had been gradually transformed into a useful utility type and was delivered first to HMRL-261 in February 1957. The UH-34 was to prove invaluable, as it shouldered much of the burden of early Vietnam operations, starting in 1962.

The Shufly Operation

Southeast Asia had been a battleground for centuries and had known several invaders and conquerors. The French held much of the area by the 1940s known as French Indochina, and had established an uneasy truce with the Japanese until Empire forces attacked in late 1941, subjugating Thailand (then known as Siam) and much of the Indochina Peninsula. Victory over Japan reinstated French influence but another, more insidious enemy was at work. Communist rebels and insurgents began openly to fight the French and ultimately drove them out of Indochina at the climactic battle of Dienbienphu, 170 miles west of Hanoi, in 1954. As a result, Vietnam was partitioned, North and South, along the 17th parallel with a Demilitarized Zone (DMZ) in between. But the area was never at peace, and by late 1961 it was necessary for U.S. leaders to consider beefing up support for the faltering South Vietnamese forces.

Accordingly, HMM-362, under Lieutenant Colonel Archie J. Clapp, was sent to Soc Trang, 85 miles southwest of Saigon, the capital of South Vietnam, to increase the battlefield airlift capability then in-country. Squadron personnel began arriving in April 1962, bringing twenty-four

UH-34Ds, and three OE-1 Cessna for wing liaison duties; the fixed-wing two-seaters were borrowed from VMO-2. Other assets soon followed, including KC-130s, one of which was piloted by Major General John P. Condon, commanding general of the 1st MAW. The Hercules were needed to bring in the heavy bulky equipment for Marine Air Base Squadron (MABS) 16. After the usual problems in setting up and establishing base security forces, Lieutenant Colonel Clapp's squadron began operations on Easter Sunday, April 22, the UH-34s flying missions in support of U.S. Army H-21 helos moving South Vietnamese soldiers into forward areas. The Marines were quickly involved in firefights as they shuttled supplies and troops into battle areas. April 24 saw the first battle damage of a UH-34 when one aircraft was hit by groundfire and forced to land with a punctured oil line. The damage was repaired in a few hours and the helicopter returned to Soc Trang.

During these early operations, techniques were beginning to evolve which would be needed years later. One concept was the armed escort of troop-carrying helos. At times, landing zones were so heavily defended by the insurgents that it was very difficult even to get the soldiers on the ground. Initial "softening up" procedures by South Vietnamese aircraft only served to advertise the location of the landing zone (LZ) to the enemy too far in advance of the actual landings.

Therefore, the incorporation of North American T-28 prop-driven trainers from the States helped the situation. The two-seater Trojans could stay with the slow-flying helicopters, flying with the troop formations, carry bombs, rockets, and guns. As the helicopters approached the LZ, the T-28s could zoom ahead and sanitize the area. OE-1s could also be used to reconnoiter ahead of the UH-34s. Equipped with an array of radios for communication with both air and ground units, the single-engine Cessnas could control the actual landings, especially with Vietnamese interpreters aboard.

Another improvisation was the Eagle Flight. Four Marine helicopters would fly above the main landing force, looking for Viet Cong rebels who tried to escape via alternate routes. With about fifty ARVN (Army of the Republic of Vietnam) soldiers distributed among them, the Eagle Flight aircraft would land where the ARVN troops could block the enemy's escape. Night assaults by helicopter also were tried during this early period, the first such operation occurring on July 20, 1962.

HMM-163 relieved HMM-362 on August 1; HMM-362 had flown fifty combat assaults, including 4,439 individual sorties in 5,262 combat flight hours. Through all this action, no aircraft were lost; although, of course, damage was sustained on several occasions. The new unit got right into action on the 1st, but did not suffer any battle damage until August 18. It was at this time that attempts were made to arm the UH-34s with something other than hand-held weapons. Mounts for M-60 machine guns, belt-fed 7.62-mm weapons, were added and taken into battle, although the gunners were strictly admonished not to fire unless fired upon by a clearly identified enemy.

Redeployment North

By September, a move north to the coastal city of Da Nang was made. HMM-163 began arriving on September 16, having moved in by Hercules transport and UH-34. Da Nang was a larger base than Soc Trang, with an 8,000-foot paved runway. September 19 saw HMM-163 aircraft aid in the evacuation of a government outpost in the mountains eighteen miles west of Da Nang. Unfortunately, this type of mission was to repeat itself many times in the coming months, as the Communists began to build up their effort, reinforced by supplies from North Vietnam. Action was heavy throughout the remainder of September. The successful Eagle Flights had been redesignated Tiger Flights and were reinstituted in early November. There were coordination problems with the ARVN authorities from time to time as well. Unfamiliar with helicopter operations and the somewhat strict timetable necessary for an effective helicopter airlift in combat, the ARVN forces were not always ready to be loaded into the UH-34s. The problem was such that a special Marine "loadmaster" was designated, usually a senior NCO, who would leave the first helicopter and hopefully get material and troops ready to go in short order.

The new year 1963 brought monsoon weather with rain and resulting mud, which hampered flight operations. HMM-163 rotated home beginning the second week in January, HMM-162 taking its place. Under Lieutenant Colonel Robert L. Rathbun, HMM-163 had flown 10,869 hours, with 15,200 sorties. August 1962 saw a record of 2,543 hours. HMM-162, under Lieutenant Colonel Reinhardt Leu, was no stranger to Southeast Asia, having recently deployed to Udorn, Thailand, during the Laotian crisis in the spring of 1962. HMM-162 had arrived at Udorn in late June, around the time the crisis had eased and U.S. forces were being withdrawn. It was thus a fairly easy turn-around for the squadron to head for Da Nang.

HMM-162 joined combat operations on January 19, 1963, and participated in many helicopter assaults, losing three UH-34s in combat. Use was also made of the armed helicopters with door-mounted M-60 machine guns. HMM-162 flew extensive combat until relieved in early June by HMM-261, Lieutenant Colonel Frank A. Shook commanding. Like its predecessors, HMM-261 had moved from its base at New River, North Carolina, to El Toro en masse, to be flown to Japan where the squadron personnel were inoculated and briefed within a 24-hour period.

They were finally flown to Da Nang where they picked up the equipment and aircraft left behind by the preceding unit. Actually, HMM-261 was the first squadron to serve its full tour at Da Nang. The old French Army compound served as the new Shufly headquarters, and eventually those of the 1st MAW in Vietnam. The Officers' Club had elaborate iron doors above which a sign greeted visitors with the inscription "Far Eastern Indochina Jungle Fighters & Combat Pilots Association LTD."

First Lieutenant H.C. Brown was a co-pilot with the unit's UH-34s, and he remembers the ever-present clouds and dampness of the South Vietnamese weather and the lush green foliage and undulating mountains over which much of Shufly's operations flew. The helicopters flew mainly supply missions to ARVN outposts, usually situated on a hill overlooking the civilian population of the individual villages. The UH-34s flew everything from livestock to people in and out of the meandering trails and rivers, which flow through the area.

However, sometimes the helos and their crews were caught in vicious firefights, and Brown recalled a mission in the summer of 1963 when he took so much ground fire that he put in a call for help. Within minutes, a flight of South Vietnamese Skyraiders roared in and threw themselves at the Communist positions. Brown and his crew watched incredulously as the Vietnamese aircraft actually flew below his helicopter in an effort to put their ordnance square on target. He called the Skyraider pilots "superb." Efficiency of ARVN forces varied considerably, the more professional units being those manned by career officers from the Air Force and the South Vietnamese Marines. The other end of the spectrum apparently included the regular field teams which probably numbered many unwilling conscripts within their group. HMM-261 began operations and flew combat until October 2, when HMM-361 came over.

Lieutenant Colonel Thomas J. Ross led HMM-361 and was the winner of five DFCs for action in World War II and Korea. By the time HMM-361 arrived and began combat operations in early October, it was painfully apparent that the VC had gotten over their initial fear of helicopters and were firing on the Marine aircraft without hesitation. Shufly helicopters of HMM-361 had been hit eighteen times in just one month.

Events in Saigon, namely the overthrow and assassination of the South Vietnamese president, as well as the returning monsoon, slowly brought Shufly operations to a halt, until at least the political situation stabilized. Of course, besides the assassination in Saigon, there had been an assassination in the U.S., when President Kennedy was shot dead in Dallas in November. Kennedy's successor, Lyndon B. Johnson, immediately froze all the units in South Vietnam, who had begun to think that they might be rotated home. There were many rumors to that effect.

It looked as if Kennedy was trying to disengage U.S. forces from Southeast Asia, but Johnson began beefing up those units and talk of returning home vanished. On January 3, 1964, after operations resumed their previous intensity, HMM-361 sustained an aircraft loss during a medical evacuation mission west of Da Nang. Hit several times, the UH-34D crashed in the jungle and was destroyed by U.S. Green Berets to prevent its falling into enemy hands. After a month's flying, HMM-361 was relieved in February by HMM-364, commanded by Lieutenant Colonel John H. La Voy. HMM-364 was scheduled to be the last Marine helicopter unit to operate during Shufly operations, and plans were underway to train South Vietnamese crews to take over the work. Monsoon clouds still periodically curtailed flight operations until early April. On April 14, HMM-364 suffered its first combat loss when a UH-34 was hit by VC groundfire while trying to take off after a medevac. The aircraft crashed forty miles west of Da Nang, and the crew sustained minor injuries. On the 18th, a large-scale assault by Shufly Marines, including twenty UH-34Ds and five Huey gunships—specifically armed escort helicopters—struck an area in the A Shau Valley near the Laotian border, a thick VC stronghold. Code-named Lam Son 115, this operation included close air control of all aerial resources, a harbinger of things to come. It was during this and subsequent assaults that the VC tried a clever trick of lighting off smoke-signal flares at a second LZ, hoping to confuse the helo crews and catch them in a crossfire.

April 27, 1964, saw the largest airborne assault in the three-year history of Shufly and it was also the most costly. Operation Sure Wind 202 called for the airlifting of 420 troops of an ARVN battalion in company with U.S. Army helicopters. South Vietnamese A-1H Skyraiders were assigned escort and suppression duties. (The South Vietnamese Air Force had been flying the big Douglas attack planes since 1960 when a contingent of Navy personnel—pilots and crews—had come to South Vietnam to train the South Vietnamese pilots, a repeat of Marines ferrying F4Us to Saigon during Korea for the French.)

The first Marine helicopters, escorted by Army UH-1B gunships, approached the LZ a little after noontime, and were met with a barrage of defensive fire from the Communists on the ground. The pre-assault attentions from the Skyraiders appeared to have had little effect on the enemy, and the UH-34s touched down in a storm of bullets. Several helos were hit, and one crashed in the LZ itself, although the crew was rescued.

A second wave met the same fire, although somewhat diminished due to the eventual spreading-out of the ARVN troops from the first wave. Several Marine aircraft had been damaged and only a reduced effort could be mounted for continued assault on the following morning. Sure Wind 202 was not completed until May 25, by which time HMM-364 had flown 983 sorties in 800 flight hours. The squadron rotated home in June, relieved by HMM-162.

The Shufly operation continued well into 1964, and as the situation rapidly deteriorated, with the VC attacking everywhere in the south and the August 1964 Gulf of Tonkin incident, which brought direct American involvement, it was clear that the Shufly effort had fallen far shot of its expectations. What, then, did Shufly accomplish? Lieutenant Colonel Archie Clapp, the first Shufly squadron commander, writing in the October 1963 issue of the U.S. Naval Institute's *Proceedings*, tried to give an answer. Although written some two years before the greater American effort of the summer of 1964, his words are worth quoting:

What did Operation Shufly add to the store of knowledge . . . ? It certainly did *not* produce a group of anti-guerrilla experts who have all the answers. It is believed, however, that most of the participants did come away with a keen awareness of the unique characteristics of this type combat . . . . And if an appreciation of the problems inherent in this facet of military operations is all that was gained, then the deployment can still be considered productive . . . .[33]

The original intention of Shufly was twofold. First, to increase U.S. presence, and particularly, as far as senior officers were concerned, Marine presence, in South Vietnam. Marines wanted first-hand knowledge of the situation, though not originally as combatants, but as observers, to relay information back to Washington for political and military policy-making. Secondly, Shufly helicopters were to be used to help the South Vietnamese move themselves around more easily in their fight against the Communist insurgents. This "taxi" service was to last only until the South Vietnamese had enough properly trained crews to operate their own helicopters.

With the above in mind, Shufly could be deemed a fair success. The South Vietnamese did gain valuable experience and confidence, proving themselves a viable force when used in conjunction with other services. The fixed-wing pilots of the South's air force were openly admired for their aggressiveness and dedication in support of the American helicopters.

In a sidelight consideration, the C-130 Hercules had proven its worth from the very beginning, bringing in heavy and valuable equipment, often into very short fields, where no other heavy transport was able to operate. Major General Condon considered Shufly "a remarkably well-planned operation" using the 130 transport as an "essential tool."

Viewed from a lower stratum, the days of Shufly were vastly different from those to come, especially during the ferocious Tet offensive and battle for Khe Sanh in 1968. Lieutenant Brown later likened the period of Shufly in 1963 to "an Appalachian Family Feud." "In 1968," he said, "It was war!" In cold reality, perhaps, the Shufly effort was only an early indication of just how tough the coming eight-year war was going to be for American servicemen, contending with not only weather, terrain, equipment limitations, and the confusion of their South Vietnamese allies, but also a tough, stoic little enemy who was prepared to wait it out, secure in the belief that the end would surely turn his way after all.

Training of South Vietnamese pilots had been scheduled for completion by March 1964, but an extension pushed the date into the summer. By that time the Gulf of Tonkin incident had heated things up and a call for more South Vietnamese pilots necessitated additional training. December saw Shufly renamed; its title now was Marine Unit Vietnam, MUV. By the spring of 1965, as U.S. men and material began pouring into South Vietnam, Shufly was eventually absorbed into the greater effort which was to come. The operation had given valuable experience to half of the Corps' medium helicopter transport squadrons. (March 8, 1965, can be considered an effective end-date for Shufly. On that date U.S. Marines landed at Da Nang in the first amphibious operation of the war for U.S. servicemen.) The men of Shufly had ceased to be the only Marines in the Republic of Vietnam.

The Development of the Armed Helicopter

One of the major developments to come out of Shufly was the helicopter which could shoot back. Of course, helo crewmen, from Korea onwards, had carried hand weapons with which to fire back on enemy troops, but for the most part helicopters remained unarmed and unarmored, with very little protective plating. One of the reasons for the lack of armor plate was the lack of lifting power of the early machines. The armor plate was just too heavy and until the advent of the more powerful HR2S and UH-34, armor was a luxury which could not be afforded.

Early Shufly combat underlined the need for armor and Lieutenant Colonel Clapp immediately took steps to place protection over the more vulnerable areas of his machines, the engine and oil lines in particular. Crew-protection was developed later in 1964, although all the additional weight, no matter how judiciously placed, imposed severe limitations on the UH-34's capabilities, especially in the hot, humid air of Vietnam.

Besides the obvious measure of providing armed fixed-wing escorts, the other alternative for helicopter protection was to arm the UH-34s themselves. At first, Lieutenant Colonel Clapp decided not to place machine-gun mounts in the doorway of the aircraft because of the obstruction placed in the way of fast-dismounting ground troops. Clapp felt the less time spent on the ground, the better. However, as the VC began to fire with increasing regularity on Marine helicopters, Clapp realized that he had to change his ruling and mount M-60s in the door-

way of the UH-34s. New instructions allowing gunners more leeway as to
when to fire were also forthcoming. Additional M-60s were installed as
the need was recognized and UH-34s were carrying two to four machine
guns by the spring of 1964. It was still not enough. The Communists were
becoming increasingly bolder.

Arming helos was not a new thought. It had been conceived by
military strategists in the late 1940s, and the British writer George Orwell
had used the armed helicopter in his novel of the future *1984*. But like
many ideas, this one had to wait until it was needed and had developed a
circle of support. Experiments had shown relative success with air-to-
ground anti-tank missiles launched from helicopters in the late 1950s.
These experiments were conducted by Army units. The Army could not
have armed fixed-wing aircraft and was therefore trying to develop its
own airborne firepower. The Marine helicopter community was watching with increasing interest, but there was a lot of anti-helicopter pre-
judice to be overcome, especially from jet fixed-wing proponents.

Marine Corps Commandant General Wallace M. Greene, Jr., was very
sympathetic to the need for armed Marine helicopters, and he directed
that an armament kit for the UH-34s be developed as soon as possible.
Since April 1963, the Marine transport helicopters had been escorted by
Army UH-1B gunships in Vietnam. These Hueys were armed with four
7.62-mm machine guns and 2.75-inch rockets in pods. But Greene was in
favor of the Marines providing their own protection. HMX-1 developed
the TK-1 (Temporary Kit-1), consisting of two rocket pods and two
machine guns mounted on platforms between the main landing gear and
fuselage, the guns being placed on the right side so that the ejected cas-
ings would not strike the left-mounted tail rotor. It was a somewhat successful arrangement, but in the opinion of many crews, the TK-1 was only a stopgap until a real gunship was allocated to the Marines, i.e., the
UH-1. The gun kits were sent to HMM-365 in November 1964, and their
success was only minimal. (Even 20-mm gun pods had been tried by
HMX-1 at Quantico in 1961-62.)

The only viable solution to the Marines' need for a gunship helicopter
seemed to be to give them one. Therefore, Marine UH-1Es were outfitted
with TK-2 kits, four electrically fired M-60s and 2.75-inch rocket pods,
and sent to the Fleet Marine Force. VMO-2 took the armed Hueys to Da
Nang in May 1965.

The Helicopter Pilot Shortage

The other pre-war problem facing Marine aviation was the pilot
shortage of the early 1960s. Admittedly, the helicopter was not as
glamorous a flying machine as the sleek, speedy jets; it took a special
type of pilot to want to fly helos. Promotion possibilities for helicopter

pilots were not the greatest either. By 1962, the Marines were facing an acute shortage of helicopter pilots. Several possible solutions were considered, including recruiting from warrant-officer and NAP programs. Although programs from these areas were initiated, the results were disappointing and the shortage continued. Forty percent of all Marine aviators were needed adequately to man the helicopter squadrons; only 29 percent were being utilized.

There was little to do except to *force* a switch. Accordingly, Major General N.J. Anderson, in charge of Marine aviation, forwarded a plan to the Commandant whereby 500 fixed-wing aviators would be ordered to transition to helicopters. Some attempt was made to soften the impact of this edict. Pilots selected would have already finished a tour in fixed-wing squadrons, and would be due for rotation anyway. Predictably, the program was a source of consternation among those pilots selected—usually first lieutenants and captains. But by June 1964, the transition training was well under way, and many of the pilots who had approached their new tours with feelings of being "second-class" soon began to change their attitude and throw themselves into their work. Their appreciation of their new trade and the different flying skills they developed were a source of great excitement and satisfaction for many, if not all. There were also new aircraft being developed for the Marine Corps helicopter community and the future appeared bright for budding helicopter aviators.

Vietnam:
The Early Stages

The gigantic, painful struggle that was Vietnam burst over the American public in early August 1964. On the 2nd, American destroyers were attacked on the high seas off the coast of North Vietnam by Communist patrol boats. A second attack on the 4th prompted immediate American response in the form of retaliatory air strikes against the PT-boat bases. This so-called Gulf of Tonkin incident also resulted in President Johnson preparing for possible escalation. The Marines, as well as the other services, had been involved in Southeast Asia for several of the preceding years, and as a consequence had watched the growing turmoil with more informed interest and concentration.

The 3rd Marine Division and the 1st Marine Aircraft Wing, both in Japan, were reorganized, beefed up, and alerted for duty in South Vietnam should the need arise. It was a tense period of watching and waiting. However, after the initial strikes by Navy carrier air units, the crisis appeared to ease, and the Marines were relaxed until a new period of intensive operation began late in 1964. By January 1965, the Marines of the 9th Expeditionary Brigade were off the South Vietnamese coast, near Da Nang. The situation rose and fell in intensity of action.

Early February saw more VC attacks and on February 7, the 1st Light Antiaircraft Missile (LAAM) Battalion got the word to land at Da Nang. When the unit's first HAWK missiles were landed by C-130 the following day, no one could have foreseen the tremendous effort and the staggering number of men and machines which were to follow in the next eighteen months.

As the initial programmed Navy strikes, known collectively as Flaming Darts I and II, hit the enemy from February 7-11, the Marines rode out the time in their ships off the coast. The bombing campaign, Rolling Thunder, began in early March, and on March 8, 1965, the Marines stormed ashore at Da Nang. However, there was no enemy opposition and the bemused Leathernecks set up shop under the welcoming gaze of the South Vietnamese who were in a festive mood. In company with KC-130s, the helos of HMM-162—transferred from HMM-365—carried the men and equipment in.

The Squadrons Begin to Arrive

As the buildup continued, MUV was deactivated and the helicopter air group, MAG-16, took its place. By April, the first tactical fixed-wing units began to arrive. The fifteen McDonnell F-4B Phantoms of VMFA-531, led by Lieutenant Colonel William C. McGraw, flew down from Japan of the 11th and began combat operations on the 13th, twelve F-4s flying close air support missions in South Vietnam. A second F-4 squadron, VMFA-542, arrived later in July. VMCJ-1 arrived on April 17th, bringing a detachment of EF-10Bs, the current designation of the venerable Skyknight, now used as an electronic countermeasures (ECM) platform. This type of big old jet was known as Willie the Whale, or more colloquially, DRUT, the derivation of which can be seen with the letters in reverse order.

The DRUTs flew their first ECM mission on April 21, and were heavily used for the next two years, especially for protection against Soviet-built and -supplied surface-to-air missiles (SAMs) which began to appear in April 1965. The Skyknights retained their integral armament of four 20-mm cannon, and early in the tour crews would strafe targets of opportunity when returning from a mission. They were soon ordered to abandon this practice. The EF-10s had neither the ejection seats nor the high speeds necessary for such dangerous low-level work. The EF-10s usually flew under fairly loose control wherever they were needed. This procedure caused some problems, including a near shootdown by Navy fighters from the *Ticonderoga* (CVA-14).

In March 1966, a section of F-8 Crusaders of VF-51 was scrambled to investigate an unidentified aircraft off the North Vietnamese coast, near Vinh. It was nighttime and as the two Crusaders approached their bogey, its identity was still unknown. The American pilots tensed with the excitement of possible action and scanned the sky for the quarry. The F-8s were several thousand feet above the bogey and had to roll over on a wing to see when the radar controller aboard a U.S. Navy destroyer told them they should be able to see the aircraft. The section leader's radar had locked onto a target, and he sent his wingman ahead to gain a positive visual identification, as per orders. The young fighter pilot pulled up above the bogey whose straight-winged outline looked very much like an Ilyushin Il-28 jet bomber. There was a lot of expectation concerning the possible use of these aircraft in a surprise raid by the North Vietnamese, and all the pieces seemed to fit. The F-8 wingman closed in for a closer look—only to find that it was a big old DRUT motoring along. In disgust and disappointment, the Crusader driver punched in his afterburner, with a resultant boom and long tongue of bright flame, just to let the Marine crew know how close they had come, and sped away. It was determined that the EF-10 had strayed into uncontrolled airspace and no one on the ground knew it was there.

Usually, however, the EF-10's contribution was appreciated. Lieutenant Colonel Otis W. Corman, commanding VMCJ-1, wrote how the Skyknight's utilization had jumped to 300%, a phenomenal rate. In fact, from their arrival in-country in April through the end of the year, EF-10s of VMCJ-1 flew 791 sorties in support of Navy and Air Force strikes into North Vietnam and Laos.

The EF-10 was remembered with varying degrees of affection by the pilots who flew it late in its life. Flying such a vintage aircraft certainly had its nostalgia value and the big airplane was rock-steady, a great vehicle for going cross-country. But it was slow and tired. By 1968, the airspeed limitation was 300 knots, and no banks greater than 90° could be made. Further, no more than three Gs could be imposed on the airframe. It was, after all, a 20-year-old aircraft, not much younger than some of the men who flew it.

By 1969, just prior to its retirement, the EF-10B found itself supporting limited air strikes while orbiting off the coast safely out of reach of most of the North Vietnamese defenses. Prior to that, in its heyday, from 1966 to 1968, the DRUT usually was flown right into the defense envelope—where the SAMs were thickest—to protect Navy and Air Force strikes. The crewmember tasked with actually running the mission was the electronic countermeasures officer (ECMO). These individuals, usually former enlisted technicians, spent most of the long flights looking into a scope, watching for emission indications from enemy radars. Jamming signals would then be used to confuse the North Vietnamese defenses and hopefully protect the strike aircraft entering and exiting the target area.

By mid-1965, the 1st MAW would include four MAGs, with Major General Paul Fontana, then Brigadier General Keith B. McKutcheon, as the commanding general. MAG-11 was the fixed-wing fighter/attack group, with VMCJ-1, VMFA-531, later VMFA-513 and VMFA-542, with later arrivals by VMFA-115 and VMFA-323. MAG-12 was the attack group, with A-4-equipped VMAs -225, -311, -214, and -211, later supplemented by VMA-223 and VMA-224. There were two helicopter groups. MAG-16, based at the Marble Mountain Air Facility, east of Da Nang, with HMM-261 and HMM-361, and HMM-161, VMO-2 with observation helos, Hueys, and the headquarters squadron, H&MS-16 at Phu Bai. An addition in September was HMH-462, a heavy helicopter transport unit which brought six CH-37Cs to be assigned to H&MS-16. MAG-36, based across from MAG-16 at Ky Ha, south of Da Nang, included HMM-362 and HMM-364, with VMO-6 and H&MS-36. Except for the CH-37 detachment and the Hueys of the VMOs, the helicopters used by the majority of the Marine squadrons were UH-343Ds.

By the end of the year, additional squadrons had arrived to fill out the wing. VMF(AW)-312 brought F-8Es on December 19, the first of three Crusader-equipped Marine squadrons to fly from Da Nang. A fourth Marine F-8 squadron, VMF(AW)-212, had arrived in the *Oriskany* (CVA-34) off Vietnam on May 8, and flown its first combat missions of the war the same day as part of Navy Attack Carrier Wing (CVW) 16. (The unit had converted from A-4s in 1963, and changed its VMA designation to VMF.) Led by Lieutenant Colonel Charles H. Ludden, the Lancers brought twelve F-8Es to the combat zone, flying in support of Marine and South Vietnamese ground operations. The Echos carried 5-inch Zuni rockets mounted on cheek racks behind the cockpit, but no underwing ordnance. That capability would come in June when the Crusaders were modified to carry Mark 82, 83, and 84 iron bombs on wing hard points.

From May to November, when the *Oriskany* sailed for home, the Marine aviators of VMF(AW)-212 flew 1,588 sorties in strikes ranging up and down the entire length of Vietnam, north and south. Many missions consisted of escorting A-4s in strikes near Hanoi, the North Vietnamese capital; others were solo bombing missions. Crusaders of VMF(AW)-212 were hit on twenty-six occasions, with one aircraft lost on November 5 on a raid near Hanoi. The pilot, Captain H.P. Chapman, ejected safely. He was captured however, and spent seven years as a prisoner of war.

An interesting turn of events occurred in September when the Navy wing commander, Commander James B. Stockdale, was shot down and imprisoned. As the senior squadron commander, it fell to Lieutenant Colonel Ludden to lead CVW-16, making him one of the few Marines to command a carrier air wing. (Of course, during World War II, the all-Marine groups (MCVGs) aboard the CVEs were led by Marine aviators.) This was the last time that a Marine squadron operated aboard an attack carrier for the next seven years.

Chu Lai

Outside of the actual dedication of Marine aviation assets and the subsequent buildup throughout 1965, perhaps the most important event during the year was the construction and opening of the airfield at Chu Lai, some fifty-five miles south of Da Nang. The need for a second tactical jet base was readily apparent. Da Nang could not handle all the traffic pouring into South Vietnam, fixed-wing and helicopter. With the activation of Ky Ha and Marble Mountain, the helicopters had their own fields. Da Nang could host the Phantoms and also serve as a central point, but another field was needed to support the action areas in I Corps. With the planned installation of Short Airfield for Tactical Support (SATS) equipment, Chu Lai looked a likely area for development. SATS involved an aluminum plank runway, taxiways, and parking ramp as well as utilization of catapult and arresting gear, similar to that on a carrier, for heavily loaded jets.

Marines of the Brigade hit the beach at Chu Lai on May 7, 1965, led by now-Brigadier General Marion Carl, one of the Corps' most celebrated World War II aces. By May 31, Navy Seabees had constructed 4,000 feet of runway and installed the arresting-gear portion of the SATS apparatus. On June 1, Colonel John D. Noble, commanding MAG-12, brought A-4s from VMA-225 in to a landing at the new base. That same day, four Skyhawks from VMA-311 arrived. Also on the 1st, aircraft from VMA-225 flew the first combat missions from Chu Lai. There was still a lot to be done, and Chu Lai was not declared officially complete and ready for business until July.

Rain turned the unfinished field into a sea of mud, and the A-4s had to take off with JATO (Jet-Assisted Take Off) and refuel in the air from orbiting KC-130s of Aerial Refueler Transport Squadron (VMGR-152) which maintained a four-plane detachment at Da Nang.

The intensity and amount of the buildup had apparently taken the VC by surprise, and they took no major action. But by July, the enemy had recovered from any timidity and launched attacks against Da Nang on the 1st. Several Air Force and Marine aircraft were damaged or destroyed. August saw a tremendous effort to oust the Marines from Chu Lai. In Operation Starlite, the Americans fought an intense battle with Communist forces from the 18th to the 24th. Battle citations and medals were won aplenty as the Marines repelled the determined attacks. Skyhawks and Phantoms from MAG-11 and MAG-12 flew day and night in support of the Marines on the ground. The helicopters of MAG-16 and MAG-36 were kept busy shuttling men and supplies in and out of battle. The fighting was the most vicious to date, but the Marines fended off the enemy attempt to retake the air base. Chu Lai remained in Marine hands and became a major part of the war effort in years to come.

Who Controls Marine Air?

As in every military action where the Marines took their aircraft, the subject of who controlled them in Vietnam came up early. And, as usually occurred, the Air Force laid claim to that responsibility. The Marines were understandably leery of letting their aircraft come under the junior service's control once again, as had happened in Korea. Marine air for Marines, first! Unfortunately, it was not to be, and the Air Force's Major General J.H. Moore was designated as the coordinating authority for all aircraft, including those of the Marines.

After some political haggling by Brigadier General McCutcheon, it was decided that although overall command rested with General Moore, McCutcheon would decide which Marine units would actually be dedicated for Air Force use. This arrangement would leave specific assets readily available for Marine commanders in the field.

Operational control of Marine aircraft came through the Tactical Air Direction Center (TADC), located at Da Nang. Subordinate organizations were the Tactical Air Operations Center (TAOC) and Direct Air Support Center (DASC). TAOCs provided for air surveillance and air defense coordination, and during the initial stages of Vietnam, relied upon various radar information being plotted by hand on display boards. It would be two years before a major step could be taken with the arrival of computer-oriented, semi-automatic TAOCs. The new Marine Tactical Data System (MTDS) was compatible with Navy systems and was set up at the Monkey Mountain complex near Da Nang. The MTDS represented a quantum leap in handling capability for the Marine controllers. Up to 250 aircraft tracks could be addressed at any one time. Eventually, information from the Air Force systems was also absorbed, making the Marine TDCC at Monkey Mountain the hub of information management in Vietnam in 1969.

Of course, the growth of air control and management took time, and in 1965 the system was still very much in its infancy. One capability which was available at this time, however, was the TPQ-10 radar which involved ground-based radar and computers guiding receiver-equipped Phantoms, Skyhawks, and later, Crusaders, to specific areas and telling the pilots when to release the bombs. In the rain and low clouds which constantly made such missions difficult, the TPQ-10 setup proved its worth as operations began to accelerate once Chu Lai was fully operational.

As 1965 progressed, Marine aviation assets were heavily utilized, not only in support of ground troops but in conjunction with other services. On May 6, the Air Force requested assistance with a rescue attempt in North Vietnam. Four Phantoms of VMFA-531 flew antiaircraft-suppression runs with Air Force planes while an Air Force helicopter recovered the downed pilot. By the end of the year, Marine F-4s had flown eighty-seven missions over the North.

In December, aircraft from MAG-11 and MAG-12 struck Communist supply routes in Laos in coordination with Navy and Air Force missions. Nearly 300 sorties were flown between December 6 and 31 in this interdictive effort. The strikes were not without losses. First Lieutenant Thomas F. Eldridge of VMA-211 was lost on December 29 while on a mission escorting helicopters. Even though his aircraft was hit and he was wounded, Eldridge dropped his ordnance through clouds and poor light, and tried to get back to Chu Lai. But his A-4 crashed short of the field and he was killed.

MAG-16 and MAG-36 supplied helicopter support for resupply and troop-movement efforts in the face of heavy enemy opposition. On September 19, all seven UH-34Ds of an HMM-161 flight were hit during a helilift; one aircraft went down. Captain Manuel O. Martinez, pilot of another helo, immediately landed beside the downed UH-34 in the midst of strong enemy fire, and waited until the downed crew had scrambled aboard. Martinez was awarded the Silver Star.

With the development of the ubiquitous UH-34 and the projected introduction of the Sikorsky CH-53, the CH-37, nicknamed the "Deuce," had not found a decent mission for itself. It was too big and temperamental to conduct vertical assaults, but Vietnam gave it a brief moment of glory and usefulness. In early September 1965, six CH-37s of HMH-461 deployed to Da Nang where they provided heavy-lift capability for MAG-16. They airlifted damaged helicopters from battle areas, thus saving them for possible repair or at least the salvage of valuable parts. They flew the first such mission on September 12.

In one case, two Deuces were dispatched to lift the stripped fuselage, transmission, and rotor blades of a downed UH-34. The first CH-37 returned safely, but the second, while lifting the fuselage, was struck by enemy groundfire which punctured the fuel lines to the port engine. The helicopter was forced to land, and another CH-37 was sent from Marble Mountain. The damaged Deuce was repaired and struggled back to its base.

By mid-1966, the end of the road was in sight for the CH-37, although the type was to soldier on until May 1967. By that time, the aircraft had flown over 5,300 hours in Vietnam and transported 12.5 million pounds of cargo.

By the end of 1965, Marine aviation was largely in place in Vietnam. Major air facilities had been established at Da Nang and Chu Lai, and thousands of sorties had been flown in support of ground action. The VC had periodically attempted to disrupt operations. On October 27, coordinated sapper attacks on the Marble Mountain Air Facility left the base decimated. MAG-16 flew in from Phu Bai, and MAG-36 arrived from Ky Ha three miles north of Chu Lai, to bolster the Marble Mountain Marines. UH-1Es at Chu Lai had also been attacked, although damage was nowhere as severe as at Da Nang. The enemy penetrated nearly every security arrangement provided; it was a basic fact of life in Vietnam. But the Marine airplanes were there for the duration.

Caribbean Interlude

While events in Southeast Asia promised increased combat to come, Marine helicopter forces halfway round the world were put to combat test in April 1965. An attempted coup by Army rebels in the Dominican Republic had plunged that country into civil war. Americans had to be evacuated. HMM-264 aboard the *Boxer*, now LPH-4, arrived off the coast on April 26 and the next day began evacuating civilians by airlift.

On the 28th, Marines were landed to cover the airlift, while UH-34s of HMM-264 flew shuttles between ships and Ciudad Trujillo, the capital city, using a polo field as a landing zone. An additional 684 refugees had been evacuated by midnight. Operations continued through the next day. On May 5, HMM-263 arrived aboard the *Okinawa* (LPH-3) to relieve HMM-362, as the flights continued, sometimes under rebel ground fire. Fortunately, only one UH-34 was hit. Its pilot, Captain T.P. McBrien, was seriously wounded but was able to land his damaged aircraft back on the polo field before being evacuated himself. McBrien thus became one of the few Marine aviators to be wounded in combat in the Western Hemisphere.

By May 26, HMM-263 was headed home aboard the *Okinawa*. HMM-264 left two weeks later in the *Boxer*. The Marines had had a brief taste of combat in an unexpected theater before being committed to a much larger war thousands of miles away.

The Skyhawks

In January 1966, the 1st Marine Aircraft Wing was spread out all over South Vietnam. Indeed, its aircraft ranged up and down the Indochina peninsula, participating in every capacity from close air support to cargo-hauling to strategic strikes. But, of course, Marine air's main mission was close air support. Writing in the August 1967 issue of the *Marine Corps Gazette*, Major General McCutcheon, commanding the 1st MAW, said:

Marine aviation is a tactical air arm. Its sole mission is to provide support to the ground forces. It is organized, trained, and equipped to perform a spectrum of functions to accomplish this mission . . . . The 1st MAW is doing all of these today in Vietnam . . . .[34]

The wing was very active indeed.

Perhaps the most active fixed-wing Marine aircraft were the little A-4s of MAG-12, out of Chu Lai. It is difficult to describe their role and the incredible impact they had in a few short paragraphs. When the SATS complex became fully operational, the Skyhawks of the seven squadrons which rotated in and out of South Vietnam were kept constantly on alert, if not in the air. VMAs -121, -211, -214, -223, -224, -225, and -311 all flew long and repeated tours of hard combat through early 1970. As one writer put it:

It is difficult to single out for comment any individual sortie or mission flown by Marine A-4s, because all such missions were strictly routine close air support operations . . . . Marine A-4s did perform workhorse close support missions, busting tanks with rockets or hitting enemy personnel concentrations and weapons sites with combinations of bombs, napalm and 20-mm cannon fire . . . .[35]

So important were the Skyhawk VMAs that it was finally decided to keep the squadrons continuously at Chu Lai and rotate personnel and aircraft on an individual basis. This allowed a continuity in operation, without the unavoidable disruption caused by the replacement of whole squadrons. While all VMA squadrons did their share of the work, VMA-311, with over 50,000 combat sorties flown by the war's end in 1973, was, perhaps, the most active of the A-4 units. The Tomcats had arrived with the opening of Chu Lai in May 1965 and, in company with other MAG-12 and MAG-11 squadrons, flew the length of Vietnam.

VMA-311 had been active during Starlite, when the VC attempted to overrun Chu Lai in August 1965. Tomcat pilots flew in support of Marines on the ground in March 1966 during the vicious fighting in the A Shau Valley. It was here that the first VMA-311 pilot was lost in combat. First Lieutenant A.M. Xavier, maneuvering in the steep mountains in predawn darkness, never pulled out of a strafing run against North Vietnamese Army (NVA) positions. VMA-311 supported Operation Hastings, the biggest and most profitable Corps operation to date in July 1966. August saw the 7,000th combat mission and the 10,000th combat flight hour achieved. Squadron pilots were flying a combined average of 600-700 combat hours a month. It was, quite naturally, dangerous work. A-4s were hit time and again, but the simple, sturdy construction of Ed Heinemann's little "Scooter" allowed heavily damaged aircraft to reach home more often than not.

During the bloody fighting at Khe Sanh in 1968, VMA-311 A-4s supported the embattled 26th Marines. In January, the second A-4 of the squadron was shot down in as many days, its pilot, Major William E. Loftus, ejecting right over the besieged Marine base. Loftus landed just outside the perimeter but a group of Marines gallantly ran to rescue the major, who had become entangled in his parachute's shroud lines, and bring him to the relative safety of the camp where he was helicoptered back to Chu Lai.

The model Skyhawk most used by VMA-311, as well as by other Marine squadrons in Vietnam, was the A-4E, originally the A4D-5, which included a more powerful engine, increased avionics, and two additional underwing stations for greater weapons load. Five hundred Echos were produced for the Navy and Marines. However, the "Charlie" model did see some service with the Marines at Chu Lai, notably with VMA-223, which apparently operated a mix of Charlies and Echos from time to time. (The squadron operated the A-4E from 1964 until 1970.)

VMA-223 had arrived in Vietnam in December 1965, operating as part of MAG-12. During the period of intense operations, the Bulldogs set a record for a day's sorties on February 3, 1966, with fifty-nine combat sorties. Milestone flight hours were rapidly achieved and surpassed. On June 16, 1966, two Bulldog Skyhawks were over a contested area where NVA activity had pinned down a Marine patrol. Captain Lynn A. Hale, the flight leader, took his section down through the mountainous area in early morning light, and in the face of heavy enemy fire, made repeated runs with ordnance and 20-mm cannon. Having expended their weapons, the two A-4s returned to Chu Lai, were refueled and rearmed, and scrambled a second time back to the same area. Captain Hale received the Distinguished Flying Cross for his determined support of the Marines on the ground.

In 1966, operations for VMA-223 continued to be intense right through the beginning of the monsoon season in October and November. In December, the squadron returned to Japan to rest and regroup. VMA-223 continued to operate in Vietnam until January 1970, when, in company with other Marine units, it left Southeast Asia as part of the planned withdrawal of U.S. forces. By that time, VMA-223 had flown over 32,000 sorties and expended over 34,200 tons of ordnance during its six years at Chu Lai.

One other model of the A-4 was used during Marine operations, the TA-4F, a two-seater originally ordered as a trainer to replace the Navy's Grumman TF-9J Cougar, then in use as advanced trainers in the Navy's Training Command. The faithful Grummans had served long and well in several capacities and had the unique distinction of being used in combat in Vietnam at the same time they were operating in a training role. The story deserves special mention, as it is not widely known.

As the pace of U.S. participation began to intensify, it became necessary to employ aircraft in a forward air control (FAC) role. Also, helicopters were in need of a capable escort, although armed UH-1Ds served well in that capacity. Fixed-wing aircraft had the speed, range, and load-toting capability to fill the escort role more efficiently, however. With all these factors in mind, the Marines decided to try some surplus TF-9Js. Being a two-seater, the Cougar could carry two pilots, which could be an advantage in a low-level, high-speed flight in a "hot" area.

Four or five Cougars arrived at Da Nang with H&MS-13 in 1966 and operated with MAG-11 and MAG-12 for about a year, alternating between Da Nang and Chu Lai. Carrying rocket pods under the wings, as well as nose-mounted 20-mm cannon, the old jets served well, roving ahead of troops on the ground or beyond helicopters approaching their landing zones, to scout and sanitize the forward areas. By late 1967, however, the new TA-4Fs were ready and they began to replace the aging Cougars in Vietnam, although the Skyhawks were not integrated into the training command back in the U.S. until 1969.

TA-4Fs performed valuable service as escorts and as airborne tactical air coordinators (TACs) above the helicopters and accompanying escort A-4s and F-4s. Two-seater Skyhawks were also employed as gunfire-spotters for Navy ships, particularly the refurbished battleship *New Jersey* (BB-62), which arrived off Vietnam in October 1968 and served only six months before being retired. During the big ship's tours, her giant guns pounded North Vietnamese positions to the delight and gratitude of the men on the ground. And above the *New Jersey* Marine TA-4s usually coordinated and advised the ship's gunners.

The composite squadron, VMCJ-1, based at Da Nang, received two new types during 1966. Both were highly specialized derivatives of airplanes already in fleet service. The first McDonnell RF-4B Phantoms arrived in October to replace the squadron's RF-8A Crusaders which had been flying not only from Da Nang but also with carriers of the Seventh Fleet's Task Force 77 offshore, some since before the Gulf of Tonkin in-cident in August 1964. The RF-4B was born in 1961 when the Air Force put forth a proposal for a reconnaissance version of the F-4, then just entering widespread service. Actually, the RF-4B was preceded by the Air Force's RF-4C prototype. The Navy lost interest in acquiring RF-4Bs and allocated them instead to the Marines, who were only too glad to ac-cept the long-nosed Phantoms. Forty-six RF-4Bs were turned over to VMCJ-2 and VMCJ-3 in 1965, but it was VMCJ-1 that took the aircraft into combat a year later.

The big RF-4B provided greater power, twin-engine safety, two crewmen, and a variety of imagery sensors never before available to the Marines. Additionally, the reconnaissance Phantom was capable of ac-quiring imagery at night, an improvement over the RF-8, whose after-dark capabilities were severely limited and seldom used.

Arriving just after the RF-4Bs on November 1, the A-6A Intruders of VMA(AW)-242 brought another tremendous jump in combat capability to Marine forces in Vietnam. The big, ugly Grumman two-seater, originally designated the A2F, carried a highly advanced bombing computer, as well as several more thousands of pounds of bombs than the gallant little A-4. Along with the attack version of the Intruder came the EA-6As for VMCJ-1. Identifiable by a big blister atop its vertical tail and the large electronic jamming pods usually carried under its wings, the EA-6A was the successor to the venerable EF-10B. The EA-6A was especially valuable against the network of SAMs which had been growing at an alarming rate and were already responsible for a number of losses from all U.S. air services. With the arrival of the EA-6A, the strike forces had an airplane which could accompany them right into the target areas, into the deepest thickets of SAM activity, maneuver with the bombers, and bring them through the enemy defenses. EA-6s were also used in conjunction with Air Force B-52 strikes which were becoming somewhat routine.

One of the greatest threats of the Vietnam War was the growth and efficiency of the North Vietnamese radar network, especially around the major cities and industrial complexes of Hanoi and Haiphong. As American strike aircraft passed over the DMZ into the North, or launched from their carriers, it was a sure bet they were being tracked and eventually locked up by enemy radar which fed the information to the greatest array of computer-directed guns and missiles ever assembled in the history of aerial warfare. An ECM platform of equal capability was desperately needed, and the EA-6A certainly went a long way to filling the requirement.

Rounding out the fixed-wing jet lineup were the F-8Es of VMF(AW)s -312, -235, and -232. This was the only use of fighter -8s made by the Marines in combat, in addition to VMF(AW)-212 aboard the *Oriskany* as already related. (The RF-8 recce bird continued to serve until completely replaced by the RF-4B, and, of course, the type formed integral parts of Navy carrier wings, in both fighter and reconnaissance versions, until the early 1970s.) The Marines had made good use of the F-8 series, but its stay in Southeast Asia was relatively brief—barely two years. Under Lieutenant Colonel R.B. Newport, VMF(AW) -312 arrived at Da Nang on December 19, 1965, and by the end of June 1966, its aircraft had flown 718 combat missions. However, that was the extent of VMF(AW)-312's operations in Vietnam. Actually, VMF(AW)-312 was scheduled to rotate back to the States just as the massive influx of Marine air squadrons gathered steam. Much to their chagrin, the pilots, officers, and men of the Crusader squadron watched as their F-4-equipped brethren of VMFA-513 and VMFA-542 prepared to go into combat. It would not do for VMF(AW)-312 to be denied a chance to fight. The squadron raised such a fuss that it was decided to extend VMF(AW)-312's tour to include two months' duty in South Vietnam, but no more, which accounts for its unusually short combat tour. The unit turned over its Crusaders to incoming VMF(AW)-235 and returned home to be redesignated VMFA-312 and be worked-up on Phantoms. Thus, the bulk of F-8 operations was to fall to two squadrons.

VMF(AW)-235 arrived on February 1, 1966, under Lieutenant Colonel P.A. Gibson, and was replaced by VMF(AW)-232 on November 15. Led by Lieutenant Colonel N.M. Trapnell, Jr., the Red Devils were assigned to MAG-11 in keeping with most of the fighter squadrons' duties, and were equipped with TPQ-10 bombing radar receivers. The F-8Es of VMF(AW)-232 began combat in December, flying 571 sorties by month's end. The squadron's aircraft were hit by ground fire on a number of occasions. (Being the only aircraft capable of carrying a 2,000-pound bomb, the Crusaders were heavily involved in close air support until the arrival of the A-6s.) On May 4, 1967, the first loss was registered, although the pilot was rescued. But two weeks later, on the 19th, the first Red Devil to be killed in Vietnam combat was lost when Captain H.J. Hellbach radioed that he was being hit over his target. The Crusader exploded before the pilot was able to eject. When VMF(AW)-232 rotated home on July 30, 1967, the squadron's record stood at 5,785 sorties. The Red Devils would return to Southeast Asia as VMFA-232 with F-4Js in 1969.

New Helicopters

While new fixed-wing jets arrived in 1966, the helicopter community also received its first examples of the CH-46 Seaknight. The CH-46, or HRB-1 as it was called prior to 1962, was a Boeing Vertol design featuring twin engines with equal-size rotor mounted in tandem, fore and aft. After some delays, the aircraft flew for the first time on October 16, 1962; the first production machines were delivered to HMM-265 at New River in June 1964.

The CH-46 was intended as the follow-on replacement for the faithful old UH-34 which was being utilized to the limit in Vietnam. The first CH-46s of HMM-164 began to arrive in Vietnam on March 8, 1966, when twenty-seven aircraft landed at Marble Mountain after flying off the *Valley Forge*. The Marines already at Marble Mountain welcomed the new arrivals with great expectations and the CH-46s were immediately put into combat operations. HMM-265 arrived with twenty-four aircraft in June.

Problems with the new helicopters, capable as they were, began to arise. Two were major considerations. The gritty, dusty South Vietnamese soil infiltrated the engines with alarming alacrity, causing all sorts of maintenance nightmares. Screens and filters were placed over the engine intakes to reduce the problem, with some success.

The CH-46 was also armed. The Shufly experiences, as well as subsequent combat, had decisively shown the need for helicopter self-protection. Therefore, Vertol-designed kits were incorporated into the Seaknights. The kit included a .50-caliber machine gun, or the regular 7.62-mm M-60, roughly equivalent to a .30-caliber weapon. Two machine guns were placed in each aircraft, one on each side. The first kits were actually installed by the Navy, the Marines not wishing to pay the nearly $3,000,000 demanded by Vertol. Naturally, the extra armament and accompanying armor reduced the CH-46's performance. The troop-carrying capability was reduced from twenty-five to fifteen. The 1,000 pounds of armor also reduced the amount of fuel which could be carried, thereby decreasing the aircraft's operating endurance. It was recommended that the lighter M-60s be carried as the standard machine gun and the amount of armor be considerably reduced.

An improved model of the CH-46 was being developed which incorporated changes and modifications, many of which were the result of experience in Vietnam. The CH-46D featured more powerful engines, new transmissions, and rotor drive components. HMM-161 took the first Deltas to Vietnam in December 1966.

Another new helicopter which arrived late in December was the long-awaited replacement for the elderly CH-37. Also a Sikorsky design, the CH-53A Sea Stallion was the largest operational helicopter in the free world. The Marines had been in desperate need of a helicopter for years but the CH-53 did not fly until October 1964 after much political and developmental haggling between Sikorsky and the Defense Department. Even after its first flight, the aircraft was hamstrung by continuous hassling. Finally, the first helos were officially accepted by the Marines in September 1966 as Major W.R. Beeler, commanding officer of HMH-463, took delivery of four CH-53As.

As the Sea Stallion crawled its way to operational status, plans were already being made to introduce the new type quickly to Southeast Asian combat as heavy retrievers. Accordingly, newly-promoted Lieutenant Colonel Beeler took the four new aircraft to South Vietnam, arriving at Marble Mountain on December 31, 1966. Two weeks later, on January 13, 1967, the first cargo missions were flown and, four days later, the first battle damage was sustained, two aircraft being hit, but not seriously hurt, by VC groundfire. From January to May, CH-53s also retrieved over 100 downed helicopters, 72 UH-34s, 13 CH-46s, and 16 Hueys. It was a clear demonstration of the CH-53's value, and the rest of HMH-463 was hurried along in its pre-deployment training.

The War

In 1966 the war continued to expand, demanding more supplies and personnel, and the combat action was both heavy and costly. Added to this was general dissatisfaction and rebellion among the Vietnamese. Anti-government demonstrations, led by Buddhist monks and nuns (some with violent, macabre displays such as self-immolation), cropped up continuously throughout the spring with resulting injuries and disorder. All U.S. military services did their best to remain clear of the civil strife but were not always able to do so.

Hampered by the lack of results of the strategic bombing campaign against the North, growing antiwar sentiment at home, and the general inability of the Vietnamese government to control its own populace, the Johnson administration began to enlarge and escalate the war on the ground in hopes of gaining at least a clear-cut military victory, if not a popular one. Therefore, 1966 became a year of constant operations, sweeps and strikes, against the invisible VC and their North Vietnamese Army compatriots. "Harvest Moon," "Country Fair," "Double Eagle," "Hastings," and more operations continued to carry the war to the enemy, searching out and destroying the Communist forces wherever and whenever possible.

Naturally, Marine aviation resources were utilized constantly. March was a particularly active month. Several aircraft—fixed-wing and helicopter—were lost to enemy action. On March 10, word came that an Air Force A-1E had gone down in the A Shau Valley, scene of especially vicious combat, and a rescue attempt was being mounted. Another A-1E landed beside the first aircraft and Major Bernie Fisher waited as Major D.W. Myers raced through a hail of bullets to the waiting Skyraider. Myers scrambled aboard and Fisher thrust his plane down the pockmarked strip. Fisher received the first Medal of Honor for aerial action in Vietnam.

While all this was going on, Brigadier General Marion Carl, then deputy commander of the 1st MAW, was being briefed by a helicopter squadron commander about the feasibility of rescuing the American and South Vietnamese garrison trapped in A Shau. The junior pilot said the weather was too bad to attempt a helilift. Carl decided to see for himself and flew his own Huey over the mountainous terrain. Carl was actually in the air and 20 minutes' flying time from the scene of the dramatic rescue by Major Fisher; he had just about decided to make his own attempt to rescue Myers when word came of Fisher's success.

Later that afternoon, Carl strongly recommended that a rescue attempt be made as soon as possible before the weather became even worse. In the evening, UH-34s of HMM-163 and Hueys of VMO-2 made the run into the Valley under intense and accurate enemy fire. One

UH-34 was shot down and the crew of three was forced to hide because of the approaching darkness, to wait till the next light for rescue. In the three-day operation, March 10-12, the defenders, Army Green Berets and South Vietnamese troops, were rescued. Two UH-34s, three F-4s, two A-4s, and two Hueys were shot down.

As Marines assets grew, the Air Force still held overall control of the aerial activity in Vietnam. Major General McCutcheon, commanding general of the 1st MAW, furnished the Air Force with Marine support requirements with the understanding that anything in excess was left for the Air Force. There was also the continuing discussion of defense against a North Vietnamese air attack. Although the problem was discussed and agreements arrived at and promulgated, the subject of air control was always sensitive. Nearly two years passed before a "single management" alternative was introduced in the spring of 1968.

Pilot and Weapon Shortages

An insidious problem which became more apparent in 1966 was the lack of pilots and certain types of ground personnel. The pace of the overall buildup had caught the U.S. military air services short. The Marines, however, particularly the helicopter Marines, were especially hard-pressed. With more than half of the FMF resources committed to combat in Southeast Asia, there were not enough pilots to fly the helos and jets. Pilots were rotated back to Vietnam more rapidly, or in some case, simply extended for up to a year.

It was not a morale-building situation, no matter how dedicated an individual might be. It was with ill-concealed bitter humor that Major General McCutcheon, now Deputy Chief of Staff(Air), remarked during a 1967 conference, " . . . there is no pilot shortage; it's merely that requirements exceed resources." Part of the problem lay with the lucrative positions being offered by commercial airlines to young military aviators; another aspect was the increasing frustration many servicemen felt over the incredible restrictions placed, seemingly arbitrarily, over combat operations by a government on the other side of the world.

Arguments raged back and forth within the military and between Congressional committees investigating the problem. Solutions were generated, discussed, and reevaluated. (In the forefront of all the verbal action was the tireless, utterly dedicated Major General Keith McCutcheon who would spend any amount of time and effort to get his points across.) The obvious solution was to increase the number of trainees going through the pipeline, as well as drafting pilots into the helicopter community. A shortened training syllabus would also provide more pilots eventually, while decreasing such "plum" assignments as staff and post-graduate schooling would give a more immediate boost.

Aid for the Marines came from an unexpected source when in 1967 the Air Force offered to train a number of fixed-wing pilots as a result of the cancellation of a West German contract. Thus, many Marine fixed-wing aviators received silver Air Force wings, while freeing slots in the Navy's training command for rotary-wing students. Even the Army was tasked with helping the Marines, although there were several differences between Army and Marine requirements. The shortage problem has so many facets, solutions and requirements, that only an overview can be given here. The author can recall that when he was going through Navy training in 1968 nearly one-half of the students in some classes were Marines, and that special attention appeared to be given to getting the "grunts" through. The young second lieutenants were fully aware of the situation and those men who were encountering difficulties in training and were considering the possibility of washing out, were heard to remark "What're they going to do, send me to Nam?" There was no bitterness, just a verbal shrug in recognition that there was a problem that had no quick solution.

Another area which began to give problems in late 1965 was the shortage of armament, especially bombs. Again the culprit seemed to be the speed and intensity of the buildup. Had President Johnson and his Secretary of Defense Robert S. McNamara gone to war before the country and its resources were ready? Through 1966 and well into 1967, it was not unusual to see Phantoms and Skyhawks taking off with minimal underwing stores. Indeed, there were cases of completely *unarmed* aircraft launching from carriers merely to create another sortie for the record, "going along for the ride," due to "snafus on the flight deck," according to one unit's combat log. Whatever the reason, the problem became acute in 1966 and pilots of all services were troubled. One young Phantom pilot wrote, "There is nothing more demoralizing than the sight of an F-4 taxiing out with nothing, not a pair of 81s or 82s (250- and 500-pound bombs, respectively) nestled among its ejector racks . . . ." It would be a while before production could match the pace of combat employment.

1967

As 1967 opened, the war, both on the ground and in the air, began to establish its pace and intensity. It was becoming clear to both sides that the Communists could not win a decisive military victory—indeed they were losing in a military sense—as long as the vast might of the U.S. bolstered its ally, South Vietnam. Although the North Vietnamese were receiving aid from all areas of the Communist world, especially from the Soviet Union and People's Republic of China, these countries never attempted to introduce the level of personnel and machines which the

American had committed, avoiding a direct confrontation between superpowers. And yet, for all the overwhelming U.S. strength, no clear-cut victory was in sight, and the VC just kept up the pressure.

The war, with very few amphibious assaults, had allowed the 1st MAW to concentrate strictly on the sustained ground combat. Fully 50 percent of Marine aviation was employed in supporting the III MAF in Vietnam. By this time the wing included five MAGs and over twenty squadrons, fixed- and rotary-wing. MAGs -11, -12, and -13 included the VMA and VMFA assets. (MAG-13, which arrived in September 1966, included VMFA-115, which arrived in June 1967, VMFA-314, and eventually VMFA-323 and VMFA-542.) MAG-16 and MAG-36 remained the helicopter groups, including, at the opening of 1967, seven transport squadrons and three observation units, which operated the smaller Hueys for a variety of duties.

The success of Marine air at this juncture, especially with the increased all-weather capabilities exemplified by the A-6s and the radar-directed F-4s and A-4s, was cause for some jealousy on the part of the Air Force which was always sensitive about its supposed authority over all air operations in Southeast Asia. The continuing high level of activity along the Ho Chi Minh Trail, the circuitous 1,500-mile network along which men and supplies flowed into South Vietnam, became the focal point of the Air Force's attentions. If aircraft were not involved in a strategic air strike against the North's industrial and POL facilities, then the Air Force, under General William Momyer, felt air assets, particularly those of the 1st MAW, would be best utilized against the activity on the trails.

As far as the Marines were concerned, interdiction was fine, but the men on the ground came first; that was the way it had always been and that was why the Marines had airplanes. The Marines' view was recently restated by Major General Norman J. Anderson, USMC (Ret.), who commanded the 1st MAW for one year beginning in June 1967. Reviewing General Momyer's book *Air Power in Three Wars* in the May 1981 issue of the *Marine Corps Gazette*, General Anderson castigated General Momyer for his parochial views on air power in general, and Marine air power in particular. Addressing Momyer's charge that the Marines "employed aviation as though they were still conducting an amphibious operation," Anderson wrote:

Nothing could be further from the truth than this spurious charge of inflexibility. Marine Corps sorties were applied where needed most and frequently to other than Marine Corps units. They were diverted with caution, though, as anyone responsible for pulling support aircraft should understand, for a commander must not be suddenly stripped of expected support . . . It was of such poppycock, however, that the infamous "single management" was born and adopted . . . .[36]

Anderson believed that the Air Force's preoccupation with the so-called "single management" concept grew out of neglecting its duties regarding Army requirements. It was only when the Marines were tasked with supporting units of the 1st Cavalry Divison, as part of III MAF in the northern provinces of South Vietnam in 1967 (a move designed to increase pressure on the VC infiltration routes along the border), that the problems began to take definite shape. Acknowledging the order by Army General William Westmoreland "to make certain that the needs of the Army divisions for tactical air support were satisfied," General Anderson wrote that he immediately knew Westmoreland's directive could not be implemented because the Army could not be included in the Marines' air-control system. However, Anderson apparently prevailed upon some departing units to give the 1st Cavalry some air-communications equipment which alleviated the problem to some extent. But, according to General Anderson, Marine air's reputation vis-a-vis the Seventh Air Force and its commander, General Momyer, was never able to satisfy its opponents.

In the last analysis . . . voluntary sharing which was extensive in Vietnam (although Momyer gives its very short shrift) will not effectively thwart "single management" . . . .[37]

It was a battle never fully reconciled.

Skyhawk Operations

In keeping with the pace of combat in 1967, the VMA units at Chu Lai accelerated their effort, often using a section of A-4s on "hot pad" alert, awaiting a scramble call: the pilots in the cockpits, the aircraft armed, and the engines turning. Sometimes the Skyhawks were already airborne. (These procedures were considered wasteful by the Air Force's General Momyer and only added to the control debate. But the Marines maintained their method of operation.)

In early 1967 MAG-12 (VMAs -121, -211, -214, and -311) flew day and night in support of U.S., ARVN, and South Korean Army operations; every month seemed to set new records for total sorties and combat flight hours. Eventually, the idea of rotating personnel rather than entire squadrons, as previously mentioned, was instituted in 1968. VMA-311 remained at Chu Lai from mid-1967 to late 1969.

Problems with the CH-46

By mid-1967, the CH-46 was well on its way to becoming the standard Marine medium transport helicopter. There were ten squadrons equipped with the type and the improved Delta version was coming into use. (The UH-34s were to soldier on for another year, however.) The CH-46 was a welcome addition. But a series of fatal accidents began to overtake the Seaknight; some occurred in the U.S., others in Vietnam. A "CH-46 Reliability Review Conference" was convened on August 1, 1967, at the Vertol plant in Pennsylvania. Recommendations from the conference included modification to the airframe and operating systems, especially in the aft rotor assembly, which was the main suspect. A CH-46 repair facility was established at MCAF Futema on Okinawa. Eventually 325 CH-46s and Ds went through the extensive overhaul program, but the result was reinstatement of a valued member of the Marine assault team.

Naturally, the grounding of CH-46s after the accidents imposed additional burdens on the rest of the helicopter community, especially the trusty old UH-34s which had been scheduled for retirement. "HUSSs" were shipped from the States to fill some of the gap, and ten CH-53s were sent in from California. Even Army Hueys were tasked with helping the Marines until the CH-46 problems were resolved.

It was during the heavy combat of 1967 that the action for which the only Medal of Honor to be awarded a Marine aviator in Vietnam occurred. On August 19, Captain Stephen W. Pless, a UH-1 pilot with VMO-6, responded to a rescue call. Four Marines were pinned down by forty to fifty VC on a nearby beach. Arriving at the scene, Pless made repeated strafing runs with rockets and machine guns before landing to pick up the Marines on the ground. After the four men had scrambled aboard his damaged Huey—Pless had sustained shrapnel hits from debris of his ordnance, so low had he flown—the intrepid pilot tried to take off. Pless attempted liftoff four times before his overloaded helicopter remained in the air, all the while under heavy Communist fire. He made it on the fourth try and brought his helicopter and men home.

Captain Pless was presented with his Medal of Honor in 1969 at ceremonies in the White House. (His two crewmen and co-pilot were awarded the Navy Cross.) At the time, he was serving as the military officer for the Navy Aviation Schools Command in Pensacola, Florida. The author remembers Pless as a compact, beribboned, tough major—he had been promoted after his exploit as the youngest major in the Corps—complete with swagger stick. He epitomized the tough, professional, no-nonsense aviator for the sweaty young hopefuls going through precommissioning training. Unfortunately, Pless was killed in a traffic accident shortly after receiving his award.

As the 1967 holiday season approached, the customary truces and standdowns were initiated. It was hoped that the Communists would honor this American idealism, but this hope was dashed as reconnaissance missions showed violation after violation of the Christmas truce. For the men of the reconnaissance squadrons ashore and aboard the carriers in the South China Sea, there was no holiday that year;

Christmas 1967 came and went with barely a notice from the hard-working photo interpreters. The trails were clogged with men and supplies all heading south. The biggest, bloodiest, and most costly period of the war was about to erupt.

Realizing they could not win a military victory, the North Vietnamese, led by General Vo Nguyen Giap, victor of Dienbienphu in 1954 which forced the French out of Indochina, had planned a major military and psychological offensive against the towns and hamlets of South Vietnam in an effort to convince the South to join in the war and throw the Americans and their Saigon allies out. It was a desperate but well-planned gamble.

Tet and Khe Sanh

Chronologically, the offensive began with a series of probes against the outpost at Khe Sanh in the extreme northwestern corner of South Vietnam in January. After the loss of the A Shau Valley in 1966, Khe Sanh had taken on major importance, and the Americans were constantly on the alert against a Communist attempt to overrun the base. The 26th Marines were about to fight for their lives over a period of seventy-seven days, while all the assets of American air power in Southeast Asia were brought into play.

Along with the battle for Khe Sanh, the Communists also launched a series of devastating attacks to coincide with the Lunar New Year—Tet—which began on January 27, 1968. Throughout the holiday truce, there were repeated violations and rocket attacks against the major U.S. air facilities at Da Nang, Marble Mountain, and Chu Lai. The real hell spot, however, for the men on the ground, was the old Imperial Vietnamese capital of Hue, near Phu Bai. It was here that the VC conducted some of the most intensive and bloody battles of the entire war. The walled inner city became a killing ground for both Communists and Americans. At least eight battalions of North Vietnamese Army troops, along with VC sympathizers, were arrayed against three undermanned U.S. Marine battalions. Over 5,000 NVA were killed in house-to-house fighting; 142 Marines died in action. But the Communists were eventually repelled, as they were all over South Vietnam, their gamble lost.

While the Tet Offensive was mainly ground combat, the battle for Khe Sanh, essentially a confrontation between ground forces, involved major elements of air support. On the ground, Khe Sanh was largely a Marine operation. However, although Marine air power was utilized to the utmost during the seige, so were air assets of the Navy and Air Force.

Khe Sanh had always been an objective for Communist forces, for it represented a major military and political roadblock to victory in the South. As long as Khe Sanh remained in American and South Vietnamese hands, it would hinder movements into South Vietnam from Laos. Marines repelled a three-week siege in April and May of 1967, but the stakes were increased considerably when the second, and final, battle for Khe Sanh began in late January 1968. The intensity and frequency of NVA attacks made it obvious that air power was needed, fast and constantly.

Supplies were the first concern. The isolated base would not last for long without massive airlift support. VMGR-152 and the helicopter groups, MAG-16 and MAG-36, were the Marine units first used in the multi-service operation to keep Khe Sanh operating. Problems were compounded by the horrible weather, for the battle had begun at the height of the infamous monsoon season. More often than not, aircraft flew into Khe Sanh on instruments, the clouds and surrounding mountains making approaches and takeoffs tests of piloting skills, to say nothing of the intense ground fire from the NVA gunners nearby. The C-130s were especially vulnerable as they flew down the ground control approach (GCA) path to the airstrip and several aircraft were hit by Communist gunfire.

On February 10, Chief Warrant Officer Henry Wildfang was approaching Khe Sanh in his C-130, loaded with bladders of fuel, when his Hercules was hit and began to burn. His 15,000 flight hours gave Wildfang, one of the last NAPs on operational duty, the experience to bring in his blazing transport. As the plane slid along the runway, crash crews raced to cover it with foam. Wildfang and his co-pilot were able to escape, but several others inside the heavily loaded C-130 were killed. Wildfang was awarded his *fifth* DFC.

Because of this and other damage to C-130s, landings at Khe Sanh for the big four-engined turboprops were suspended until a way could be found to decrease the danger to the transports. A partial solution came in the form of an Air Force procedure—the Low Altitude Parachute Extraction System (LAPES). Approaching from the east, which would put the aircraft nearer the loading area of the camp, the Hercules pilot would open his tail ramp doors and as he neared the planned touchdown point, an electrically operated parachute would be deployed, pulling the pallet-mounted cargo out. The C-130 never actually landed and thereby kept to a minimum its exposure to gunfire. Another method was to simply air-drop by parachute, which called for close coordination between the men on the ground and the transport crews. There was the danger of the supplies being damaged or scattered by a hard landing. The helicopters were also fully utilized during the Khe Sanh airlift. Helo crews flew day and night on medevac and supply missions, continuously exposing themselves to enemy fire.

VMO-6 helicopter crews were in the thick of the fighting. February saw several aircraft hit, some seriously, as they flew low-level escort and medevac missions. But resupply of the Marine outposts around the main base was critical, if Khe Sanh was to remain in American hands. The crews of the UH-34s, CH-46s, and CH-53s, escorted by Huey gunships, were in a class by themselves. But a more effective escort was needed. The operation known as the Super Gaggle was developed. A-4s were pressed into service from MAG-12 at Chu Lai.

The first Super Gaggle went off on February 24, 1968, and involved twelve A-4s, twelve to sixteen CH-46s, four UE-1E gunships, and one TA-4F for coordination. The TA-4F would scout the area for weather information. If the ceiling was sufficiently high, the two-seater would call in the A-4s and, simultaneously, the CH-46s would launch from their bases. The slower speed of the helicopters would allow enough time for the Skyhawks to sanitize the immediate area with everything from napalm to tear gas and 20-mm cannonfire.

As the helicopter transports descended to the landing zone, they would be followed by the gunships who would scoop up crews that were shot down at this point. Of course, the Super Gaggle depended on timing, weather, skill, and luck, but the operations were more successful, more so than before its introduction. Everything, water, ice cream, soda pop, and mail, as well as the necessary war supplies, was flown in in an effort to support the Khe Sanh defenders.

Lieutenant Colonel David L. Althoff was the executive officer of HMM-262 during that Seaknight-equipped unit's activities in the Khe Sanh airlift. In a later account of the helicopter operations at Khe Sanh, he described Super Gaggle mission-planning as follows:

Each night we'd pick the hill we were going into the next morning and brief the fixed-wing people. We planned all the takeoff times so that when the fixed-wings arrived from Chu Lai, the Huey slicks would be there to control them. Meanwhile, we'd have launched the twelve CH-46s from Quang Tri, gone into Dong Ha, picked up our external loads and be heading for the objective.[38]

Questioned about the weather and the high rate of instrument flying, Lieutenant Colonel Althoff gave a good picture of the conditions:

Normally during that time of the year the weather would be socked in at Dong Ha, and then clear, or at least broken, at Khe Sanh. So we had to climb out IFR . . . with our . . . loads.

We'd line up at Dong Ha, pick up our loads one at a time, and take off into the soup. We'd break out at six or seven thousand feet, regroup and fly on up to Khe Sanh.[39]

He also detailed how GCA approaches were tailored for the environment at Khe Sanh:

You had to stay above the glide slope. I remember four different nights I got in there with the weather below GCA minimums. People would come up to Quang

Tri, where my squadron was based, and drop off supplies that were needed urgently at Khe Sanh . . . . we'd just have to go.

I'd get to where Khe Sanh had me on radar and I'd ask the controller there to bring me down paralleling the glide slope, about 700 feet above it. The North Vietnamese would hear me coming and open fire, but it would mostly go below me.

I'd have the controller tell me when I was over the threshold of the runway. He'd lose me on radar at this point, so then it was up to me. I'd slow down to about 20 knots and start a very slow descent to the runway. I watched my radar altimeter, and when I got to 100 feet if I wasn't visual then, I'd just take it around . . . . The CH-46 is a real stable instrument ship and she handles very nicely under these conditions.[40]

Even though the American camp at Khe Sanh would be dismantled in June, action around the area in northern Quang Tri Province remained high throughout the summer months. Former Shufly pilot, H.C. Brown, now a major, had arrived at Khe Sanh in early May with HMM-262, the same outfit with which Lieutenant Colonel Althoff served as the executive officer. Brown flew several resupply missions during the final stages of the siege and his CH-46D was hit on several occasions.

During a mission in August, Brown was called upon to insert a Marine ground reconnaissance team near the Laotian border. After dropping the team, Brown stood off in his helicopter waiting for the routine message that everything was all right and the team was proceeding. He waited anxiously, as the minutes went by with no sight or sound from the men he had just deposited in extremely hostile territory. An hour went by and still nothing. By this time, the two Huey gunship escorts were running low on fuel; so was Brown. He dispatched the gunships back to an outpost with a refueling capability and when they returned, he himself left to refuel. Upon return, he found the team had immediately run into heavy enemy action and could not call for fear of being heard, so close were they to the VC.

During the same month, Major Brown participated in a major effort to insert a battalion of Marines near Con Thien and the DMZ. So important was the operation that the pre-insertion landing-zone sanitizing was conducted by Air Force B-52s! As Brown and his squadronmates waited at Quang Tri, they could see the big bombers off to the north pounding the area. It was a strange feeling knowing that they would soon be headed directly for that area. In company with aircraft from HMM-161, Brown led a flight of four CH-46s, using an old church as a landmark over which the helicopters would turn and head directly north toward the LZ.

The HMM-161 flight turned over the church and was immediately caught in heavy groundfire, two of the Seaknights being so badly damaged as to be out of action. The leader of the flight, who was also the commanding officer of HMM-161, passed the lead of the entire operation to Brown, who found himself in charge of some twenty-five aircraft. The battalion was dropped off, to be picked up that afternoon.

The afternoon pickup proved to be just as interesting as the morning's mission. (Brown did not fly that afternoon.) The flight leader of the afternoon pickup was hit by a radio-controlled mine and had to land. His wingman was hit by a similar weapon and nearly blown apart. The two pilots escaped miraculously; but the crew chief was killed. The helicopter aircraft commander (HAC), Major Harvey Britt, and his co-pilot immediately joined the Marines on the ground, awaiting rescue.

After spending some time thinking about their predicament, Britt looked at the first downed chopper, which had landed intact and was covered with dirt from the mine explosion. Acting on a hunch, Britt collected the surviving members of his squadron, and together the Marines cleaned off the CH-46, climbed in, started the engines, and to everyone's surprise, took off. (Britt had gained something of a reputation for being an extremely capable and daring pilot, and was given the moniker "Blades" because he always seemed to bring his aircraft back from dangerous escapades with the rotors damaged and in need of repair.) The battalion could not be airlifted out of its position, and it remained for them to literally walk out from Con Thien.

Operation Niagara

The aerial defense of Khe Sanh was given the code name Operation Niagara, and it was a veritable deluge of support. Not only the 1st MAW aircraft, but all the other air services, including mammoth B-52s, were called in. Generally, close air support, B-52 Arc Light strikes, and radar-directed bombing were the three types of missions flown during the operation.

Tactical aircraft from the Navy's Task Force 77 or 1st MAW were available around the clock and were usually under a tactical air controller (airborne) TAC(A). Although sometimes the TAC(A)s were flying TA-4Fs, the versatile little Cessna Birddog, a single-engine, tandem-seated, conventionally geared airplane, which had been around since 1950 and had seen action from Korea onwards, was the usual mount of the TAC(A)s. Marine O-1C pilots, according to one source, controlled nearly 95 percent of air strikes around Khe Sanh. The Birddog carried three radios, two FM for communication with ground units and a UHF set for communicating with aircraft. Birddogs controlled strikes day and night, from Chu Lai to inside North Vietnam.

There was never a problem getting air power for Khe Sanh. Indeed, the problem was just the opposite. The controllers had their hands full with literally stacks of aircraft from all the services orbiting—sometimes up to

35,000 feet—waiting the call to come down and drop their ordnance. (Pre-1967 photos show the area around Khe Sanh to be dense foliage, a jungle. But by late 1968, the terrain had taken on the appearance of a Martian landscape, the thick carpet of trees killed by defoliants and the bare red clay pockmarked with bomb and shell craters.

A-4s of VMA-311 and F-4s of VMFA-323 were especially active during the actual siege. Lieutenant Colonel Harry T. Hagaman, commanding officer of VMFA-323, and his radar intercept officer, Captain Dennis F. Brandon, had a close call in late January when their Phantom was mortally hit by enemy fire. Brandon, with over 300 combat missions, knew the sound of a fatal hit and did not wait; he ejected immediately. Lieutenant Colonel Hagaman stayed a while longer, fighting to maintain control of the F-4, but finally he too punched out, as the stricken aircraft began to roll and tumble a scant 100 feet above the ground. The two Marines aviators sustained minor back injuries from their ejections, but were eventually rescued by helicopters. Captain Brandon went on to amass 400 missions, the first RIO to do so.

The TPQ-10 radar system really showed its value during the battle for Khe Sanh. The weather was rarely even fair, and the TPQ-equipped aircraft, such as the A-6s, were invaluable. Their heavy loads could be released from ground-control positions without their crews ever seeing the actual target. A-6s and F-4s were used to complement the B-52 Arc Light missions and, as a result, the enemy took a tremendous pounding almost daily from the massive air strikes.

By April, successful ground sweeps had all but driven the NVA from the main area, and Khe Sanh was officially declared secured, although mopping-up operations continued for the next two months. Outside of the strategic-bombing strikes of Rolling Thunder, the aerial umbrella over Khe Sanh had been the largest and most successful air operation of the war. General Westmoreland said that over 300 sorties were flown daily—one every five minutes—and some 35,000 tons of ordnance expended during the 77-day period of January 22-March 31, 1968. Air Force General Momyer later wrote:

Khe Sanh was probably the turning point in the enemy's strategy for Tet. If Khe Sanh had fallen, the regular NVA forces would have moved against the major cities that were initially assaulted by VC local forces. The fact that there were no significant actions by regular forces indicated the enemy backed away from a combined military-political offensive . . . .[41]

VMO-6 acquired its first fixed-wing aircraft sometime in July 1968, the Cessna O-1C Birddog. The pilots who flew the O-1 were TAC(A)s. O-1s had been very active during the Tet offensive of January 1968 and had controlled air strikes throughout South Vietnam and just above the DMZ into North Vietnam, day and night.

The O-1 detachments used the radio call sign "Fingerprint" and served until 1969 when the Birddog was retired from first-line service. The O-1C carried two FM and one UHF radios, acting as an airborne link between air and ground forces. They also conducted low-level reconnaissance missions with hand-held cameras. (Sometimes, the O-1s, on a seemingly quiet recce mission, would spook Communist troops in an "abandoned" bunker into firing on the aircraft, thereby revealing their position. The O-1 would then spend the rest of its time directing air strikes against the enemy.)

Single Management Arrives

March 10, 1968, saw the controversial control doctrine known as "single management" put into practice, the Seventh Air Force obtaining complete control of air assets and operations in Vietnam. One of the more practical aspects of the Khe Sanh fighting was the realization that this method of controlling tactical air power could work. The Marines had fought long and hard against its implementation, but control of 1st MAW's fixed-wing assets, as integrated into the massive effort of Operation Niagara, was imperative. Basically, the Marines were directed to convey to the Seventh Air Force their daily capabilities, as opposed to the previous method of detailing their own needs first, and then allowing any additional aircraft to be tasked by the Air Force. The Air Force, apparently in an attempt to smooth ruffled feathers, did its best to take care of Marine requirements, especially those of helicopter escort and landing-zone preparation. The system took a little getting used to, mainly from the Marines' point of view; but both sides tried to make it work and, as seen at Khe Sanh, generally succeeded.

OV-10As Become Operational

On July 6, 1968, a new aircraft arrived at Da Nang with VMO-2. After a lengthy development period, the LARA (light-armed reconnaissance aircraft) of 1962 arrived in Southeast Asia. Looking something like a World War II fighter with its twin propellers and twin tailbooms, the North American OV-10A Bronco was the result of a call for a lightly armed aircraft capable of operating in the counterinsurgency (COIN) role. The Navy, Marines, and Air Force were all subscribers and the first aircraft flew in 1966. (The Navy's VAL-4 "Black Ponies" operated the type for a while in 1971 as the last Navy fixed-wing squadron in South Vietnam. The Air Force probably utilized the Bronco more than did the other two services.) The Marines, however, employed the Bronco as a helicopter escort, a TAC(A) vehicle, and general reconnaissance aircraft. VMO-6 took delivery of the plane in the summer of 1968 while attached to the Provisional MAG-39, based at Quang Tri, home of many of the helicopter squadrons which took part in the Khe Sanh airlift. (Quang Tri was a veritable beach, though far inland from any coastal area. The base was built upon gritty white sand which caused constant maintenance headaches, as well as permeating everything from clothing and bedding to food. MAG-39 had been the command and control element of MAG-36's Det Alpha until it was redesignated on April 15. VMO-6 had been attached to MAG-39 at the same time.)

Having the ability to loiter on station with a variety of weapons, the Bronco was a welcome addition to the ground war waged by the hard-pressed helicopter crews. Four M-60 machine guns were fixed armament, and the high-tailed aircraft could also carry Zuni air-to-ground rockets, as well as Sidewinder air to air missiles, although the latter were rarely used. The Bronco, although it had a high degree of maneuverability, was not at its best in a high-threat area with large-caliber flak guns, or even the possibility of interception by enemy MiGs. As an air-to-ground weapon, the Bronco could carry additional guns and rocket pods in a variety of combinations.

The Bombing Halt

For the U.S. government, 1968 was a difficult year. Civil unrest at home, spurred on by the seemingly endless involvement in Vietnam, constricted the President's abilities to decide and act. Indeed, the pressure on Lyndon Johnson was so great that he decided in the spring not to seek reelection in November. It was a stunning disclosure, and set would-be candidates scurrying to make up for lost time. Johnson had been under constant advice from his Cabinet and some of his senior military strategists to disengage all U.S. forces from combat, bring the men home, and come to some sort of terms with the North Vietnamese.

It was a hard and bitter pill to swallow. Militarily, American strength could not be disputed; but a peaceful end to the war in favor of South Vietnam was impossible. Some sort of inducement had to be offered to the Communists. Therefore, on October 31, Johnson announced a unilateral bombing halt, effective the next day, November 1. All strike activity north of the DMZ would cease, except in the case of retaliatory measures against enemy violations, and unarmed reconnaissance flights. The North Vietnamese responded on November 3 by saying they would go to Paris to talk peace. Like most of the Communist diplomatic activities throughout the war, these peace talks would turn out to be a series of ploys to gain time.

With the bombing halt, the first phase of the Marines' involvement in Vietnam came to an end. From the first, tentative Shufly operations to the initial buildup in 1965, Marine aviation in Southeast Asia had by 1968 become a compact and powerful force. The Marine close air support doctrine, the *raison d'etre* of Marine air, had been restated and restructured, but was still an important aspect of combat operations in Southeast Asia.

New aircraft such as the A-6/EA-6A, the OV-10A, CH-46, and CH-53 had shown themselves to be valuable members of the Marine team. The older veterans, like the F-8, UH-34, and CH-37, were passing from the scene, but left a no less brilliant record. Of course, the two workhorses of the conflict had been the A-4 and F-4. These sturdy, yet flexible, aircraft met each and every task, got their crews home again despite devastating battle damage, and had plenty of room left for development for future requirements. The two could be compared to the SBD Dauntless and F4U Corsair of World War II. They were a team that enabled thousands of flight crewmen to cut their teeth in combat and come home.

In 1968, 47,436 combat sorties were flown by fixed-wing aircraft, while helicopter sorties had doubled since the previous year, from 388,000 in 1967 to 639,194, reflecting greater support of the effort on the ground to seek out the enemy. Yet, for all the high numbers, the sorties, the tonnage, and the thousands of enemy soldiers killed, the war had realized very little. To be sure, some areas in the South had been pacified, the Communists thrust out (for the moment), but the rejection never lasted. For those military personnel in Vietnam, hamstrung by foolish political policies emanating from an ineffective government and vocal minority, the war was becoming an impossible situation. The North Vietnamese gleefully observed the travesty of the Democratic convention in Chicago during the summer of 1968, and knew that their policy of watching and waiting would ultimately bear fruit. The great military giant was being ripped apart from within; all the Communists had to do was wait. They were good at that.

12

The Communist Waiting
Game Pays Off

 In November 1968, the Republican Party, under the leadership of Richard M. Nixon, regained control of the White House. It was not an overwhelming victory; Hubert Humphrey and the Democrats gave a good fight. But at the center of the election was the war, and the country was tired of the war. Perhaps a change of administration would help. At any rate, Nixon was inaugurated in January 1969, and quickly set new directives into motion. A gradual phase-down and phase-out of U.S. military presence would begin by June. Troops and aircraft would begin to leave South Vietnam, and by the end of the year, many units had departed, leaving a rapidly decreasing nucleus of their comrades to continue advising the South Vietnamese. The intent was to give the war back to the South Vietnamese, who had been bolstered with huge amounts of aid and training so that they could carry on themselves with minimal U.S. assistance and presence.

For the 1st MAW, the new orders had some effect. There was still to be a considerable Marine air presence in Southeast Asia. But some of the units in-country would be redeployed to Japan, while the remainder would be consolidated. Provisional MAG-39 was deactivated, and MAG-36 departed, leaving MAG-16 in control of Marine helicopter assets in Vietnam. Most of the fixed-wing squadrons remained, MAGs

-11, -12, and -13 still playing a large role in the continuing combat operations.

Perhaps the single most important event in 1969 for Marine aviation was the arrival of the first Bell AH-1G Hueycobras, the first designed-for-the-purpose gunships to be placed in production. The UH-34 and UH-1E had been merely makeshift developments to fit the need for an armed helicopter. Successful as they had been, they were only stopgaps. What was needed was a real *attack* helicopter. By the mid-60s, several companies had been involved with a gunship but it was Bell's Model 209 which showed the most promise. With a two-man crew, and a slim, shark-like profile, the first AH-1Gs entered Army service in early 1967 and deployed to Vietnam in late August, flying their first combat missions on the 31st. Used in company with Army ground forces and helicopter units, the new Bell soon proved its worth. The Marines were very interested.

The Corps wanted some changes in the Cobras, especially an additional engine which was essential for overwater flights from LPHs. It would be two years, however, before the twin-engined AH-1J Seacobra would be in service. Therefore, thirty-eight AH-1Gs were sent to the Marines. Four of the Cobras joined VMO-2 at Marble Mountain Air Facility in April 1969. Used in concert with the OV-10, also a recent arrival, the Cobras served as escorts, and flew fire-support and armed reconnaissance missions. The new gunships were received with enthusiasm. Captain W.L. Buchanan, a highly decorated Huey pilot, stated:

The secret of helicopter escort is instantaneous fire suppression; not in 10 or 20 seconds, but *instantly*. The Emerson TAT-101, a movable gun turret, gives the Cobra this capability . . . it is undoubtedly the best helicopter escort aircraft on the market . . . .[42]

The OV-10, he wrote, was a worthy companion to the Cobra.

The OV-10A and AH-1G are not bombers. Their weapons systems were designed for two jobs; fire suppression and target marking. We have the best attack aircraft and close air support pilots in the world, and if we don't use them at every opportunity we are missing a bet . . . .[43]

A newer, more powerful model of the Sea Stallion arrived in 1969 with the introduction of the CH-53D, while the faithful old UH-34 was finally retired. The HUSS had been retired when the CH-46's problems had been rectified, but the plan was somewhat premature. Plans to give remaining UH-34s to the Reserve were rescinded when rising combat losses in 1967 necessitated the reinstatement of the UH-34 to full operational status. Every military facility was scavenged for UH-34s; only the training command was allowed to retain its helicopters.

Once operational experience with the CH-46 and CH-53 had been obtained, the UH-34 could finally retire gracefully. Oddly, and perhaps appropriately, the type's last combat flight was with HMM-362, the first Shufly squadron back in 1962. On August 18, 1969, in ceremonies at Phu Bai, a Huss's rotor blades were folded for the last time. (HMM-362 later left for the U.S. and reequipped with CH-53s as HMH-362.) By September, all UH-34s were gone from Vietnam. However, several "last" flights were claimed, but UH-34s flew in the U.S. until October 3, 1973, when the *really* last flight took place at MCAS New River. Another old timer which left the scene in 1969 was the EF-10B. "DRUT," "Willie the Whale," or Skyknight, the old jet aircraft retired from VMCJ-1 after four years of service in Vietnam.

Early Withdrawals

Throughout 1969, troops withdrawals had continued, and men and equipment remaining were consolidated. Ground combat was still going on, however, and the Marines were in the thick of the fighting. From January 22 to March 18, 1969, Operation Dewey Canyon covered the A Shau Valley in northwestern South Vietnam, scene of some of the war's bloodiest fighting. The 3rd and 9th Marines, complete with supporting artillery, were airlifted by helicopters from Quang Tri. Dewey Canyon was a real tribute to helicopter support. For two months, at the height of the monsoon, the Marines sought out and destroyed the Communist camps along the Laotian border, denying much-needed supplies and food to the NVA troops coming across. With the help of Marine helicopters, the mud-Marines hopscotched the area to attack enemy bases. Killed were 1,617 Communists and over 500 tons of food and supplies were confiscated.

VMO-6 was heavily involved in Operation Dewey Canyon. All three types of aircraft in the squadron—Hueys, Birddogs, and Broncos—saw heavy action throughout the operation. Hueys were used as escort for supply and medevac aircraft, while the two fixed-wing aircraft operated in the reconnaissance, artillery-spotting, and FAC(A) roles.

By the early part of 1970, many Marines had left Vietnam, rotating either to Japan or back to the U.S. The 1st MAW lost four squadrons—HMH-361, with its CH-53s; A-4-equipped VMA-223 and VMA-211; and VMFA-542, which took its F-4s back to El Toro. The wing now consisted of MAGs -11, -13, and -16. MAG-11 at Da Nang included VMCJ-1, VMA(AW)-225, and VMA(AW)-242, which had A-6As, along with VMO-2 with its OV-10As. MAG-13, based at Chu Lai, contained VMA-311, the faithful "Tomcats," and VMFAs -115, -122, and -314. The helo-equipped MAG-16, located at Marble Mountain, consisted of four medium helicopter squadrons with CH-46s, one

HMH with CH-53s, and two light squadrons, one with UH-1Es and the other with AH-1Gs. In all, 170 fixed-wing aircraft and 210 helicopters.

In July 1970, more departures saw VMCJ-1 leave for Japan, having flown 4,500 combat sorties since 1965, and VMA-311 leave Chu Lai for Da Nang to become part of MAG-11. HMM-161 took its aircraft back to the U.S., as did VMFA-122, VMFA-314, and VMA(AW)-242. Chu Lai was turned over to the U.S. Army. MAG-13 redeployed to El Toro, too. By September 1970, sixteen tactical squadrons had left Vietnam, and only two groups, MAG-11 and MAG-16, remained in-country. At the peak of Marine activity in 1968 and 1969, there had been twenty-six aircraft squadrons in Southeast Asia.

1971

In 1971 the South Vietnamese launched Lam Son 719, a massive incursion into Laos, ostensibly to attack VC staging areas. Ideally, the operation was meant to demonstrate the effectiveness of the ARVN forces acting on their own with little or no American aid. Marine ground forces were to provide security for various areas along the invasion route, and CH-53s of HMH-463 were to airlift equipment and troops.

Accordingly, on February 8, ARVN forces crossed into Laos. CH-53s, escorted by AH-1Gs, or the newly arrived twin-engine AH-1Js, airlifted heavy artillery pieces into position. The AH-1J Seacobra, four of which had arrived for HML-367, was a heavily armed gunship, the kind for which the Marines had begged for many years. The AH-1Js flew their first combat mission on March 2, escorting Sea Stallions.

VMA-311 was in action throughout Lam Son 719, flying hundreds of interdiction strikes against Communist trails and supply routes, hitting trucks and tanks. Air Force FACs in OV-10s controlled the strikes. Navy aircraft from the carriers were also involved.

Lam Son 719 was a costly operation for the South Vietnamese, although they inflicted heavy casualties on NVA forces. The Air Force estimated fully one-third of the helicopters involved were destroyed; Army numbers were somewhat less. Nevertheless the estimates do indicate the ferocity of the action. Thus, while Lam Son 719 did show some favorable results for the South Vietnamese, and Vietnamization, it was clear that the ARVN could not sustain itself on the battlefield without large amounts of American air power.

The might and breadth of the U.S. air umbrella was the one thing the VC and North Vietnamese feared and respected above all else. Its withdrawal in 1971, at a fairly critical stage of the war, allowed the Communists to finally contemplate massive invasion of the South and final victory. On May 26, 1971, the last Marine air combat unit, HML-167, redeployed to New River in the United States. All American squadrons had left Vietnam; the last Navy squadron, VAL-4, had taken its OV-10 Broncos out in April. MAG-11 departed on May 21, and MAG-16 left on June 1. Five hundred Marines were left in-country to provide transitional support for the Vietnamese. But the withdrawals were largely complete. President Nixon had made good on his promise to bring Americans out of combat. In doing so, he had left the South naked.

The 1972 Easter Invasion

As the American withdrawals were completed and the Communists sat at the Paris peace talks, they were plotting the invasion of South Vietnam, now divested of U.S. air power and support. On March 30, 1972, Good Friday, a massive mortar barrage signalled the beginning of the offensive. North Vietnamese Army troops flooded across the DMZ into Quang Tri Province supported by tanks and heavy artillery. Surface-to-air missiles followed the Communists into the south. Along with ground-launched SA-2 and SA-3 missiles, the NVA brought the shoulder-launched, highly mobile SA-7 heat-seeking missile, which played havoc with low- and slow-flying aircraft like transports and helicopters. The surprised ARVN forces were routed by the ferocious enemy assault. There was little to do but fall back to safer ground and wait for help.

U.S. air power in Southeast Asia had, of course, been greatly reduced during the withdrawals, until only Air Force units in Thailand and a pair of aircraft carriers patrolling up and down the coast were all that remained. The 1st MAW had been redeployed back to Japan and the U.S. As U.S. forces were once again hurriedly mobilized for the trip back into South Vietnamese combat, air units joined the flow of men and machines.

MAG-15, under Colonel Keith O'Keefe, was ordered to bring VMFA-115 and VMFA-232 back to Da Nang, while VMFA-212 flew in from Hawaii and joined the other squadrons. MAG-12, led by Colonel Dean C. Macho, took its A-4E squadrons, VMA-211 and VMA-311, to Bien Hoa air base, 15 miles northeast of Saigon. The Skyhawks arrived on May 17 from Japan, and by the 19th were ready for combat operations.

The aircraft of both groups flew sorties along the Cambodian and Laotian borders in an effort to interdict the flood of North Vietnamese supplies. VMCJ-1 and VMCJ-2 brought their EA-6As to Cubi Point in the Philippines, operating a combined detachment, rotating in and out of Da Nang as well as staging directly from their Philippine base with the in-flight refueling services of VMGR-152. Arriving in April, the composite squadrons flew ECM missions in support of Navy and Air Force strike groups. Orbiting offshore, the EA-6s of the six-to-seven-plane detachment put in a performance which was one of the minor miracles of this hectic period. From April to January 1973 they flew a sustained period of operations which earned the detachment a Navy meritorious unit commendation. Staging out of Cubi and Da Nang, the Intruders operated against enemy SAMs. April 13 saw the first loss of a crew and aircraft when Pigment 08—the aircraft call-sign—failed to return from an Alpha strike near Thanh Hoa in North Vietnam.

Part of the success of the EA-6As of the VMCJ-1/2 group was due to the fact that the Marine aircraft were the only platforms capable of jamming the new I-band frequency guidance radar of some of the North Vietnamese missiles. Another aspect was the tremendous maintenance and support effort which enabled as many as seven EA-6s to be airborne simultaneously on different missions.

One other unit of Marine aircraft which responded to the call for air power was VMA(AW)-224, one of three Marine squadrons aboard Navy aircraft carriers in the South China Sea. It had been seven years since Marines had flown into combat from carriers, but the A-6As of VMA(AW)-224 were aboard the *Coral Sea* (CVA-43) as part of Air Wing 15. In all, VMA(AW)-224 operated through six line periods on Yankee Station, the northern area of operations for carrier air power.

Arriving on line in early January 1972, CAW-15 flew strikes against major passes in Laos. The A-6As of VMA(AW)-224 also flew as pathfinders, leading other aircraft down through the low clouds to the targets, or alone at night against North Vietnamese trucks on the Ho Chi Minh Trail.

During the third line period in March, VMA(AW)-224 received three A-6Bs, variants equipped with the Air Force-developed AGM-78, Standard ARM (anti-radiation missile) for use against SAMs. The new mission was approached with some uncertainty, but eventually ninety-five A-6B sorties were flown, with over forty-seven Standard ARM missiles fired. A 39-percent success rate against the Fansong guidance radars of the SA-2 sites was obtained.

VMA(AW)-224 lost four Intruders in combat beginning in April when the squadron flew in support of Operation Linebacker, the initial major reaction to the North Vietnamese invasion. On May 9 the CAG, Commander Roger E. Sheets, led three A-6As and Navy A-7s on a mining mission into Haiphong Harbor, the main North Vietnamese port. The mining of the principal ports of North Vietnam had been a bone of contention for military planners for almost as long as the war itself. The prevailing military view was that to mine the ports would effectively close off the supply of the Communist effort in the south at its source. The timid Johnson administration had balked at what it considered such a drastic step. However, Richard Nixon was more daring and, by May,

(Text continues on page 279.)

A UH-34 lifts off from an LPH with a cargo net underneath, while a CH-37 is serviced. These two helicopters formed the backbone of the Marine Corps' pre-Vietnam assault capability. (Sikorsky Photo)

Da Nang flight line in 1963, looking north to Hi Vai Pass. Clouds were typical weather. (H.C. Brown)

An outpost, manned by U.S. advisors, thirty-five miles from Da Nang. Outposts were usually placed on high ground overlooking civilian areas. (H.C. Brown)

UH-34Ds of HMM-261 on a mission, twenty miles south of Da Nang in October 1963. Marine helicopters were used as transports for the troops of the South Vietnamese Army. (H.C. Brown)

Then-First Lieutenant Brown watches a servicing operation from the cockpit of his UH-34. Note his camouflaged fatigues and flak jacket. The aircraft is equipped with a winch immediately above the cabin door, and an M-60 machine gun. (H.C. Brown)

An EF-10B of VMCJ-1 sits in the rain at Da Nang. Vietnam was the Skyknight's swan song, and the big old jet served for four years as a radar-jammer against North Vietnamese missile defenses.

An A-4E of VMA-311 makes the first official takeoff from the SATS field at Chu Lai in 1966.

World War II ace Marion Carl led the brigade landing at Da Nang in 1965, He eventually rose to major general, capping a long, colorful career in Marine aviation.

Some of the first Phantoms to arrive in Vietnam land at Da Nang in April 1965. VMFA-531 F-4Bs taxi in, dragging their breaking chutes behind them. The buildup was rapid and massive during 1965, apparently catching the Communists off guard.

An HU-1E "Huey" gunship from Marine Squadron 6 escorts a UH-34D medical evacuation helicopter.

In October 1965, the only aircraft capable of retrieving downed or disabled aircraft was the elderly CH-37 Mojave. Here a MAG-16 "Deuce" hauls the fuselage of a UH-34D hit by ground fire and forced to land.

252

In April 1965, Marine helicopter squadrons were sent to the Dominican Republic to evacuate American citizens during an Army coup. Here, while Marines man machine guns to protect the landing field, UH-34s bring equipment in to support the evacuation.

A TF-9J takes off from Da Nang. The aircraft carries rocket cannisters, and a tiger shark marking on the nose. Cougars served for approximately one year as roving forward air controllers and reconnaissance aircraft before being replaced by the OV-10 and TA-4F.

An A-4E of VMA-223 launches for a mission using JATO in September 1966. Skyhawks flew a phenomenal number of support missions, especially at this time of the war.

A TA-4F taxis past other aircraft at Da Nang, including an A-4 of VMA-311, an F-8E of VMF(AW)-235, and an F-4B.

A TA-4F of H&MS-11 at Da Nang in 1969. Aircraft is marked as belonging to the commanding general of the 1st MAW, and carries the colorful fuselage stripe denoting the plane's status. Note the small Playboy Bunny symbol on the tail. The squadron's callsign was, appropriately, "Playboy." The aircraft would frequently carry underwing ordnance to hunt for VC troops. (Dave Seder)

254

VMF(AW)-232 replaced VMF(AW)-235 in November 1966, and took the departing squadron's Crusaders. Red Devil Crusaders are here shown at Da Nang in April 1967, just before mission takeoff. The aircraft in foreground, number 11, carries a full wingload of 250-pound bombs, while aircraft number 5 appears to tote only a single bomb beneath each wing.

A VMA(AW)-242 A-6A Intruder is loaded with 250-pound bombs in August 1967 in preparation for a night-bombing mission from Da Nang. Big and ugly, the Intruder made it possible
for the Marines to deliver bombs in almost any type of weather.

An F-8E of VMF(AW)-235 begins a mission from Da Nang in April 1966. The aircraft is armed with Zuni rockets on fuselage launchers. The squadron trim on the nose and tail is red with white stars.

A Marine lieutenant, second from left, shows off his T-38 at Laredo Air Force Base in late 1968. The Air Force was helping to train Marine aviators in order to relieve the Corps' shortage. (Peter B. Mersky)

F-4Bs of VMFA-115, the Silver Eagles, get some attention before a mission. The pilot, on the right, has begun his preflight walk-around. The aircraft has a full load of bombs and two underwing fuel tanks. (Richard Henry)

Assigned to VMCJ-1, this EA-6A takes off from Da Nang in 1970 for an ECM mission. The aircraft carries extra fuel tanks and jamming pods beneath the wings.

A Sea Stallion of HMH-463 prepares to lift a downed CH-46. No other helicopter could manage the loads of the CH-53A, which gave the Marines their first truly reliable heavy-lift helicopter.

A CH-46A deposits Marines in a rice paddy during a search operation in February 1967. The Sea Knight's arrival in March 1966 greatly enhanced helicopter capability, but the aircraft was vulnerable to maintenance problems and ever-present dust.

A Medal of Honor crew. Then-Captain Stephen W. Pless, far right, earned the Medal of Honor during a 1967 mission in which he and his crew plucked ground troops from a Communist ambush. Pless' co-pilot and two crewmen received the Navy Cross.

Seaknights on their way to Khe Sanh in March 1968 at the height of the siege. Carrying a 3,000-pound load of ammunition on a cargo hook, these aircraft are from HMM-364 based at Phu Bai.

A-6A Intruders of VMA(AW)-533 head home after a mission in South Vietnam, December 1967.

A Marine C-130 at Chu Lai in late 1968. Hercules from Navy, Marine, and Air Force squadrons made a great effort to resupply the desperate base at Khe Sanh but were withdrawn for a time due to highly dangerous ground fire.

A Cessna O-1C Birddog of VMO-6 flies low over a Marine company in February 1967. Aircraft scouted ahead for enemy activity, ready to call in air support. Note triple rocket-launchers, one under each wing. O-1Cs carried six smoke rockets to mark targets for air strikes.

An OV-10A lifts off from Marble Mountain, near Da Nang, loaded with rocket canisters on fuselage sponsons. OV-10s were flown by Navy, Marine, and Air Force squadrons.

Marine UH-1Es touch down at a fire support base during Operation Dewey Canyon in early 1969. Dewey Canyon was one of the most successful Marine endeavors of the war and became a showcase for helicopter support.

An HMM-262 CH-46A. Helicopters were hard to maintain in the dusty, wet atmosphere of northern South Vietnam, and thus looked tired and dirty even when they were operational. Note the squadron tiger on the tail. HMM-262 was based at Quang Tri in early 1968. (H.C. Brown)

Two Bell AH-1G Hueycobras, possibly of VMO-2, newly arrived in Vietnam in 1969. Their slim profile and chin-mounted turret are evident in this view.

Twin-engined AH-1Js were specifically designed for the Marines, who wanted the safety of an additional engine for overwater operation. AH-1Js arrived in Vietnam in early 1971, and were immediately put into operation during Lam Son 719, the South Vietnamese incursion into Laos.

A North Vietnamese MiG-17 takes off on an intercept mission. MiG-17s were highly maneuverable, especially against the ponderous Phantom, and carried three fuselage-mounted cannon in addition to air-to-air missiles.

Intruders of VMA(AW)-224 just before their deployment in the *Coral Sea* in early 1972. Marines flew as part of Air Wing 15, losing four aircraft in combat.

During a 1972 mission from Nam Phong, a Silver Eagle Phantom delivers its bombs through the clouds, probably on signal from Air Force F-4s which frequently accompanied Marine aircraft. Air Force planes carried Loran radar and could tell the Marines when to release their loads. Note the open chaff-dispenser door above the word "MARINES." (Joe Rice)

264

Major General Keith B. McCutcheon, right, is presented the Distinguished Service Medal by Marine Corps Commandant General Wallace M. Greene, Jr., on October 6, 1966. McCutcheon, then serving as Deputy Chief of Staff (Air) at Headquarters Marine Corps, was a strong force behind Marine aviation developments right up to his death from cancer in 1971. He was the first Marine Corps aviator to attain four-star rank while on active duty.

As South Vietnamese refugees huddle in the foreground, Marine CH-46s of HMM-164 depart on a mission in June 1972.

VMA-311 A-4Es at Da Nang in June 1972 as part of MAG-15. Having left Vietnam only a year before, the Tomcats were back in response to the North Vietnamese invasion, flying from Da Nang and then Bien Hoa.

Two VMA-321 pilots chat before a squadron Skyraider. Note the combined Navy/Marine marking on the rear fuselage. Photo was taken at NAS Anacostia.

Grumman F8F Bearcats of VMF-321 fly over the Jefferson Memorial and the Tidal Basin in Washington, D.C. in 1949. Fast and highly maneuverable, the stubby little Bearcats, the last Grumman prop fighters, were turned over to the French for use in Indochina.

VMA-321 pilots stand in front of a squadron FJ Fury. They display their flight suits and personal survival gear, as well as squadron baseball caps.

Corsairs replaced Bearcats. VMF-321 was based at NAS Anacostia, just south of Washington. This F4U-4 carries the orange Reserve band.

VMFA-321 F-4s went through several color schemes. This 1979 photo of two F-4Ns (the N was an uprated B) shows vestiges of the 1976 markings, a blue vertical tail, white stars and lettering, and a red pitchfork. The squadron had returned to its earlier "Hell's Angels" nickname.

Several T-33s operated with the squadron for currency work, as well as providing a limited adversary capability against Marine fighters. Here, an RF-8G of Navy squadron VFP-206, a reserve reconnaissance unit, flies alongside a VMFA-321 T-33.

An A-4F of VMA-142, based at NAS Jacksonville, Florida, drops a Snakeeye bomb on a range in the southwestern U.S. The bomb's fins are opening to retard its fall, stabilize it, and allow the Skyhawk to clear the blast area. The Flying Gators are one of six VMA squadrons in the Marine Reserves. (Harry Gann)

Sikorsky CH-53A Sea Stallions of HMH-772, NAS Willow Grove, Pennsylvania, participate in an exercise involving Reserve units aboard the *Iwo Jima* (LPH-2).

VMF-321 progressed to F-8K Crusaders, after sharing F-8Bs with the Navy Air Reserves at NAF Washington. The F-8Ks were given black trim with white stars, and the squadron called itself the "Black Barons," abandoning the original "Hell's Angels" sobriquet for a time. Note the extended in-flight refueling probe above the national marking.

A Bell AH-1G of HMA-773, NAS Atlanta, Georgia, in the field with Marine armored units. The squadron is the only light attack helicopter unit in the 4th MAW.

A-4Ms of VMA-331 release a string of Snakeeye bombs during weapons practice. Note that the bombs fall away from the aircraft, and then their fins open to stabilize the bomb and allow the aircraft to escape the blast area. (Harry Gann)

The AH-1T variant of the Seacobra carries a variety of ordnance, from air-to-air missiles to anti-tank weapons. (Bell Photo)

A full-scale development (FSD) AV-8B carries a full load of sixteen Mk. 82 500-pound bombs, demonstrating the considerable lifting ability of the Harrier II. (McDonnell Douglas)

A two-place TAV-8A of VMAT-203 takes off using a ski-jump. This arrangement allows an increase in takeoff weight—meaning more ordnance carried—and was used in combat during the 1982 Falklands War between Britain and Argentina. (Harry Gann)

The OA-4M might be the last version of the Skyhawk to see Marine service. Developed from the TA-4F, this variant carries a laser spot tracker below the nose, and will be used as an FAC aircraft. (Harry Gann)

A brand-new CH-53E flies over the water during test flights. The aircraft's seven-bladed main rotor is evident. The Super Stallion is powered by three engines. (Sikorsky Photo)

Bell UH-1N was a twin-engined development of the earlier UH-1E, which had one powerplant. Here a UH-1N flies off Okinawa, Japan in 1980. (Fred Lash)

The Marines are responsible for maintaining the helicopters of the presidential flight. Here, a VH-3A Seaking flies past the Washington Monument. When the president is aboard one of these helicopters, the aircraft's call sign is Marine One; a fixed-wing aircraft is called Air Force One when carrying the chief executive.

An OV-10D aboard the *Okinawa* (LPH-3). OV-10D carries nighttime sensors and a 20-mm gun turret.

274

A Seaknight of HMT-301, the CH-46F-equipped training squadron, participates in exercises aboard an LPH. Seaknights will serve through the 1990s with various modifications in avionics and such physical updates as fiberglass rotor blades.

The Douglas C-117, a super C-47/R4D, flew with the Marines in Japan until the last three were retired in June 1982. Note the squared tail of the C-117. (Hadeki Nagakubo)

Several North American T-39 Saberliners serve as fast VIP transports. (Hideki Nagakubo)

276

The McDonnell Douglas C-9B serves the Marines as a long-range transport.

An EA-6B Prowler of VMAQ-2 flies off the Libyan coast in April 1986. These ECM aircraft provided coverage for the Navy and Air Force strikes against Libyan targets in March and April. (Dave Parsons)

Marines supply the transport for the Navy's Blue Angels flight demonstration squadron. Their KC-130F follows the team's A-4Fs, transporting ground crews and maintenance equipment. (Peter B. Mersky)

Two types of Phantoms: the F-4N (left) serving with VMFA-323, and the RF-4B of VMFP-3. (Harry Gann)

Subject of much controversy, the McDonnell Douglas F-18A Hornet was developed from the Northrop-designed YF-17A. Here is an F-18A of VMFA-314, the first Marine squadron to transition to the Hornet. The aircraft is in the low-visibility paint scheme instituted Navy-wide. (McDonnell Douglas)

The twin-engined layout of the Hornet is shown to advantage in this view. Sidewinder air-to-air missiles can be carried on the wing-tip stations. (McDonnell Douglas)

Haiphong, Cam Pha, Hon Gai, Thanh Hoa, and Vinh had been sealed up.

VMA(AW)-224 continued its combat tour, losing a third aircraft on May 29, the Navy pilot and Marine bombardier/navigator ejecting into the Gulf of Tonkin, where they were rescued by a SAR helicopter. The *Coral Sea* left the line in late June after its sixth period, taking the Marines of VMA(AW)-224 back to the U.S.

A Marine Crew Scores a Kill

The chances for Marine aerial victories in Southeast Asia were next to nothing. As has been shown in the preceding pages, nearly all the assets of the 1st MAW were committed to close air support or peripheral support of larger strike groups (as in the case of the EF-10s and EA-6s of VMCJ-1 and VMCJ-2). Although most Marine aviators would have gladly paid large sums of money for a shot at a MiG, the Marines scored only three times against enemy aircraft in Vietnam. Two of these kills occurred while the Marine pilots were on exchange duty with the Air Force.

The first action took place on December 17, 1967, when Captain Doyle D. Baker shot down a MiG-17 with 20-mm cannonfire and finally a Falcon air-to-air missile. Flying an F-4D of the 13th Tactical Fighter Squadron from Udorn, Thailand, Baker was on his thirtieth mission over the North escorting F-105 fighter-bombers.

The second Marine aerial victory did not occur until August 12, 1972, when Captain Larry Richard, flying with Navy Lieutenant Commander Mike Ettel, in an F-4E of the 58th Tactical Fighter Squadron, claimed a MiG-21. Richard got a GCI call on two MiG-21s. The enemy aircraft soon came into view, and as Richard blew off his underwing fuel tanks, a slow-turning dogfight developed with Richard shooting a Sparrow AIM-7 first at one MiG then at the other. The first North Vietnamese evaded the American missile, but the second MiG had its tail blown off.

VMFA-333—the Fighting Shamrocks, Trip Trey (the unit enjoyed several nicknames)—had been the first Marine F-4J-equipped unit to deploy as part of a carrier air wing. Basically an Atlantic Coast squadron, VMFA-333 nonetheless had become part of CVW-8 in the *America* (CVA-66) in January 1971, along with another East Coast squadron, Navy VF-74. The *America* arrived on Yankee Station in July 1972, and its air wing, including VMFA-333, immediately began flying group strikes, photo escort, and various CAP missions.

During the carrier's third line period in September, the opportunity for a MiG engagement arose. On September 11, two VMFA-333 F-4Js were on patrol near Phuc Yen. The lead aircraft, flown by the squadron executive officer, Major Lee Lasseter, and Captain John Cummings, the

RIO, got a radar call on two MiG-21s. Turning rapidly into the oncoming enemy aircraft, Lasseter shot a missile which quickly destroyed one of the MiGs. The second MiG retreated some distance away from the Marine flight. However, as the two Phantoms turned back towards their ship, the MiG made a run on Lasseter's wingmen, Captain A.S. Dudley, and his RIO, First Lieutenant J.W. Brady.

Lasseter fired off another Sidewinder which apparently damaged the MiG, although not downing it. The enemy plane turned away, and the two Phantoms again turned for home. Coasting out, the pair waded through some heavy flak. Lasseter's aircraft was hit by a SAM; Dudley's F-4 had been damaged by flak and was in probable danger of running out of fuel. Both crews ejected south of Haiphong, were picked up by a helicopter and flown back to their carrier.

Even though the mission resulted in the loss of two aircraft, the first and only all-Marine kill of Vietnam was a milestone, and Major Lasseter was awarded the Alfred E. Cunningham Award as the top Marine aviator of 1972. He also assumed command of VMFA-333 when Lieutenant Colonel J.K. Cochran and his RIO were shot down by flak during a photo-escort mission on December 23. The Shamrocks returned to Beaufort, South Carolina, in March 1973, having flown throughout the final stages of the Vietnam War, gaining the Meritorious Unit Commendation for its work with Task Force 77. (Unfortunately, Lieutenant Colonel Lee Lasseter died in March 1980, after being medically retired from active duty the previous year.)

The Rose Garden

In mid-May, the remote base of Nam Phong in Thailand began receiving Marine squadrons. VMFA-115 with F-4Bs and VMFA-232 with F-4Js arrived from Da Nang in June, as did VMA(AW)-533 with its A-6As. Nam Phong was 300 miles from Hanoi and had never been completed. So austere were the surroundings that the Marines called it the "Rose Garden," in wry reference to a popular song and current Marine recruiting slogan. The Red Devils of VMFA-232 and Silver Eagles of VMFA-115 flew missions into Laos and North Vietnam, VMFA-232 losing three F-4Js between August and November; two crewmen were lost.

One of the Phantoms lost was actually shot down by a MiG-21 in the fall of 1972. Stationed as a BARCAP protecting orbiting tankers for a strike into North Vietnam, a section of VMFA-232 F-4Js heard a threat call from ground radar. The MiG was closing but was apparently hard to see. Standard procedure was to unload and run if the bogey was not seen. However, the wingman decided to haul his heavy F-4 around to meet the oncoming MiG. The Phantom slowed enough for the North Vietnamese pilot to shoot a missile; the lead saw the fireball as his wingman exploded.

The two F-4 units only flew daytime hops, leaving night flying to the crews of VMA(AW)-533, who flew singly or in pairs against the truck traffic on the darkened trails. Flying with no lights, the Intruder crews exhibited considerable skill and daring in the mountains and hilly terrain of Laos and Cambodia.

Life at Nam Phong was straight out of M*A*S*H, with wooden, tin-roofed hangars and tent-huts for living quarters. Having come from the much more modern and commodious base at Da Nang, the Marines were in for quite a shock when they arrived at their new base in Thailand. Making the best of the situation, the F-4 crews flew interdiction missions, usually under Air Force control, hitting targets in South Vietnam, Laos, and Cambodia, and taking enemy ground fire nearly 70 percent of the time. The Marine Phantoms took off from Nam Phong, checked in with an orbiting C-130 control center, which handed them off to a FAC in an OV-10 who would actually pinpoint the targets. Occasionally, the Phantoms would double-cycle, flying from Nam Phong to Da Nang and back to Nam Phong, including two missions. It was a hectic time and the only way to be sure of the date was to check a calendar watch.

Sometimes the Air Force would provide Loran bombing fixes when the weather got so bad that targets were obscured and visual bombing was impossible. Marine aircraft did not carry Loran, and one or two Air Force F-4s would fly up from Udorn and accompany the VMFA-115 or VMFA-232 birds to the target area, getting the necessary radar fix while the Marines dumped chaff to confuse the enemy defenses.

The action did not stop with the January ceasefire, as many missions were flown into Laos and Cambodia after the war had stopped in Vietnam. VMA-311 pilot First Lieutenant Charles G. Reed flew his squadron's 50,000th combat sortie of the war on August 29. The unit would eventually total 54,625 sorties by January 29, 1973. VMA-211 and VMA-311 flew in support of the ARVN forces still trying to counter the NVA thrust. On August 12, two VMA-311 A-4Es flew close air support 60 miles southeast of Saigon, hitting an enemy command post. Briefed in the air by an orbiting FAC, the two Skyhawks immediately dove on the target, bracketing it with 500-pound bombs. Several local positions were destroyed during this typical sortie. VMA-311 would deliver the last Skyhawk warload on January 28, 1973, during a mission into Cambodia. Four A-4s took off in the late afternoon, armed with specially painted red, white, and blue bombs, just for the occasion, with suitable inscriptions and messages for the VC. A little more than an hour later, the aircraft returned to Bien Hoa in a diamond formation. First Lieutenant

Thomas Boykin was the last to land. He reported taking hits in the Mekong Delta area. "I dropped the last one," he reported, "I'm glad it's over."

June 20th also saw HMA-369 begin operating its AH-1J Seacobras from the *Denver* (LPD-9) against enemy ferry and barge traffic, as well as acting as low-flying FACs for Navy carrier strikes. VMFA-212 returned to Hawaii and did not deploy to Nam Phong from Da Nang.

At the end of June, the ARVN forces were ready to begin their own counteroffensive. Driving north towards Quang Tri, the Saigon forces eventually pushed the Communists back, and South Vietnam was fairly well secured once again by late September.

Linebacker II and the Ceasefire

There was still a lot of combat, and much of it was to take place directly over Hanoi in October and December, as waves of Air Force B-52s, in company with Navy aircraft, pounded the North Vietnamese capital. At one point the Communists seemed to call for peace, and President Nixon stopped the strategic-bombing campaign. But the enemy was only stalling, and the giant Strato-fortresses were unleashed in a massive bombing offensive named Linebacker II. Throughout the week of December 18, Hanoi and Haiphong reeled under strategic bombardment. The Air Force and Navy aircraft waded into the biggest, most sophisticated network of aerial defenses in the history of warfare. The mining of the harbors had had a distinct effect, but there were still plenty of SAMs and flak to go around. The courage and skill of the B-52 crews over Hanoi in those night raids of December 1972, against flak, SAMs, and MiGs, deserves telling in any account of Vietnam combat.

As has been said, the main Marine contribution during this period was VMCJ-1/2's ECM support. Together with Navy EA-6B Prowlers, four-seat versions of the Intruder, the Marines provided indispensable anti-SAM support for the strikes. Finally after a week of intense action, the North Vietnamese sued for peace. An accord was signed in Paris for a ceasefire to take effect on January 27, 1973. Prisoners of war would be returned and the mines would be cleared from North Vietnamese harbors. Marine squadron HMH-463 was tasked with providing its CH-53A for Project Endsweep, the mine-clearing operation. HMM-164 and HMM-165 brought their helicopters along as well, for SAR services.

On February 24, the first units arrived in Haiphong Harbor, with the Navy's HM-12 and HMM-165 aboard Navy amphibious transport docks. The first sweep was conducted on February 27 by HM-12, while HMH-463 flew additional sweeps. A Marine CH-53 was lost on March 18 near Hon Gai due to mechanical difficulty, but its crew was rescued. The operation continued until mid-April when it was halted because the

North Vietnamese slowed the POW repatriation process. Eventually, the mine-clearing was resumed and was completed on July 27, after the Navy and Marine helicopters had made 3,554 sweeping runs.

On January 29, 1973, MAG-12 under Colonel Dean Macho, the last American combat aviation unit still in-country, left Vietnam. The official figures for combat losses in Southeast Asia for Navy and Marine squadrons were 529 and 193 fixed-wing aircraft, and 13 and 193 helicopters, respectively. These figures, of course, reflect the greater use of helicopters by the Corps. The strides in all phases of aviation had been tremendous, from in-flight communication and air-ground coordination to blind-bombing techniques and new equipment. However, sadly, neither the Marines nor the rest of the American military services, were through fighting in Vietnam. Navy carrier strikes continued throughout early 1973 against targets in Cambodia and Laos, as the Communists still harried the governments in these countries. By August, the U.S. Congress had had quite enough of the endless drain of Vietnam and voted to cut off U.S. support in any form. Thus, the last actual missions of Southeast Asian combat were really flown on August 15 by Navy and Marine aircraft from carriers and from bases in Thailand.

South Vietnam Falls

Ground combat in Southeast Asia never really halted with the 1973 Paris Accords. The wily North Vietnamese had effectively duped Henry Kissinger and the U.S., and, as always, bided their time. In January 1975, the NVA, which had been allowed to remain in the South, struck out in a bold new offensive. Without U.S. presence, the South Vietnamese were nearly helpless. By late April, the Communists' long-awaited victory was all but assured. All that remained was the final evacuation of American personnel from South Vietnam.

The end came on April 29 when orders to execute Frequent Wind, the evacuation of Saigon, were given. HMH-462 and HMH-463 began shuttling back and forth, carrying evacuees out to the assembled ships offshore. CH-53s and CH-46s kept up the flow, while an umbrella of Air Force and Navy jets flew protection overhead.

The pace was hectic, as the helicopters kept up a steady stream of flights back and forth from the ships to the landing pads in South Vietnam. That there were no mid-air collisions was a minor miracle, the traffic was so heavy. Because of the late start of the rescue flights—they did not get under way until 1300—the operation was still going on until well into the early morning hours, several pilots totaling up more than eleven hours of flight time when they finally left their cockpits.

One humorous story to come out of the operation concerned the rescue of the U.S. ambassador, Graham Martin, who was to be the last to leave the embassy in Saigon, thus signalling the end of the rescue. When the ambassador was safely aboard a helicopter and the aircraft airborne, the pilot was to transmit the supposedly secret call "Tiger, Tiger, Tiger," and nothing else. The rescue of the ambassador and his staff was accomplished, and as the young Marine pilot flew his airplane back to the carrier, he transmitted "Tiger, Tiger, Tiger," as per instructions.

The airborne controller responded, "Roger, confirm Tiger, Tiger, Tiger?" The excited helicopter pilot came back:

"Affirmative. Tiger, Tiger, Tiger. I have the *ambassador!*"

HMA-369 returned with its AH-1Js aboard the *Midway* (CVA-41). The Seacobras served as escorts and pathfinders for the transport helicopters, as well as TACs for the overall effort. In over forty sorties during the "Night of the Helicopters" the Marines brought out over 2,000 people. On the 30th, the last frantic flights left Saigon just as the Communists rolled into the fallen city. The Vietnam War was finally over.

13

Post-Vietnam Future

The Reserves

Like all the U.S. military aviation services, Marine aviation has a shadow complement of men and equipment: its reserve force. The reserves are an important part of the U.S. military, more important, perhaps, than would initially appear. In reality, the active-duty forces of any nation are usually compact; it is the strength of the reserves which usually determines a country's ability to fight a long-term war successfully. The regulars are the first line—the first to fight—and it is the reserves, upon mobilization, which allow the fight to continue.

Marine reserve aviation had its beginning soon after the formation of a regular Marine reserve in 1916. Many of the first Marine aircrews to see combat in World War I were reservists, the first USMCR aviator being Second Lieutenant Allen H. Boynton. These men flew long antisubmarine patrols in the Azores, as well as more publicized supply and bombing missions over the lines in France. Indeed, the first Medal of Honor to be awarded to a Marine aviator went to a reservist, Second Lieutenant Ralph Talbot, whose exploits have been detailed in earlier pages.

Postwar demobilization allowed the deactivation of much of the reserves. By March 1919, only forty-one reservists were flying in the Marines. 1928 saw the recall to active duty of five Marine reservist pilots. These World War I veterans were tasked with forming an active Marine air reserve. The program allowed for the training of *ab initio* aviators who would be obligated for one-year tours of active duty, upon completion of flight training and receipt of their commissions.

In 1935, legislation was passed which created the grade of aviation cadet in the Marine Reserve, providing for the training and pay of such individuals. Among the future "greats" who were part of the cadet program were Gregory Boyington and Robert Galer, both of whom won the Medal of Honor for their exploits in World War II.

In 1938, the Naval Reserve Act increased the pay and benefits for Marine reservists as well, and by the end of that year, over 700 Marine pilots, crewmen, and ground personnel were drilling at various sites around the country, Quantico and San Diego being the most active locations.

World War II brought the complete integration of the reserves into the active forces; 75 percent of all services were reservists. Six of the eleven Medals of Honor awarded to Marine aviators went to reservists. After the war, the reserves were reactivated with a headquarters at NAS Glenview, Illinois. Bolstered by the large number of World War II veterans, Marine reserve aviation could boast more than 6,300 officers and enlisted men, associated with forty-two squadrons, by 1949.

Korea saw a call-up of many U.S. reserve units, with eleven Marine air reserve squadrons being eventually recalled. Relatively few actually saw combat duty; one that did was VMA-121. With the 1st Marine Division saddled with the brunt of the Korean action, other resources of the organization had to be called upon. The Organized Reserve was mobilized in July 1950. Most of the men in the Marine Reserves were combat-ready. The infantry reservists were in combat by the fall of 1950, and the 1st MAW had received mobilized reservists by September. Six Marine fighter squadrons had been called up, as well as three ground-control intercept squadrons. The reservists were to be integrated into the regular squadrons already in combat or on the way.

The first Marine air reservists had just returned from their regular two-week annual stint of active duty. It involved a major exercise at Cherry Point, North Carolina. VMF-235, located in Boston, Massachusetts, flew its Corsairs to El Toro to join VMF-232 from NAS New York. VMF-143 reported to NAS New Orleans in early 1951, bringing its Corsairs to retrain many of its members who were going to the regular 1st MAW squadrons in Korea. Throughout the late 1950s and early 1960s, the Marines updated their aircraft as well as struggled to maintain flying proficiency. In July 1962, the 4th Marine Aircraft Wing was established at Glenview to replace the Marine Air Reserve Training Command. The 4th MAW consisted of eight MAGs and one support group. During Vietnam, no 4th MAW units were recalled, but the end of the war saw a great influx of seasoned combat veterans into all reserve components, and the Marines got their share.

For the most part, Marine air reserve squadrons utilized fairly modern aircraft, the F-8 Crusader and A-4 Skyhawk providing much of the tactical jet equipment. Eventually, the Crusader was replaced by the Phantom. VMFA-321, based at the Naval Air Facility, Andrews Air Force Base, got the first F-4Bs in 1973.

VMFA-321 is a fairly representative Marine air reserve squadron, and a closer look at such a unit will give an idea of the heritage of Marine reserve aviation. The Hell's Angels of VMFA-321 have their roots in a World War II Corsair squadron which enjoyed a good record, shooting down thirty-nine Japanese aircraft during that conflict. In the immediate postwar years, VMF-321 flew several aircraft, especially the Grumman F8F Bearcat and Vought F4U Corsair. While the squadron remained based at NAS Anacostia during Korea, several squadron members were recalled and saw combat duty; a few did not return.

Captain Warren York, a Washington, D.C., native, was killed in action on October 29, 1951, while serving with VMF-214. A highly decorated veteran, with two DFCs, York was flying a Corsair on a night mission when his aircraft was hit by flak and crashed. A Corsair flown by Captain Herman L. Bushong, Jr., was also hit by enemy flak late in 1952, but the recalled reservist managed to make it home with a two-foot hole in his F4U's tail.

In 1953, the squadron's Bearcats were replaced with F4U-4s because the French desperately needed more F8Fs in Indochina. When the 4th MAW was established, VMF-321 was assigned to MAG-42, and in 1959 it was reassigned to MAG-41, the group it belongs to today. Until 1968, Navy and Marine reserve pilots in Washington took turns flying the Crusaders at Andrews. This sharing accounts for the pictures of various reserve aircraft carrying both Navy and Marine markings. But in 1970, the Naval Air Reserve was drastically reorganized, largely because of its poor showing during the 1968 *Pueblo* crisis. With two tactical carrier wings, the Navy also established two reserve light-photographic squadrons, VFPs, which flew the RF-8G variant of the Crusader. Utilization of this specialized version released several F-8Ls to the Marines, and VMF-321's complement rose to nineteen aircraft. Painted with distinctive black dorsal areas and tails, spangled with white stars, the Crusaders, later F-8Ks, were an eye-catching line-up on the ramp. VMF-321 also changed its name to the "Black Barons."

By late 1962, the entire Marine Air Reserve had transitioned to tactical jets. VMF-321 at Anacostia had flown AD-5N Skyraiders, as VMA-321, through the late 1950s, but by 1962 had begun receiving FJ-4B Furies, and had also moved just across the river in October 1961 to the new Naval Air Facility at Andrews Air Force Base. By January 1965, the Furies had begun to be replaced by F-8B Crusaders, and the Vought aircraft was destined to serve the longest of any type with the Marine air reserves.

In December 1973, VMF-321 turned in its F-8Ks for F-4Bs and became VMFA-321. Transition to the Phantom, obviously a more complex airplane than its predecessor, went fairly smoothly. A big help was the large number of pilots, RIOs, and ground crewmen who had operated the type in Vietnam. One of the F-4Bs had a MiG-17 kill to its credit while it was serving as a Navy fighter with VF-51 in the *Coral Sea* (CV-43) in 1972. The F-4B gave way to the updated F-4N in 1976, and it is this variant which the renamed Hell's Angels of VMFA-321 operate today.

VMFA-321 not only serves as the focal point for Marine Air Reservists from the Washington area, but also provides various services for components of the regular services, especially in the air combat manuevering (ACM) training role. Over the course of a year, detachments of VMFA-321 crews will take their aircraft all over the U.S. and Canada, or host a detachment from other units, even Air Force, for several days of intensive flying and training.

VMFA-321 is a representative Marine Air Reserve squadron, and gives an idea of the current status of the organization. Each squadron member drills—works at the squadron spaces—for two days per month, usually more, and also participates in an annual two-week period of active duty which usually takes the squadron to MCAS Yuma, Arizona, where there are bombing and electronic ranges. The time each reservist devotes to his job and position within the squadron is important in the overall status and importance of the Marine Air Reserve.

As of this writing, the Marine Air Reserve, like other reserve components, is facing a budgetary crunch, and it is somewhat difficult to tell exactly where things will stand in the future. New equipment, such as A-4Ms and CH-53s, is beginning to enter reserve units, and there is some thought of giving Marine reserve squadrons first-line equipment such as the AV-8B and F/A-18. (The Air Force Reserve and Air National Guard, an auxiliary of the Air Force, have enjoyed the luxury of off-the-line aircraft for several years, but the Navy and the Marine air reserves have usually had to make do with relatively tired retreads from the fleet. The addition of brand new aircraft would have a tremendous rejuvenating effect on the squadrons lucky enough to get the new aircraft.)

Currently, the 4th MAW consists of six attack squadrons, flying the A-4E/F, and is assigned to MAG-42. The EA-6A has also found its way into the Marine Air Reserve, and the recently established VMAQ-4 operates the type at the NAS Whidbey Island, Washington. MAG-41 includes most of the other fixed-wing assets, including the two VMFA units, 321 and 112, flying F-4Ns. MAG-41 also includes VMO-4, with OV-10A and the refueler squadron, VMGR-234, flying KC-130s.

MAG-46 is the helicopter group and includes three HMH squadrons with CH-53As, three HMMs with CH-46Ds, three HMLs with UH-1E/Ns, and one HMA squadron with AH-1Js. HMS units also fly various transport aircraft, such as the C-12. The 4th MAW includes some ninety-seven units, with over 9,500 reservists, including nearly 600 aviators, supported by another 2,000 Marines.

The Future

After the experience of Vietnam, the Marines, as in nearly every postwar period, found themselves in a battle for survival. Equipment, personnel, and responsibilities were all being scrutinized. Marine air was coming in for a major share of reorganization and orientation. The Marines still felt that having their own air arm was essential to support amphibious operations and provide helicopter airlift for supply and troop movement, as had been emphatically proven in Vietnam.

Fixed-wing aircraft were an essential part of the Marine air effort, giving direct support when and where needed. However, being officially part of the overall Navy establishment, the Corps was caught in the traditional squeeze of Navy budgetary planning. Fortunately, one program which was already fairly well established was the V/STOL AV-8A Harrier. Developed from a British design of the late 1950s, the Harrier took off and landed vertically, like a helicopter, but could then rotate its engine nozzles and fly like a normal fixed-wing jet. Britain's Hawker Siddeley Company had created a unique military aircraft and the Marines saw immediate applications of the Harrier for their special needs.

The plane could operate right behind front lines, or from the deck of an LPH which usually accommodated only helicopters. The Harrier offered tactical jet speed and weapons delivery, yet the ability to operate right with the troops. It was a long-sought combination, and in 1968 Major General Keith McCutcheon sent to England two experienced Marine aviators, Lieutenant Colonel Bud Baker and Colonel Thomas Miller, to gain first-hand experience with the Harrier. The two Marine pilots spent two and one-half weeks flying the British jet, and returned to Washington determined to sell the Corps on the new airplane. Fortunately, they found ready ears in both McCutcheon and General Leonard F. Chapman, Jr., the Commandant. Appropriations were sought to purchase the Harrier from England "off the shelf," but Congress balked at buying foreign machinery unless a good deal of future production could take place in the United States.

Two key individuals who were difficult to recruit were Dr. Alain C. Enthoven, Assistant Secretary of Defense (Systems Analysis), and his assistant, Russell Murray, II. Both men had a history, during their tenure under Secretary of Defense Robert S. McNamara, of denying the Marines were having problems, either in personnel or equipment procurement. In 1967, it had been extremely difficult to convince Dr. Enthoven that the pilot shortage was real. He eventually was won over after much discussion, education, and haggling by both Chapman and McCutcheon.

However, Russ Murray developed into something of an "enemy" of the Marines in the aviation community, and especially where the Harrier was concerned. For some reason, he challenged the Corps' decision to buy the British aircraft, saying the plane would not be cost-effective, a watchword in military spending. He convinced his boss Enthoven to oppose the purchase, even though leading aeronautical engineers gave the Harrier high marks, favoring its acquisition by the Marines.

Senator Stuart Symington of Missouri was also opposed to the purchase, because the funds to buy the British planes would have to come from money set aside to purchase seventeen new F-4s. McDonnell, the manufacturer of the Phantom was, of course, based in St. Louis; Symington's son was a Congressman from St. Louis. It was getting very sticky; $58 million was a lot of money to take out of American pockets and give to a foreign, albeit friendly, nation. Fortunately, Colonel Miller had visited McDonnell and discussed the situation with the McDonnell family with whom he enjoyed a great rapport. The McDonnells agreed to support the foreign purchase because they believed it would be a shot in the arm for American V/STOL hopes and would provide the Marines with a unique aircraft. Of course, McDonnell would also be involved in future manufacturing rights. Miller suggested that the irate Senator from Missouri place a call to McDonnell. No more complaints were heard about buying British over American goods.

A licensing agreement was subsequently worked out between McDonnell-Douglas and Hawker Siddeley, but by 1971, the Congress had reversed itself and refused to fund further money for moving production of the Harrier to America. Thus the British filled the entire order of 110 aircraft by 1976, including 102 single-seat AV-8As and eight TAV-8A two-seat trainers.

The mark which the Marines obtained was comparable to the GR Mk 3, redesignated AV-8A in U.S. service. Minor modifications were made, including avionics and a different ejection seat. The first aircraft were delivered in February 1971, while the first Harrier squadrons were formed soon afterwards, VMA-513 in April and VMA-542 in December 1972.

VMA-231 followed in October 1973, and the training squadron VMAT-203 in 1975.

The first AV-8As actually went to the Naval Air Test Center at NAS Patuxent River in southern Maryland for initial service trials, including compatibility tests aboard LPHs and LPDs. January 1972 saw the first deployment of the Marine Harriers as VMA-513 embarked in the *Guam* (LPH-9) for the North Atlantic. VMA-231 and VMA-542 travelled to Japan in 1976 and 1977, as well as serving aboard the carrier *Roosevelt* (CV-42) during the same period, on various Mediterranean cruises.

But problems with the V/STOL program towards the end of the 1970s, plus the development program surrounding the so-called Super Harrier—the AV-8B—were causes for concern. Aside from what some considered an inordinate number of crashes, it was found that the AV-8A could not carry a satisfactory payload; either more power or greater lift was needed. The AV-8A was a demanding aircraft. It incorporated a powerful engine in a light-weight airframe, and it flew through a wide spectrum of flight regimes, which demanded a high degree of motor skills and reflexes from its pilots. With cutbacks in flight time, leave, or other responsibilities, Harrier pilots had a greater need to stay current than, say, their A-4 counterparts.

A proposed AV-16A design was abandoned because of the development costs for a new airframe and Rolls-Royce engine. McDonnell-Douglas redesigned the aircraft, incorporating a larger wing and various lift improvement devices; the Pegasus 11 turbofan of the A remained. The new aircraft's payload and radius were doubled and the Harrier became a true V/STOL airplane. In fact, the AV-8B carries one of the heaviest payloads in modern tactical jet aviation.

When President Jimmy Carter took office in January 1977, twenty-eight AV-8As had crashed since the introduction of the type, and although this number was not as catastrophic as would appear at first glance, given the total number of flight hours achieved, criticism of the entire V/STOL program was hot and heavy. Russ Murray led a group opposed to the AV-8B and succeeded in convincing Secretary of Defense Harold Brown to delete the AV-8B from the FY 79 defense budget. In a hard-hitting paper, Murray called the AV-8B

a small, single-engined, subsonic aircraft of British lineage, developed as an improvement over the Marines' current AV-8A. The Harrier is a relatively undistinguished aircraft in all respects save one—its unique ability to use very short runways . . . at some sacrifice in range and payload . . . .[44]

Murray claimed that the forthcoming F-18 would be a much better acquisition than the AV-8B, and his group pointed to the B's high cost and relative weakness in the field of air-to-air combat. They downplayed, however, the type's obvious advantages in tactical proximity to the battlefield.

The Marines fought alone. The Navy, occupied with its floundering F-14 program, did not lend any support, and the Air Force and Army chose not to show much concern either. Besides, the Air Force was having enough problems keeping its own B-1 program afloat. Chief champion was, of course, Lieutenant General Miller, now D/CS (Air). He talked to anyone and everyone who would listen, and eventually assembled a group of influential supporters at the Congressional level, as well as Commandant General Louis H. Wilson. Through Miller's efforts and those of his allies, funding for the AV-8B through FY 81 survived.

The YAV-8B first flew in 1978, after some budgetary problems, and the first pre-production prototypes flew in November 1981. There are currently plans for over 300 AV-8Bs to be produced, though not before 1984.

The Marine use of the British aircraft was cause for public interest; certainly the plane's unique flight characteristics were reason enough for attention. (Use of British aircraft, though rare, was not unheard of. During World War II, Army Air Force units reaching Europe utilized Spitfires, Mosquitos, and even Beaufighters, until U.S.-manufactured equipment arrived in strength.) The Harrier, while primarily employed as a ground-attack aircraft, was also well equipped for air-to-air combat. Armed with Sidewinders and cannon, and having an unusual ability to "turn square corners," through VIFFing (Vectoring in Forward Flight), the rapid control of the moveable engine nozzles to quickly decelerate and almost stop in mid-air, the Harrier boasts a true air-superiority potential. This potential was finally realized in the 1982 Falklands war between Britain and Argentina, when British Harriers destroyed twenty Argentine aircraft with guns and missiles.

The introduction of the AV-8A brought new demands for the Marine aviators selected to fly it. They had to learn new terminology and skills before even setting foot in the aircraft. Proponents of the plane saw limitless possibilities in the roles of close air support and air combat. All was not rosy, however. The AV-8A's lifting power, particularly with any useful combat load, was not all it could be, and steps were taken to improve it. These steps resulted in the AV-8C, which incorporated lift improvement devices and additional avionics. The "Charlie" model will fill the performance gap until the AV-8B enters service.

The Skyhawk Continues to Serve

No tactical jet aircraft had come to mean as much to the Marines as the tough and capable little A-4 Skyhawk. There was a certain empathy between the A-4 and the Corps. Indeed, they were quite similar in background and experience; small, but ideally suited to their combative roles, and endowed with a durability born of long service. In the post-Vietnam period, the Marines were loath to retire the A-4, although the number of squadrons operating the aircraft was reduced to five—VMA-211, -214, -223, -311, and -331. Although the older Echo and Foxtrot models were still retained, a new development soon began to appear in strength. The Marines had considered obtaining the Vought A-7 Corsair in the late 1960s to replace the Skyhawk, but in the final analysis, it was decided that the Corsair was too sophisticated for the close air-support mission flown by Marine aviators, and that funds would be better used to further develop the A-4.

Designated A-4M, the new Skyhawk flew in April 1970. It incorporated a larger engine and cockpit canopy, nose-mounted bombing radar, and other internal refinements. VMA-324 received the first A-4Ms in 1971; 158 were finally produced. On February 27, 1979, the Skyhawk reproduction line finally closed with the delivery of the 2,960th aircraft to VMA-331, at MCAS Cherry Point, North Carolina. While the number of squadrons still flying the Skyhawk will no doubt diminish more rapidly in the near future, development of the basic aircraft continues to fit the needs of the Marines.

A new variant entered service in 1979 with the introduction of the OA-4M, a reconfigured TA-4F, to be used as FACs by headquarters squadrons. The OA-4M incorporates a laser spot tracker, a device which "sees" a target illuminated by a laser beam pinpointed by a ground facility. This capability allows the FAC to see his target more readily. Now, even in the twilight of its life, the little A-4 still forms an integral part of Marine aviation.

Helicopter Developments

The Marine Corps has continued operating the same four basic helicopters which it utilized in Southeast Asia: AH-1, CH-46, and CH-53. Of course, development of these versatile helicopters has continued as well. The single-engine UH-1E was given an additional engine and redesignated UH-1N. The first UH-1Ns were delivered to the Marines at New River in North Carolina on April 7, 1971. Some actually flew in the last frantic stages of the Vietnam War.

The AH-1 had gone from the single-engined, Army-funded "G" to the twin-engined "J" built expressly for the Marines. A postwar development is the AH-1T, fifty-seven of which will replace Marine AH-1Gs. The "T" carries TOW (tube-launched, optically-guided, wire-controlled) anti-tank missiles manufactured by Hughes, as well as Sidewinder missiles for an air-to-air capability against Soviet gunship helicopters.

The A/D versions of the veteran CH-46 continue to serve the medium-helicopter community. A new development will be the Echo, which incorporates more powerful engines, more effectively armored interior, engine exhaust suppressors to decrease vulnerability to heat-seeking missiles, and other internal refinements. CH-46E s arrived in FMF units in October 1977. Other developments for the Seaknight include a new infrared (IR) paint scheme which reduces sun reflections and thereby IR signatures, various radar warning receivers and jammers, and modified cockpit lighting for better nighttime operations. The metal rotor blades will also be replaced by fiberglass ones which promise longer life. With all these improvements, the CH-46 appears capable of serving past the turn of the century.

The last member of the Vietnam quartet of helicopters is the Sikorsky CH-53 Sea Stallion, the largest production helicopter in the free world. Ever in need of a versatile heavy-lift helicopter, the Marines have made the new CH-53E their best bet in the 1980s. Based on the Delta, the Echo still incorporates many changes, the most advantageous of which is probably the addition of a third engine. Scheduled to be produced at the rate of approximately fourteen aircraft a year until 1985, CH-53E's total will amount to about fifty units. With its name changed to Super Stallion, it offers the capability of lifting any tactical aircraft used by the Corps, including another CH-53E. This "retriever" capability was the CH-53A/D's forte in Vietnam and still remains a very desirable asset.

Development of the Echo began as early as 1967 and preliminary studies were concluded in early 1972. The Department of Defense had authorized further development and the first prototypes flew on March 1, 1974. On August 10th, a YCH-53E lifted an external load of 17.8 tons into a hover, for a total gross weight of 71,700 pounds, the heaviest load ever lifted by a helicopter in the free world. Production problems at the Sikorsky plant, however, prevented the introduction date of May 1980 from being met. But HMH-464 was established at MCAS(H) New River in March 1981 to receive fifteen new Echos in June. A second squadron, HMH-465, received its first aircraft in February 1982 at MCAS(H) Tustin, near El Toro. As the situation now stands for the Marines, many of the veteran aircraft used for so many years are programmed to remain in service to the end of the 1980s and some even well into the 1990s. The A-4 will be the first to leave fleet service as, by FY 85, VMA-331 will have relinquished its A-4Ms and transitioned to the AV-8B which then will be coming off the production lines. As the A-4M leaves active service, it will naturally find its way into the reserve force, with the first Ms programmed to go to El Toro-based reservists in FY 83. By 1990 all squadrons now operating the A-4M will have transitioned to the Harrier, the last being VMA-214.

The A-6 Intruder will continue to serve for a very long time, with various additions to its already large array of electronics. VMA(AW)s

-121, -242, -224, -332, and -533, along with the training squadron, VMAT(AW) -202, are programmed to fly the Intruder into 1990, but actually have no end-date in sight. There just is no aircraft in the near future ready to take the A-6's place with the Marines, a high tribute to the Grumman Corporation's design.

One area undergoing a more noticeable change is the forward air controller, the FAC, used so much in Vietnam. One of the problems facing this specialized community is the increasing proliferation of air defenses, both missile and electronic. Even relatively poor Third World countries can afford to field a staggering array of sophisticated and dangerous antiaircraft weapons. The Vietnam scenario of a slow-moving FAC orbiting his target area as he directs a strike is not in keeping with the facts of modern combat. Even the OV-10 Bronco is too slow to operate in such a hazardous environment. More standoff distance is needed for the FAC, as well as greater speed, agility, and firepower. In this regard, therefore, many Marine strategists are seriously hoping to add to the attack-helicopter lineup, with three additional HMAs being considered. The AH-1Ts in these squadrons would contain additional weaponry to take care of themselves, as well as being able to remain outside the main target area, away from the enemy's defenses.

Fixed-Wing Fighters

Perhaps no area of Marine aviation has caused so much concern, developmental and administrative, as that of a tactical jet fighter to replace the F-4 Phantom. The F-4 reached Marine squadrons in 1962/63, served throughout Vietnam and, through several modifications and updates, continues to operate with VMFA squadrons. But a replacement was, and is, necessary. From an air-superiority standpoint the Grumman F-14A Tomcat seemed a likely candidate. This ultra-sophisticated weapons system first flew in 1970 and began reaching Navy fleet squadrons in 1973.

The Marines, at one point, in the person of then-Brigadier General Philip D. Shutler, D/CS(Air), tried to strike a deal with the Navy for the purchase of Harriers and Tomcats. Shutler believed the Navy and Marines should operate the same aircraft, either on carriers or from shore bases. Why, argued Shutler, could not the Marines fly Harriers from land bases, in advance of the main forces, while the Navy operated the AV-8s from carriers. (The AV-8A has nearly the same attack capability as the F-18; indeed, the ranges are nearly equal.) With wing-folding, nearly twice as many Harriers could be accommodated on current ships as could A-7s, the standard Navy light attack bomber. It was an interesting concept, but given the rivalry that has always existed between Navy and Marine air, it was stillborn.

The F-14, with its huge, highly capable radar, could also serve as an advance early-warning system, able to defend itself, something which the E-2s and Air Force E-3 AWACS could not do. If there were a real hot war, it is doubtful that the expensive AWACS aircraft would be sent right into the high-threat areas. The risk of their being shot down, by missile or interceptor, would make such use prohibitive. The Tomcat, on the other hand, with Phoenix missiles and integral cannon, would not be at a disadvantage.

Initially the Marines had asked the Secretary of the Navy, John Warner, for a number of F-14s. Discussions and counterproposals naturally followed. The F-14 was too expensive, too difficult to maintain in the rough field conditions in which the Marines usually found themselves. Too many squadron personnel would be needed just to maintain the weapons systems, let alone the airplane itself. The money would be better spent on the F-4, a proven aircraft, while the F-18 was being developed. However, as money became scarce and the per-unit cost of the F-14 seemed to be running away, the decision was made to take nearly $600 million earmarked for Phantoms and put it towards F-14s for the Marines. The first F-14 squadron was to be VMFA-122 at Beaufort, South Carolina, with three other units to follow. It was somewhat of a strong-arm method, as the Commandant was forced to purchase the Tomcats, nearly seventy in all. However, to those who had originally wanted the Grumman fighter, it was a blessing to be embraced enthusiastically. But when James R. Schlesinger became Secretary of Defense, he decided to get the Marines out of the F-14 controversy. On July 2, 1975, General Louis H. Wilson announced that the twelve VMFA F-4-equipped squadrons would continue to operate the Phantom until the F-18 became available.

The F/A-18 Hornet

The Marines knew what they needed: a moderately fast, capable yet simple aircraft, with room for development, but without the overpowering avionics and systems which distort the plane's mission: to operate in a fast-paced, hazardous environment in defense of the ground troops. The ability to dogfight at 30,000 feet would be a secondary advantage.

The twin-engined, twin-tailed Northrop-designed YF-17 Cobra, the losing competitor to the General Dynamics F-16 in the Air Force's Air Combat Fighter (ACF) runoff, now became the front-runner for the Navy/Marine new fighter/attack aircraft, the VFAX. Having lost a major Air Force and NATO competition for the next-generation light fighter, the YF-17 was quickly developed, with McDonnell Douglas's help, into the F/A-18 Hornet. This aircraft was to have both superb light-attack and air-combat capabilities, thereby eliminating both the F-4 and A-7 from the Navy's inventory, as well as the F-4 and A-4 from the Marines' lineup. Opponents of the Harrier, among them Russ Murray, quickly pointed to the F/A-18 as the only choice for the Corps against the AV-8B.

Of course, the Hornet has had its own share of detractors, including the Secretary of the Navy, John Lehman, who demanded that McDonnell Douglas reduce the cost of the aircraft or face cancellation of the production contract. But the Hornet is undeserving of a lot of the "bad press" it has received. As the F-18 nears operational deployment— VMFA-314 took official charge of its Hornets in January 1983, while VMFA-323 and VMFA-531 will be ready for deployment by July 1983—the final arguments are perhaps best left until the actual performance of the squadrons, aircraft, and personnel concerned can be observed. Initial reports indicate widespread acceptance, by Navy and Marine personnel, of the F-18. Its serviceability and combat capability have given it the highest marks of any new aircraft in the last twenty years.

Consider the aircraft which the Hornet is destined to replace, the F-4 Phantom, arguably the most successful of all Western post-World War II military aircraft. Air superiority and close air support are still the main Marine missions. The F-4 has had several limitations over its long career, age having little to do with its leaving active service. The Phantom uses a lot of fuel, especially during air combat engagements when its afterburner is used a great deal. The Phantom is big and heavy and is a relatively poor dogfighter; its success in Vietnam and the Mideast is due mainly to its tremendous power and speed, which enable its pilot to disengage from most combat situations. Then, too, the Phantom's radar has been the subject of many problems. Some units in Vietnam suffered a 20-30% reliability rate at times. The radar required constant maintenance. And an engine change took a great deal of time as well. The F-4 has been updated with slats for maneuverability and its radar has been constantly upgraded to a solid-state technology, which resulted in a much better record. Still, the F-18 promises so much more.

Design considerations in the Hornet demanded deletion of some components, like air-intake ramps which enable an airplane to go faster. Thus, the F-4 is somewhat speedier than the F-18, but the latter is much easier to maintain. The F-18 has a gun, whereas Navy and Marine Phantoms carry only missiles for air-to-air combat.

The Hornet has a self-starting capability, due to its auxiliary power unit (APU), which releases the aircraft from dependence on a massive ground-support facility. It can take off, depending on the load, from a 2,600-foot roll, with a 600- 900 foot maximum performance takeoff also within its capability. The Hornet is finding acceptance from its pilots, both in air combat exercises and around aircraft carriers. Early carrier qualification periods have produced a 93-100 percent boarding rate, the percentage of actual arrestments, a remarkable accomplishment for a new aircraft.

An engine change is also made much easier by the aircraft mounted accessory drive (AMAD), which shortens the disconnect/connect time for most of the engine accessories, an area which is a tedious and time-consuming part of mounting a new powerplant. The Marine Hornet will also include forward-looking infrared radar (FLIR) and a laser designator (LSD), which will give the Marines their first night and marginal-weather capability in a fighter/attack airplane. The integral cannon is palletized for ease of maintenance and loading.

Combat in the 1980s

In August 1982, Marine air was part of the task force of ships and planes which covered the landing of 800 Marines at Beirut, Lebanon, a replay of such an occasion in 1958. Throughout the tense months which followed, Marine helicopters stood by the ships, ready to support the men ashore, as well as evacuate civilians and embassy personnel. The catastrophic bombing of the Marine barracks in late October 1983, with the loss of 241 Marines and Navy personnel, raised tension to the highest level of the deployment.

However, Marine aviators had been more actively engaged in the Caribbean. Supporting the US-led invasion of the tiny island of Grenada, Marine helicopters flew their first combat missions since the *Mayaguez* rescue mission eight years before. Only one Marine aviation squadron was involved, HMM-261, a composite squadron from MCAS New River, North Carolina. Embarked in USS *Guam* (LPH-9), HMM-261 used CH-46E Sea Knights, CH-53D Sea Stallions, and UH-1N Hueys to move men and weapons into and out of the battle zones during the operation, codenamed Urgent Fury. Four AH-1T Sea Cobras were also assigned to HMM-261 for the invasion.

Action was sporadic, but occasionally intense, especially during the first hours of the invasion. The four Sea Cobras from HMM-261 were heavily engaged covering the initial assaults on October 25. One AH-1T was hit by ground fire in the mid-afternoon. Capt. Tim Howard crash-landed the Cobra well within sight of the Cuban defenders. Howard had his right forearm severed by the intense fire, and his right leg badly wounded. He barely managed to bring the helo down. As the aircraft landed, it began to burn, and Howard yelled, trying to rouse his co-pilot gunner Capt. Jeb Seagle, knocked unconscious by the initial defensive fire.

Seagle regained consciousness and both men jumped from their burning plane amidst a hail of fire from the Cuban positions only 40 yards away. Pinned down, the two Marine aviators were trapped. Howard yelled for Seagle to save himself, but Seagle said he would try to run for help. He had barely covered 40 yards before Cuban machine gun fire killed him.

A second Sea Cobra, orbiting the scene tried to suppress the Cuban fire while directing a rescue helo toward Howard. This Cobra, too, was hit, and it crashed into St. George's Harbor, killing both pilots, Capt. John P. Giguere and 1/Lt. Jeffrey R. Scharver.

Finally a CH-46 landed near Howard and its crew chief, Gy/Sgt. Kelly Neidigh, carried the injured Marine to safety under enemy fire. Capt. Howard recovered, and remained in the Corps, despite the loss of his right arm. Capt. Seagle was awarded a posthumous Navy Cross and Air Medal. Capt. Howard received the Silver Star and Distinguished Flying Cross.

Working with Army helicopters, and supported by fixed-wing aircraft of CVW-6 from the carrier *Independence,* detoured from a Mediterranean deployment, the Marine helicopters contributed to the success of Operation Urgent Fury, which resulted in the denial of Grenada to Soviet and Communist Cuban forces, and the rescue of nearly 1,000 US citizens, including the medical students at St. George's University.

The continuing conflict in the eastern Mediterranean increased US Navy carrier presence, and along with those carriers, US Marines made the first Atlantic deployment in the F/A-18A.

Learning their new aircraft was a full-time job for the Marines in the carrier. The Hornet's futuristic avionics and capabilities combined tremendous potential with problems concerning a pilot's ability to keep up with the aircraft. This situation is not limited to the Navy and Marines, and is an unwelcomed by-product of the great advances in aircraft design and avionics of the late '70s and early '80s.

Nevertheless, by the time *Coral Sea* entered the Med, her air wing was ready, just in time. Something had to be done to control the terrorists, who seemed to be getting aid and instructions from the Libyan dictator, Colonel Khaddafi.

Threats by Libya and a so-called "line of death" across the Gulf of Sidra could not be long ignored. Accordingly, on March 24, 1986, after Libyan ground forces fired a spread of Soviet-supplied SA-5 SAMs at Navy aircraft, the US carriers present—*Saratoga, America,* and *Coral Sea*—launched selective strikes over a two-day period against the SAM sites and Libyan patrol boats which approached too close to the task force. Navy and Marine F/A-18s flew combat air patrols alongside the F-14s of the *Saratoga* and *America.*

Three weeks later, on the night of April 14th, aircraft from the *America* and *Coral Sea* launched strikes against the Libyan city of Benghazi while Air Force F-111s attacked Tripoli. Alongside the Air Force strike, Navy and Marine F/A-18s fired HARM missiles, against anti-aircraft sites, standing off from the main attack. Thus, the Hornet has flown its first combat missions. More

Hornets with Navy A-7s hit additional targets an hour later. EA-6Bs of VMAQ-2 in the *America* also provided valuable ECM services for both the Air Force and Navy strikes.

14

Fighting Terrorism in the 1980s

For the last half of the 1980s, American foreign policy focused on the volatile Middle East and Southwest Asia. After having left Lebanon in 1984, the United States became concerned with the ongoing bloody war between Iran and Iraq, which began in September 1980. Though generally kept ashore in the vast desert between the two countries, the fighting sometimes spilled out to the adjacent Indian Ocean and Persian Gulf. ("Persia" is another name—albeit ancient—for Iran, and political sensitivities sometimes require the name to be changed to the more generic "Arabian Gulf." Iranians do not consider themselves Arabs.

Since a great deal of the world's oil supply travelled in and out of this vital region, the free conduct of the tanker fleets was of great concern to the United States. Coupled with a rising rate of terrorism which was sponsored by both rogue states, the Iran-Iraq conflict took on major international importance.

Iran began threatening tankers (one source lists 111 attacks), mining approaches to the Gulf, and harassing water traffic. On March 7, 1987, the U.S. agreed to reflag Kuwaiti tankers as American ships, and thus, provide escort and protection in the dangerous tanker channels.

On May 17, the frigate USS *Stark* (FFG-31) was hit by two Exocet anti-shipping missiles fired by an Iraqi Mirage F.1 eighty miles northeast of Bahrain. Thirty-seven sailors were killed. There were many repercussions to the tragedy, several of which focused on the ship's lack of preparedness to meet the threat. But questions about the Iraqi pilot's true intentions—and those of his government—persisted after the official investigation. Four years later, this incident was recalled by some as a disregarded warning, and perhaps an opening shot of the Persian Gulf War.

In late July, Operation Earnest Will, the escort of reflagged tankers, started. Although protected by American task forces, the tankers still encountered threats in the form of mines, and several ships were damaged by these underwater weapons. In September, Army helicopters attached to Navy ships discovered a small Iranian ship laying mines and attacked it with rockets and machine gun fire. The situation continued to escalate, and on October 19, 1987, the U.S. task force attacked two Iranian oil platforms that were being used as communication centers. But even with this confrontation, the Iranians continued their operations. On December 12, a Cypriot-flagged tanker was sunk by Iranian speedboats.

The final straw came when USS *Samuel B. Roberts* (FFG-58) struck a mine on April 14, 1988. No one was killed, and the badly damaged ship was towed to Dubai for repairs and eventually returned to service.

Operation Praying Mantis was the answer to this accumulation of terrorist attacks, and on April 18, Navy and Marine units fought what was termed the largest purely naval action by American forces since World War II. A combination of naval gunfire and rockets from Marine Corps AH-1T gunships of HMLA-167 struck armed Iranian oil platforms in strategic positions in the Gulf. A Cobra and its crew were lost, although the reason was never clear. A month later, the bodies of Captain Stephen C. Leslie and Captain Kenneth W. Hill were recovered. Both pilots received posthumous Purple Hearts and Distinguished Flying Crosses.

The Iranians tried to respond, sending several Boghammar speedboats and an F-4 Phantom toward the American task force. Aircraft from the nuclear carrier *Enterprise* quickly attacked the speedboats and the Iranian frigate *Sahand*. Another Iranian frigate, the *Sabalan*, was also badly damaged and dead in the water. The delay in authorizing a *coup de grace*, however, allowed Iranian units to rescue the *Sabalan* and tow her to the port of Bandar Abbas. By December, Operation Earnest Will was concluded. Some 270 merchant ships had been escorted through the Gulf.

While events around the world took center stage, other milestones in Marine Corps aviation included the deaths of Lieutenant General Christian F. Schilt on January 13, 1987, and of Pappy Boyington on January 11, 1988. Schilt had received the Medal of Honor for action in Nicaragua in 1927 and had risen to three-star rank by the time he retired in

1957. He was ninety-one. Boyington was seventy-five when he died of cancer. He had also received the Medal of Honor for his record as an F4U Corsair ace in the Pacific during World War II. In 1987, Marine aviation celebrated—albeit somewhat quietly—its seventy-fifth anniversary, and on January 5, 1987, VMA-331 began the first extended deployment with the AV-8B Harrier II, sailing in USS *Belleau Wood* (LHA-3) to the Pacific. The Harrier II was already involved in a lengthy development program, and the first night-attack AV-8B made its first flight at St. Louis on June 26, 1987.

VMA-211 celebrated a thirty-year anniversary of flying the A-4 on September 9, 1987, and on October 1, VMFAT-101, the Marine's fleet training squadron for F-4s, officially transitioned to the FA-18 Hornet.

The Phantom was in the waning days of its great career with the naval service. The Navy had long ago relegated the big fighter to reserve squadrons, fleet defense being taken over by Grumman's F-14. Light-attack and strike duties were the responsibility of A-7E squadrons, but by 1984, an increasing number of squadrons were equipped with the Hornet.

The FMFPAC squadron VMFA-235 had retired the last F-4s in October 1989, moving to the Hornet and leaving only VMFP-3 flying RF-4Bs in the fleet. "P-3," as it was affectionately called, had taken over tactical reconnaissance duties on some carriers when the Navy retired the venerable RF-8G photo-Crusader from the fleet in 1982. The long-nosed photo-Phantoms cruised in *Midway* and *Coral Sea*. However, by the late 1980s, even these long-serving variants of McDonnell's masterpiece were looking at the end of the road. Only the reserve squadrons, VMFA-112 at Dallas, and VMFA-321 at NAF Washington, D.C., flew the F-4. And finally, even the reserves retired their last Phantoms in January 1992.

There were many changes afoot as the 1980s gave way to the 1990s. Old aircraft that had served long and well continued giving way to new types, and with drastic funding reductions and drawdowns, the entire U.S. military service faced incredible face-lifts in both the number of squadrons and also the number of bases that hosted them.

A major organizational change at the Marine Corps squadron level occurred in 1988 when the Headquarters and Maintenance Squadrons (H&MSs—usually pronounced "Hams") became Marine Aviation Logistics Squadrons (MALSs). The MALSs gained a more sharply-defined mission and new responsibilities. Concerned that the H&MSs had developed a "garrison mindset," which could only support a specific aircraft (e.g., H&MS-31 could only service MAG-31's FA-18 Hornets), HQMC redesigned the concept as a contingency support package. MALSs could now deploy with their MAGs, allowing the group to bring their "house" with them.

Perhaps the most important changes involved a helicopter and the tactical-jet side of Marine aviation. The Boeing Vertol CH-46 Sea Knight had been the true medium-lift workhorse of the Navy and Marine Corps since its introduction in June 1964 when HMM-265 took delivery of the first CH-46As. The first Sea Knights arrived in Vietnam with HMM-164 in March 1966, and the helicopter served throughout the war.

Inevitable development and changes in capability accompanied the twin-rotor Sea Knight, often called "Frog." By 1982, all Marine Corps squadrons were flying the CH-46E, while the Navy continued operating several variants. Upgrades and close inspection of existing aircraft could not keep the Sea Knight from aging, however, and as the mid-1990s approach, the need for a replacement for the faithful Frog is becoming more immediate with every deployment. On May 13, 1990, the Marine Corps grounded its CH-46 fleet. The Navy followed on July 3.

A lot of interest, therefore, was shown toward a revolutionary aircraft from Bell, the V-22 Osprey, which offered the combination of vertical takeoff and landing capabilities, with the greater speed of the traditional fixed-wing aircraft. The first V-22 was rolled out at the Bell facility in Arlington, Texas, on May 23, 1988, with the first flight taking place on March 19, 1989.

Built largely with composite materials and using fiberglass rotor blades, the boxy V-22 soon attracted its share of proponents and detractors. The various military services lined up for a closer look, each seeing the V-22 as the next generation of its own particular mission aircraft. For the Marine Corps, the need was straightforward: a replacement for the Sea Knight. But, even as the V-22 made its first flights, Congress began slashing the defense budget, including continued funding of the Osprey's development. On September 4, 1989, the V-22 made its first flight in the traditional aircraft configuration.

As the helicopter question plagued the Marines, the Corps was also trying to modernize its fixed-wing fleet. Thus, the A-6E Intruder was scheduled for retirement in the early 1990s, with a gradual, but steady phaseout of the few remaining Marine A-6 squadrons.

The Intruder's replacement was already well established. On February 14, 1989, VMFA-225 had received the first FA-18Ds, a two-seater variant of the Hornet. Previously, the FA-18B had been a two-seat trainer version for transition training. But the FA-18D retained much of the single-seater's weapons capabilities, and in fact, included several avionics upgrades, which gave the new Hornet the ability to act as FAC as well as deliver its own ordnance. The Delta thus boasted a light- to medium-attack ability that promised a replacement for the Intruder.

The new FA-18D squadrons were redesignated VMFA(AW)s and also provided a place for the cadre of Marine naval flight officers (NFOs), who had seen their carrier paths disappear with the demise of the F-4 and A-6 programs. Using the Air Force term "weapons system officer"—or WSO (pronounced "Wizzo")—the Hornet backseater became an integral part of the mission. Other Delta squadrons stood up quickly. VMFA(AW)-121 got its aircraft in May 1990. VMFA(AW)-242 soon followed. The new Hornet would soon get to test itself and its new mission in combat.

The Marines also began their long farewell to another veteran aircraft, the Douglas A-4 Skyhawk. On February 27, 1990, VMA-211 sent its last A-4Ms to MAG-42 of the 4th MAW, the Marine Corps Air Reserve. The little jet bomber flew with reserve squadrons in Massachusetts, Tennessee, and California, but even these second-line units' time was growing short. By 1992, only one of the former reserve A-4s had survived to transition to FA 18s. There were more reorganizations and decommissionings to come, but first, the Marines had to fight alongside an international coalition in a major unpredicted war in the desert of Southwest Asia.

Taking the Measure of Saddam

There had been very little public indications of the action to come. U.S. intelligence officers had been watching, and a few even tried raising warning flags, but the Iraqi invasion of Kuwait on August 2, 1990 caught the world largely by surprise. America's military had been piecing together the results of its operation in Panama in December 1989. Operation Just Cause had deposed strongman Manuel Noriega whose resume included conflicting, almost double-agent activities such as working as an operative for the CIA while selling drugs.

The two-week action rid Panama of the dictator, and several components of the American military took part. The Marine Corps sent 700 troops, losing one in action.

The invasion of Kuwait presaged something infinitely bigger, however. Iraq had long maintained that Kuwait was its nineteenth province and constantly threatened its smaller neighbor to the east.

On August 3, President George Bush sent the *Eisenhower* and *Independence* battle groups into the Red Sea and the Indian Ocean. As the two forces rushed to the Persian Gulf, diplomatic messages and charges flew. Iraq then threatened to invade Saudi Arabia. Its million-man army would have made short work of the smaller army of the wealthy sheikdom.

The following weeks brought several escalations—the taking of hostages by Iraq, closing of embassies, military buildups, economic sanctions, threats, and counterthreats. The entire Southwest Asia region was boiling over.

President Bush, determined not only to free Kuwait but also to keep its oil and that of the Arabian peninsula out of Iraqi hands, began hammering together a surprising coalition of improbable allies, not the least of which were several Arab states which had seldom worked together and had often made war on each other. The Egyptians and Syrians cautiously joined the alliance, as did several European and Asian nations that relied on oil shipments from Iraq.

Operation Desert Shield became the most massive buildup of military men and material since World War II, all aimed at facing down one apparently deranged, or dangerously wily, dictator.

While Desert Shield gathered steam, the Marines answered another call. The west African nation of Liberia had been fighting a civil war for nine months and three different factions were tearing the country apart.

By May 1990, it was clear that the action endangered American citizens, and a four-ship amphibious ready group, with 2,100 Marines, prepared to extract them. On August 4, with the situation ashore quickly deteriorating—one of the rebel leaders had threatened to take American hostages—the president issued the order to start Operation Sharp Edge. Elements of the 22nd Marine Expeditionary Unit (MEU) launched from USS *Saipan* (LHA-2). Covering the operation were Sea Knights (HMM-261) and Sea Stallions (HMH-362), escorted by four Sea Cobras (HMLA-167) and two Harriers (VMA-223).

The transports brought Marines to reinforce the embassy compound and help the evacuation. On the first day 72 people were rescued, and eventually, more than 1,600 people—including 132 Americans—were taken out of the country. The helicopters then flew in medical supplies, fuel, and water. The operation continued through August, finally concluding on December 3 after a ceasefire in Liberia on November 28. A total of 226 American citizens and 2,200 other nationals had been rescued.

Desert Shield Gathers Momentum

On August 12, President Bush announced a naval quarantine of Iraq to reinforce a U.N.-established economic embargo. Six days later, the first incident saw two Navy frigates confront two Iraqi tankers. The next two months included several other incidents as more supplies and people poured into bases in the region, building a wall around Iraq and its leader, Saddam Hussein.

Marine aviation was in the buildup immediately, along with every other component of the Corps. Older veteran aircraft and their squadrons accompanied the latest types to the Gulf area. Two A-6E squadrons—VMA(AW)-224 and VMA(AW)-533—arrived in Bahrain in August and December, respectively. VMO-2 flew its OV-10A/D Broncos 10,000 miles from California to Saudi Arabia. VMO-1's Broncos hitched a ride across the ocean on board USS *America*, while VMAQ-2 transpaced two-thirds of its complement of Prowlers, twelve EA-6Bs deploying to Sheik Isa Air Base in Bahrain. For many of the Leatherneck Prowler crews, this unexpected combat deployment was an exciting introduction to real-world operations. "I had about 500 EA-6B hours," Captain Joel Strieter said. "My two junior ECMOs—First Lieutenants Daniel Friedel and John Fulp—had arrived in VMAQ-2 in the spring of 1990. My senior ECMO—Captain William Fiser—was on his second tour in the squadron."

Marine CH-46 and CH-53 squadrons rode over on LPHs and LHAs, accompanied by AH-1T/Ws, and even older AH-1Js from two reserve squadrons. Reserve HMM and HMH squadrons also made their way to the Gulf. Reserve KC-130 tankers supplemented FMF VMGRs. Every community contributed. FMF Hornet squadrons transpaced, including an FA-18D squadron, VMFA(AW)-121.

Maritime interdiction missions were some of the first offensive operations in the Gulf and usually involved intercepting various tankers, freighters, and smaller ships that might be carrying contraband. There was always the chance of a hostile reception by the boarded ship's crew, and the Navy SEAL and Marine teams were, in turn, always ready to meet any threat. There were few incidents, although contraband was occasionally discovered.

In one case, however, an elderly Swedish passenger seemed to have a heart attack after a SEAL team had boarded her ship. She needed immediate medical attention and the CH-53E squadron on board USS *Iwo Jima* got the call. Captain Rick Mullen and his crew flew the woman, who was later determined to have a bad case of food poisoning, to Muscat. Captain Mullen did his best to calm the woman's fears about riding in his huge, noisy helicopter. He wrote her a letter explaining who he and his crew were and what their mission was. He included a photo of his helicopter—he was an avid photographer. When they landed, the woman grasped Captain Mullen's hand and said, "Thank you. You people are so kind. Thank you."

"It felt especially good to be an American that day," he recalled.

By January 1991, the enormous coalition of 500,000 men and women representing some thirty-five countries was in position, waiting as the diplomatic clock wound down to the inevitable. Yet, even as the Marines and their coalition compatriots prepared to face down the Iraqis, another side show developed.

As in Operation Sharp Edge only six months before, Operation Eastern Exit was launched to rescue U.S. citizens caught in a civil war in Africa—this time in Somalia. Although the ten-day operation in early January 1991 was overshadowed by events in the Gulf, it resulted in the rescue of 281 people from thirty countries. USS *Guam* and USS *Trenton* (LPD-14) received orders on January 2 to head for the waters off the Somalian capital, Mogadishu. The CH-53Es of HMH-461 in *Guam* would provide the primary lift support.

Three KC-130s from VMGR-252 and VMGR-352 left their Desert Shield base in Bahrain to provide aerial refueling services for the big Sea Stallion helicopters. Allowing for the low-grade, but very real threat of SAMs, the Marine crews planned a low-altitude approach to the American embassy.

On January 5, at 0245, two CH-53s of HMH-461 launched from *Guam* with sixty Marines and nine SEALs, refueled from orbiting KC-130s, and headed toward Mogadishu, 460 miles away. The helicopters crossed the beach, avoiding the northern areas of the city where the fighting was reported to be the heaviest.

The helo crews ran into trouble picking out their objective because of old, out-of-date maps. Major Dan Schultz, the det commander, decided to fly back over the water to get his bearings. As they headed back over the city, the two Marine helicopters flew over a band of Somali trucks, several of which were armed with .50-caliber machine guns. The operators, however, jumped off their vehicles and ran.

Finally, the pilots spotted the embassy, which seemed to be under attack by a group of Somalis. These people also ran as the helicopters approached.

Setting their aircraft down inside the compound a little after 0700, the Marine crews waited for an hour, loading sixty-one people, before taking off for the safety of their ship. After depositing the evacuees on the *Guam*, the two CH-53s headed for the *Trenton*, their home ship, to the enthusiastic greetings of the ship's crew.

Alerts continued throughout the day, with CH-46Es from HMM-263 and HMM-365, and armed UH-1Ns from HMLA-269, ready to fly back to the embassy. *Guam* and *Trenton* had steamed to a point where the CH-46s, which lacked in-flight refueling capability, could launch to get the remaining civilians. The final wave retrieved the remaining Marines and SEALs out of harm's way, leaving the building to the violent attentions of the Somali populace, who rocketed, then looted, the embassy.

Back to the Gulf

One gap in Marine Corps support in the Gulf was tactical reconnaissance. For three decades, VMFP-3 had flown its RF-4Bs. The photo-

Phantoms had become the last fleet Phantoms in naval service. But P-3 decommissioned on October 1, 1990, incredibly, leaving the Corps without a valuable set of eyes on the eve of what would be the largest military action since Vietnam. The squadron had once flown as many as twenty-one RF-4Bs and included some 800 people on its rolls.

The hole left by P-3's retirement was to be filled to an extent by unmanned aerial reconnaissance vehicles (UAVs), specifically Pioneer reconnaissance drones. These small unmanned aircraft, originally obtained from Israel and delivered to the Marine Corps in 1987, could be launched from ships or from shore launch points close to the battlefield. Their size limited the number of sensors and thus, they could not offer the depth of coverage of the RF-4B. But in the coming months, the drones, used by the Navy and the Marine Corps, would sometimes be the only battlefield reconnaissance assets available.

UAVs flew with Marine, Navy, and Army units, and generally received high marks for their performance. Crews became intensely loyal to their little aircraft, and since the war, have become great boosters of the UAV program, citing their slogan, "No widows, no POWs with UAVs."

Marine Corps UAV battalions used all three types of UAVs: the Israeli-manufactured Pioneer, the Pointer, developed by and for the Army, and the new BQM-147A Exdrone, which was still under development but was taken from testing units because of the great need for them in the Gulf.

Writing in the September 1991 issue of *Marine Corps Gazette*, Major Christopher P. Gutmann, an experienced RF-4B backseater, made several telling observations:

VMFP-3 for years played an unsung and unglamorous role in Marine aviation . . . the RF-4B did not represent our only reconnaissance asset, but surely it was our most significant and most capable reconnaissance asset . . . . P-3's greatest problem was its lack of visibility within the Marine Corps . . . . At the time of its retirement, the RF-4B, still very capable, had long past seen its best days. The airframes and reconnaissance systems were tired and subject to excessive failure . . . . What was difficult for officers within the reconnaissance community to understand was how the RF-4B could be retired with no replacement in sight. My feeling was that unmanned aerial vehicle (UAV) employment . . . must have existed for the Corps to disband its only reconnaissance squadron . . . . Undeniably UAVs are very important . . . but they can't currently replace manned aircraft . . . .

Lieutenant General Royal Moore, commanding general, 3D MAW, commented on the intelligence problem in the Gulf: "Our own aircraft supplied us with the best intelligence. We had 177 airplanes at Sheikh Isa, both Air Force and Marines, and some Air National Guard RF-4Cs. I retired the last Marine Corps RF-4Bs two days before I left California in August 1991. We looked very hard at bringing those RF-4Bs back; we just could not do it." [45]

General Moore also assessed the UAV contribution, saying, "We used the Pioneer system extensively. We had all the Pioneer companies out there . . . the RPVs caught some SA-6s coming down the road to Jabar, and we knocked them stiff . . . ." [46]

16

Desert Storm

 The boldness of the Iraqis, and particularly their president, seemed to many observers a sign that they would not leave Kuwait, and thus, a conflict was inevitable. With his coalition in place and prepared after six months of training in the Saudi Arabian desert, President Bush delivered a final deadline for the Iraqis to acquiesce to U.N. demands, retreat back to their traditional borders, vacate Kuwait, and avoid war. The January 15 deadline passed, and the first strikes of the war occurred in the early hours of January 17.

Captain Strieter commented that Marine Corps aviation activities were divided into four phases during Desert Storm—"preplanned waves," which lasted for the first four days, strikes on high-value targets such as air defense, command and control, air fields, and logistics areas, battlefield interdiction, then close air support. "During Phase II," he said, "we would receive the Air Tasking Order in the evening, and plan for the next day's missions. This was different from Phase I where we had received the ATO months before." Phase III included artillery raids and border skirmishes, which the Playboy Prowlers supported.

At 0300, Playboy Prowlers were in the air supporting the first coalition raids into Iraq, and along the border of Saudi Arabia and Kuwait. One Prowler crew could shield six different missions at once with its jamming facilities, as well as with HARMs, fired against enemy SAM and anti-aircraft radars. Captain Strieter and his crew helped defend a force of more than forty Marine FA-18s, as well as Navy strike aircraft as they headed into and out of Iraq.

Strieter observed, "My orbit's southern point was the 'crotch' of the Iraq-Saudi-Kuwait border . . . . We had no dedicated CAP—alone, unarmed, and unafraid! Looking left, right, and out front, all we could see were AAA and SAM launches. It wasn't any better turning around." Strieter tried to call his wingman, but after several attempts without a reply, he feared the worst. Happily, they regained contact with the other Prowler as they were heading back to their base. He recalls, "In retrospect, holding to land was probably the most dangerous phase of the flight. All aircraft coming home were not under positive control, so there were about fifty aircraft all within twenty miles of each other . . . . It seemed like everyone was out to kill you!"

The squadrons of the four MAGs which made up 3D MAW—which had come from redesignating and reorganizing MAG-70—flew from shore bases and ships. MAG-70 had been the air-combat element (ACE) of the 7th Marine Expeditionary Brigade (MEB), and was what retired Brigadier General E.H. Simmons had called a "pocket air force . . . flying a great variety of aircraft."[47]

In reality, however, the shore-based Marine squadrons reported appropriately to the senior Marine commander, Lieutenant General Walter E. Boomer, commanding the I Marine Expeditionary Force (I MEF). However, the various helicopter squadrons and VMA-331, the AV-8B squadron on board *Nassau*, were under the control of Vice Admiral Stan Arthur's Seventh Fleet organization.

It was a somewhat disjointed arrangement brought on as much by Marine Corps stubbornness as by more traditional interservice rivalries. As usual, the Air Force wanted a large piece of the Marine aviation assets, and so did the Navy. The Marine Corps, of course, wanted to fly its aircraft in support of its Marines on the ground, with a distinct secondary role in support of other services. It was an argument as old as Marine Corps air, itself, and like so many times before—in World War II, Korea, and Vietnam—the situation was never satisfactorily resolved, even when the shooting started.

The Marines also wanted to be ready to support any amphibious operation that might be launched, which, after all, was at the heart of Marine air's *raison d'etre*. But, in truth, the massive from-the-sea invasion of Kuwait that so troubled the Iraqis was never planned. It was considered for a short time but never really given any more thought, primarily because such an operation would have been much too costly for what it might have gained.

The depth of the Marines' resentment of having to split their forces showed up during General Moore's interview in the November 1991 issue of the U.S. Naval Institute's *Proceedings*. When the interviewer noted that the Marine Corps had lost five Harriers to enemy action, the 3D MAW commander quickly and strongly corrected him: "First we did not lose five; we lost four, and the 4th Marine Expeditionary Brigade, which was under the Naval Commander, Central Command control, lost one on the last day. . . ." It may have been a fine point, but it was one that the Marines felt strongly about. (VMA-331, embarked in USS *Nassau*, had lost the last AV-8B during combat operations. Although considered a combat loss, the reason was never specifically determined to be as the result of enemy action.)

The first offensive mission by Marine Corps aviation in the Gulf began at 0400 on January 17. Forty-eight Marine aircraft from Sheikh Isa and Bahrain International Airport, along with twenty other allied planes, hit Iraqi airfields and SCUD missile shelters.

As dawn broke, MAG-13 Harriers and OV-10s went in against targets in southern Kuwait. By the end of the first day of Desert Storm, Marine aircrews had flown 144 combat sorties, the first of more than 18,000 during the war.

While largely successful, the Marines did have losses. On January 18, an OV-10A from VMO-2 was shot down, its two-man crew interned as POWs. The pilot was the squadron CO, Lieutenant Colonel Cliff Acree, and the observer, CWO-4 Guy Hunter.

The Leatherneck Intruder squadrons were also at work, flying day and night missions in the terrible weather that enveloped the region. These precision bombing missions led the A-6 crews into Iraq and Kuwait against convoys of armored and supply vehicles, as well as troop concentrations. Even when the Iraqis used ecological terrorism and torched hundreds of Kuwaiti oil wells, releasing towering plumes of thick, black smoke that eventually curtained off the region, the Intruders responded.

VMAQ-2's Prowler crews were constantly in demand to support coalition strikes. It was not uncommon for the Playboys to be jamming for raids involving more than fifty aircraft. On February 21, Captain Strieter and his crew defended twenty-five separate flights of Harriers and Hornets. Strieter's Prowler was carrying three ECM pods and two HARMs. It had been less than a week since Marine Prowlers had fired their first anti-radiation missile on February 15.

The controller told the Marine Prowler to support a B-52 raid near Al Jaber. An Iraqi mobile SAM's radar came up near the target and Captain Strieter shot a HARM at the enemy site, gaining a possible kill.

Magill's MiG

One Marine fighter pilot continued a long-established tradition by shooting down an enemy MiG while flying an exchange tour with the

Air Force. Captain Charles Magill was assigned to the Air Force's 58th Tactical Fighter Squadron, flying the F-15C Eagle which was, along with the Navy's Tomcat, the world's premier air superiority fighter.

A Hornet pilot by trade, Captain Magill launched as part of an eight-plane escort early in the afternoon of January 17. By this time, the war's first strikes had yielded the first kills by other F-15 pilots in the pre-dawn darkness over Iraq. As Magill and his four-plane division topped off from an orbiting tanker, the omniscient AWACS aircraft warned of Iraqi MiG-29s over the target airfield at Al Taquaddum.

"As we drew nearer the target," Magill commented later, "I directed the second division to continue their sweep to the north while I led three Eagles toward the south."

He bore down on the MiGs, just as he saw two SAM launches. The F-15 pilots jettisoned their external fuel tanks, but the missiles flew past without detonating.

The two blue MiG-29s had turned south toward Magill's flight, and as they approached the F-15s, Magill fired two AIM-7 Sparrows. His wingman, Captain Rhory Draeger, also fired a missile. For the Marine and Air Force fighter pilots, time slowed down as their missiles seemed to hang in midair. Finally, the Sparrows' rocket motors lit off, and the missiles sped toward their targets.

Draeger's Sparrow got to his MiG first, blowing it into a huge fire-ball. Then, Captain Magill's Sparrows struck another MiG, one right after the other, sending the Iraqi fighter toward the desert below. The elated Eagle pilots turned back toward their strike group of F-16s, avoiding a spread of SAMs. Arriving back at their base, Magill and Draeger indulged in the traditional victory roll to the delight of their ground troops. (Draeger, who would get another kill—a MiG-23 on January 26—was one of eight Air Force pilots to score two kills.)

Marine Air in the Ground War

The strategic air campaign against Iraq continued throughout most of February. The results were a mighty confirmation of air power's role in modern war, but the ultimate action of the war was yet to come: the ground war. Everything else had been in preparation for confronting the enemy on the desert floor.

All coalition factions prepared for the kickoff of the ground war, the main act of which would include lifting massive numbers of coalition troops into fighting areas. All squadrons would be used to cover the battlefield, from AH-1Ws to CH-46s and CH-53s.

The long-awaited ground war kicked off at 0400 on Sunday, February 24. Coalition forces thrust deep into Iraq and Kuwait, cutting into Iraqi positions with surprising ease that caught the Allies off guard as much as the Iraqis.

HMLA-367 Cobras were in the thick of the action. On the morning of February 24, after flying several armed reconnaissance missions, they took out several enemy 120mm mortar batteries that were firing on advancing Marine tanks, and then went after three Iraqi tanks, destroying them as well. Seeing their comrades' fate, the remaining Iraqi troops quickly surrendered to the Marines, who were quickly advancing toward the Iraqis.

As thousands of Iraqi POWs stretched the limits of the coalition's ability to detain and care for them, the push quickly went far ahead of schedule, and coalition units scrambled to catch up with those who had gone before them.

Captain George Caulkins, a Cobra pilot with HMLA-367, proudly recalled his squadron's record: "There is really no doubt that Scarface was the best. I am as susceptible as the next guy to unit pride, but we feel that we went beyond that. We did not have the most assets in theater, but no one answered the call the way we did."

At the ceasefire on February 28, HMLA-367 had accounted for ninety-six kills against Iraqi equipment, as well as being directly responsible for thousands of Iraqi POWs who surrendered to the approaching Scarface Cobras.

Major John S. Stollery, Jr., USMCR (FTS), had arrived with HMM-774, a reserve CH-46E squadron from Norfolk, Virginia, originally scheduled for an exercise in Norway that year, but now one of several Marine reserve squadrons mobilized for duty in the Gulf. HMM-774 loaded its Sea Knights onto USAF C-5s, and their people and material onto eight C-141s. They landed at Jubail, the main USMC helicopter base in Saudi Arabia, on January 5, 1991, having left the U.S. on January 3.

For the next two weeks, the squadron reassembled and flight-tested their aircraft, set up their operations, acclimatized to the desert, and practiced with their new ANVIS-6 night vision goggles. They had no chance to train with the new NVGs in the States, but the new goggles were easier to use then the ANVIS-5 models the squadron had used at home. The ANVIS-6 was also more capable than the earlier model.

HMM-774 moved to the forward base called Lonesome Dove on February 22 to be ready for the ground war. Lonesome Dove was eight miles southwest of the Kuwait-Saudi border, merely a point in the desert known only to the Bedouin nomads as a crosspoint. It was chosen because of its proximity to Kuwait and to projected "breech" points for the ground war through which Marine ground forces would pour into Kuwait once the ground war began. Stollery called it "a mixture of gravel, and camel and goat turds."

Unlike Jubail, which featured a terrain of small hills, Lonesome Dove was flat and allowed the squadron to practice "turfing"—flying at fifty feet above the desert with little fear of running into an unexpected hill, especially while using NVGs.

Stollery tried to calm his pre-combat jitters by reading and walking. He read a book while sitting in the cockpit of his helicopter the day before the ground war. He wore his full NBC MOP gear, however, as long as he did not move too much, the gear was not too uncomfortable. Communication was a problem, though, and could only be done on ICS.

On February 24, Stollery launched with forty-six other Marine helicopters—transports (46s and 53s) and their Cobra escorts. He was in Red group, a four-plane section from 774. They had gone to LZ Sandy at 1500 on the 23rd, and slept in their helicopters waiting for a white star shell, which would signal that they had twenty minutes before launch.

The launch was briefed to start at 1200 on the 24th, however, by 1500, no signal had come. Finally, at 1530, the shell was fired. The crew got into their NBC gear. Stollery's copilot was nervous and furiously tapped his fingers. Fortunately, it was not too distracting through all the NBC gear. They would be hauling a two-man TOW-missile team and their jeep-launcher. A sergeant drove around to all the aircraft in a jeep to tell the crews that it had been determined that there was no NBC threat and that they could, thankfully, discard their cumbersome protective gear. The messenger also warned they would launch in eight minutes.

The wind had shifted from the west to the north. As the large gaggle of helos lifted, the rotor wash stirred up the sand and dirt, mixing it into a huge cloud that obscured vision for the helo crews, especially those in the rear of the formation. A half mile ahead of Stollery's aircraft, one plane rolled over as its pilots lost ground reference in a brownout. No one was killed although the H-46 incurred strike damage.

Stollery lifted off and gingerly sidled off to the right to clear the cloud directly in front of him. His torque warning horn blared in the cockpit. His aircraft was fully loaded at maximum gross weight of 24,000 pounds. He had fuel for an hour and forty-five minutes of flight—1,200 pounds—and besides the TOW team and their jeep, he had two door-mounted M-60 machine guns with 700 rounds per gun.

The Marine helicopters joined up, and the huge formation headed toward the Kuwait border. The sun was setting in the late afternoon and what was to have been a daylight operation was becoming a nighttime hop, complete with night vision goggles. Whereas the sun could be a problem as it sank below the horizon, the hazard was replaced by the glare of the raging oil fires which made seeing the aircraft around him difficult for Major Stollery. He likened the scene with NVGs to taking a picture directly into the sun: he could only see a featureless silhouette of the aircraft in front of him, and could not tell how far away the next helicopter was from him, except as the profile changed in size. He made slight movements with his H-46 to keep the formation in sight as they flew at 200 feet.

The radio frequency was clobbered. Everyone was talking, making communication difficult. Since there was no threat from the Iraqis, precautions were dropped. Escorts were having a tough time staying with their transports. Stollery's lead announced that he would abort the flight unless control cleared up the confusion. "The fog of war," Stollery said, "made it hard."

The formation crossed into Kuwait directly over a breech line. The word came that the ground forces were having great success. Stollery and his four-plane formation decided not to deliver their troops because of the confusion and obscured visibility, and turned around for home.

As they recrossed the border, the MAG-16 aircraft broke off and headed for Tanijib, their home base, while Stollery's formation flew toward Lonesome Dove. Everyone was low on fuel. The MAG-16 choppers would try to make the FFARP, while the reserve planes pressed on. It was a dangerous point in the flight as planes broke away from the formation and struck out in new directions. HMM-774 recovered at Lonesome Dove in an open space near their tents.

Staff Sergeant William Chambers, a regular Marine assigned to HMM-774, was in a CH-46E in the third string. They were to carry a jeep and its four-man crew to the landing zone, but the mayhem of the brownout ahead of them made it nearly impossible.

Chambers, a designated aerial gunner manning a .50-caliber machine gun, eventually flew into Kuwait International, his pilot touching down by the passenger terminal. HMM-774 had been the first Marine aviation squadron into Kuwait City, just behind the exultant ground troops who liberated the city. The reserve helo crews had taken replacements for the lead troops into the city, which Chambers remembers as "war-torn, gutted."

For Staff Sergeant Chambers, the strongest memory of Desert Storm were the oil fires. "You could see the fires as soon as you crossed the border. Everything was black from the fires. You could see the smoke from fifteen miles away."

Captain G.J. Mazenko, flying CH-46s with HMM-268 from USS *New Orleans* also considered the fires and smoke the most troubling part of any mission. When the plans for an amphibious assault changed to supporting the ground war, the Red Dragons moved ashore to the airfield at Tanajib, Saudi Arabia. "The most dangerous enemy we faced," Captain Mazenko reported, "was not the Iraqi Army, but the thick, dense, black smoke from the hundreds of oil fires. High-tension power lines across the open desert were sometimes masked by the smoke."

On one occasion, a flight of eight helicopters, including six CH-46s and two Cobra escorts entered what appeared to be a thin cloud of smoke. The visibility in the smoke, however, quickly dropped to zero, and with the tight formation often within two or three rotor diameters of each other, the danger of a midair collision was great. Fortunately, the Marine helos got out of the cloud before such a tragedy could happen.

Marine gunship helos were busy during this last phase of the war. At 0400 on February 26, six UH-1Ns from HMLA-269, armed with 2.75-inch rockets and machine guns, launched from USS *Nassau* and headed for Iraqi-occupied Failaka Island. The raid was meant to be part of a feint to keep the enemy off guard while diverting attention from the real invasion further inland.

Flying on night vision goggles, the Huey crews flew the seventy-two miles to the island. The smoke and flames from Kuwait's burning oil wells and from Kuwait City were plainly visible, as was random flak from Bubian Island to the north. But the Huey crews pressed on, arriving at their pre-attack position. Flak from Bubian was still peppering the sky around them, but after making a night tactical turn, all six helicopters fired their rockets at targets along the northwest beach of Failaka.

The Iraqis quickly responded with defensive fire, and the sky was lit with bursts from both sides. The Hueys spread out, finally reversed their direction, and headed back to their ship, having reinforced the bogus threat of an amphibious invasion of Kuwait in the minds of the Iraqis.

AH-1W crews of HMLA-169 had brought an experimental system to the Gulf. The Nite Eagle laser identification system had literally been taken from its testing laboratory for a combat evaluation with Hellfire laser-guided missiles. The enthusiastic Viper pilots scored several kills against Iraqi tanks with the new system.

It was on February 26, that Lieutenant Colonel Michael M. Kurth, the commanding officer of HMLA-369, earned one of only two Navy Crosses awarded to Marines during the Gulf War. Having led five AH-1Ws from Lonesome Dove to Al Jaber, he then launched in a UH-1N to scout for the ground forces. Contending with near-zero visibility because of the smoke from oil well fires, he repeatedly flew near and sometimes under powerlines. Eventually, he located the Marines on the ground, then returned to the AH-1s he had left at Al Jaber, and soon, the Cobras were providing support for the ground forces, using laser designation from Lieutenant Colonel Kurth's Huey.

Major General J.M. Myatt, who commanded the 1st Marine Division during the war, commended Lieutenant Colonel Kurth during a magazine interview:

. . . So here's . . . the 3rd Armored Division . . . needing some help, and you've got Mike Kurth flying from the area south of all the smoke, in a Huey, guiding a division of helicopters under three big high-tension wire systems, flying under them, going north to support Task Force Ripper . . . .[48]

Besides the EA-6Bs and A-6Es, two other fixed-wing tactical jets flew with the squadrons of MAG-11, 3D MAW. Derived from the preliminary, quick-reaction organization of MAG-70, 3D MAW, under Major General Royal Moore, carried the brunt of Marine Corps aviation activities in the war in the Gulf. During the forty-two days of the war, MAG-11 aircraft posted more than 7,500 sorties in 16,500 flight hours. MAG-11 aircraft dropped more than 17,000,000 pounds of ordnance, including Mk-80 series bombs, Maverick, HARM, and Rockeye.

Perhaps the most anticipated sorties were those of the highly-touted AV-8B, flying in its first combat since the AV-8A entered USMC service in 1971. Four full squadrons (VMAs 311, 542, 231, and 331), and a six-plane detachment from a fifth (VMA-513 Det B), of Harrier IIs flew in the war, most from shore bases. VMA-331 flew from USS *Nassau*, however, eventually making the first ship-launched missions for Marine Corps Harriers, beginning on February 20. The VSTOL attack squadrons mainly flew the CAS missions for which they were designed, ahead of advancing Marines on the ground.

Harrier missions were not without cost, however, and five Harriers were lost in combat. Two pilots ejected and were captured. Another ejected after nursing his crippled plane close to friendly lines. But two Harrier pilots died in action, one while attacking an enemy tank at night, and the second in unspecified circumstances during a mission.

U.S. Marine Corps AV-8Bs were not the only Harriers in theater, although they alone saw combat. Britain's Royal Navy stationed the carrier HMS *Ark Royal* with a complement of Sea Harrier FRS.1s of 899 Squadron in the Red Sea along with other coalition ships. The British Harriers were held in reserve, however, as the Royal Navy's helicopter units were that service's most active aviation groups.

The Royal Air Force was in the middle of a major transition from its old GR.3 Harriers—comparable to AV-8As—to the GR.5 and GR.7. Since the RAF had sent many other types of aircraft to the Gulf, and because Vice Admiral Stanley Arthur, commanding the U.S. Navy's Seventh Fleet and U.S. Naval Forces Central Command, decided that he did not need the British Harriers, the RAF aircraft remained at home.

The first major Harrier actions involved the Battle for Khafji on January 28-29. Originally thought to be an Iraqi feint, the attack on the border town quickly became the first full-fledged ground battle of the war, with probes, thrusts, and artillery duels. On the night of January 29, the Iraqis took the lightly-defended town. Harriers from VMA-542 flying from King Abdul Aziz East airfield, ninety miles from Khafji, responded to the call.

Major Jim Lee and his four-plane flight headed toward an Iraqi column of personnel carriers, which were right in the middle of Khafji. Major Lee and his wingman, Captain Dennis Hass, made the first runs, dropping their Mk-82 500-pound bombs. Captain Dan Claney and his wingman followed with Rockeye anti-tank cluster bombs. Angered by the first attack, the enemy was waiting for the second section of AV-8Bs. The Iraqis fired at least seven SA-9 heat-seeker SAMs at the oncoming Harriers whose pilots evaded all of the missiles.

Harrier attacks against Khafji continued throughout the following day, disposing of a number of Iraqi tanks and FROG surface-to-surface missiles. Shortly after dawn, VMA-311 AV-8Bs hit an Iraqi artillery battery that had been shelling the town and an adjacent oil refinery. An orbiting OV-10 crew called in the Tomcat Harriers, which obliterated the enemy position with 1,000 pound bombs and cannon fire. Eventually, the Iraqis were evicted from Khafji.

Khafji also saw widespread use of Marine AH-1W Cobra gunships from the beginning of the Iraqi attack. HMLA-367 crews constantly engaged Iraqi tanks and armored columns, destroying several vehicles.

Harrier pilots flew their own missions or in company with another important Marine Corps jet, the FA-18 Hornet. No less than seven VM-FAs flew in the Gulf as part of MAG-11 (VMFAs 212, 232, 235, 314, 333, 451, and VMFA(AW)-121, with its new two-seat FA-18Ds). The single-seat Hornet squadrons flew both FA-18As and FA-18Cs, staying mostly within the Kuwait Theater of Operations (KTO) after the first week of the war. Following extensive training in Desert Shield, the MAG-11 Hornet squadrons were ready for Desert Storm, flying strike missions as well as CAPs in the northern Gulf, and a single mission against targets close to Baghdad. Marine Hornets flew more than 5,100 combat sorties during the forty-three-day air campaign, and although several aircraft were hit by Iraqi ground-fire and missiles, none was lost in combat.

Captain A. Morrison, an FA-18A pilot with VMFA-333, reported that the Shamrocks had a young Navy intelligence officer "who did a superb job and probably saved several pilots."

Recalling various missions, Captain Morrison remembered that the Iraqis "threw 'orange pumpkins' at us—flak." But unlike Vietnam, where getting permission to go after the flak sites was complicated, the Marine FA-18 pilots in the Gulf War, after finding the sites, would actually troll for fire. When the flak guns—usually 85mm-100mm weapons—opened up, the Hornet drivers went after them, frequently with Rockeye cluster-bomb canisters, a very effective weapon against stationary ground targets.

Having traded its A-6Es for the two-seat Hornets in April 1990, VM-FA(AW)-121 barely had time to get to know its new mounts before heading out to the Gulf on January 7, 1991, little more than a week before the shooting started. With six aircraft and 118 people, the squadron set up at Sheikh Isa, followed by six more Hornets and flight crews.

Their mission was largely battlefield preparation and reconnaissance in the KTO. Carrying 2.75-inch rocket pods, 20mm cannon, and white-phosphorous marking rounds, the Green Knights flew among the oil fires, scouting Iraqi positions for the coalition ground units. The first mission came on January 18 when, after topping off from KC-130s, squadron Hornets marked targets for a strike group. As the war continued, the 121 crews flew around the clock, using NVGs during night missions, spotting the muzzle flashes of Iraqi artillery, and quickly either directing strikes against the artillery battery, or going after the enemy position themselves.

Like their Harrier compatriots, the FA-18D crews helped defend the town of Khafji, in one case stopping an Iraqi armored column threatening a Marine position. Captain Robert Turner (pilot) and his WSO (Major Michael Pedersen) used rockets and their cannon to strafe Iraqi tanks, which came as close as 1,500 meters from the Marines on the ground.

Lieutenant Colonel Stephen F. Mugg, the commanding officer of VMFA(AW)-121, remarked: "Every crew flew every day, and each crew was paired up. They got to know their relatively small area very well."

The surprisingly fast pace of the ground war brought a quick end to the overall conflict. By February 28, the Iraqis had retreated from Kuwait, back across the extreme southeastern border with their "nineteenth province." Even when the Iraqis could muster and launch an offensive or counterstrike of their own, it did not last long. Allied air power would usually pull the plug. Marine Corps fixed- and rotary-wing squadrons roamed free to give whatever support was needed.

AH-1W Super Cobras were especially active during the ground war phase, using TOW anti-tank weapons and their turret-mounted 20mm cannon to good effect. AH-1T and AH-1J (the Juliets were from the two Marine Air Reserve squadrons, HMA-773 and HMA-775) escorted transport helicopters over the battlefield.

The ceasefire announced by the United States on February 28, 1991, ended the immediate hostilities, but there was a lot of cleaning up to do, and the Iraqis still had a few scores to settle.

Provide Comfort

The United States had hoped that one of the results of its victory over Iraq would be the deposition of Saddam Hussein by his own people. The Kurds, tribesmen who composed twenty percent of the Iraqi population, had been oppressed by Saddam for years as subjects of bombing raids and gas attacks. The U.S. hoped that the Kurds would be the driving force behind an uprising, but after a few days of rebellion, the Iraqi army, which had been decimated and demoralized by the coalition's overwhelming conquest, reformed and went after the Kurds with a vengeance that could only come from the frustration of being defeated by a more powerful enemy.

The Kurds fled into the mountains bordering Iraq and Turkey, some 750,000 of them flooding refugee camps by late March. The disheartened, sickened Kurds soon presented a massive humanitarian problem for the allies of the coalition. With 1,500 refugees dying every day, the U.S., which was still dismantling its huge war machine, assessing the results of Desert Storm and the frustrating continuing presence of Saddam in power, knew it had to help.

Along with units still in the Gulf, the Marine Corps ordered other Marines from around the world to head for the area to participate in the largest humanitarian effort in Marine Corps history. Besides its own CH-46Es, many of which were battle-scarred veterans of Vietnam more than fifteen years before, HMM-264, a composite squadron embarked in USS *Guadalcanal* (LPH-7), brought elements of HMH-461 (CH-53Es) and HMLA-167 (UH-1Ns and AH-1Ts) to what had been labeled Operation Provide Comfort.

As they began flying missions on April 15, the Marines struggled to establish primitive landing zones and base camps among the inhospitable mountains and hills of northern Iraq. They also had to contend with the seas of humanity that pressed forward to meet each helicopter, little caring of the danger from whirring rotor blades and heavily-laden helicopters.

For the next two months, the Marines of HMM-264 and of various ground units tended to aiding the huge allied operation of first resuscitating the Kurds and then trying to relocate them back in Iraq. Fighting weather, Kurdish fears, and the vengeful Iraqis were no easy tasks, but by mid-June, when the Marines left the hills of Kurdistan, the tribesmen were much healthier and the future held promise, even among the ruins and tensions of Saddam's country.

In addition to helping the Kurdish refugees, Marine aviation participated in another large-scale humanitarian effort, Operation Sea Angel, a massive relief operation to help survivors of a huge cyclone in Bangladesh. The storm struck the impoverished country on April 29, 1991, and the country's prime minister appealed for help.

Soon a world-wide rescue involving thirty-two countries was mounted. President Bush sent in elements of III MEF, including 5th MEB and

MAG-50. The squadrons of this aircraft group were looking forward to returning home after the Gulf War but their homecoming would be delayed.

HMLA-169, HMM-265, VMA-513's Det B, and HMH-772, a reserve squadron, were sidetracked to the Bay of Bengal. From mid-May to early June, the MAG's heavy- and medium-lift helicopters brought food and medical supplies to the devastated countryside.

Much has been written and said about the overall contribution of naval aviation during the Gulf War of 1991. The USAF usually claims the lion's share of credit so far as the impact of air power on the Iraqis, pointing to the effect of its strategic air campaign and the success of its F-15 pilots against Iraqi MiGs, whose pilots seldom flew their advanced aircraft in an aggressive or knowledgeable manner. However, while the USAF and other coalition partners certainly did well in the one-sided war, the Navy and Marine Corps did not spend the conflict on the sidelines.

For the Marines, the war was a chance to exercise, much like the wish of an athlete who has spent a lot of time and effort training in a gym, and who longs to try himself in competition. Indeed, it may be argued that Marine Corps aviation found itself more of a tangible role than did the Navy's vaunted carrier-based squadrons, whose dedicated crews had to deal with the Air Force's complicated air-tasking order and fight for the junior service's aerial tankers.

The Marines, with their highly trained Harrier and Hornet crews, as well as their own KC-130 tankers, were more independent, and in more demand by the ground units, who, after all, ultimately fought the ground war that was the centerpiece of Allied strategy.

Colonel John P. Oppenhuizen had been serving as the deputy commander of the Naval Safety Center in Norfolk, Virginia, when he was asked to volunteer to serve as the air officer for I MEF. An A-4 pilot in Vietnam with VMA-223, he commented on Marine aviation in the Gulf:

Marine air was probably not used as much in the CAS role before the ground war. There *were* CAS missions since we had people along the border the whole time . . . . Harriers were definitely used at Khafji . . . . Marine air was used a lot for interdiction and SEAD—most of it was interdiction . . . .[49]

Colonel Oppenhuizen was correct in assessing the use of Marine aircraft as battlefield interdictors, a role that Marine aircrews seldom trained for.

Major William R. Cronin commented in the March 1992 issue of *Marine Corps Gazette*: ". . . The release of Marine air for Marine use was delayed . . . by a spate of bad weather over many of the strategic targets in Iraq and northern Kuwait, and by a lack of confirmed bomb damage assessment assets . . . ." BDA *was* a problem that was never resolved during the war. Cronin concluded, "Unlike deep air support and armed reconnaissance, battlefield air interdiction (BAI) is a mission seldom practiced by Marine tactical aviation, and prior to Desert Storm, was most often associated with Air Force tactical doctrine . . . ."

17

New Challenges for All

 Desert Storm and its fortuitous conclusion was only a pause in the larger activities that involved all the U.S. military, including the Marine Corps. Hard budgetary considerations in Washington forecast a shrinking lineup of squadrons and people. And even though squadrons may have participated with distinction in the Gulf War, they were not protected from the ax. Several aviation squadrons were decommissioned by 1993, with more to follow by mid-decade.

Important programs like the V-22 Osprey were never safe, especially when crashes and operational mishaps seemed to dog the Navy and Marine Corps. Safety stand-downs, by the direct orders of the Chief of Naval Operations, the Commandant, and their respective heads of aviation programs, strove to reorient people's attention toward safety and making do with a declining budget and supply chain.

Seventy AV-8Bs were grounded for five days in March 1996 after two mishaps. A similar grounding followed in June of all Navy and Marine Corps CH-53E and MH-53E helicopters to permit inspection of the big helos' main-rotor heads. Concern developed after the fatal crash in May of a CH-53E, which killed four Sikorsky employees on the pre-delivery flight.

The Harrier community, however, also scheduled a partial grounding of the AV-8B fleet—90 of 170 aircraft—in October after another series of fatal mishaps, which brought the number of AV-8Bs lost in 1996 to seven. The investigations focused on the Harriers' new 406 engines. By October, sixty-eight Sea Stallions remained grounded because they were waiting for parts to prevent crashes like the one in May.

Veteran aircraft finally left the inventory. The unique OV-10 Bronco and its squadrons—VMO-1 and VMO-2 in the FMF, and VMO-4 in the reserves—retired in 1993. Entering Marine Corps service in 1964, the big A-6 Intruder also retired in April 1993, VMA(AW)-332 having the nostalgic honor of flying the last Leatherneck sortie with Grumman's attack bomber. And reserve squadron VMFA-112 at NAS Dallas held a retirement ceremony in January 1992 to bid farewell to McDonnell's F-4 as it left naval squadron service.

Other changes included the deactivation of VMAQ-4, the reserve Prowler squadron in September 1992, followed by its immediate reactivation as part of a four-for-one split in the USMC EA-6B community. In an unusual move, the Marines reconstituted their sole VMAQ, the Playboys of VMAQ-2, with three detachments (X,Y, and Z) into three separate squadrons, VMAQs 1, 2, and 3. The reserve 4th MAW's VMAQ-4 was disestablished, then stood back up as the fleet's VMAQ-4. The reorganization occurred on July 1, 1992, and permitted better coverage around the world and throughout the Navy and Marine Corps.

Besides the changes in hardware and organization, the Marines also found themselves changing geographic location in some cases. Servicewide base closings and realignment necessitated Marine Hornet squadrons on both coasts to shift. MCAS El Toro would be closed, and the west coast Hornets would have to move south to the Navy's tactical jet base at Miramar, outside San Diego. Likewise, VMFA(AW)-533, having given up its A-6s after the Gulf War, had transitioned to the FA-18D and would take up residence at MCAS Beaufort, South Carolina.

Marine Corps aviation had a full plate with new missions, new squadrons, new groupings and new responsibilities. But the world went on, and new crises in different parts of the globe required that Marine squadrons participate.

The Marines also found themselves dealing with the sociological changes affecting the entire American military. Women were now entering naval flight training for the express purpose of becoming Marine aviators. By August 1996, two women had pinned on their wings of gold, one as a pilot and one as a naval flight officer. First Lieutenant Sarah Deal would fly CH-53Es, while First Lieutenant Jeanne Buchanan would fly EA-6Bs as an electronic countermeasures officer (ECMO).

Back to Africa

For the third time in two-and-one-half years, the Marines were called to action in Africa, and once again, the place was the strife-torn, famine-ridden coastal nation of Somalia, where rival factions were ruled by avaricious warlords who plundered their country and kept the rest of the civilized world at bay. More than 300,000 Somalis had died since the Marines' last visit in January 1991. The United States and other U.N. member-countries wanted to send in medical supplies and food, but could not risk entering the unsecured ports and airports. Thus, it fell to the Marine Corps' 15th MEU(SOC) to land on December 9, 1992, launching Operation Restore Hope.

The uncontested landing was carried out in a light atmosphere in front of enthusiastic news cameras. However, the risk was real, and on January 12, 1993, a Marine was killed during a gun battle near the airport at Mogadishu.

HMM-164 (REIN) from USS *Tripoli* (LPH-10) provided air support with CH-46Es, CH-53Es, UH-1Ns, and AH-1Ws. On December 12, 1992, a Huey took small-arms fire, and shortly afterward, two AH-1Ws came under fire from armed Somali trucks, called "technicals," near the road to Baledogle, a few kilometers inland. The Cobras returned fire, making short work of the light trucks and their foolish drivers.

Soon, other Marine squadrons arrived, including HMLA-169, HMLA-369, HMH-363, HMH-466, and VMGR-352. By December 23, Marines had set up radar and a control tower at Mogadishu airport. Although action was heavy in the first weeks, by late February, Somalia was sufficiently secure to allow some squadrons to leave. When they happened, fire fights between American forces and Somali irregulars could be vicious. One such encounter led to the downing of an Army helicopter, the entrapment of its crew and Army Rangers, and eventually, the awards to two Army troopers—albeit posthumous—of the first Medals of Honor since Vietnam.

Operation Deny Flight Over Bosnia

The world had changed greatly since the start of the 1990s. There had been a unpredicted war in the Persian Gulf, which had changed the way the United States and the rest of the world saw the pecking order in the rank of international standing. Another, arguably more substantial and indicative change was the collapse of Communism in Europe and the demise of the world's second super power, the Soviet Union. Marine Corps helicopters helped evacuate U.S. citizens from former Communist Albania in March 1997, as well as in the war-torn African countries of Zaire and Sierra Leone in April and May.

As the regions of the former U.S.S.R. fell to squabbling among themselves, establishing their own new independence and ranking, they also faced periods of frightening internal strife, perhaps none so dangerous as in the always volatile nation-state of Yugoslavia. Loosely constructed and barely held together, because of surging ethnic, racial, and religious differences, this area had always been a simmering pot, ready to boil over at a moment's notice. (It was, after all, the assassination of a minor Austrian archduke in Sarajevo in 1914 that led directly to World War I, the cataclysmic struggle that changed world history forever.)

Finally, factional problems became too great and the country was quickly torn apart by an especially bloody civil war. There were old scores to settle, some harkening back to World War II, before the Communist takeover of the late 1940s, and although the United States and NATO tried desperately to monitor the situation, find solutions, and simply prevent violence, it was soon clear that the warring parties would not be ruled by outside interference.

NATO, working for the U.N., could moderate the war in one area, however. In much the same way as they tried to prevent Iraq from mounting aerial attacks against its ethnic minorities such as the Kurds, NATO and the U.N. imposed an embargo in Yugoslavia, primarily against the Serb faction, which had the best-equipped air force.

In July 1993, eight FA-18Ds from VMFA(AW)-533 arrived at Aviano Air Base in Italy to participate in Operation Deny Flight, the enforcement of the so-called no-fly zone over Yugoslavia, now called Bosnia-Herzegovina. VMFA(AW)-224 would also bring its FA-18Ds to Aviano.

The Marine fighters patrolled the skies over the Adriatic, and on April 11, 1994, two FA-18Cs from VMFA-251 attacked Serb targets outside the town of Gorazde, which had been besieged by the Serbs. Other Hornet squadrons from MAG-31 would participate in Deny Flight.

On November 21, 1994, a major strike involved more than thirty NATO planes from eight Italian air bases. The force, which included six FA-18Ds from VMFA(AW)-332 at Aviano, hit Ubdina Air Base in Croatia, which had been used as a staging field for Serbian air attacks in Bosnia. The Moonlighter Hornets were the first in, launching HARMs against SA-6 sites.

VMAQ-4 Prowlers, which had only arrived at Aviano and Sigonella the previous day, provided ECM support. For the next two months, Seahawk crews flew more than 220 missions, which included firing several HARMs.

On May 25, 1995, a NATO strike hit Serb positions, and a week later, on June 2, a Serb missile downed an F-16. The young Air Force pilot,

Captain Scott O'Grady, hid from the Serbs trying to find him, sometimes passing within a few feet of where O'Grady was crouching in the underbrush. Efforts to recover him failed. Finally, early on the morning of June 8, the tired and hungry F-16 pilot made contact with a member of his squadron on a patrol, and the rescue force was sent in.

The Marines of the 24th MEU(SOC) had trained for just such a mission, and they were ready. HMM-263(REIN), on board USS *Kearsarge* (LHD-3), provided three CH-53Es, three AH-1Ws, and four AV-8Bs. Two FA-18Ds of VMFA(AW)-533, out of Aviano, also joined the flight, as did two Navy Prowlers from USS *Theodore Roosevelt*. The EA-6Bs were crewed by members of VAQ-141 and recalled Naval Air Reservists of VAQ-209.

The Cobras, led by Major Scott Mykleby, escorted the CH-53Es toward O'Grady's position. Launching at 0505, the helicopters were feet dry by 0549, heading into Croatia from the Adriatic, then into Bosnia. By a little after 0600, the Harriers had launched to provide further escort. The FA-18Ds flew passes to check for SAMs and to try to contact the young F-16 pilot. The Marine Hornet crews pinpointed O'Grady's position, and at 0640, as the AH-1s circled the area to defend against enemy action, the CH-53Es landed in a rocky landing zone.

The F-16 pilot dashed from his cover and as the Marine troops hauled the bedraggled Air Force pilot into the shuddering helicopter, the pilots lifted off, heading west toward the coast. However, still over Serbian territory, the rescue force came under fire, several rounds from small-arms fire hitting the helicopter carrying Captain O'Grady. Surface-to-air missiles were also fired at the rapidly departing CH-53Es. Except for a few holes in their aircraft, and momentarily elevated heart rates, the Marines and their thrilled evacuee were safe. It was a happy ending to a tense week for the FA-18 squadron, several of whose crews had befriended Captain O'Grady at Aviano.

Despite the success of Captain O'Grady's rescue, NATO's patience was wearing thin, and on August 30, it was finally exhausted. When the Serbs lobbed a shell into a busy marketplace in Sarajevo, killing thirty-seven innocent civilians, NATO decided the time had come for a strong show of force and resolve. Accordingly, a sustained air campaign called Operation Deliberate Force began, which lasted until September 14, with several breaks to allow the Serbs to come to the peace table. Hundreds of sorties blasted the Serb position, and Marine Hornets were in the thick of the action. VMFA(AW)-533's two-seater Hornets flew 180 sorties, which included SEAD and interdiction.

VMFA-312 flew its single-seaters from the *Roosevelt* against the Serbs, delivering HARMS and bombs. VMFA-251, flying from USS

America as a part of CVW-1, also participated in the latter stages of Deliberate Force. Having departed its home port of Norfolk in late August, *America* received orders to steam ahead of its battlegroup to arrive in the Adriatic to relieve *Roosevelt*, and also to provide additional support for the intense campaign over Bosnia. Arriving on September 8, CVW-1 quickly began combat operations, with Thunderbolt Hornets delivering the wing's first ordnance during a CAS mission.

The four-week air campaign finally got the Serbs to agree to a round of peace talks in the improbable locale of Dayton, Ohio. Administered by the U.S. State Department, the talks produced a ceasefire agreement, which if not the ideal solution for all parties, at least gave each faction a portion of its goals, allowed them to agree to stop the fighting, and permitted a NATO force to enter the country to prevent a resumption of hostilities.

Development of existing aircraft as well as new types continued, but at a slower pace in the mid-1990s. The night-attack version of the Harrier II began arriving in squadrons in 1991. Using forward-looking infrared (FLIR), night-vision goggles (NVGs), and a digital moving map, the AV-8B(NA) also received an engine upgrade, with fifteen percent more thrust. VMA-211 got its first night-attack Harrier in March 1991.

The AV-8B Harrier II (Plus) brought continued improvements with a characteristic bulbous nose, which added seventeen inches to the standard Harrier II airframe, to house an improved bombing radar, the Hughes APG-65. Included in the program was the remanufacture of seventy-three older Bs to II (Plus) standard, thereby saving twenty-two percent of the cost of a new aircraft. The first rebuilt AV-8B II (Plus) made its first flight on November 29, 1995. Only twenty-seven new aircraft have been built.

To consolidate CH-53D lift resources, all Delta squadrons migrated to Kaneohe in Hawaii, while a new squadron, HMH-366, joined them on September 30, 1994.

"It's no secret that the CH-46 is in trouble," wrote Major Jay Anderson in the November 1995 issue of the U.S. Naval Institute's *Proceedings*. "By the time the MV-22 is fielded in sufficient numbers . . . around 2008, the CH-46 will have been in service approximately forty years."

In March 1994, with the V-22 Osprey still having funding problems, the Marine Corps began a modernization program to keep its remaining Sea Knights flying up to the 12,500-hour level, some 4,000 hours more than what most airframes had logged. The program involved replacing rotor heads, drive systems, transmissions, and rotor-control systems within the coming five years.

By the middle of the decade, the Marines were becoming anxious, if not downright desperate, to find a replacement medium-lift helicopter. Major Frederick J. Whittle lamented in the Spring 1995 issue of *Wings of Gold*, the quarterly journal of the Association of Naval Aviation (ANA):

(If) the USS *Guam* possessed the MV-22 . . . during Operation Eastern Exit in January 1991, the rescue of 300 diplomats in Mogadishu, Somalia, (we) could have completed the mission in under eight hours, vice the eighty-four it took . . . .

The V-22 was a battle-scarred veteran even before the first full-scale aircraft took flight. Intended as a multi-service aircraft, the Osprey lost one third of its USAF sponsorship in 1986. Defense Department support also wavered and finally disappeared when Secretary of Defense Richard Cheney canceled the program in April 1989.

There were, however, five development aircraft flying, and the flight-test program continued. But, on June 11, 1991, a V-22 test aircraft crashed at Wilmington, Delaware. The remaining four Ospreys were grounded, but returned to flight status in October. On July 20, 1992, V-22 No. 4 was destroyed when it crashed into the Potomac River near Quantico after a long ferry flight from Florida. Seven civilian and military crewmembers were killed. In May 1993, a board of inquiry determined that the Potomac mishap involved faulty maintenance and design flaws, but not the tilt-rotor technology at the heart of the V-22's design. The flight program began again.

On October 22, 1992, Bell and Boeing got a $550,000,000 contract for testing and development, including four new V-22s and a modification of two existing Ospreys.

Finally, in December 1994, DoD made a commitment to produce the V-22 for the Marine Corps and the Air Force's special operations units, with a tentative IOC of 1999. Four special operations aircraft would be initially built along with thirty-three MV-22s for the Marines. Navy combat SAR (CSAR) would eventually receive forty-eight Ospreys. Ultimately the production run would see some 400 aircraft manufactured from 1997 to 2021. On December 5, 1995, Osprey No. 7's wing was mated to its fuselage. This example is the first engineering-and-manufacturing-development V-22, which is basically the first production Osprey. All internal and external features should be the same as on those aircraft that will follow.

At the time of writing, DoD budgetary cuts have decreased the initial production lot of V-22s. The Marine Corps' request for 425 MV-22s, including 65 so-called "attrition aircraft," has been reduced to 360. However, an accelerated production program would see thirty Ospreys a year by 2004. Delivery schedules call for the first MV-22As to reach the redesignated VHMT-204 training squadron by 1999, with an initial operating capability by 2001.

Changes in the Reserves

Chapter Thirteen begins with an assessment of the Marine Corps Air Reserve. Perhaps these final pages of this new edition are a good place to bring that portion of this history quickly up to date. As with the U.S. Naval Air Reserve, the Marine reserves are dealing with downsizing and restructuring.

Several Marine Air Reserve squadrons—mostly helicopter units (but also various support units and two VMGR aerial refueling squadrons)—were mobilized for combat duty in 1991. Although very few air reservists saw actual combat, and of those, none saw sustained action, they were very much a part of the overall Corps participation in Desert Shield and Desert Storm, providing support and backup when needed.

However, with their return home, the reserves had to deal with the business of force restructuring and squadron decommissionings. As noted earlier, VMAQ-4, while on duty during Desert Storm to replace the single FMF VMAQ squadron, was decommissioned, then immediately reconstituted as a regular squadron. VMO-4 retired altogether, along with its OV-10s. Other reserve squadrons that retired by the mid-1990s were VMA-133, VMA-322, VMA-124, and VMA-131, along with their trusty A-4s. VMFA-112, VMFA-134, and VMFA-321 gave up their Phantoms for Hornets, while VMA-142 traded its A-4s for FA-18s and will move from Cecil Field, near Jacksonville, Florida, to NAS Atlanta, Georgia. Several helicopter squadrons also retired, or were redesignated and given different missions.

The Marine Air Reserve adversary squadron, VMFT-401 at MCAS Yuma, Arizona, flew leased Israeli Kfirs, indigenously-produced modifications of the French Mirage, from 1987 to 1989. After returning the delta-winged Kfirs to their owners in September 1989, the Snipers have flown the F-5E and F-5F and will do so for the foreseeable future, one of the few survivors of the U.S. military's once mighty adversary program.

Altogether, twelve fleet and eight reserve squadrons have decommissioned since 1989, with an additional two fleet and two reserve units to retire in 1997. Many squadrons are moving—from El Toro (near Los Angeles) to Miramar (San Diego) or Hawaii, or from Cherry Point to Beaufort. Several of the survivors will change equipment and missions as noted above.

As with some Naval Air Reserve squadrons, Marine Air Reserve units are also being tasked to support the huge anti-drug effort in the Caribbean and South America. In September 1995, HMLAs 773 and 775 sent detachments to Trinidad and Tobago for a joint drug-interdiction exercise in the island-nation's forests. AH-1Ws and UH-1Ns carried the Marine Corps reservists into the so-called "marijuana belt" to help destroy the illicit crop, which enjoyed a street value of $3,000 per pound. The two-week operation—called "Weedeater"—destroyed $500,000,000 of marijuana plants, according to the American ambassador.

Various communities will see changes and upgrades as the new century approaches. Marine Corps helicopter squadrons will see continuous upgrades in their aircraft, including new cockpit systems, radar and weapons systems, and ECM suites.

To give the light-attack helo units (HMLA) more punch, they will receive more Cobra gunships, with a proportion of eighteen AH-1s to nine UH-1s. UH-1Ns and AH-1Ws will benefit from major upgrades. The remanufcaturing of 280 Hueys and Cobras will give these veteran helicopters more powerful engines and four-blade main and tail rotors. Increased weapons and fuel capacity will also be included.

The Sea Stallion squadrons—there are six CH-53E and four CH-53D squadrons in the fleet—will consolidate and improve their equipment. The two reserve squadrons that now fly RH-53Ds, HMH-769 at El Toro, and HMH-772 at Willow Grove, will have transitioned to CH-53Es by the end of 1997. The Echo is the only heavy helicopter still in production in the U.S., and there are no plans for a replacement. The CH-53E's use in Somalia and during the rescue of USAF Captain O'Grady in Bosnia points out the Echo's long range and load-carrying capabilities.

Incredibly, the CH-46 is scheduled to serve for another twenty years, by which time its career will have spanned some fifty years. This extension comes even with the introduction of the V-22. Today, the aging Frog remains the Corps' medium assault helicopter transport for troops, weapons, and supplies.

The Marines' two main tactical fixed-wing jets—the AV-8B and the FA-18A/C—while still at the heart of the CAS mission, are already facing replacement by the end of the first decade of the Twenty-first century. The joint strike fighter—more than 600 of which are planned to be built for the Marines—will consolidate the Harrier and Hornet roles, as well as serve in other services.

Other types of aircraft, namely the KC-130 Hercules and EA-6B Prowler, will continue to serve, again, with the help of upgrades in systems and instrumentation. The KC-130 is the Marine Corps' oldest type, and equips three fleet and two reserve squadrons. Thus, the tankers are much in demand, and can be found across the globe.

UAVs have also reorganized and are now part of Marine aircraft groups, just as any other squadron. Whereas until January 1996, UAVs served in companies—1st Remotely Piloted Vehicle Company 1 and 2—

providing aerial reconnaissance services for all four elements of the Marine Air-Ground Task Force, they have since been redesignated VMU-1 and VMU-2 (Fixed-Wing, Marine, Unmanned 1 and 2).

As Marine Corps aviation heads toward the new millennium, there are many obstacles to be faced and overcome. The world is not what it was even ten years ago when this book's second edition appeared, let alone what it was at the end of World War II fifty years ago. Old enemies are now cautious allies, and old scenarios against which we all trained no longer hold true, or at least completely true. The dangers and threats are still out there, but they have different names and faces.

To negotiate all that lies before us, we need to continue to build and maintain a strong military force, perhaps smaller, leaner, and decidedly more intelligent, but we need it, nonetheless. And we definitely need a Marine Corps and its dedicated air arm.

A Marine UH-1N flies over Beirut International Airport during a patrol for the multinational peacekeeping force in September 1983. (US Navy)

A Sikorsky CH-53 Sea Stallion lands on the deck of the USS *Guam* (LPH-9) off the coast of Lebanon in December 1982. The amphibious assault ship and its aircraft were part of the multinational peacekeeping force deployed in the eastern Mediterranean. (US Navy)

Marines board a CH-46 Sea Knight for the flight back to their ships as the 22nd Marine Amphibious Unit leaves Lebanon in February 1984. (US Navy)

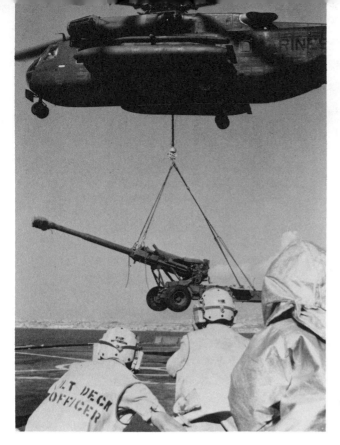

A Marine CH-53E Super Sea Stallion lifts a 155mm howitzer from the flight deck of the USS *Austin* (LPD-4) in January 1983. (US Navy)

A CH-53 Sea Stallion operating from the USS *Guadalcanal* (LPH-7) off the coast of Lebanon in May 1983. (US Navy)

A Marine AH-1T Sea Cobra of HMM-261 prepares for takeoff from the USS *Guam* (LPH-9) on the first day of Operation Urgent Fury, the invasion of Grenada in October 1983. (US Navy)

A Marine AH-1T Sea Cobra of HMM-261 heads toward the beach during the invasion of Grenada, October 1983. The helicopter carrries three-barrelled 20mm cannon in the nose turret, TOW anti-tank missiles and 2.75-inch unguided rockets. (US Navy)

CH-53 helicopter of HMM-261 takes off after depositing Marines near Pearls Airport during the invasion of Grenada, October 1983. (US Navy)

A Marine CH-46 Sea Knight of HMM-261 takes off after landing Marines in a field during the invasion of Grenada, October, 1983. (US Navy)

McDonnell Douglas AV-8B of VMAT-203, the training squadron, MCAS Cherry Point, North Carolina. (author)

F/A-18A Hornet of VMFA-323 taxis toward the runway at NAS Norfolk, August 1985. VMFA-323 and VMFA-314 had flown from El Toro to conduct carrier qualifications aboard USS *Coral Sea* prior to deployment to the eastern Mediterranean. This cruise saw the first combat use of the Hornet during strikes against Libya in April 1986. (author)

A pilot of VMFA-323 makes last-minute adjustments to his flight gear before manning his F/A-18A Hornet. Scene on the NAS Norfolk ramp in August 1985 taken during El Toro squadron's deployment to conduct carrier qualifications aboard USS *Coral Sea* prior to cruise to eastern Mediterranean. (author)

The scene on the flight deck of the USS *America* (CV-66) just after midnight on 15 April 1986. An EA-6B of VMAQ-2 is ready for launch from the number 4 waist catapult. The Marine Prowlers provided ECM services for USAF and Navy strike aircraft during attacks on Libyan cities, Tripoli and Benghazi. (US Navy)

A McDonnell Douglas F/A-18A Hornet prepares to launch from the aircraft carrier USS *Constellation* (CV-64) during carrier qualification training in 1983. Aircraft belongs to VMFA-314, the first Navy or Marine fleet squadron to begin operations with the Hornet. Three years later, this squadron participated in the 1986 raids against Libya as part of the embarked air wing in USS *Coral Sea* (CV-43). (McDonnell Douglas)

A McDonnell Douglas AV-8B Harrier II rises vertically before a sortie from MCAS Cherry Point in July 1985. (McDonnell Douglas)

McDonnell Douglas AV-8B Harrier IIs from training squadron VMAT-203 fly formation. VMAT-203 provides training in the Harrier II before pilots join their regular FMF squadron. (McDonnell Douglas)

Two VMFP-3 RF-4Bs tank from a KC-130 from VMGR-352 in 1987.

Ordnancemen load an AIM-9 Sidewinder onto the starboard weapons pylon of an AH-1W on board USS *Guadalcanal* (LPH-7) during operations in the Persian Gulf in August 1987. (PH3 Cleveland)

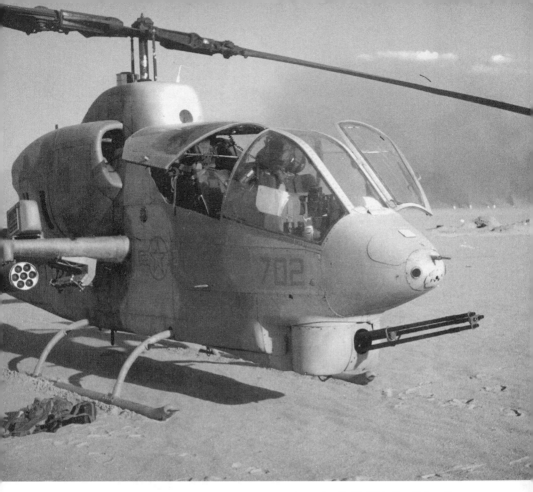

Two reserve squadrons brought their older AH-1Js to the Gulf. This Sea Cobra from HMA-775 frames the smoke and flames from numerous oil-well fires. (R.S. Doty)

Armed with Sidewinders, this AH-1W of HMLA-169 flies up the starboard side of USS *Okinawa* (LPH-3) in the Persian Gulf in 1987. (Carl D. Siegmund)

A CH-46E of HMM-774 passes an oil refinery in the
Kuwaiti wastelands. (John Stollery)

An FA-18D of VMFA(AW)-121 over a field of oil well fires shortly after the war. The two-seat Hornets, relatively new to service, quickly got their baptism of fire during the Gulf War, taking over the role of Fast FAC and battlefield interdictor. (McDonnell Douglas)

The Playboys arrive. VMAQ-2 Prowlers inbound to Sheikh Isa, 1990.

The latest in NBC gear. A CH-46 pilot of HMM-774 models his protective kit. (John Stollery)

CH-53Es of HMH-464 at LZ Lonesome Dove sported names and low-visibility paint schemes. (Rick Mullen)

The crowded flight deck of USS *Nassau* as the ship steams in the Persian Gulf during the late weeks of Desert Shield. AV-8Bs, CH-46s, AH-1s, and UH-1s jam the aft portion of the relatively small flight deck. (Joe Doyle)

CH-53Es line the stern of USS *Iwo Jima* (LPH-2) while the amphibious assault ship is moored at Manama, Bahrain in December 1990. Many of the large helicopters were transported to the Gulf lashed to the decks of whichever ships could carry them. (PH2 Susan Marie Carl)

An AH-1W of HMLA-269 prepares to head out on a mission during the ground war. The Cobra is armed with Hellfire anti-tank missiles and 2.75-inch air-to-ground rockets. (R.S. Doty)

OV-10D of VMO-2.

VMA-542 Harriers at King Abdul Aziz Naval Base, Jubail, Saudi Arabia. The AV-8Bs all carry Rockeye canisters, the weapon of choice for most of the VSTOL squadrons.

Captain Charles Magill, on exchange duty with the Air Force, shot down an Iraqi MiG-29 on January 17, 1991, the only Marine aviator to score a kill in Desert Storm. Captain Magill stands by his F-15C, which now carries a small red, white, and black facsimile of the Iraqi flag below the windscreen. (via Charles Magill)

A busy flight-deck scene shows three types of Marine Corps helicopters—CH-53E, UH-1N, and AH-1W. (Rick Mullen)

This CH-46E of HMM-264 stands on an airfield near the first tent city constructed as part of Operation Provide Comfort in April 1991. (JO1 Greg Snaza)

Technicians prepare a Pioneer reconnaissance drone for a mission from Naval Air
Warfare Center, Point Mugu. (U. S. Navy)

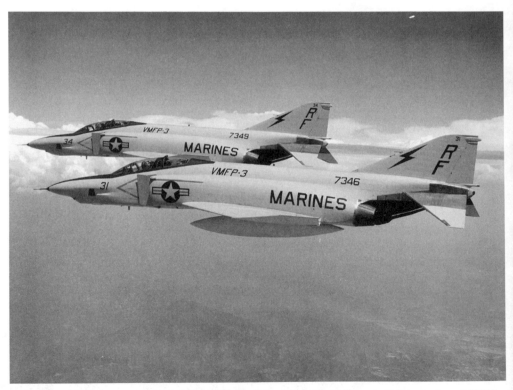

At the end of their tour: two immaculate RF-4Bs fly over the mountains near their home base, MCAS
El Toro, in July 1990. A month later, the squadron was decommissioned and its unique, valuable
aircraft retired. Less than six months later, Marines embroiled in a major war pleaded for the type
of battlefield photography that only the photo-Phantoms could provide. (Robert Lawson)

KC-130s—this one is from VMGR-252—continue to provide airlift and aerial refueling services for the Corps. The Hercules is the Marines' oldest aircraft type.

A CH-53E of HMH-461 lifts off during an exercise in Europe. (Rick Mullen)

AV-8Bs of VMA-331 prepare to launch on a mission from USS *Nassau* in February 1991. (Joe Doyle)

A member of HMLA-367 fires a .50-caliber machine gun from a UH-1N during training in the Philippines, August 1991. (PH3 Robert Foster, USN)

In August 1990, Marines guard supplies that a CH-46E of HMM-261 has just delivered to the U.S. embassy in Monrovia, Liberia. A few days later, these Marines and helicopters will evacuate people from the war-torn African country. (JO2 William G. Davis, III)

A Marine Air Reserve AH-1W lifts off for an anti-drug mission in Trinidad. (via Peyton DeHart)

Members of an SPMAGTF board a Navy SH-60F on the flight deck of USS *Theodore Roosevelt* in May 1993 while the nuclear carrier is on station in the Adriatic to support NATO Operation Deny Flight in Bosnia. The Marines will participate in a training exercise in Italy. (PHAN Sean Griffiths)

A CH-53E and CH-46E of HMM-263 (REIN) land in a field of scrub in famine-ridden Somalia in 1993. (CWO2 N.H. North, USMC)

An unusual view of an EA-6B Prowler of VMAQ-1 during its landing approach. (Ted Carlson)

Somalis bear bags of precious food from a CH-46E of HMM-263 (REIN). (CWO2 N.H. North, USMC)

WK 505 and its two-man crew get last-minute checks before heading out for a mission over Bosnia from the Italian air base at Aviano.

An A-6E of VMA (AW)-224 with a load of Rockeye at Sheikh Isa. The Intruder will launch on a mission to support the Coalition advance. The ground war is one day old.

Vertical assault in the future will feature waves of Marines delivered by MV-22 Ospreys. These two "demonstrators" running from a Bell V-22 prototype show the technique if not the intensity of the action. (Bell Textron)

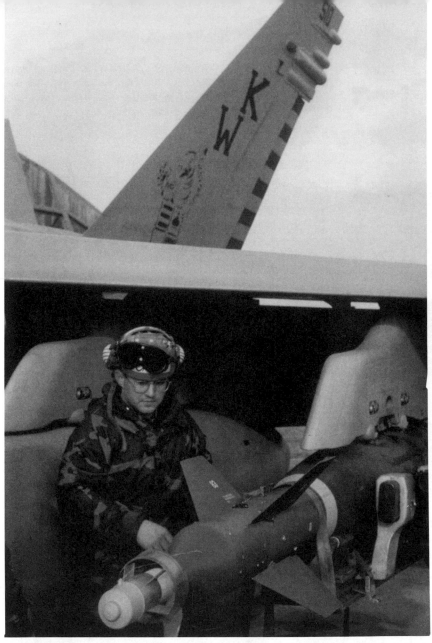

An ordnanceman checks a laser bomb on an FA-18D of VMFA (AW)-224 at Aviano air base in Italy.

An FA-18A Hornet of VMFA-122. (Ted Carlson)

AH-1W Super Cobras and CH-53 Super Stallions of HMM-263 (REIN) lift off to carry out the TRAP mission of USAF Captain Scott O'Grady in June 1995. (Sgt. Dave A. Garten, USMC)

USS *Inchon* underway in the Caribbean off the coast of Haiti during Operation Support Democracy in June 1994. (PH2 John Sokolowski)

A UH-1N leaves a Marine position during Rescue Eagle, a search-and-rescue exercise involving units of the U.S. Navy and Marine Corps, in Albania, July 1995. (PH2 Brett Siegel)

A CH-53E launches from USS *Wasp* during operations in the Adriatic. (P. Croisetiere)

A clean AV-8B of VMA-542 approaches a tanker during an exercise in September 1996. The Harrier II's huge intakes and large clamshell cockpit canopy show up well. (Ted Carlson)

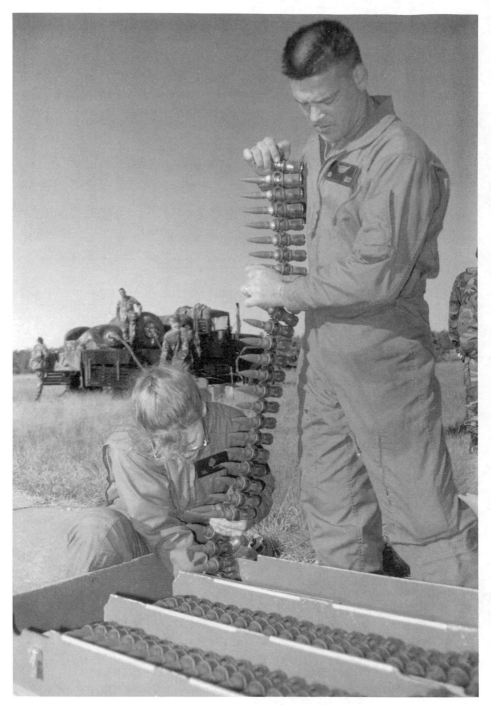

Reservists of HMLA-773 load 20mm rounds into a Cobra's ammo can. (via Peyton DeHart)

Notes

1. Major A.A. Cunningham, quoted in *Marine Corps Aviation: the Early Years 1912-1940,* Lieutenant Colonel Edward C. Johnson, USMC. History and Museums Division, Headquarters, USMC, 1977.
2. *Ibid.,* p. 25.
3. *Ibid.,* p. 27.
4. *Ibid.,* p. 31.
5. *Marine Corps Gazette* (hereafter cited as *MCG*), September 1929.
6. *Ibid.*
7. *Eagles of Mitsubishi: the Story of the Zero Fighter,* Jiro Horikoshi. University of Washington Press, Seattle, Washington, 1981.
8. *The Cactus Air Force,* T.G. Miller, Jr. Bantam Books, New York, 1981, p. 117.
9. *Naval Aviation News* (hereafter cited as *NAN*), May 1982.
10. Quoted in *History of Marine Corps Aviation in World War II,* Robert Sherrod. Presidio Press, San Rafael, California, 1980, p. 117.
11. *The Battle for Guadalcanal,* Brigadier General Samuel B. Griffith II. Nautical & Aviation Publishing Company of America, Baltimore, Maryland, 1979, p. 244.
12. *Baa Baa Black Sheep,* Gregory Boyington. Putnam's, New York, 1958, p. 127.
13. *Hell in the Heavens,* John M. Foster. Zenger Publishing, Washington, D.C., p. 193.
14. *Ibid.,* p. 193.
15. *Ibid.,* p. 203.
16. *Ibid.,* p. 221.
17. *The Wartime Journals of Charles A. Lindbergh.* Harcourt Brace Jovanovich, New York, 1970, p. 921.
18. *Marine Aviation in the Philippines,* Major Charles W. Boggs, Jr., USMC. U.S. Government Printing Office, Washington, D.C., 1951, p. 79.
19. *Ibid.,* p. 135.
20. *Ibid.,* p. 135.
21. *History of the Second World War,* Marshall Cavendish Promotions, Ltd., 1974, p. 2,465.
22. Sherrod, p. 394.
23. *The United States Marines 1775-1975,* Brigadier General E.H. Simmons, USMC (Ret). Viking Press, New York, 1974, p. 168.
24. *Semper Fidelis: The History of the United States Marine Corps,* Allan R. Millett. MacMillan, New York, 1980, p. 441.
25. *Marines and Helicopters 1946-1962,* Lieutenant Colonel Eugene W. Rawlins, USMC. History and Museums Division, Headquarters, USMC, 1976, p. 26.
26. *NAN,* November 1952, p. 10.
27. *Leatherneck,* October 1953, p. 70.
28. Simmons, p. 196.

29. *The American Weekly,* August 23, 1953.

30. *Ibid.*

31. "The Douglas Navy F4D Ford," *Journal of the American Aviation Historical Society,* Summer 1979, p. 129.

32. *Ibid.,* p. 131.

33. *The Marines in Vietnam: 1954-1973, An Anthology and Annotated Bibliography,* History and Museums Division, Headquarters, USMC, 1974, p. 53.

34. *MCG,* August 1967.

35. "Marine Corps Skyhawks," in *Replica in Scale*, vol 3, no. 1, p. 11.

36. *MCG,* May 1981.

37. *Ibid.*

38. *MCG,* May 1969.

39. *Ibid.*

40. *Ibid.*

41. *Airpower in Three Wars,* General William Momyer, USAF (Ret). Government Printing Office, p. 311.

42. *MCG,* May 1968.

43. *Ibid.*

44. "The AV-8B-rising vertically through the air, invulnerable to runaway cuts." Russell Murray II. A treatise on the AV-8B, 1978.

45. "Marine Air: There When Needed, interview with Lieutenant General Royal N. Moore," *U.S. Naval Institute Proceedings*, November 1991.

46. *Ibid.*

47. "Getting the Marines to the Gulf," *U.S. Naval Institute Proceedings*, May 1991.

48. "The 1st Marine Division in the Attack, an interview with Major General J.M. Myatt, USMC," *U.S. Naval Institute Proceedings*, November 1991.

49. Interview, June 26, 1991, Norfolk, Virginia.

Recommended Reading

For those who would like to read more about a specific area of Marine aviation or a specific squadron or aircraft, I would suggest the following books and sources.

General:

Semper Fidelis: The History of the United States Marine Corps. Allan R. Millett. MacMillan, New York, 1980.

The United States Marines 1775-1975. Brigadier General E.H. Simmons, USMC (Ret). Viking, New York, 1974.

Aircraft Carriers: A Graphic History of Carrier Aviation and its Influence on World Events. Norman Polmar. Doubleday, Garden City, N.Y., 1969.

History of Marine Corps Aviation in World War II. Robert Sherrod. Presidio Press, San Rafael, Cal., 1980 edition.

The Battle for Guadalcanal. Brigadier General Samuel B. Griffith II. Nautical & Aviation Publishing Company of America, Baltimore, Md., 1979.

The Cactus Air Force. T.G. Miller, Jr. Bantam Books, New York, 1981.

Baa Baa Black Sheep. Gregory Boyington. Putnam's, New York, 1958.

Two pictorial books are also worth reading, although one is out of print:

U.S. Marine Corps Aircraft 1914-1959. William T. Larkins. Aviation History Publications, Concord, Cal., 1959.

Flying Leathernecks in World War II. Thomas E. Doll. Aero Publishers Inc., Fallbrook, Cal., 1971. This book is still available.

The History and Museums Division of the Headquarters, Marine Corps, in Washington, D.C., is responsible for an ambitious writing program, and to date, has published several useful volumes on Marine operations in Vietnam, as well as six squadron histories: *VMA-223, VMA-311, VMFA-312, VMFA-232, HMM-161,* and *VMO-6*. There is also a volume on the period 1912-1940, entitled *Marine Corps Aviation: the Early Years*. A new series on the Persian Gulf War of 1991 will also include a volume on Marine Corps air operations. All of these Marine-produced and -sponsored works are nominally priced and should be read by anyone interested in the subject.

For specific aircraft, I recommend the following works:

United States Navy and Marine Corps Fighters 1918-1962. Bruce Robertson, ed. Harleyford Publications Ltd., UK, 1962.

The Dauntless Divebomber in World War II. Barrett Tillman. U.S. Naval Institute, Annapolis, Md., 1976.

Hellcat. Barrett Tillman. U.S. Naval Institute, Annapolis, Md., 1979.

Marine Fighting Squadron Nine (VF-9M). Jess C. Barrow. TAB Books, Blue Ridge Summit, Pa., 1981.

United States Naval Fighters of World War II in Action. Michael O'Leary. Blandford Press, Ltd., UK, 1980.

MiG Master: the Story of the F-8 Crusader. Barrett Tillman. Nautical & Aviation Publishing Company of America, Baltimore, Md., 1980.

The Wildcat in World War II. Barrett Tillman. Nautical & Aviation Publishing Company of America, Baltimore, Md., 1983.

Certain periodicals are also worthwhile sources of material on military aviation in general. Two of those dealing specifically with Navy and Marine aviation are *Naval Aviation News*, the U.S. Government's oldest military publication, and *The Hook*, a quarterly journal from the Tailhook Association of California, a well-produced publication dealing primarily with carrier aviation. The highly respected U.S. Naval

Institute's *Proceedings* also carries articles dealing with aviation, both current and historical.

Several books on the 1991 Gulf War give good overviews of the conflict, as well as of the various equipment and organizations that fought it. One of the best written of these overviews is: *The Generals' War: The Inside Story of the Conflict in the Gulf* (Michael R. Gordon and General Bernard E. Trainer. Little, Brown, Boston, Ma., 1995). *Gulf Air War Debrief* (Aerospace Publishing, UK, 1992) remains one of the best surveys of aircraft, weapons, and squadrons during the war. It is replete with color photos and drawings, and personal experiences of Coalition aircrewmen.

Appendix A

First 100 Marine Corps Aviators

Number	Name	Date of Designation	Naval Aviator Number
1	Alfred Austell Cunningham	17 Sep 1915	5
2	Bernard Lewis Smith	1 Jul 1914	6
3	William Maitland McIlvain	10 Mar 1915	12
4	Francis Thomas Evans	9 Mar 1916	26
5	Roy Stanley Geiger	9 Jun 1917	49
6	David Lukens Shoemaker Brewster	5 Jul 1917	55
7	Edmund Gillette Chamberlain	9 Oct 1917	96 1/2 & 768
8	Russell Alger Presley	9 Nov 1917	100 3/4 & 769
9	Doyle Bradford.	5 Nov 1917	111 1/2
10	Clifford Lawrence Webster	5 Nov 1917	112 1/2
11	Arthur Houston Wright	6 Dec 1917	148 & 803
12	Herman Alexander Peterson.	2 Nov 1917	163 1/2
13	George McCully Laughlin III	12 Dec 1917	165 & 790
14	Charles Burton Ames	21 Dec 1917	193
15	John Howard Weaver	21 Jan 1918	251 & 794
16	Alvin Lochinvar Prichard	21 Jan 1918	279
17	George Conan Willman	22 Jan 1918	299 & 795
18	Herbert Dalzell Elvidge	12 Mar 1918	424
19	Hazen Curtis Pratt	8 Mar 1918	426
20	Sidney "E" Clark	8 Mar 1918	442 & 800
21	Frederick Commodore Schley	8 Mar 1918	443 & 801
22	Charles Alfred Needham	14 Mar 1918	444
23	John Bartow Bates	25 Mar 1918	449
24	Ralph Talbot	10 Apr 1918	449
25	Thomas Carrington Comstock	26 Mar 1918	473 & 789
26	Francis Osborne Clarkson	28 Mar 1918	474 & 788
27	Guy Mowrey Williamson	25 Mar 1918	477
28	Grover Cleveland Alder	25 Mar 1918	479
29	Edward Kenealy	23 Mar 1918	480
30	Donald Newell Whiting	1 Apr 1918	503
31	Howard Albert Strong	2 Apr 1918	505
32	John Parke McMurran	1 Apr 1918	508 & 791
33	James Kendrick Noble	1 Apr 1918	510 & 792
34	Vincent Case Young	1 Apr 1918	519
35	Province Law Pogue.	19 Jun 1918	522 & 782
36	Duncan Hugh Cameron	26 Mar 1918	527 & 787
37	George Fred Donovan	26 Mar 1918	532 & 798
38	William Herbert Derbyshire	28 Feb 1918	533 & 770
39	Frederick Brock Davy	28 Feb 1918	534 & 771
40	Douglas Bennett Roben	14 Mar 1918	535 & 774
41	Arthur Hallett Page, Jr.	14 Mar 1918	536 & 775

Number	Name	Date of Designation	Naval Aviator Number
42	Gove Compton	14 Mar 1918	537 & 773
43	Thomas James Butler	10 Apr 1918	541 & 786
44	Thomas Rodney Shearer	4 Apr 1918	559
45	Ford Ovid Rogers	14 Apr 1918	560
46	Homer Carter Bennett	11 Apr 1918	562 & 797
47	John Edmond Powell	4 Apr 1918	563
48	William Morrison Barr	8 Apr 1918	567 & 799
49	Harry Eldridge Stovall	11 Apr 1918	568
50	Harvey Byrd Mims	4 Dec 1917	576
51	Winfield Scott Shannon	17 Apr 1918	583
52	Everett Robert Brewer	17 Apr 1918	585
53	John George Estill Kipp	17 Apr 1918	586
54	Frederick Louis Kolb	17 Apr 1918	587
55	George Franklin Kremm	17 Apr 1918	588
56	Jesse Arthur Nelson	17 Apr 1918	589
57	Herman Judson Jesse	17 Apr 1918	590
58	William Webster Head	17 Apr 1918	591
59	Gustav Henry Kaemmerling	17 Apr 1918	592
60	Jesse Floyd Dunlap	17 Apr 1918	593
61	Trevor George Williams	17 Apr 1918	594
62	Clyde Noble Bates	17 Apr 1918	595
63	Melville Edward Ingalls Sullivan	17 Apr 1918	596
64	Francis Patrick Mulcahy	17 Apr 1918	597
65	Benjamin Louis Harper	17 Apr 1918	598
66	Walter Harold Batts	17 Apr 1918	599
67	Henry Teasdale Young	17 Apr 1918	600
68	Karl Schmolsmire Day	17 Apr 1918	601
69	Fred Sevier Robillard	17 Apr 1918	602
70	Melchior Borner Trelfall	17 Apr 1918	603
71	Harold Cornell Major	17 Apr 1918	604
72	Robert Sidney Lytle	17 Apr 1918	605
73	Thomas Caldwell Turner	14 Mar 1918	772
74	Kenneth Brown Collings	26 Mar 1918	776
75	Donald Buford Cowles	4 Apr 1918	777
76	Maco Stewart, Jr.	4 Apr 1918	778
77	Henry Sidney Ehret, Jr.	6 Apr 1918	779
78	Raymond Joseph Kirwan	8 Apr 1918	780
79	Frank Nelms, Jr.	19 Jun 1918	781
80	Harvey Chester Norman	23 May 1918	783
81	Delmar Leighton	23 May 1918	784
82	John Thomas Brecton	11 Apr 1918	785
83	William Wheelwright Torrey	22 Mar 1918	793
84	Joseph White Austin	23 Mar 1918	796
85	Bunn Gradon Barnwell	28 May 1918	804
86	Walter Josephs Willoughby	19 Jun 1918	805
87	Chester Julius Peters	19 Jun 1918	806
88	Roswell Emory Davis	19 Jun 1918	807
89	Horace Wilbur Leeper	25 Jun 1918	808

Number	Name	Date of Designation	Naval Aviator Number
90	Byron Brazil Freeland	25 Jun 1918	809
91	Robert James Paisley	19 Jun 1918	810
92	Charles Thomas Holloway II	1 Jul 1918	811
93	Frank Henry Fleer	2 Jul 1918	812
94	Maurice Kingsley Heartfield	2 Jul 1918	813
95	Robert James Archibald	8 Jul 1918	814
96	Arthur Judson Sherman	8 Jul 1918	815
97	Philip William Blood	8 Jul 1918	816
98	Albert Aloysius Kuhlen	28 Jun 1918	817
99	Earl Francis War.....................	30 Jun 1918	818
100	August Koerbling.....................	1 Jul 1918	819

NOTE: Aviators with two designation numbers generally transferred from the Navy to the Marine Corps, receiving a second number from the Marines. The lower number is used to establish precedence. Numbers with fractions resulted from several aviators being given the same designation number. Also, dates of designation should not be confused with dates of precedence, which are reflected by naval aviator numbers and are often much earlier than designation dates.

Appendix B
Directors of Marine Corps Aviation

MAJ Alfred A. Cunningham . . . . 17 Nov 1919—12 Dec 1920
LCOL Thomas C. Turner. . . . . 13 Dec 1920—2 Mar 1925
MAJ Edward H. Brainard . . . . .3 Mar 1925—9 May 1929
COL Thomas C. Turner. . . . . 10 May 1929—28 Oct 1931
MAJ Roy S. Geiger . . . . .6 Nov 1931—29 May 1935
COL Ross E. Rowell . . . . .30 May 1935—10 Mar 1939
BGEN Ralph J. Mitchell . . . . 11 Mar 1939—29 Mar 1943
MGEN Roy S. Geiger . . . . 13 May 1943—15 Oct 1943
BGEN Louis E. Woods . . . . .15 Oct 1943—17 Jul 1944
MGEN Field Harris. . . . . .18 Jul 1944—24 Feb 1948
MGEN William J. Wallace .24 Feb 1948—1 Sep 1950
BGEN Clayton C. Jerome . . . . .1 Sep 1950—1 Apr 1952
LGEN William O. Brice . . . . 1 Apr 1952—31 Jul 1955
LGEN Christian F. Schilt . . . . 1 Aug 1955—31 Mar 1957
LGEN Verne J. McCaul. . . . . .1 Apr 1957—2 Dec 1957
MGEN Samuel S. Jack . . . . 14 Jan 1958—20 Feb 1958
MGEN John C. Munn . . . . .21 Feb 1958—14 Dec 1959
MGEN Arthur F. Binney. . . . . .15 Dec 1959—10 Sep 1961
COL Keith B. McCutcheon . . . . 11 Sep 1961—17 Feb 1962
COL Marion E. Carl . . . . 18 Feb 1962—4 Jul 1962
BGEN Norman J. Anderson. . . . . .5 Jul 1962—20 Oct 1963
MGEN Louis B. Robertshaw. . . . . 21 Oct 1963—15 Jun 1966
MGEN Keith B. McCutcheon . . . . 15 Jun 1966—18 Feb 1970
MGEN Homer S. Hill . . . . 19 Feb 1970—24 Aug 1972
MGEN Edward S. Fris. . . . . 25 Aug 1972—27 Aug 1974
BGEN Philip D. Shutler . . . . 28 Aug 1974—Jan 1975
MGEN Victor A. Armstrong . . . . Jan 1975—21 Aug 1975
LGEN Thomas H. Miller, Jr.. . . . . .22 Aug 1975—29 Jun 1979
LGEN William J. White . . . . 30 Jun 1979—30 Jun 1982
LGEN William H. Fitch . . . . 1 Jul 1982 — 31 Aug 1984
LGEN Keith A. Smith . . . . .1 Sep 1984—29 Apr 1988
LGEN Charles H. Pitman . . . . 30 Apr 1988—16 Aug 1990

LGEN Duane A. Wills . . . . 17 Aug 1990—30 Jun 1993
LGEN Richard A. Hearney. . . . . .1 Jul 1993—15 Jul 1994
LGEN Harold W. Blot . . . . .16 Jul 1994—21 Jul 1996
LGEN Terrence R. Dake . . . . .22 Jul 1996—

On 1 Apr 1936 the title of the senior aviator attached to Headquarters, Marine Corps, changed from Officer-in-Charge, Aviation, to Director of Aviation, and on 25 Apr 1962 became Deputy Chief of Staff (Air).

Index